MAJESTIC

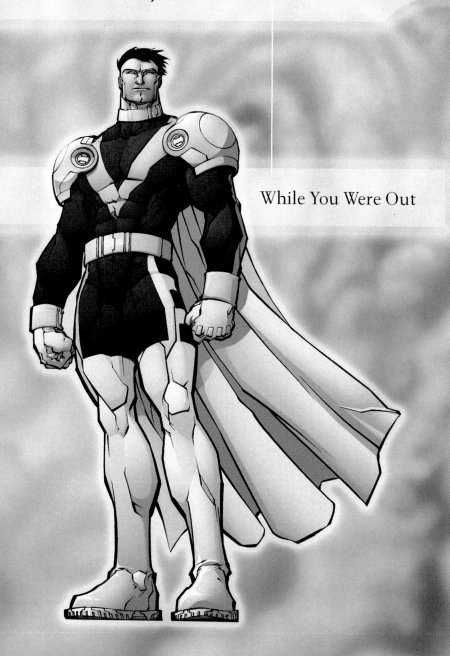

While You Were Out

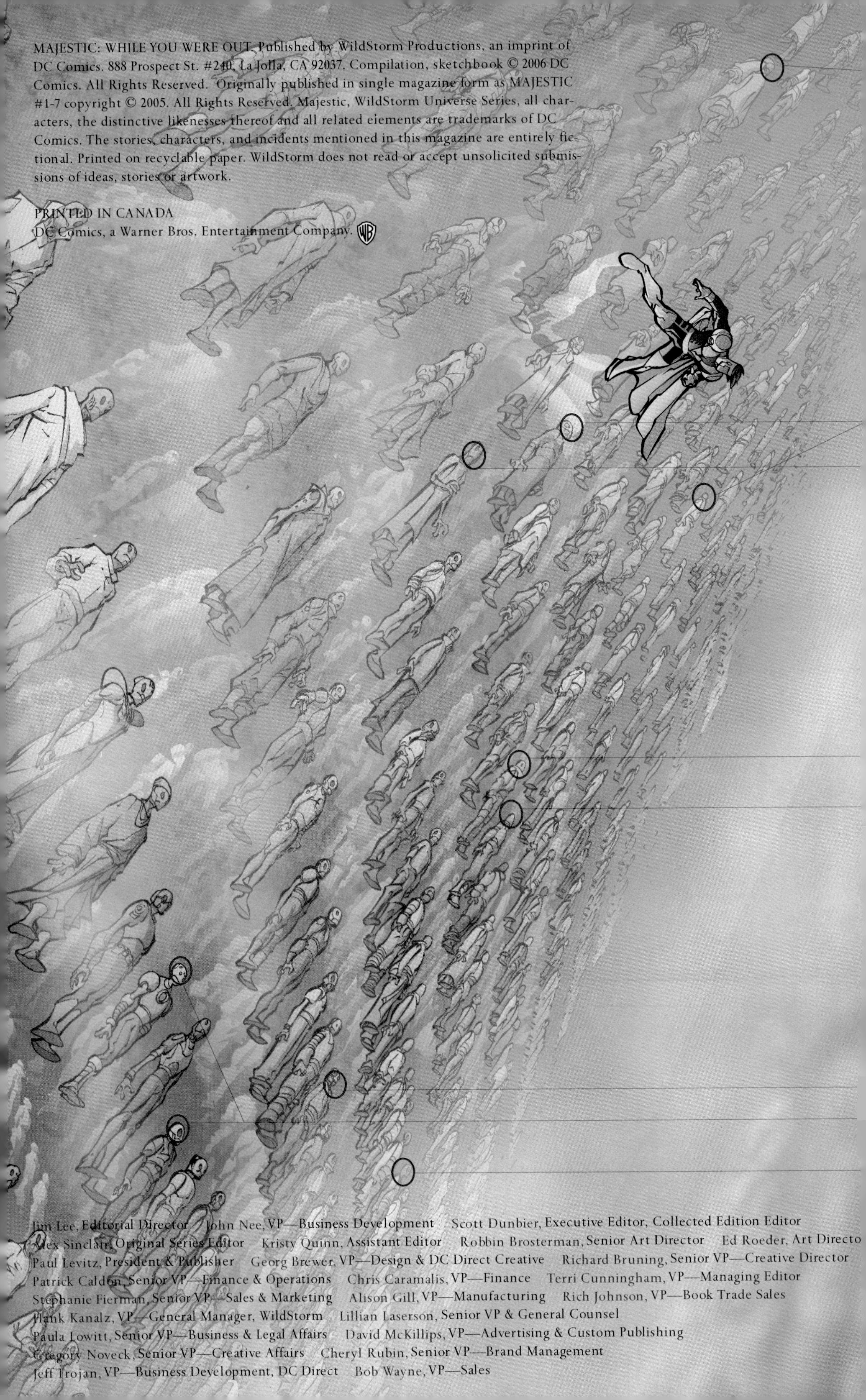

PRINTED IN CANADA

DC Comics, a Warner Bros. Entertainment Company.

Written by
Dan Abnett and
Andy Lanning

Penciled by
Neil Googe (#1-4, 7)
Juan Santacruz (#5)
Googe with Juan Santacruz (#6)

Inked by
Trevor Scott (#1-2, 4, 6)
Scott with Sal Regla (#3)
Sal Regla (#5)
Scott with Neil Googe (#7)

Colored by
Carrie Strachan (#1-3, 6-7)
Strachan with Randy Mayor (#4) Tony Aviña (#5)
Lettered by
Phil Balsman

Collected Editon Design by
Larry Berry

Original Series Covers
Ed McGuinness & Dexter Vines (#1-3, 5-7)
Ed McGuinness & Andy Lanning (#4)
Variant cover to #1: Josh Middleton

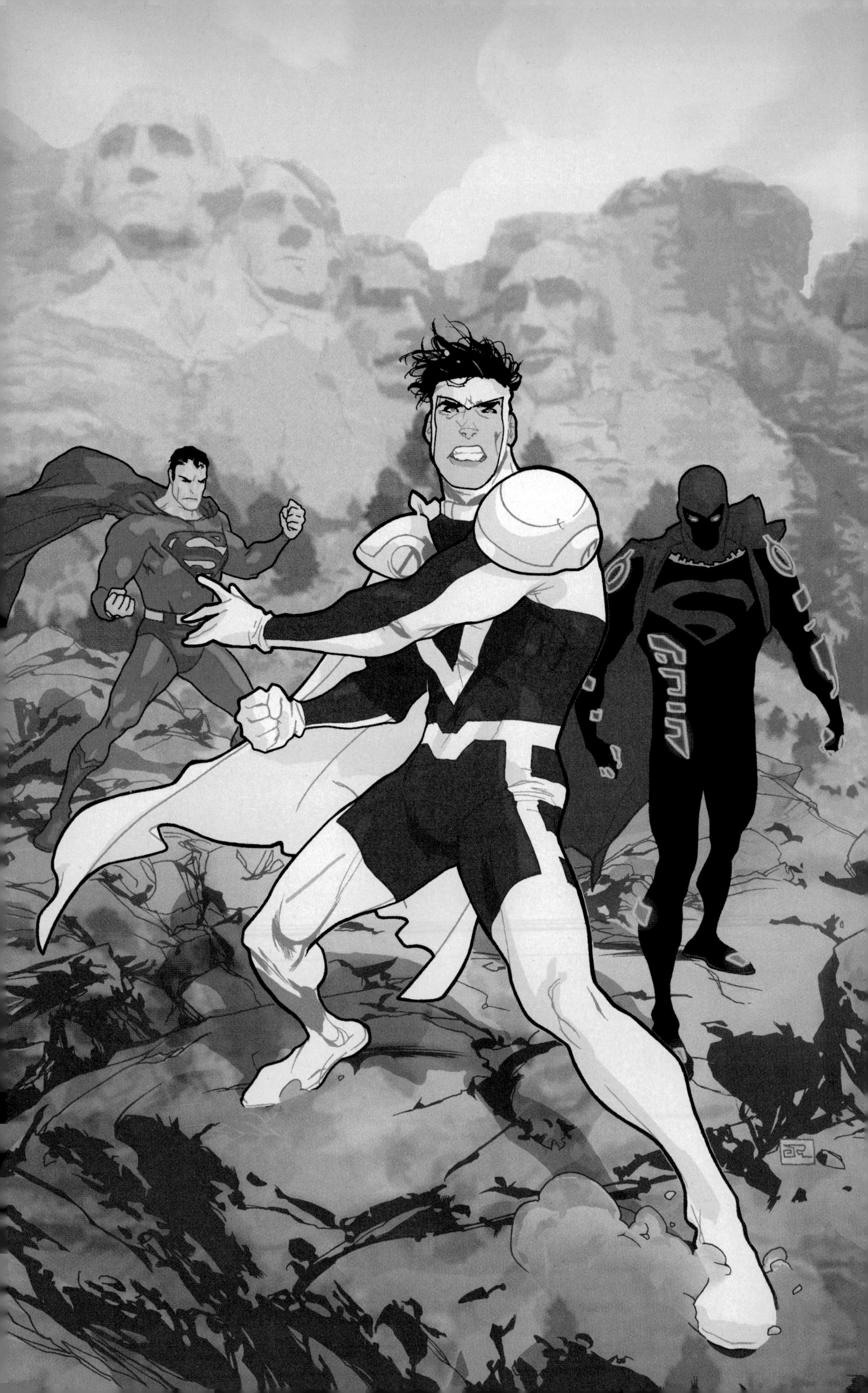

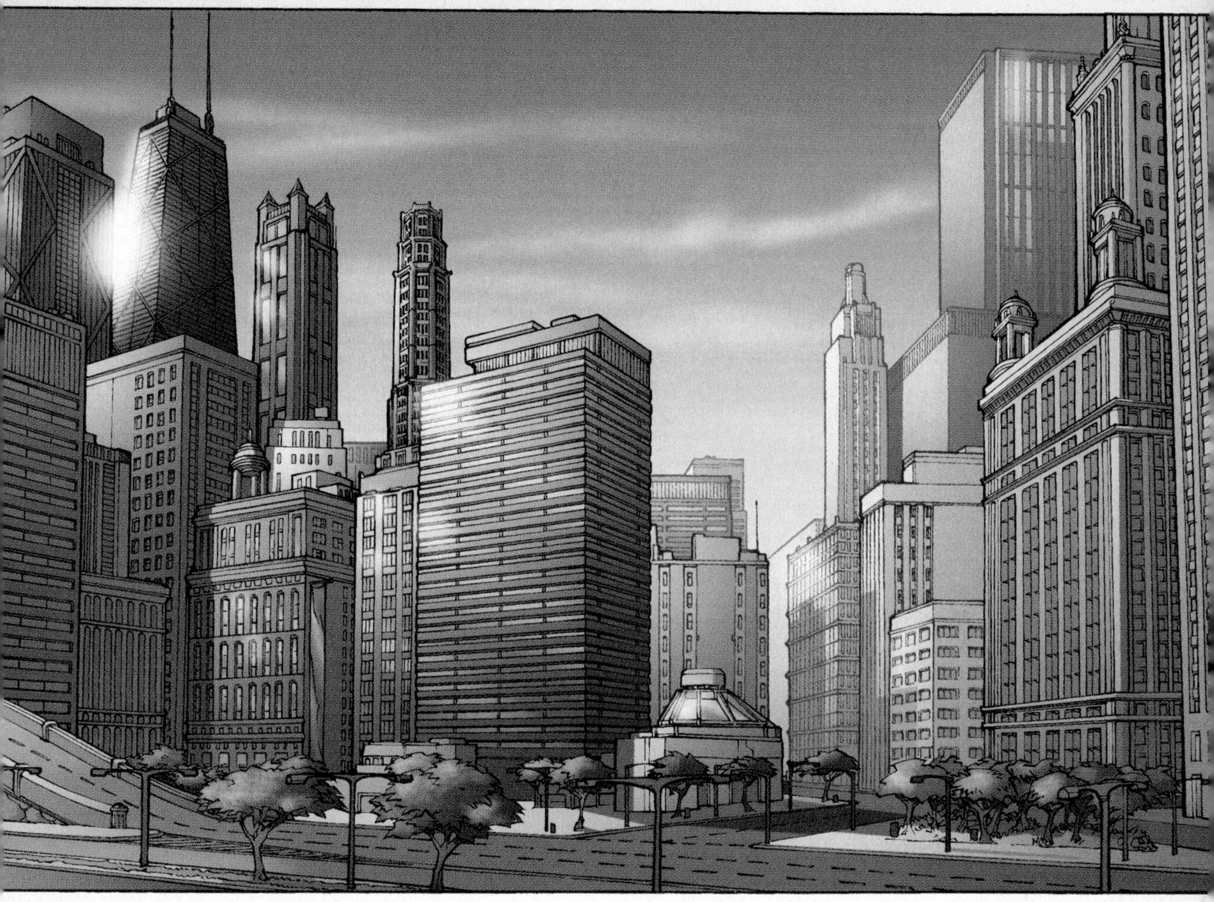

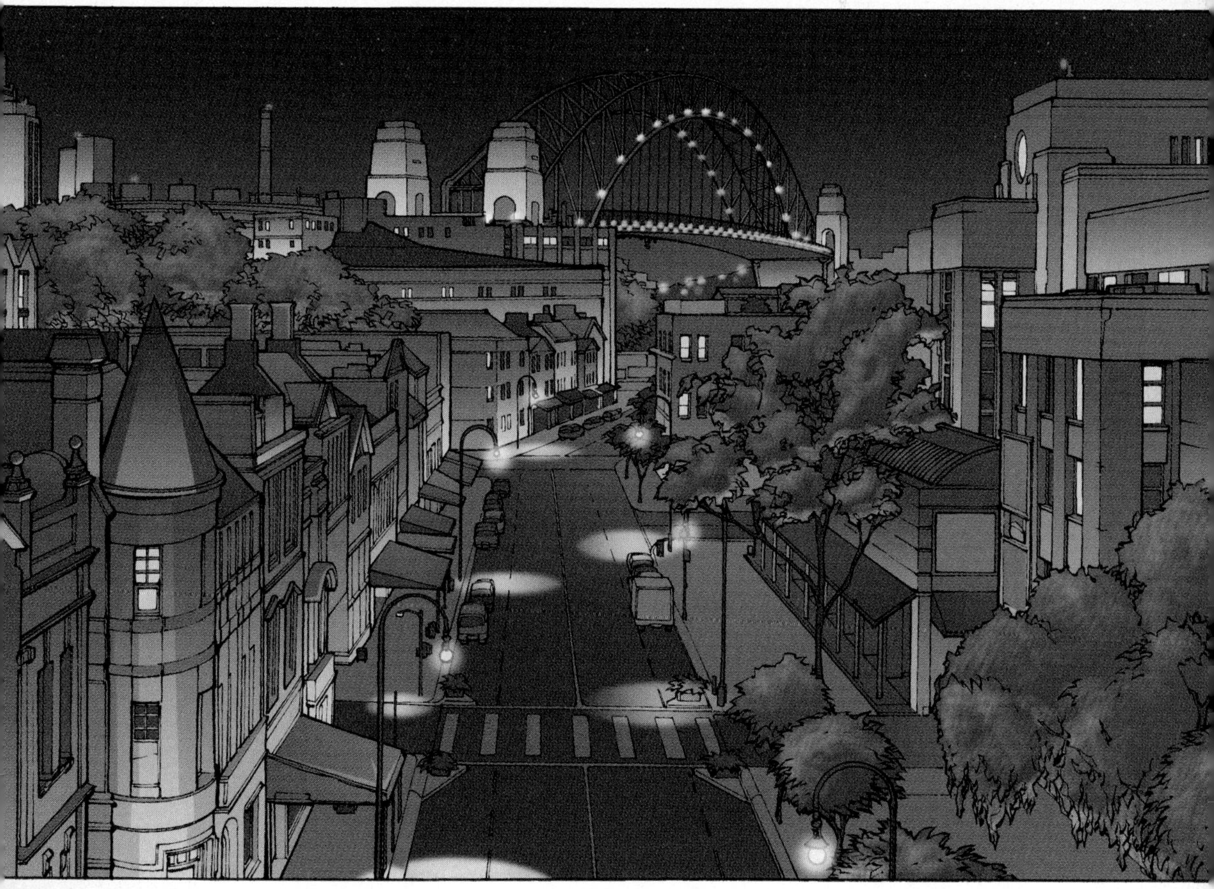

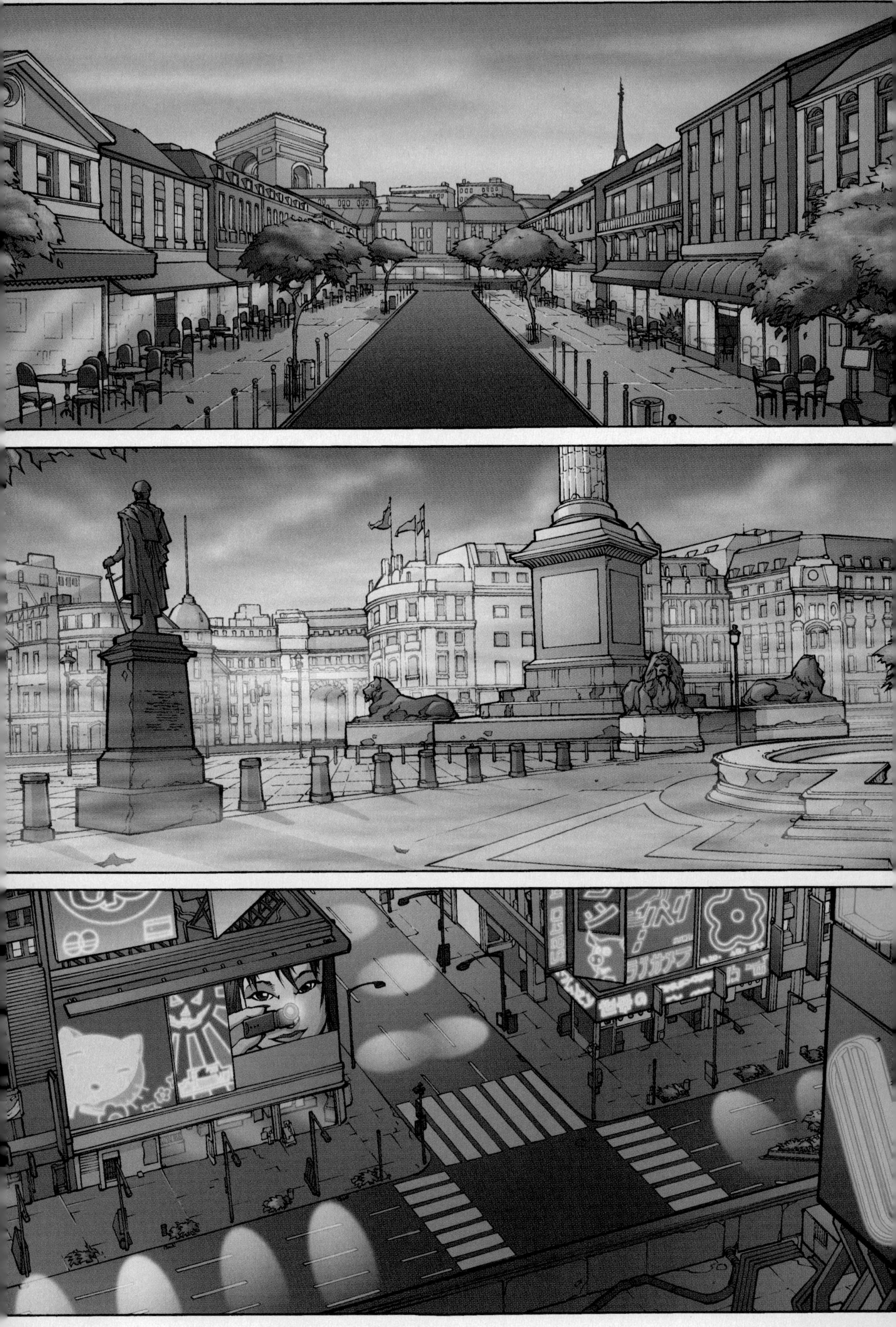

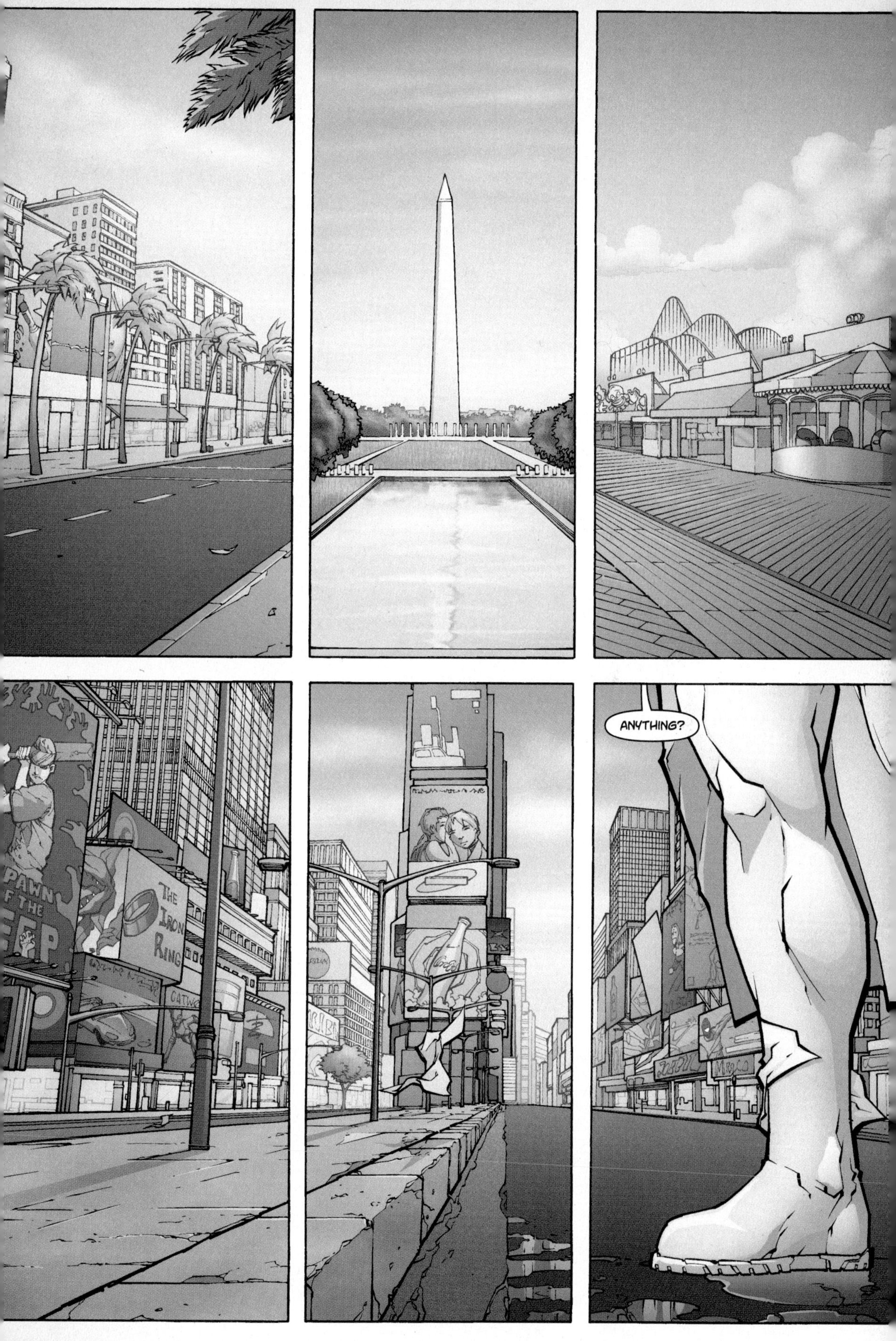
THE IRON RING
ANYTHING?

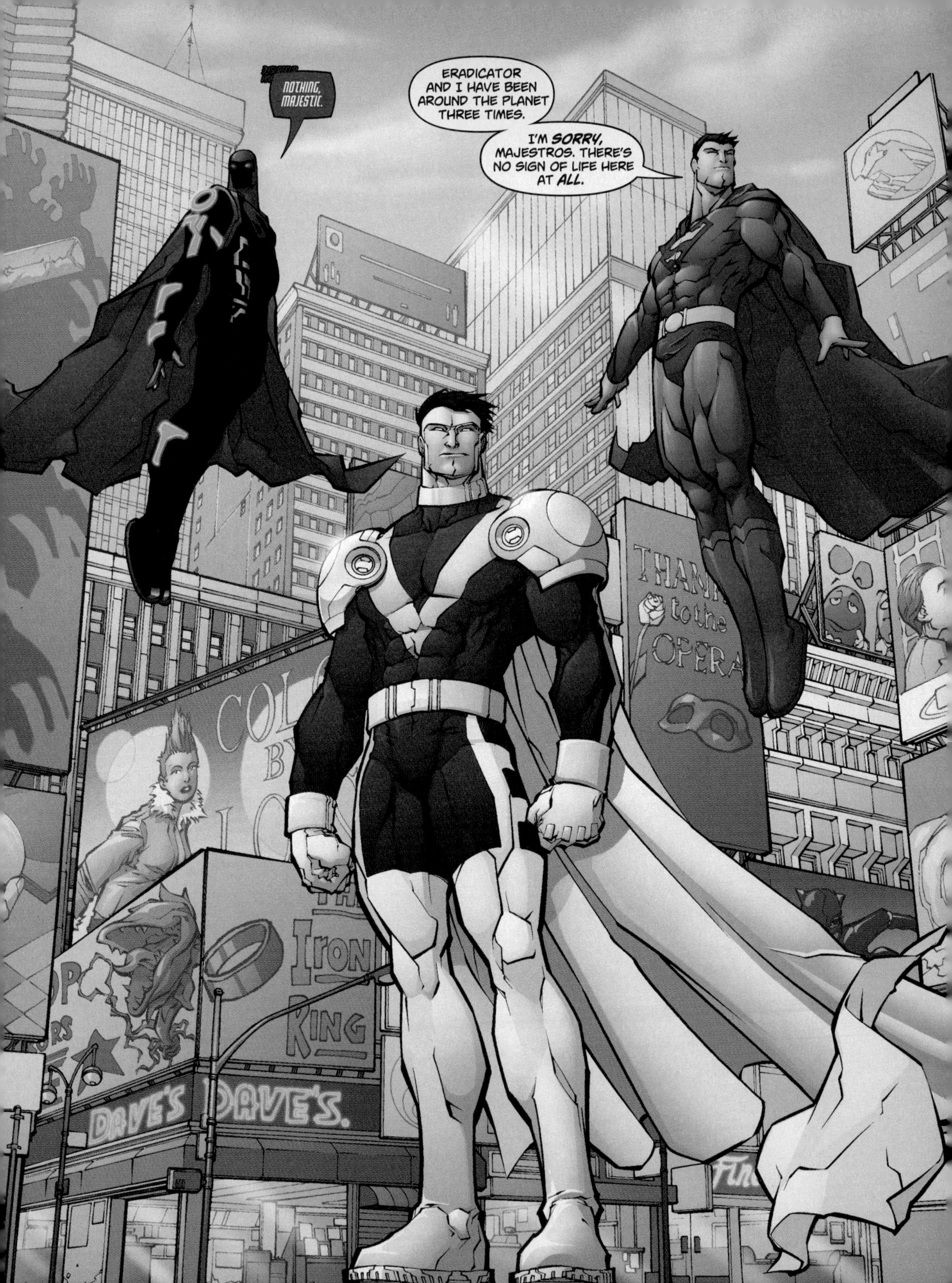
NOTHING, MAJESTIC.
ERADICATOR AND I HAVE BEEN AROUND THE PLANET THREE TIMES.
I'M SORRY, MAJESTROS. THERE'S NO SIGN OF LIFE HERE AT ALL.
to the OPERA
Iron
RING
DAVE'S
DAVE'S.

WHILE YOU WERE OUT

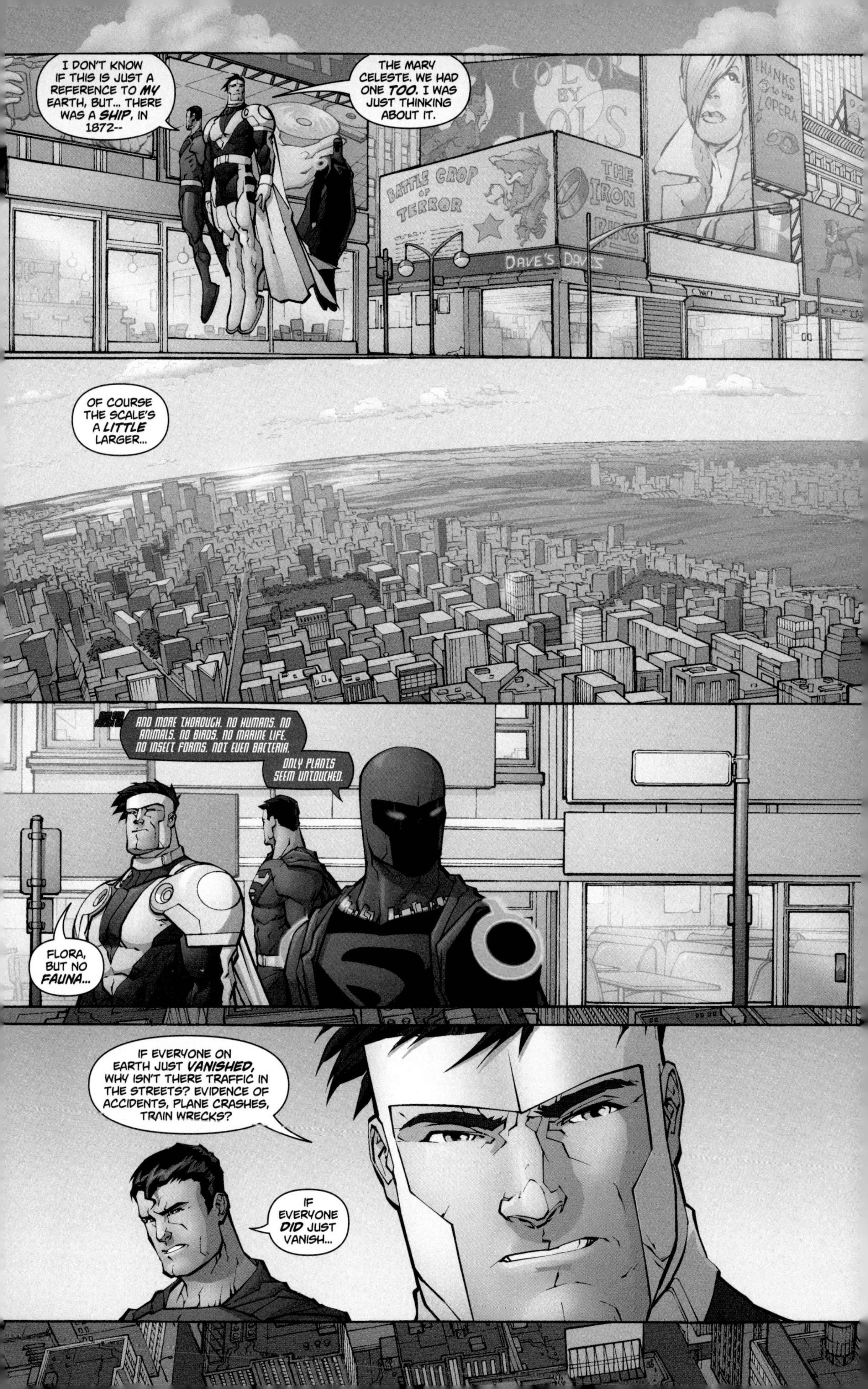
I DON'T KNOW IF THIS IS JUST A REFERENCE TO MY EARTH, BUT... THERE WAS A SHIP, IN 1872--
THE MARY CELESTE. WE HAD ONE TOO. I WAS JUST THINKING ABOUT IT.
BATTLE CROP OF TERROR
THE IRON RING
DAVE'S DAVE'S
OF COURSE THE SCALE'S A LITTLE LARGER...
AND MORE THOROUGH. NO HUMANS. NO ANIMALS. NO BIRDS. NO MARINE LIFE. NO INSECT FORMS. NOT EVEN BACTERIA.
ONLY PLANTS SEEM UNTOUCHED.
FLORA, BUT NO FAUNA...
IF EVERYONE ON EARTH JUST VANISHED, WHY ISN'T THERE TRAFFIC IN THE STREETS? EVIDENCE OF ACCIDENTS, PLANE CRASHES, TRAIN WRECKS?
IF EVERYONE DID JUST VANISH...

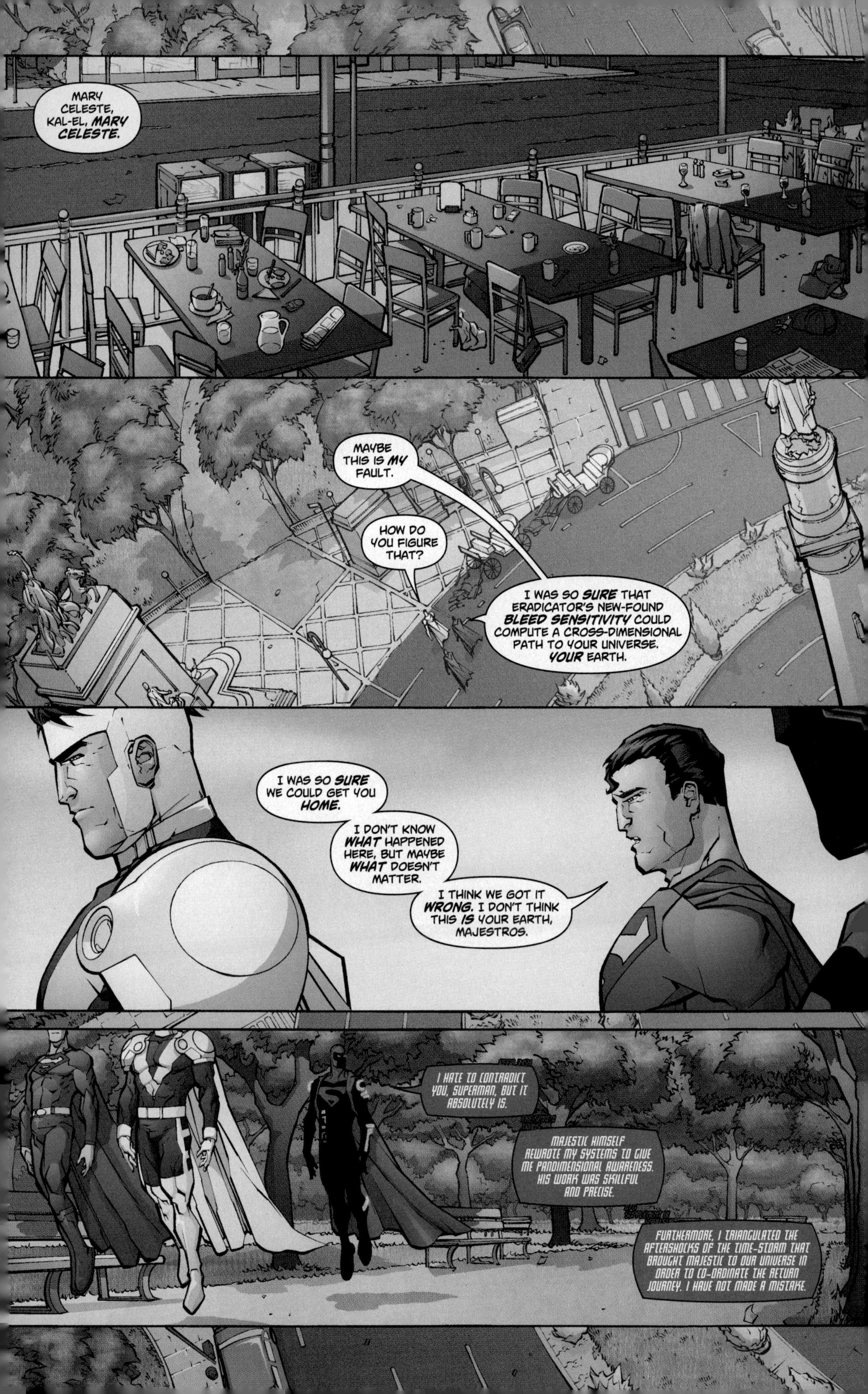

MARY CELESTE, KAL-EL, MARY CELESTE.
MAYBE THIS IS MY FAULT.
HOW DO YOU FIGURE THAT?
I WAS SO SURE THAT ERADICATOR'S NEW-FOUND BLEED SENSITIVITY COULD COMPUTE A CROSS-DIMENSIONAL PATH TO YOUR UNIVERSE. YOUR EARTH.
I WAS SO SURE WE COULD GET YOU HOME.
I DON'T KNOW WHAT HAPPENED HERE, BUT MAYBE WHAT DOESN'T MATTER.
I THINK WE GOT IT WRONG. I DON'T THINK THIS IS YOUR EARTH, MAJESTROS.
I HATE TO CONTRADICT YOU, SUPERMAN, BUT IT ABSOLUTELY IS.
MAJESTIC HIMSELF REWROTE MY SYSTEMS TO GIVE ME PANDIMENSIONAL AWARENESS. HIS WORK WAS SKILLFUL AND PRECISE.
FURTHERMORE, I TRIANGULATED THE AFTERSHOCKS OF THE TIME-STORM THAT BROUGHT MAJESTIC TO OUR UNIVERSE IN ORDER TO CO-ORDINATE THE RETURN JOURNEY. I HAVE NOT MADE A MISTAKE.

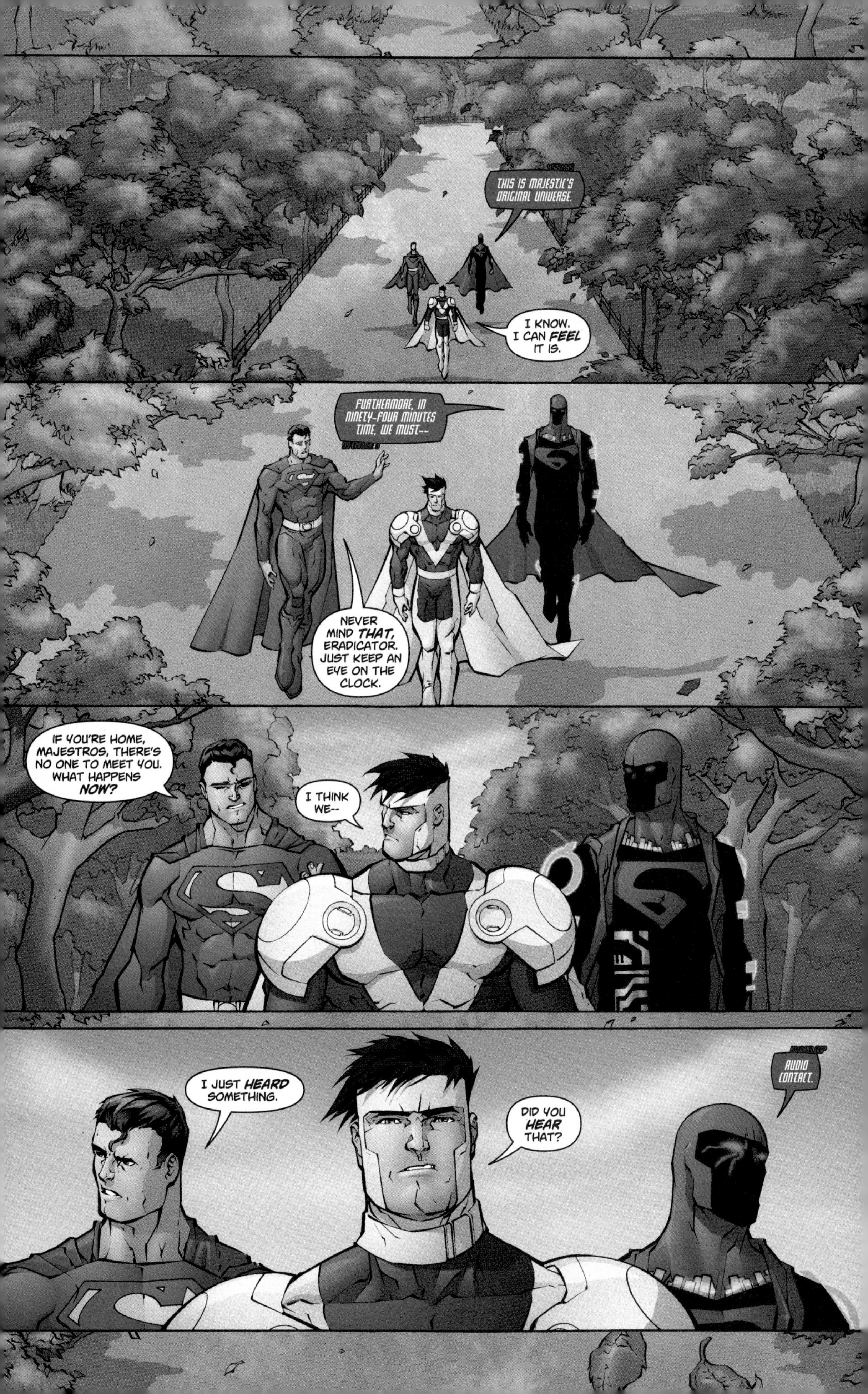
THIS IS MAJESTIC'S ORIGINAL UNIVERSE.
I KNOW. I CAN FEEL IT IS.
FURTHERMORE, IN NINETY-FOUR MINUTES TIME, WE MUST--
NEVER MIND THAT, ERADICATOR. JUST KEEP AN EYE ON THE CLOCK.
IF YOU'RE HOME, MAJESTROS, THERE'S NO ONE TO MEET YOU. WHAT HAPPENS NOW?
I THINK WE--
I JUST HEARD SOMETHING.
DID YOU HEAR THAT?
AUDIO CONTACT.

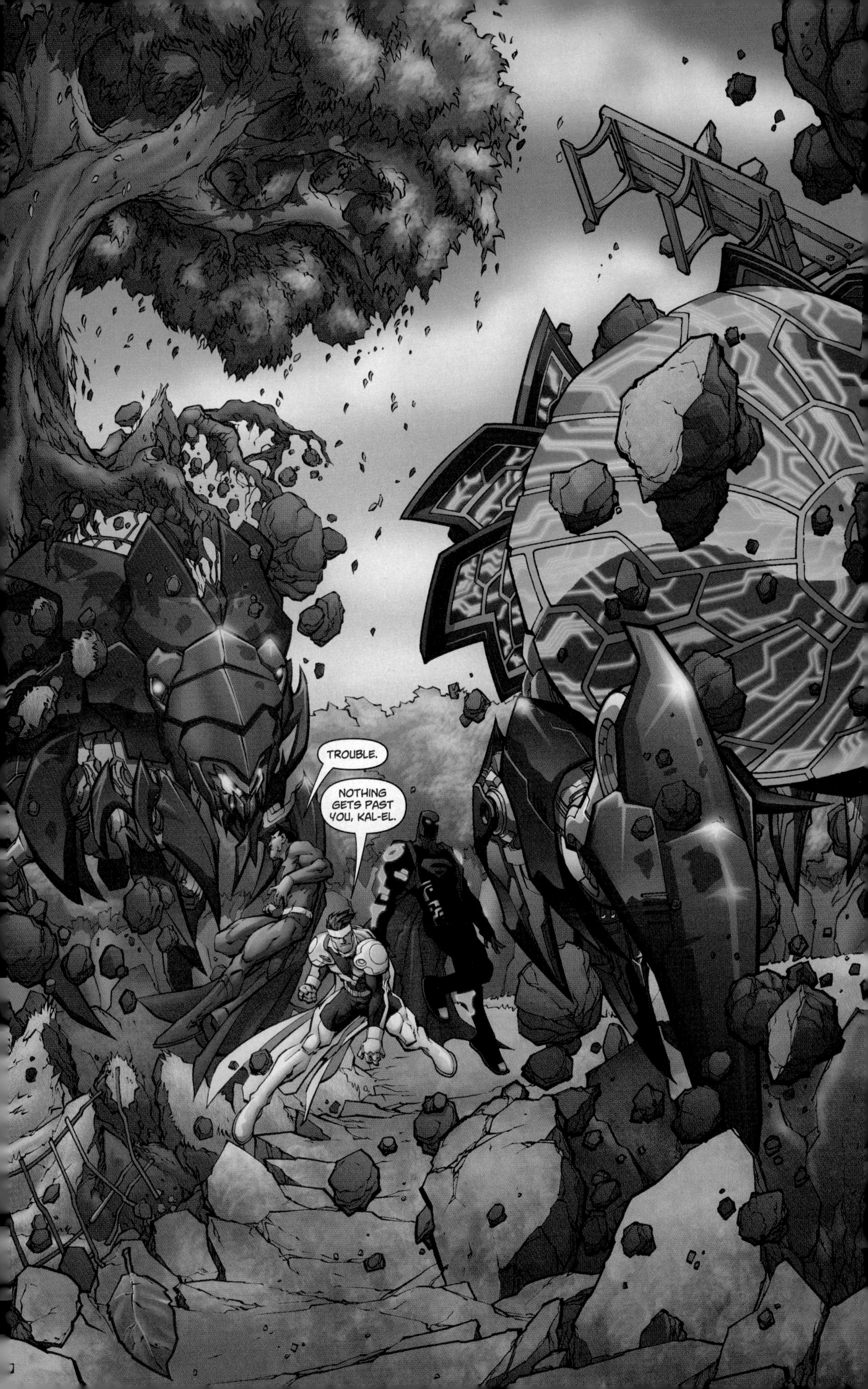
TROUBLE.
NOTHING GETS PAST YOU, KAL-EL.

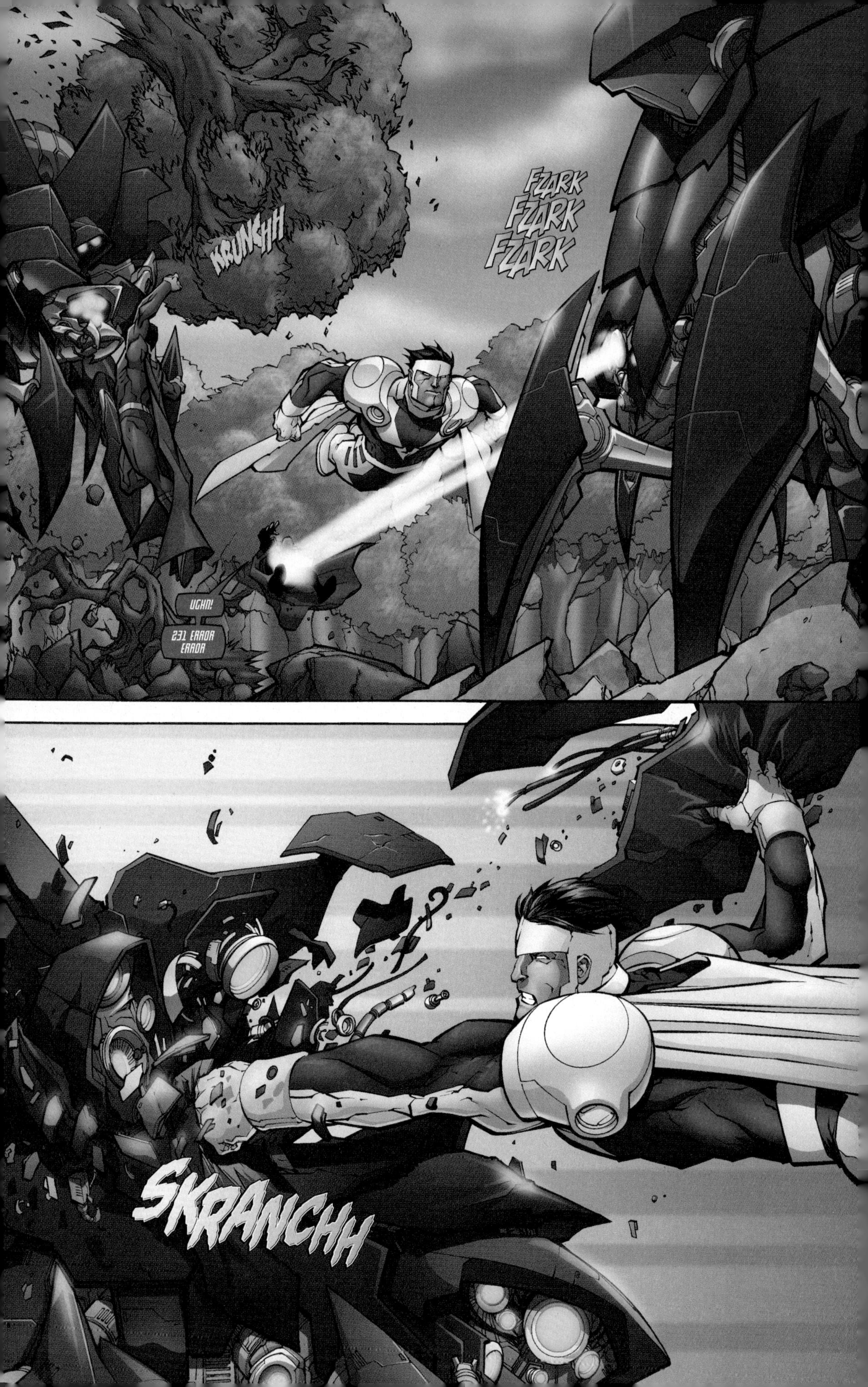
KRUNCHH
FZARK FZARK FZARK
UGHN!
231 ERROR ERROR
SKRANCHH

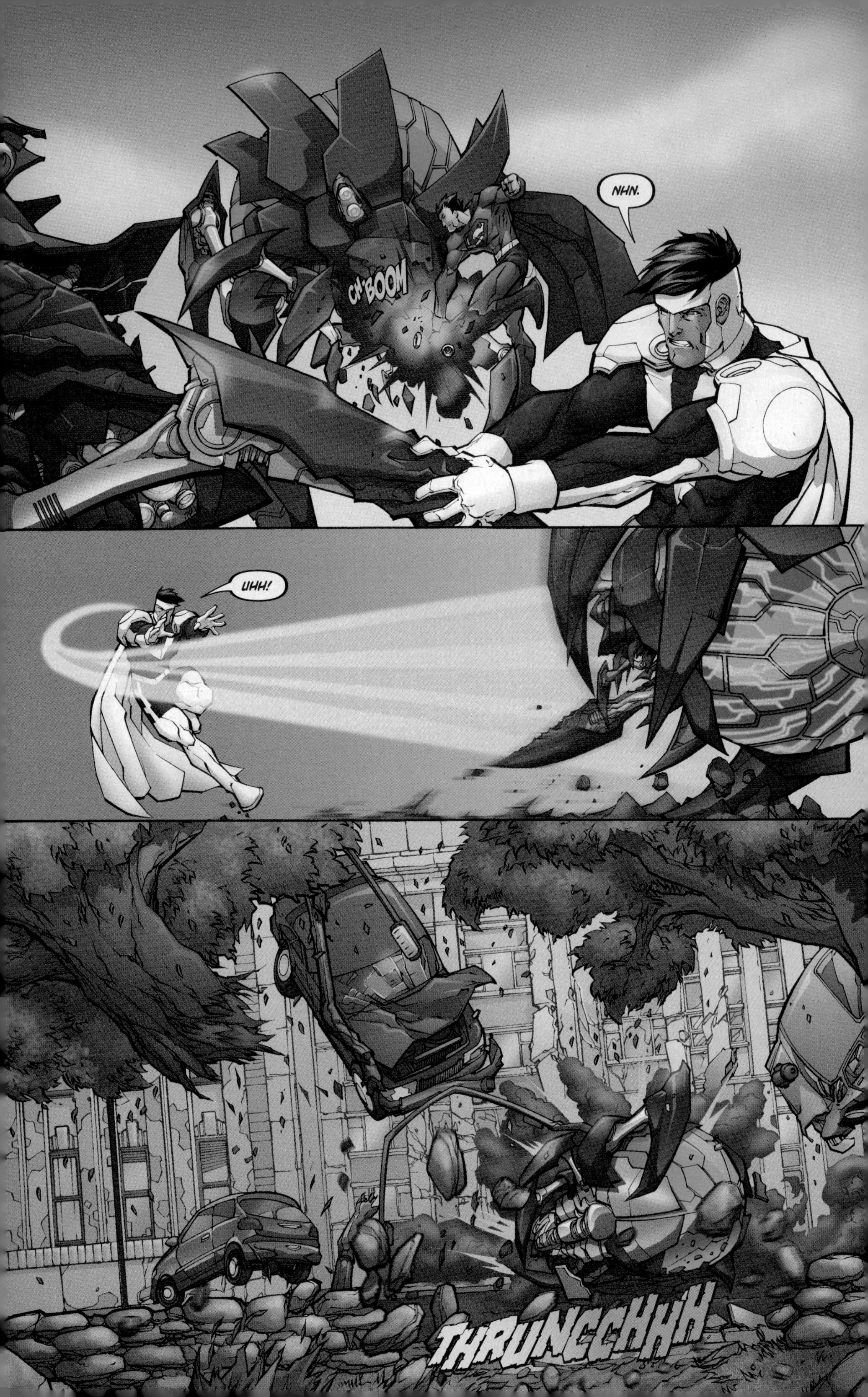
NHN.
CH-BOOM
UHH!
THRUNCCHHH

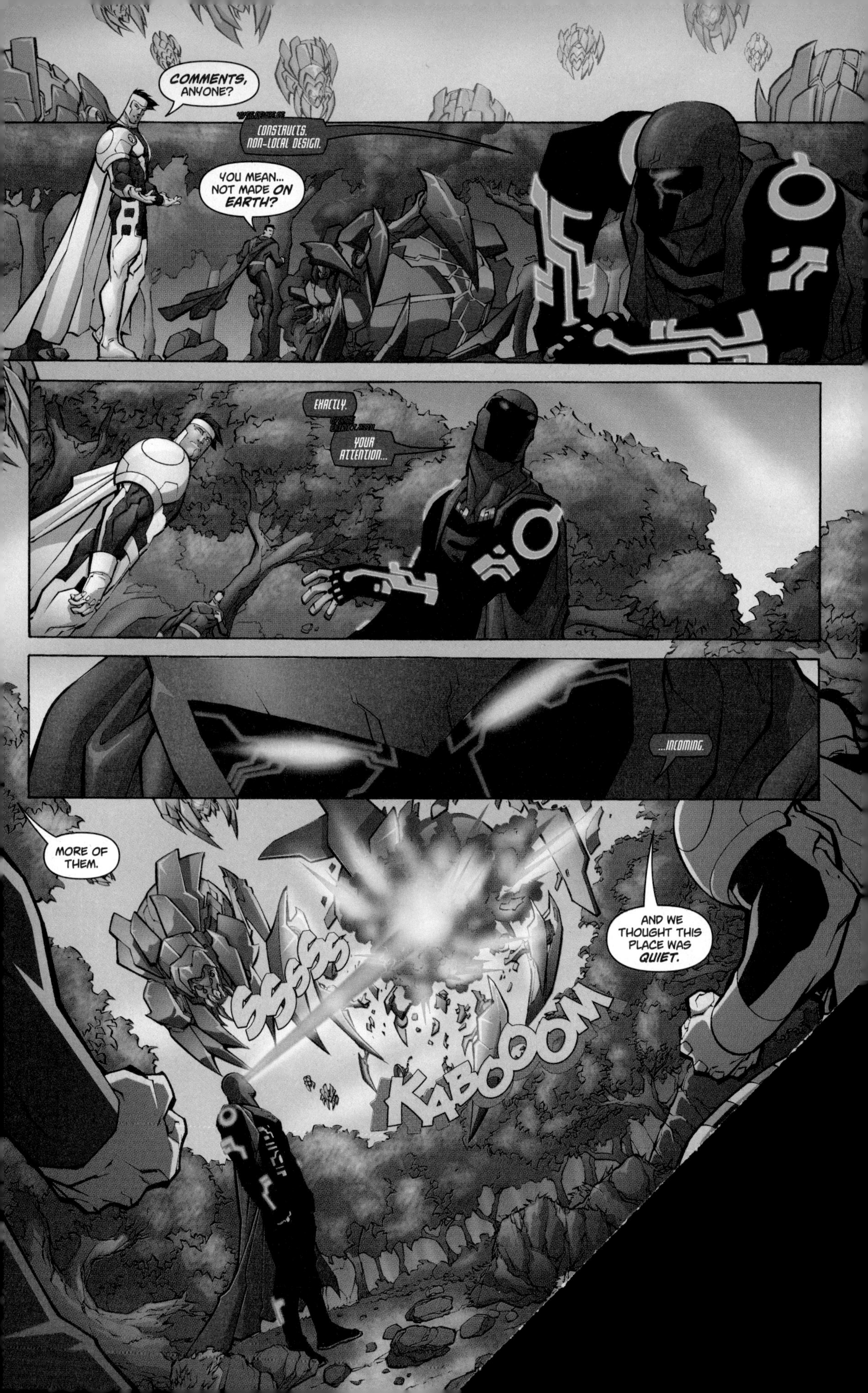
COMMENTS, ANYONE?
CONSTRUCTS. NON-LOCAL DESIGN.
YOU MEAN... NOT MADE ON EARTH?
EXACTLY.
YOUR ATTENTION...
...INCOMING.
MORE OF THEM.
SSSSS
KABOOOM
AND WE THOUGHT THIS PLACE WAS QUIET.

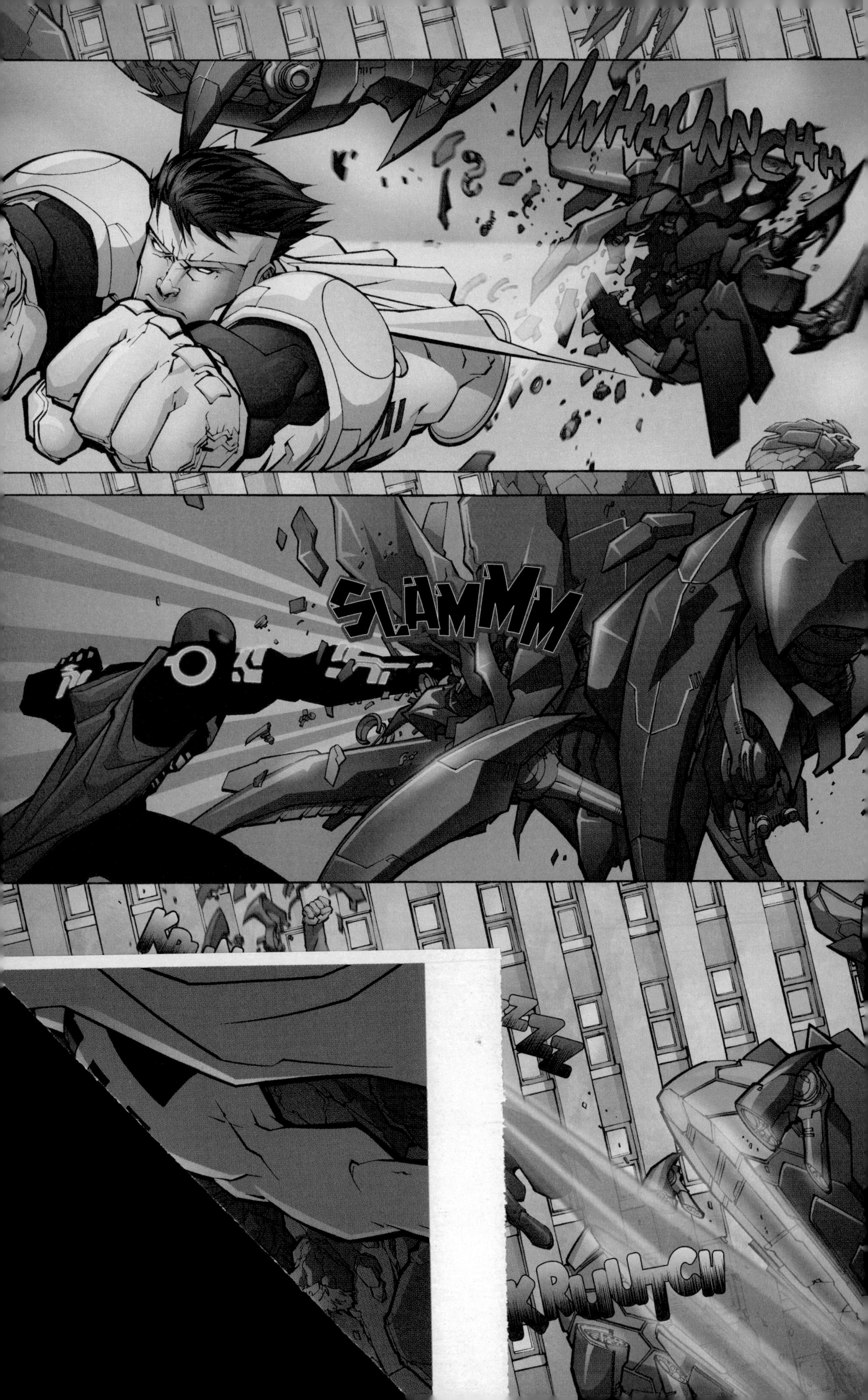
WHHUNNCHH
SLAMMMM
KRUUTCH

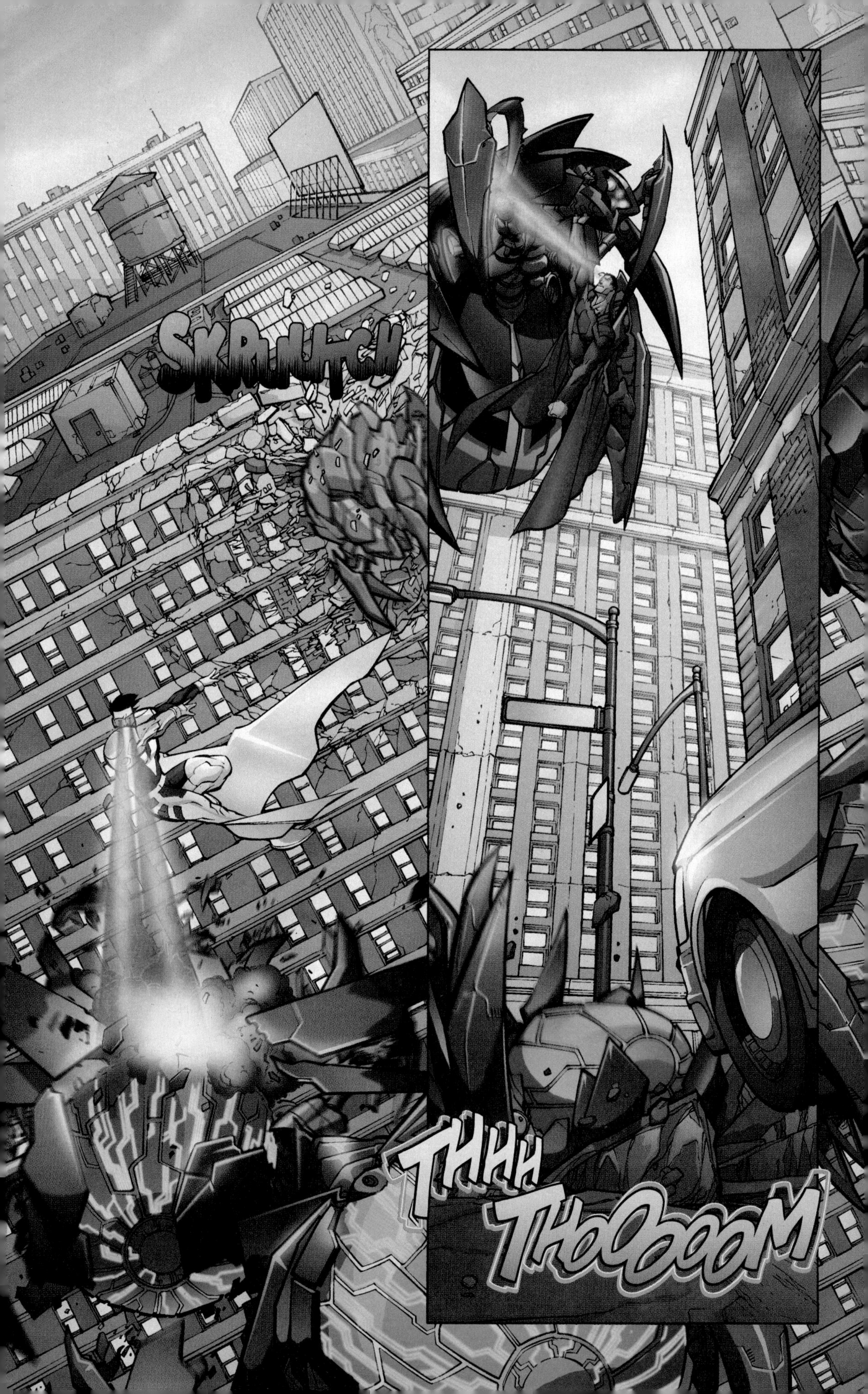
SKRUNCH
THHH
THOOOOOM

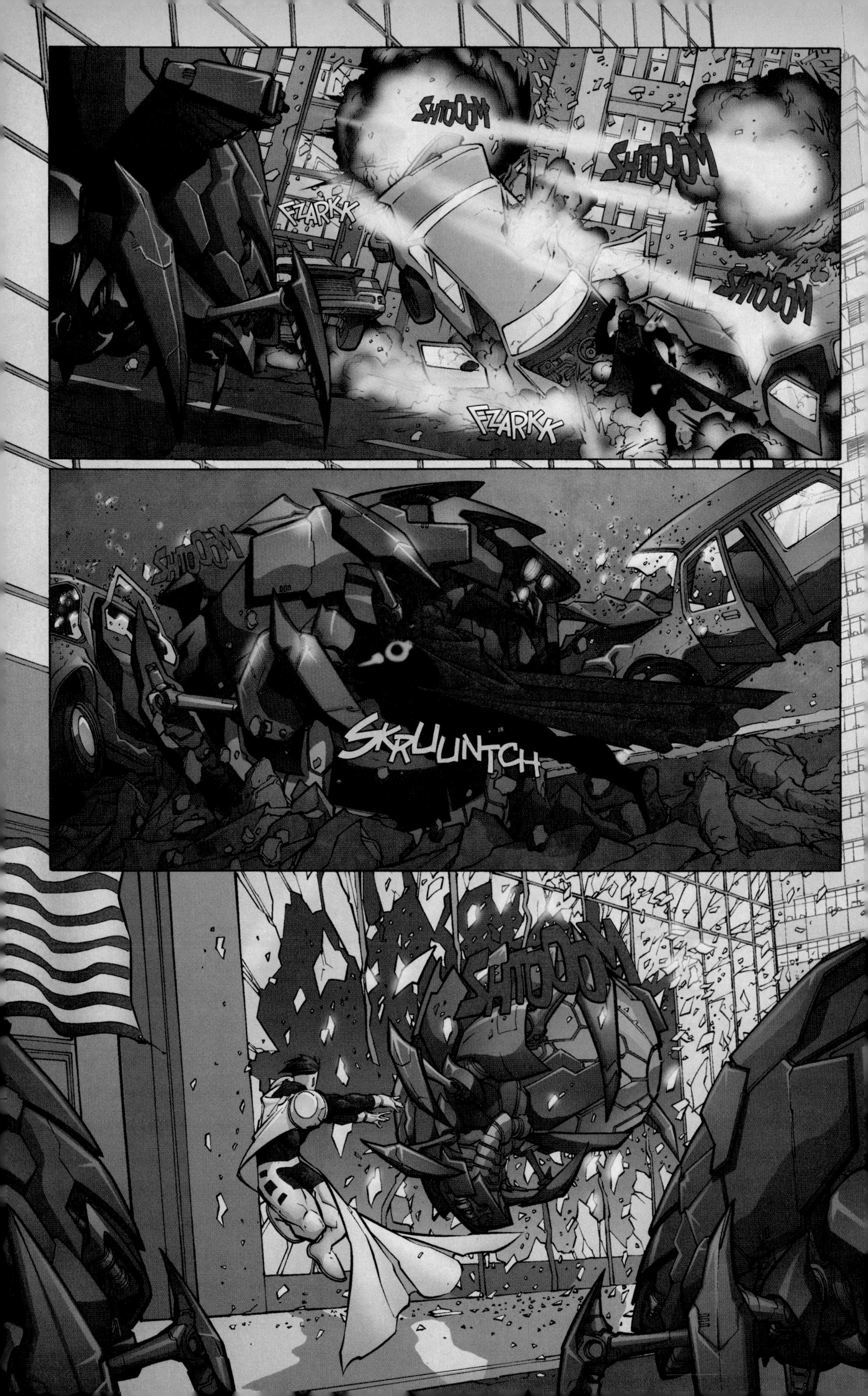
SHTOOOM
SHTOOOM
FZARKKK
SHTOOOM
FZARKKK
SHTOOOM
SKRUUNTCH
SHTOOOM

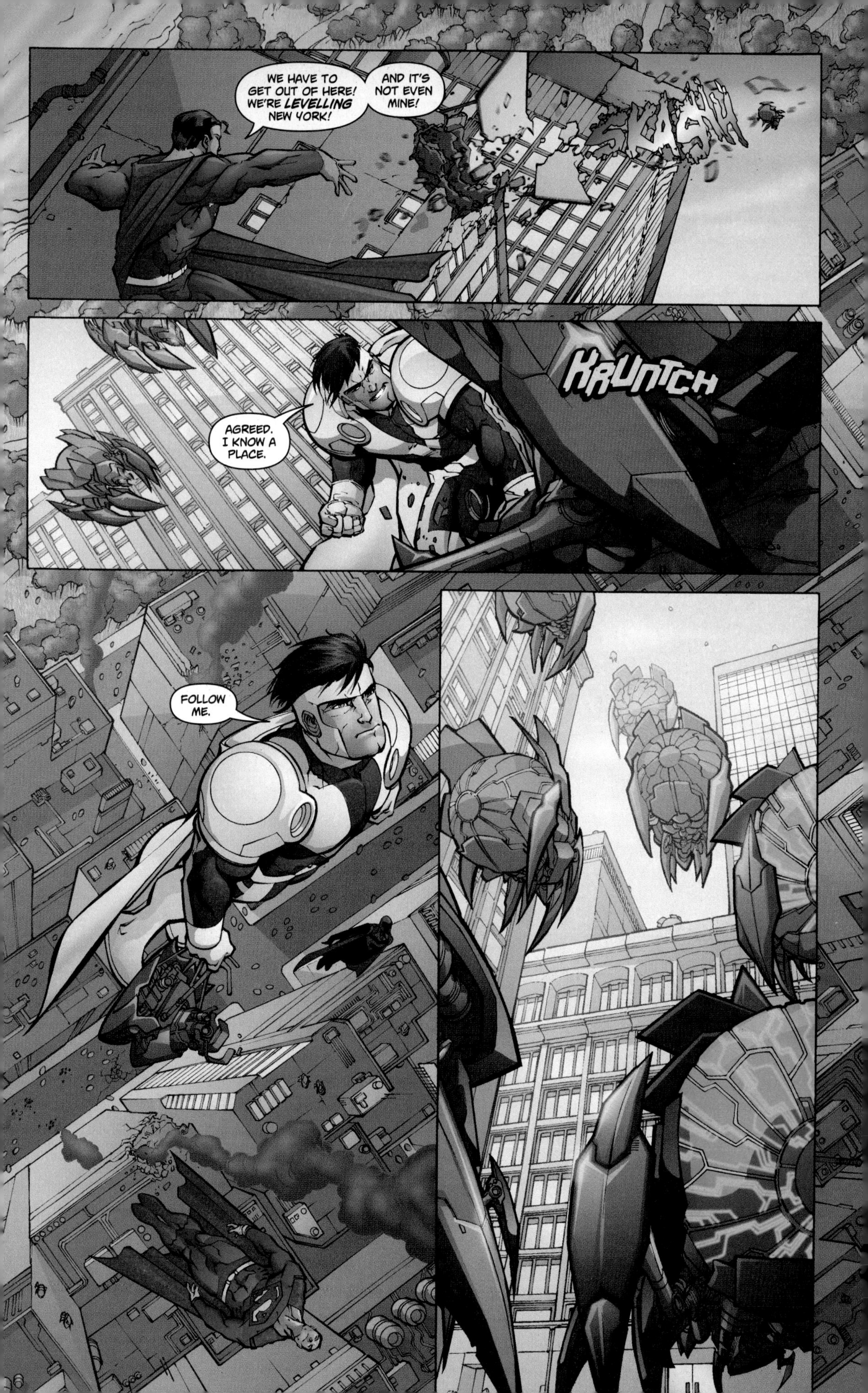
WE HAVE TO GET OUT OF HERE! WE'RE LEVELLING NEW YORK!
AND IT'S NOT EVEN MINE!
SKACH
KRUNTCH
AGREED. I KNOW A PLACE.
FOLLOW ME.

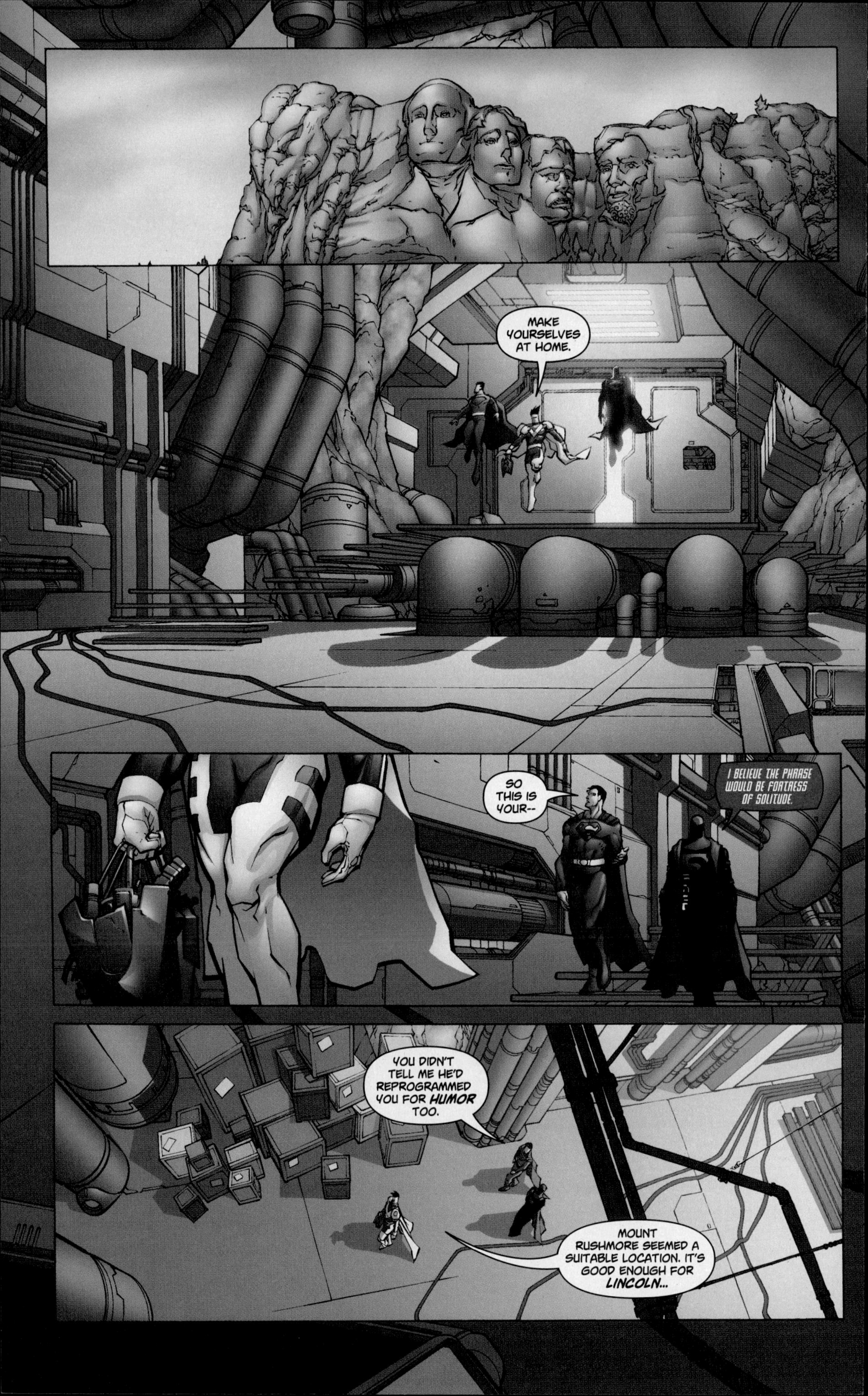
MAKE YOURSELVES AT HOME.
SO THIS IS YOUR--
I BELIEVE THE PHRASE WOULD BE FORTRESS OF SOLITUDE.
YOU DIDN'T TELL ME HE'D REPROGRAMMED YOU FOR HUMOR TOO.
MOUNT RUSHMORE SEEMED A SUITABLE LOCATION. IT'S GOOD ENOUGH FOR LINCOLN...

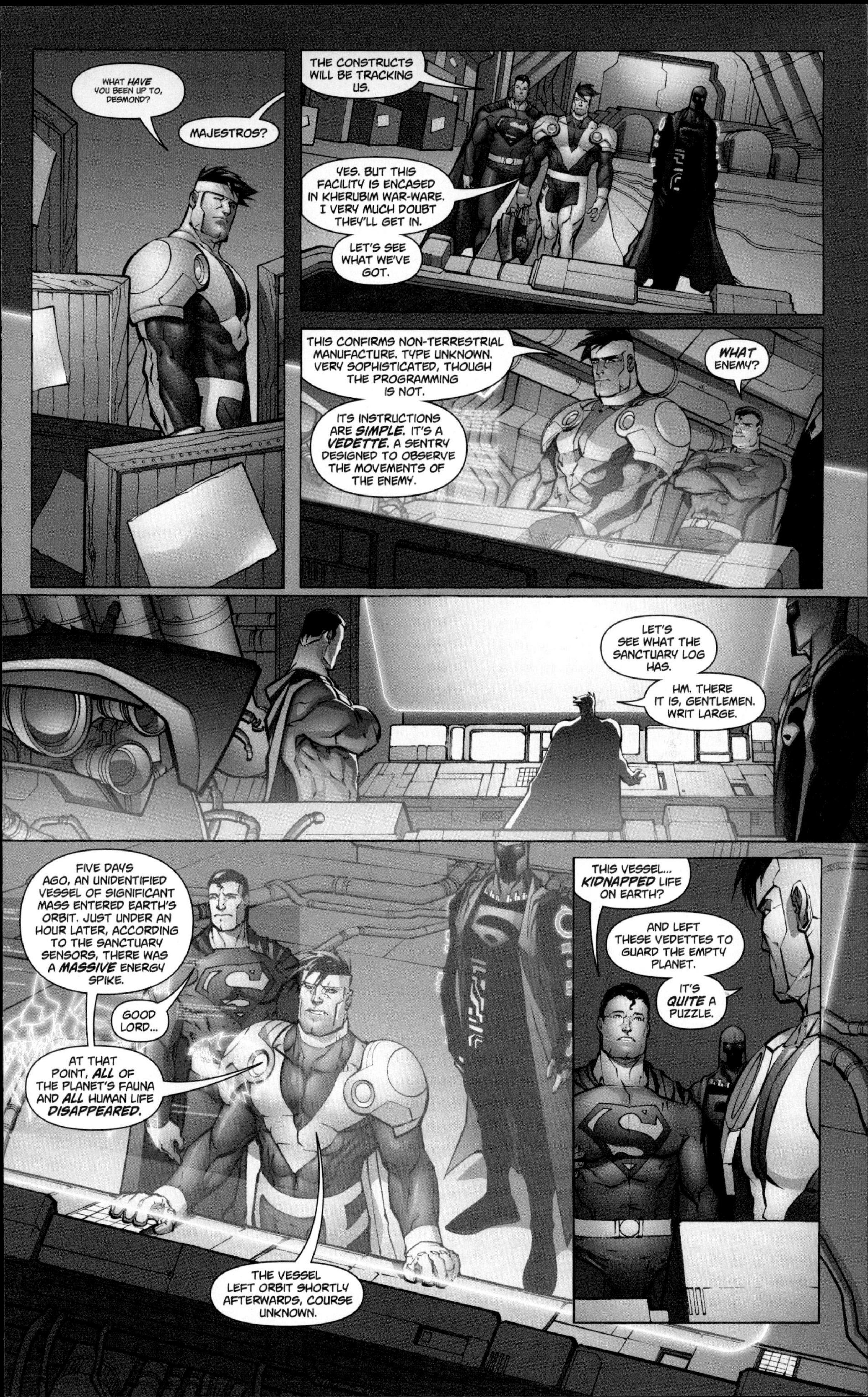
WHAT HAVE YOU BEEN UP TO, DESMOND?
MAJESTROS?
THE CONSTRUCTS WILL BE TRACKING US.
YES. BUT THIS FACILITY IS ENCASED IN KHERUBIM WAR-WARE. I VERY MUCH DOUBT THEY'LL GET IN.
LET'S SEE WHAT WE'VE GOT.
THIS CONFIRMS NON-TERRESTRIAL MANUFACTURE. TYPE UNKNOWN. VERY SOPHISTICATED, THOUGH THE PROGRAMMING IS NOT.
ITS INSTRUCTIONS ARE SIMPLE. IT'S A VEDETTE. A SENTRY DESIGNED TO OBSERVE THE MOVEMENTS OF THE ENEMY.
WHAT ENEMY?
LET'S SEE WHAT THE SANCTUARY LOG HAS.
HM. THERE IT IS, GENTLEMEN. WRIT LARGE.
FIVE DAYS AGO, AN UNIDENTIFIED VESSEL OF SIGNIFICANT MASS ENTERED EARTH'S ORBIT. JUST UNDER AN HOUR LATER, ACCORDING TO THE SANCTUARY SENSORS, THERE WAS A MASSIVE ENERGY SPIKE.
GOOD LORD...
AT THAT POINT, ALL OF THE PLANET'S FAUNA AND ALL HUMAN LIFE DISAPPEARED.
THE VESSEL LEFT ORBIT SHORTLY AFTERWARDS, COURSE UNKNOWN.
THIS VESSEL... KIDNAPPED LIFE ON EARTH?
AND LEFT THESE VEDETTES TO GUARD THE EMPTY PLANET.
IT'S QUITE A PUZZLE.

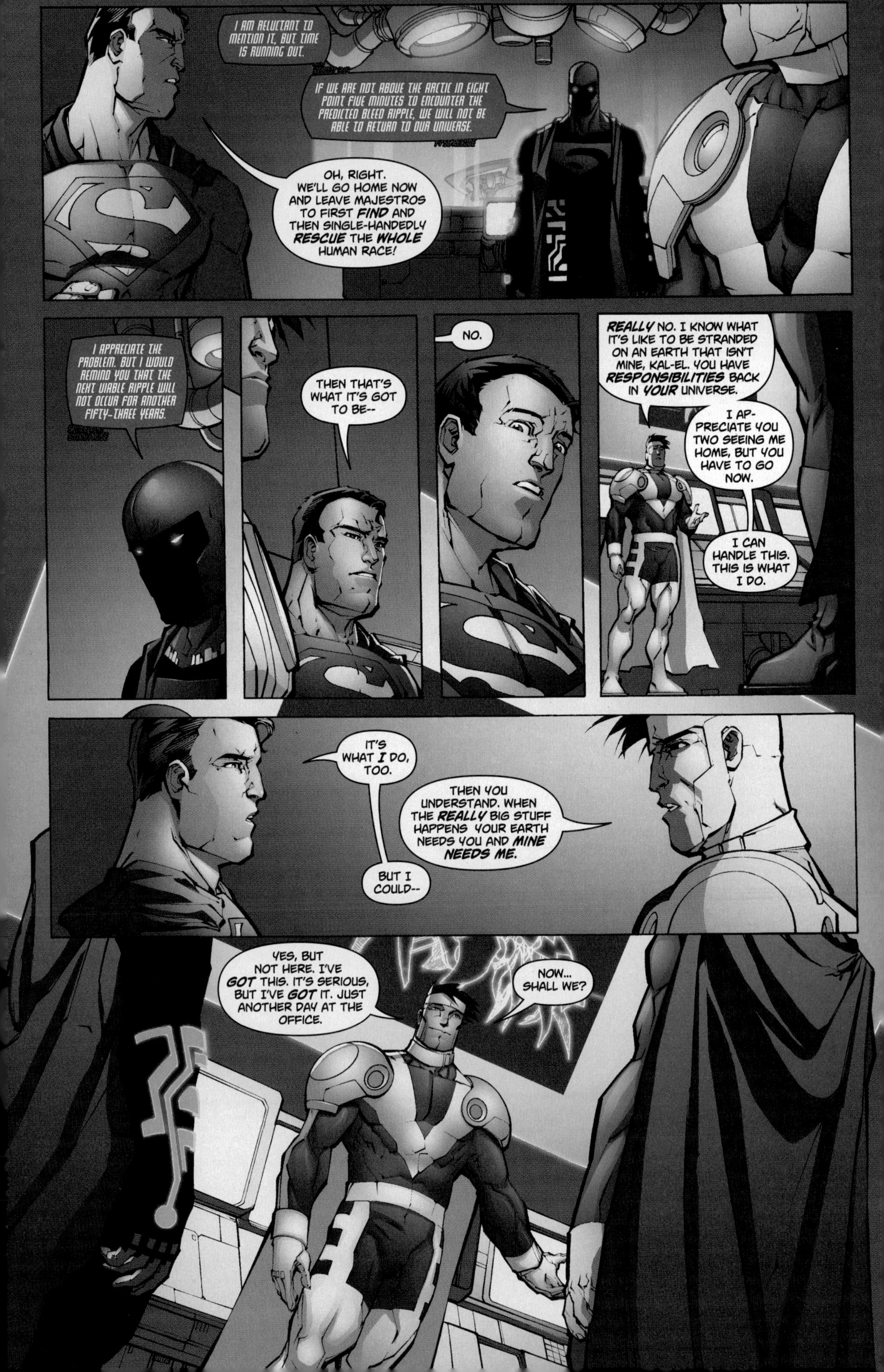

I AM RELUCTANT TO MENTION IT, BUT TIME IS RUNNING OUT.
IF WE ARE NOT ABOVE THE ARCTIC IN EIGHT POINT FIVE MINUTES TO ENCOUNTER THE PREDICTED BLEED RIPPLE, WE WILL NOT BE ABLE TO RETURN TO OUR UNIVERSE.
OH, RIGHT. WE'LL GO HOME NOW AND LEAVE MAJESTROS TO FIRST FIND AND THEN SINGLE-HANDEDLY RESCUE THE WHOLE HUMAN RACE!
I APPRECIATE THE PROBLEM. BUT I WOULD REMIND YOU THAT THE NEXT VIABLE RIPPLE WILL NOT OCCUR FOR ANOTHER FIFTY-THREE YEARS.
THEN THAT'S WHAT IT'S GOT TO BE--
NO.
REALLY NO. I KNOW WHAT IT'S LIKE TO BE STRANDED ON AN EARTH THAT ISN'T MINE, KAL-EL. YOU HAVE RESPONSIBILITIES BACK IN YOUR UNIVERSE.
I APPRECIATE YOU TWO SEEING ME HOME, BUT YOU HAVE TO GO NOW.
I CAN HANDLE THIS. THIS IS WHAT I DO.
IT'S WHAT I DO, TOO.
THEN YOU UNDERSTAND. WHEN THE REALLY BIG STUFF HAPPENS YOUR EARTH NEEDS YOU AND MINE NEEDS ME.
BUT I COULD--
YES, BUT NOT HERE. I'VE GOT THIS. IT'S SERIOUS, BUT I'VE GOT IT. JUST ANOTHER DAY AT THE OFFICE.
NOW... SHALL WE?

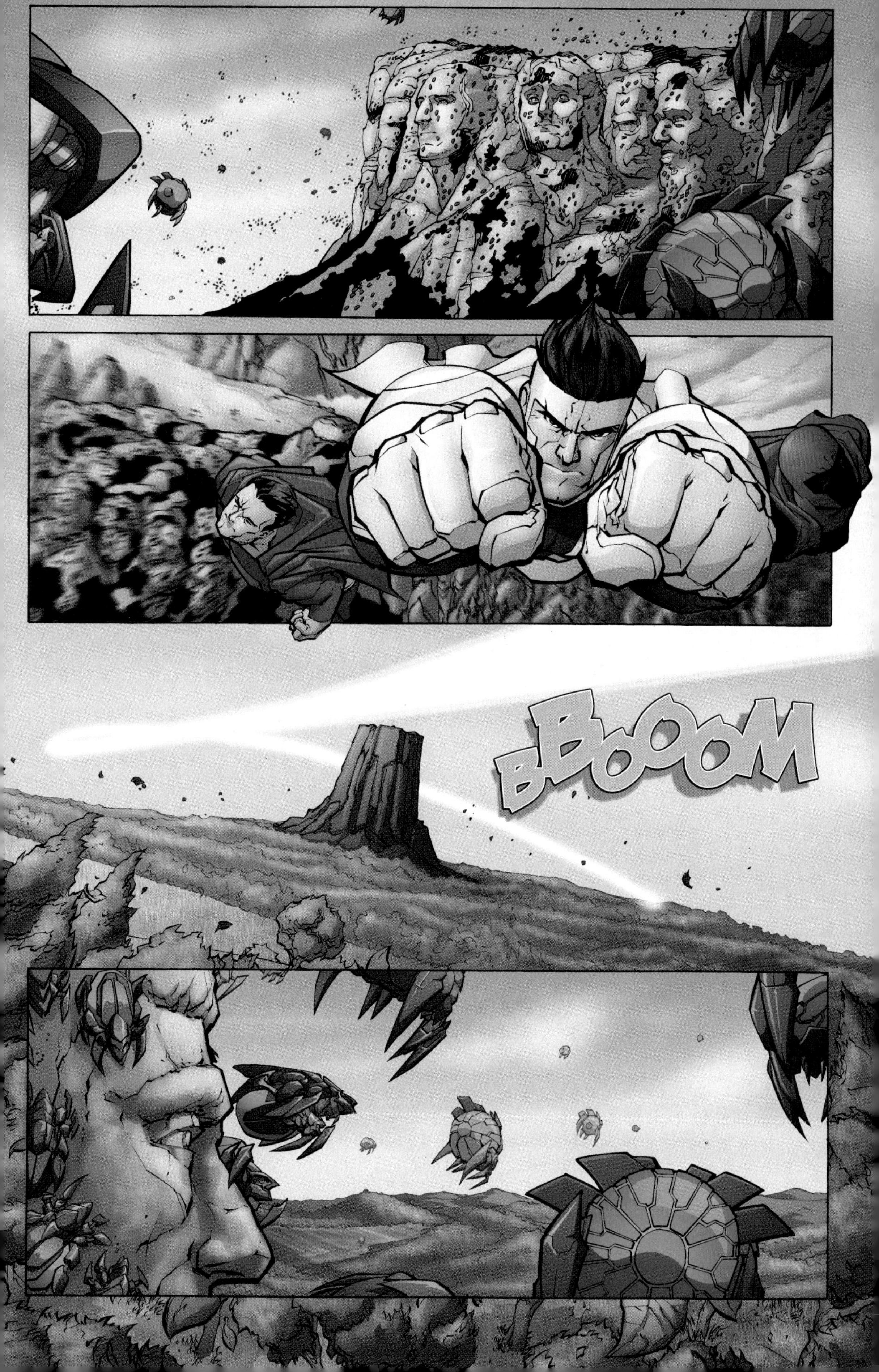
BBOOOM

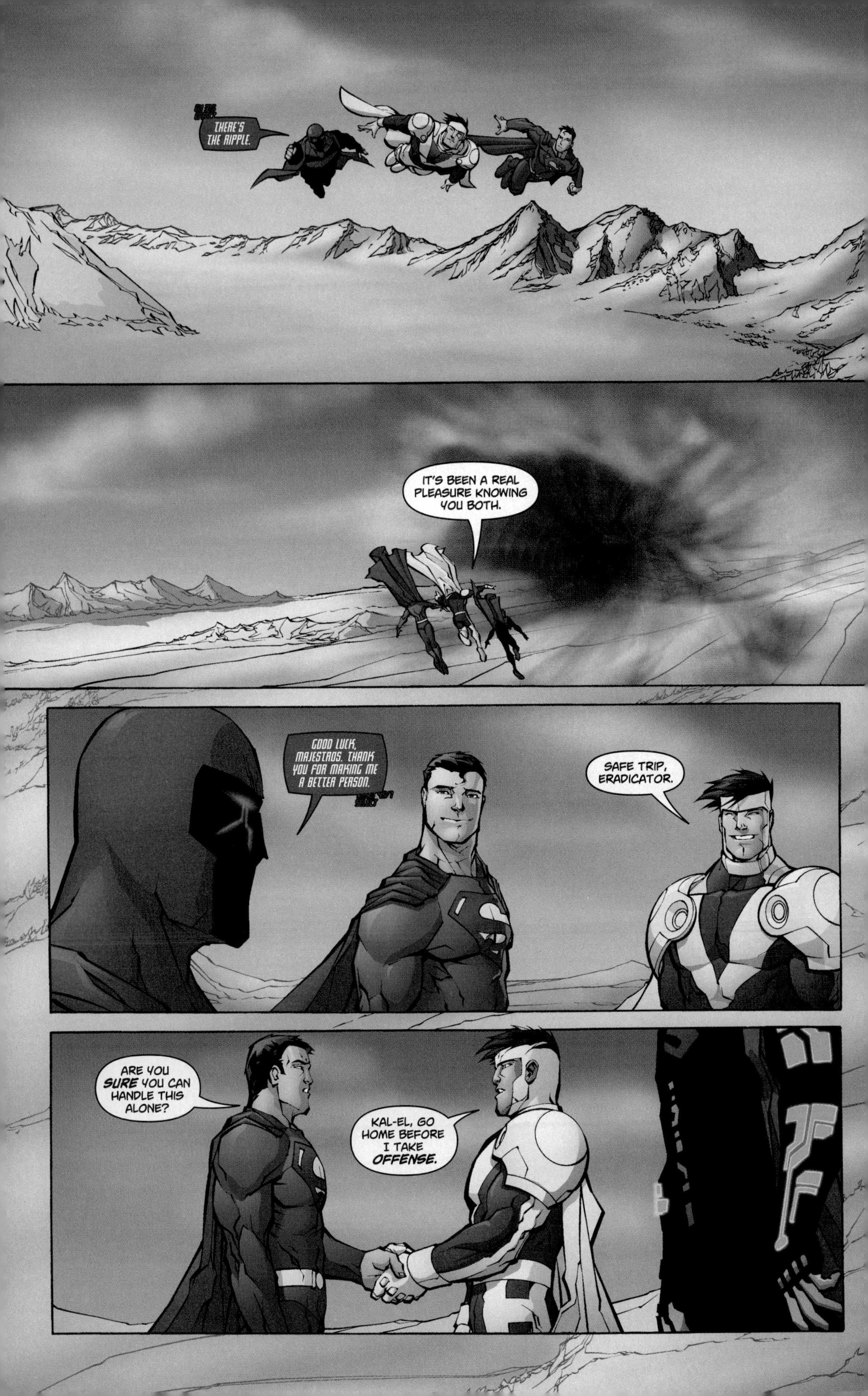
THERE'S THE RIPPLE.
IT'S BEEN A REAL PLEASURE KNOWING YOU BOTH.
GOOD LUCK, MAJESTROS. THANK YOU FOR MAKING ME A BETTER PERSON.
SAFE TRIP, ERADICATOR.
ARE YOU SURE YOU CAN HANDLE THIS ALONE?
KAL-EL, GO HOME BEFORE I TAKE OFFENSE.

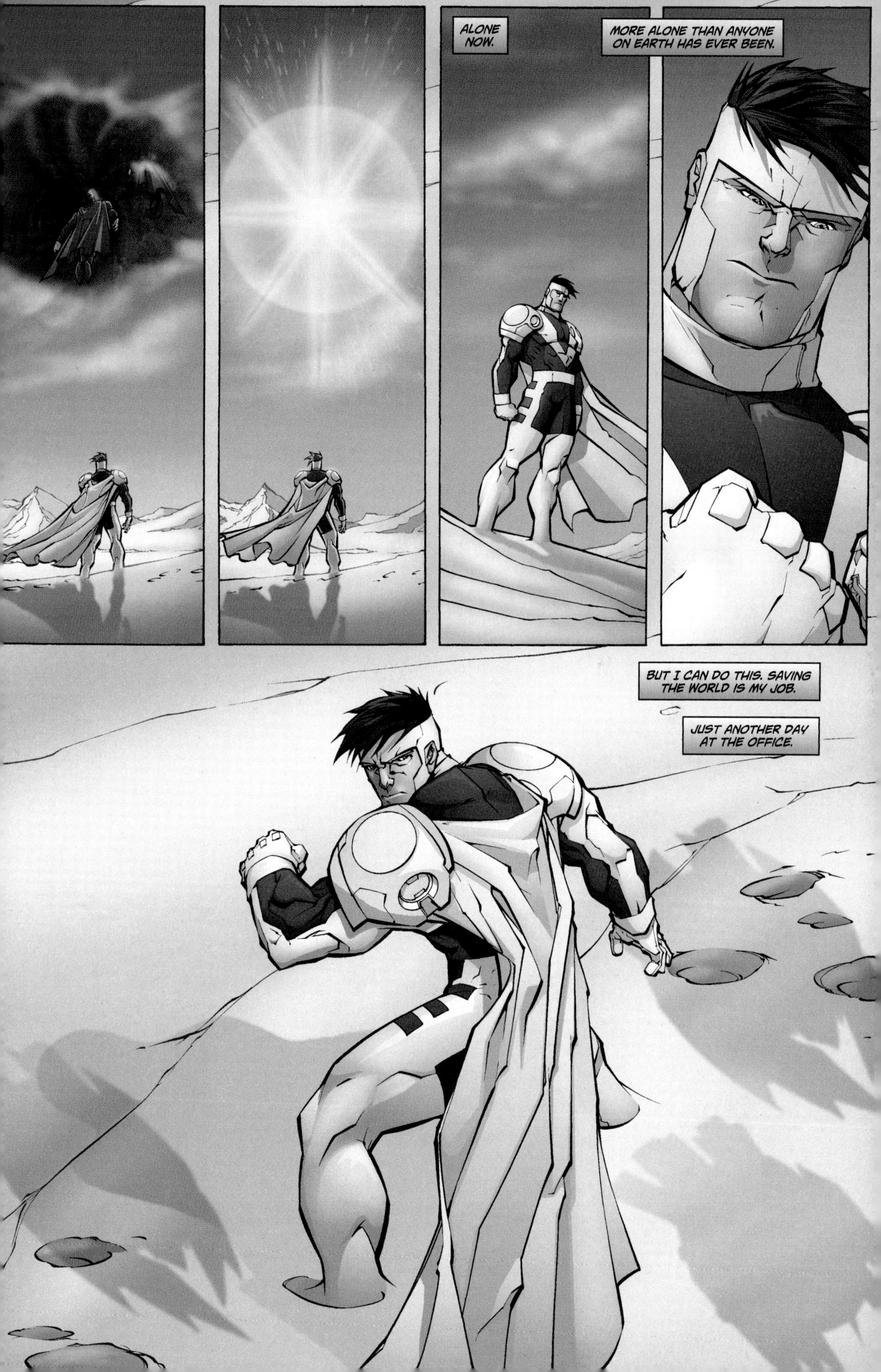
ALONE NOW.
MORE ALONE THAN ANYONE ON EARTH HAS EVER BEEN.
BUT I CAN DO THIS. SAVING THE WORLD IS MY JOB.
JUST ANOTHER DAY AT THE OFFICE.

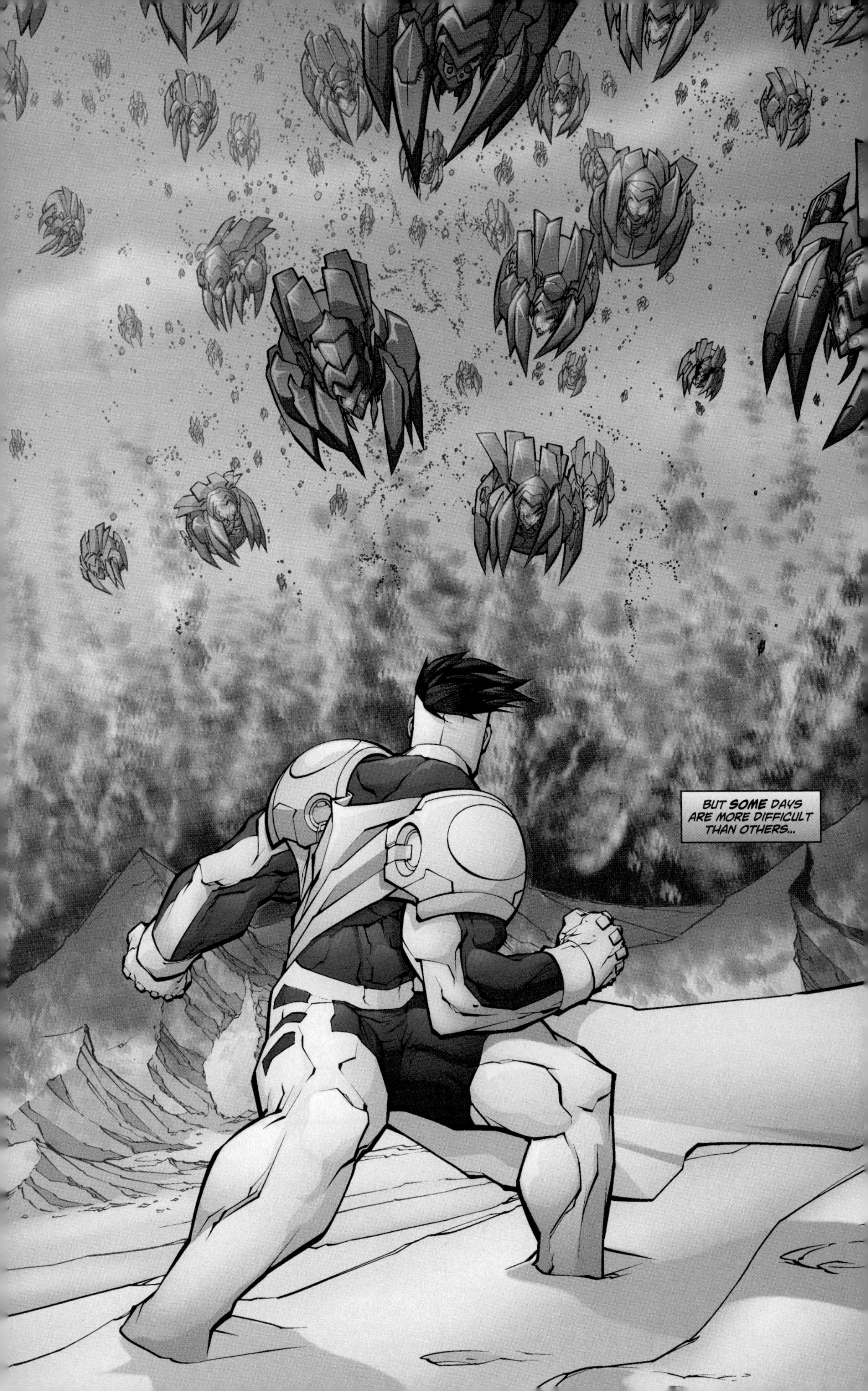
BUT SOME DAYS ARE MORE DIFFICULT THAN OTHERS...

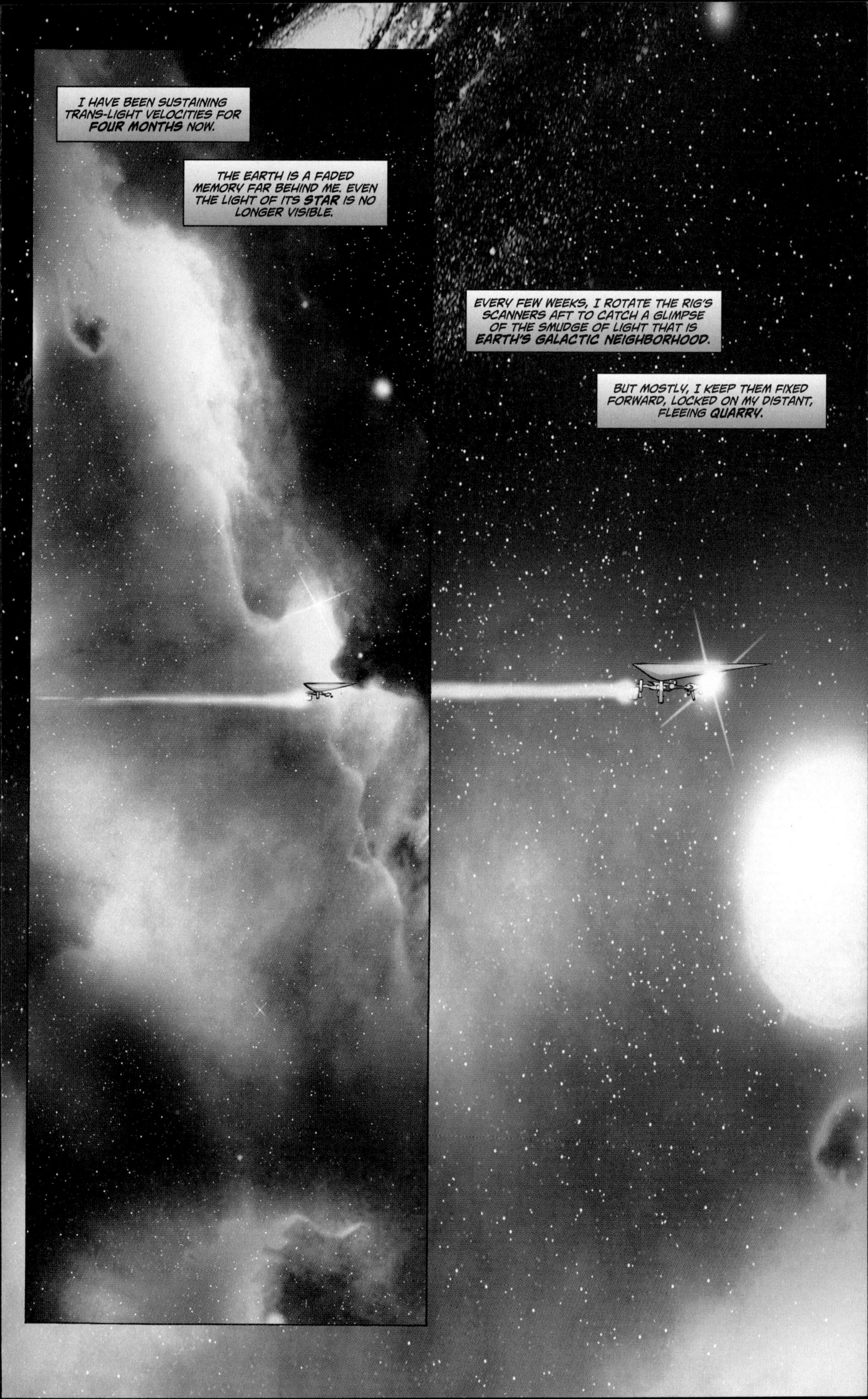
I HAVE BEEN SUSTAINING TRANS-LIGHT VELOCITIES FOR FOUR MONTHS NOW.
THE EARTH IS A FADED MEMORY FAR BEHIND ME. EVEN THE LIGHT OF ITS STAR IS NO LONGER VISIBLE.
EVERY FEW WEEKS, I ROTATE THE RIG'S SCANNERS AFT TO CATCH A GLIMPSE OF THE SMUDGE OF LIGHT THAT IS EARTH'S GALACTIC NEIGHBORHOOD.
BUT MOSTLY, I KEEP THEM FIXED FORWARD, LOCKED ON MY DISTANT, FLEEING QUARRY.

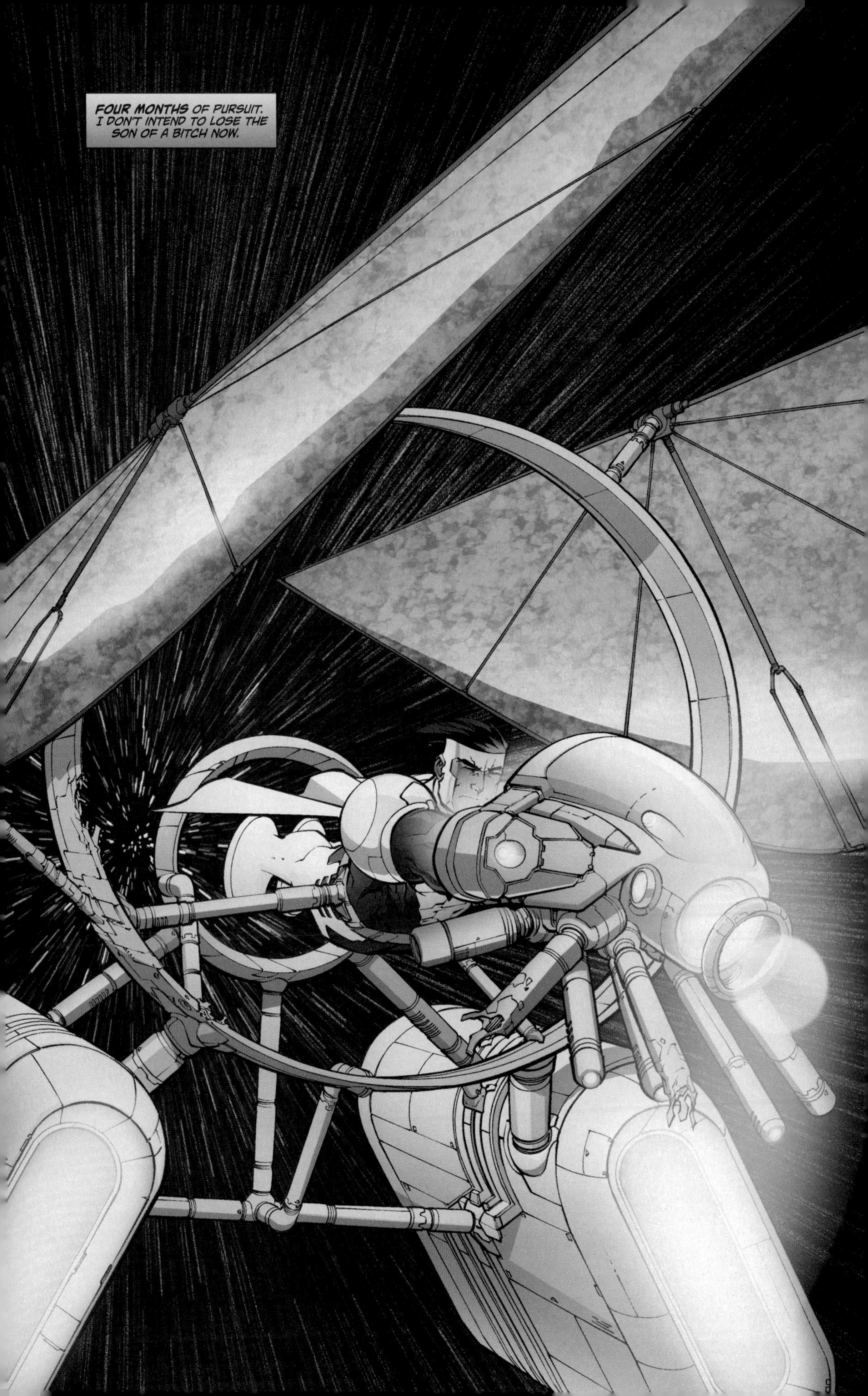
FOUR MONTHS OF PURSUIT. I DON'T INTEND TO LOSE THE SON OF A BITCH NOW.

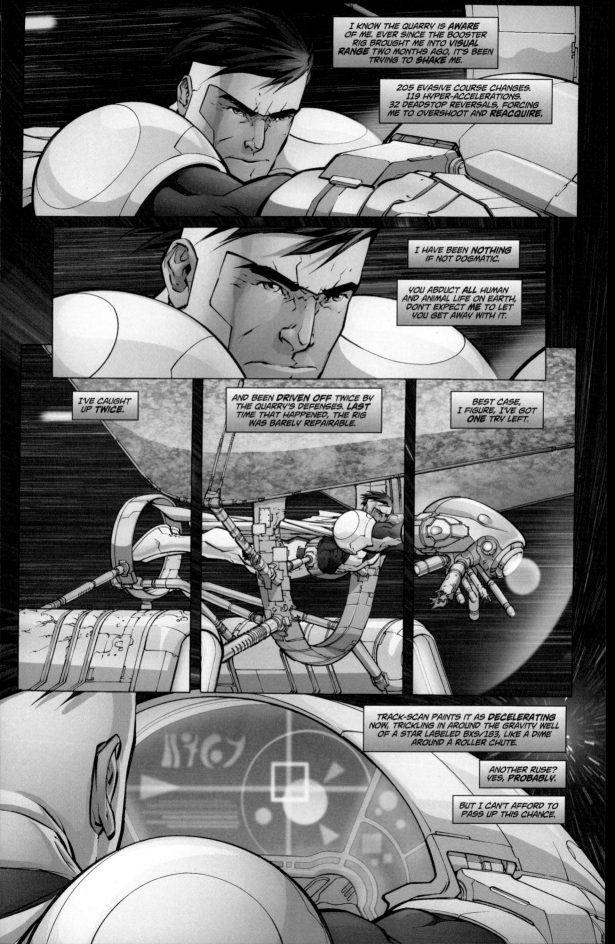

I KNOW THE QUARRY IS **AWARE** OF ME. EVER SINCE THE BOOSTER RIG BROUGHT ME INTO **VISUAL RANGE** TWO MONTHS AGO, IT'S BEEN TRYING TO **SHAKE** ME.

205 EVASIVE COURSE CHANGES. 119 HYPER-ACCELERATIONS. 32 DEADSTOP REVERSALS, FORCING ME TO OVERSHOOT AND **REACQUIRE.**

I HAVE BEEN **NOTHING** IF NOT DOGMATIC.

YOU ABDUCT **ALL HUMAN** AND ANIMAL LIFE ON EARTH, DON'T EXPECT **ME** TO LET YOU GET AWAY WITH IT.

I'VE CAUGHT UP **TWICE.**

AND BEEN **DRIVEN OFF** TWICE BY THE QUARRY'S DEFENSES. **LAST** TIME THAT HAPPENED, THE RIG WAS BARELY REPAIRABLE.

BEST CASE, I FIGURE, I'VE GOT **ONE** TRY LEFT.

TRACK-SCAN PAINTS IT AS **DECELERATING** NOW, TRICKLING IN AROUND THE GRAVITY WELL OF A STAR LABELED BXS/183, LIKE A DIME AROUND A ROLLER CHUTE.

ANOTHER RUSE? YES, PROBABLY.

BUT I CAN'T AFFORD TO PASS UP THIS CHANCE.

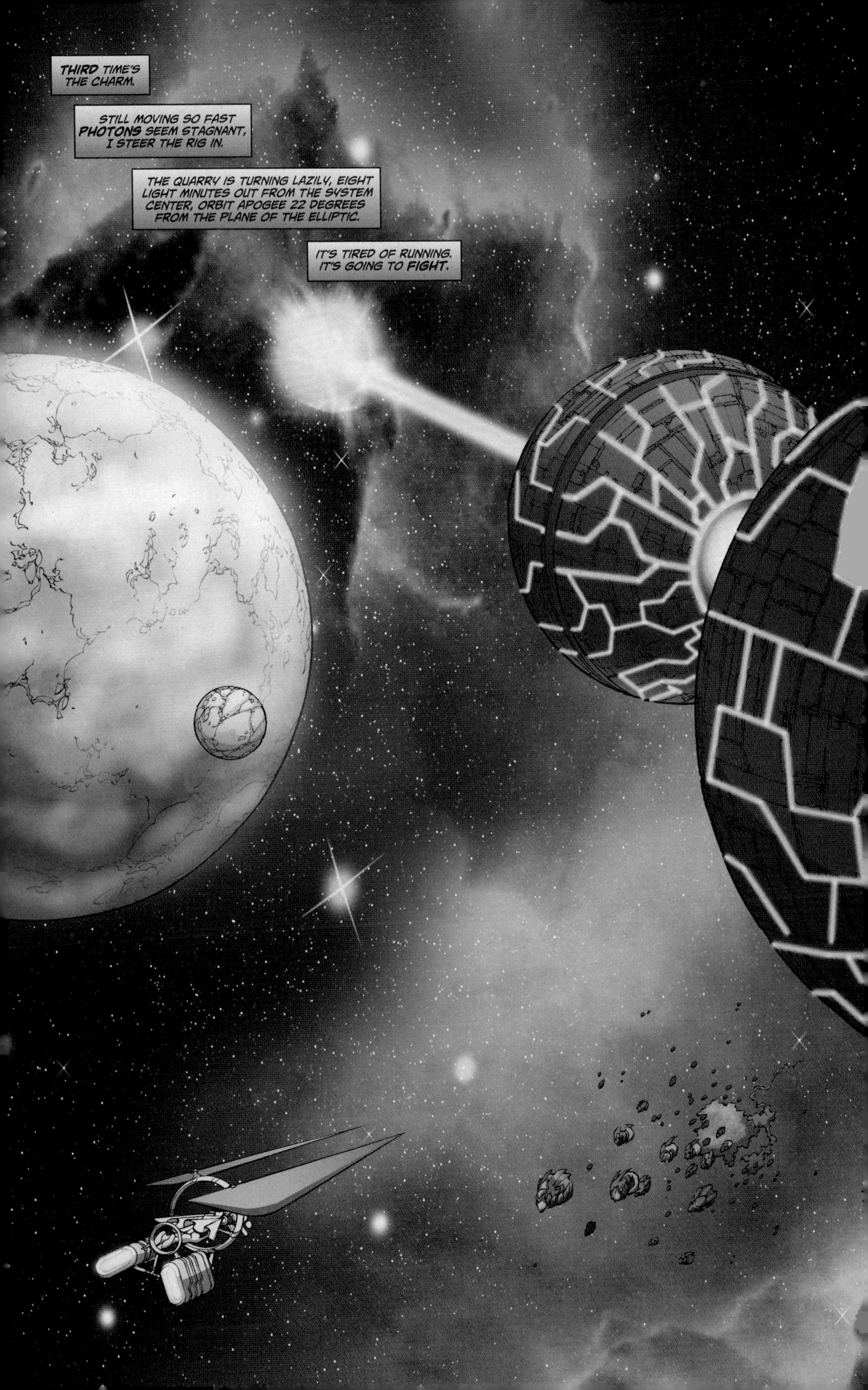
THIRD TIME'S THE CHARM.
STILL MOVING SO FAST PHOTONS SEEM STAGNANT, I STEER THE RIG IN.
THE QUARRY IS TURNING LAZILY, EIGHT LIGHT MINUTES OUT FROM THE SYSTEM CENTER, ORBIT APOGEE 22 DEGREES FROM THE PLANE OF THE ELLIPTIC.
IT'S TIRED OF RUNNING. IT'S GOING TO FIGHT.

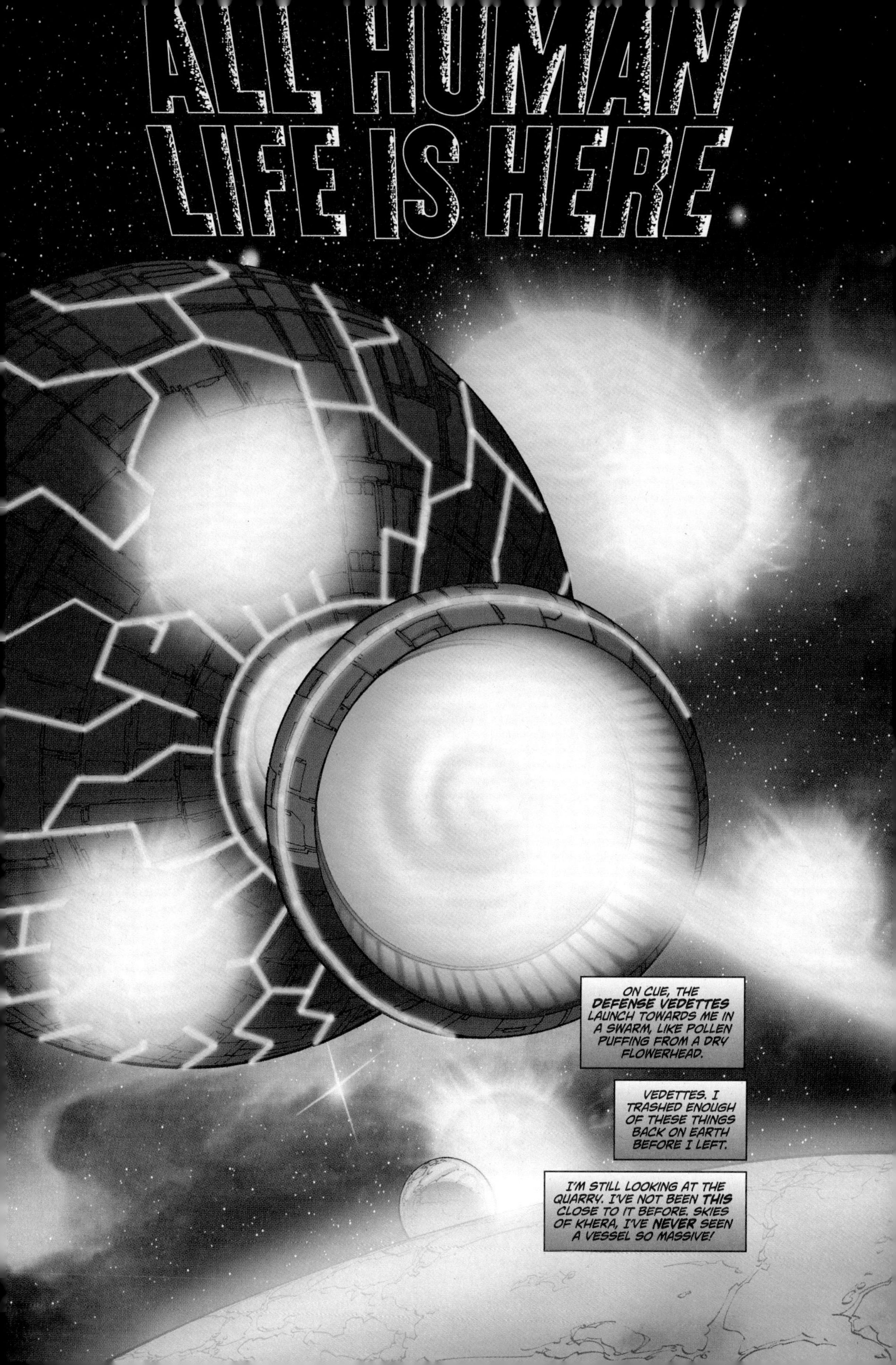
ALL HUMAN LIFE IS HERE
ON CUE, THE DEFENSE VEDETTES LAUNCH TOWARDS ME IN A SWARM, LIKE POLLEN PUFFING FROM A DRY FLOWERHEAD.
VEDETTES. I TRASHED ENOUGH OF THESE THINGS BACK ON EARTH BEFORE I LEFT.
I'M STILL LOOKING AT THE QUARRY. I'VE NOT BEEN THIS CLOSE TO IT BEFORE. SKIES OF KHERA, I'VE NEVER SEEN A VESSEL SO MASSIVE!

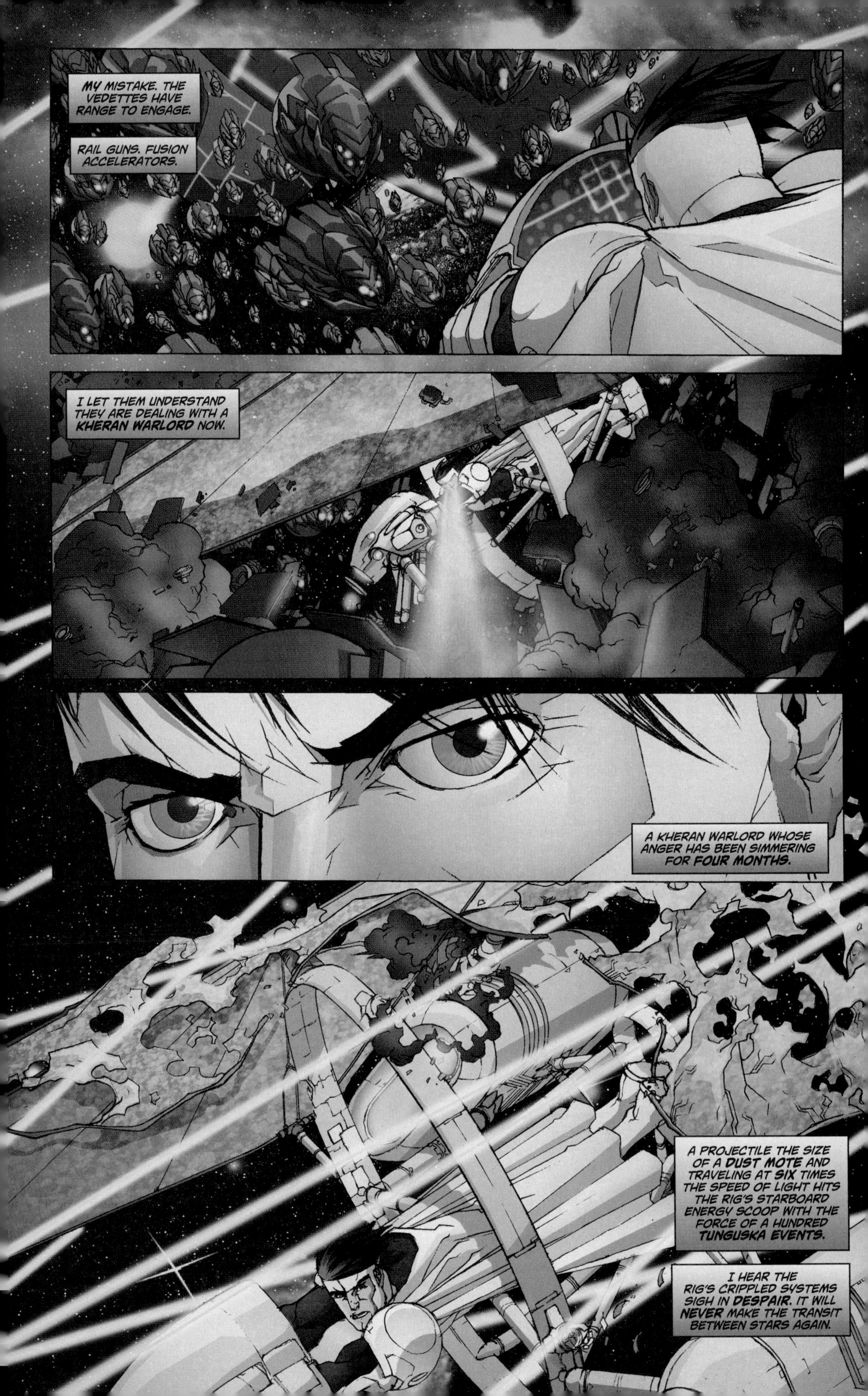
MY MISTAKE. THE VEDETTES HAVE RANGE TO ENGAGE.
RAIL GUNS. FUSION ACCELERATORS.
I LET THEM UNDERSTAND THEY ARE DEALING WITH A KHERAN WARLORD NOW.
A KHERAN WARLORD WHOSE ANGER HAS BEEN SIMMERING FOR FOUR MONTHS.
A PROJECTILE THE SIZE OF A DUST MOTE AND TRAVELING AT SIX TIMES THE SPEED OF LIGHT HITS THE RIG'S STARBOARD ENERGY SCOOP WITH THE FORCE OF A HUNDRED TUNGUSKA EVENTS.
I HEAR THE RIG'S CRIPPLED SYSTEMS SIGH IN DESPAIR. IT WILL NEVER MAKE THE TRANSIT BETWEEN STARS AGAIN.

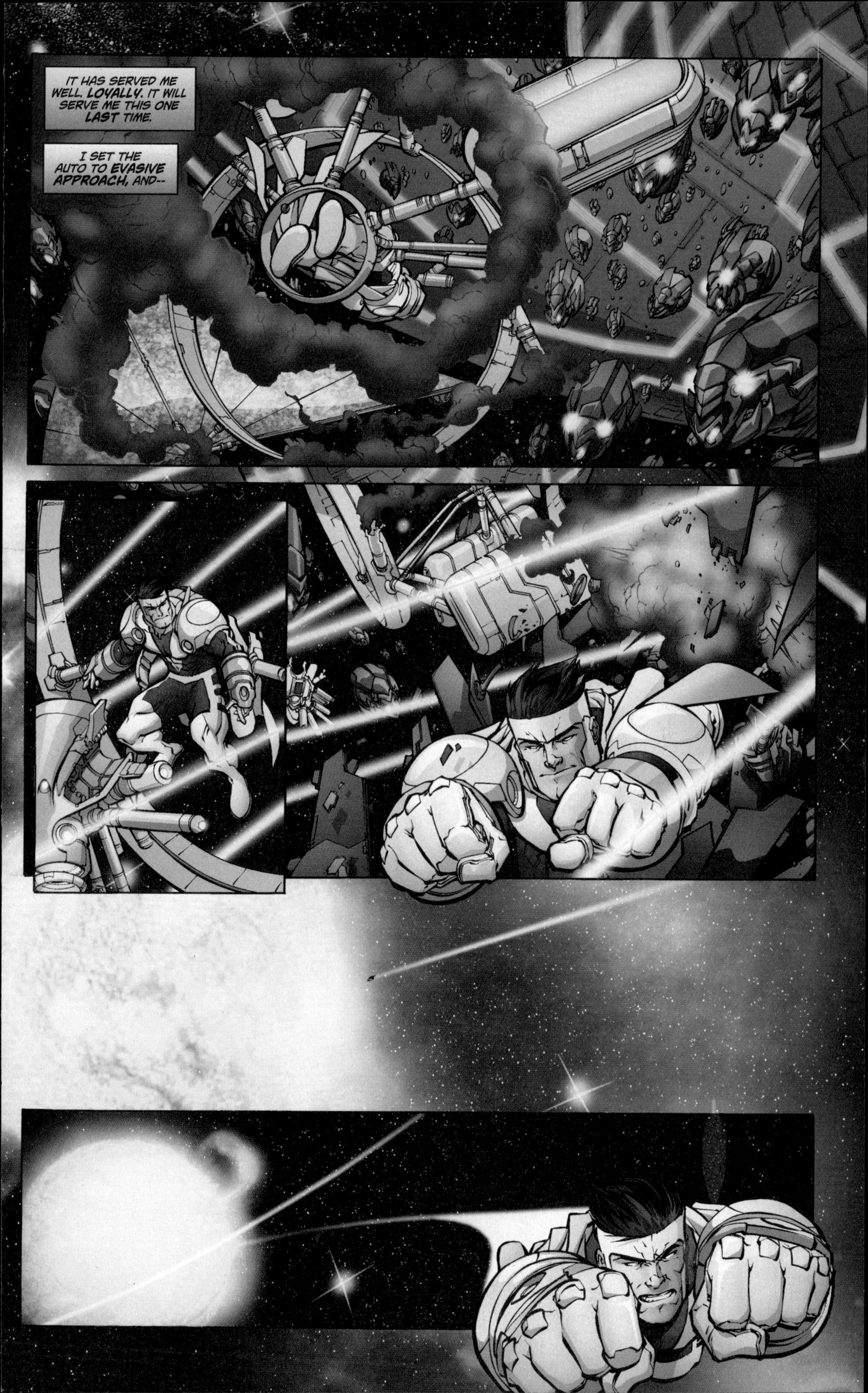
IT HAS SERVED ME WELL. LOYALLY. IT WILL SERVE ME THIS ONE LAST TIME.
I SET THE AUTO TO EVASIVE APPROACH, AND--

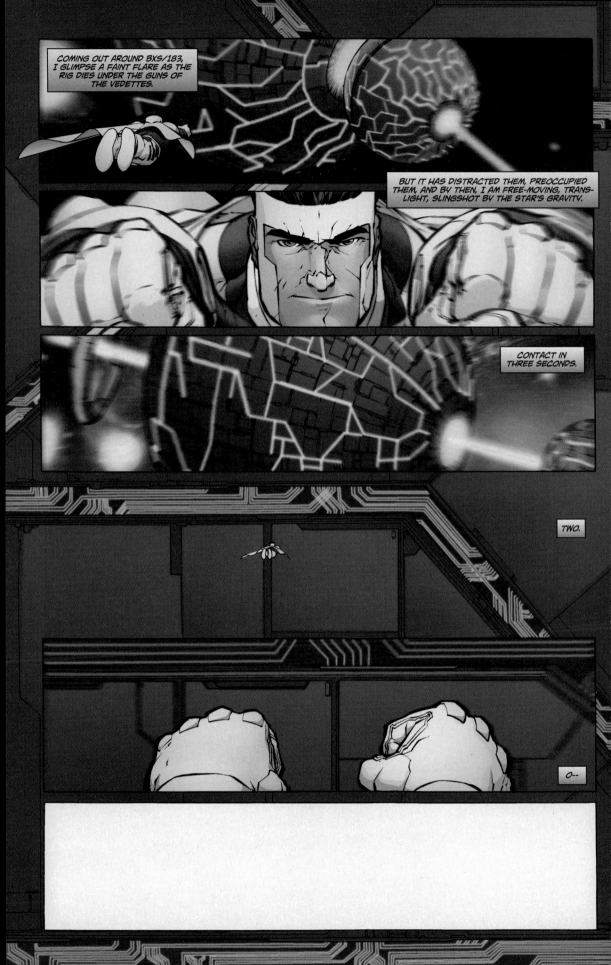

COMING OUT AROUND BXS/183, I GLIMPSE A FAINT FLARE AS THE RIG DIES UNDER THE GUNS OF THE VEDETTES.

BUT IT HAS DISTRACTED THEM, PREOCCUPIED THEM, AND BY THEN, I AM FREE-MOVING, TRANS-LIGHT, SLINGSHOT BY THE STAR'S GRAVITY.

CONTACT IN THREE SECONDS.

TWO.

O--

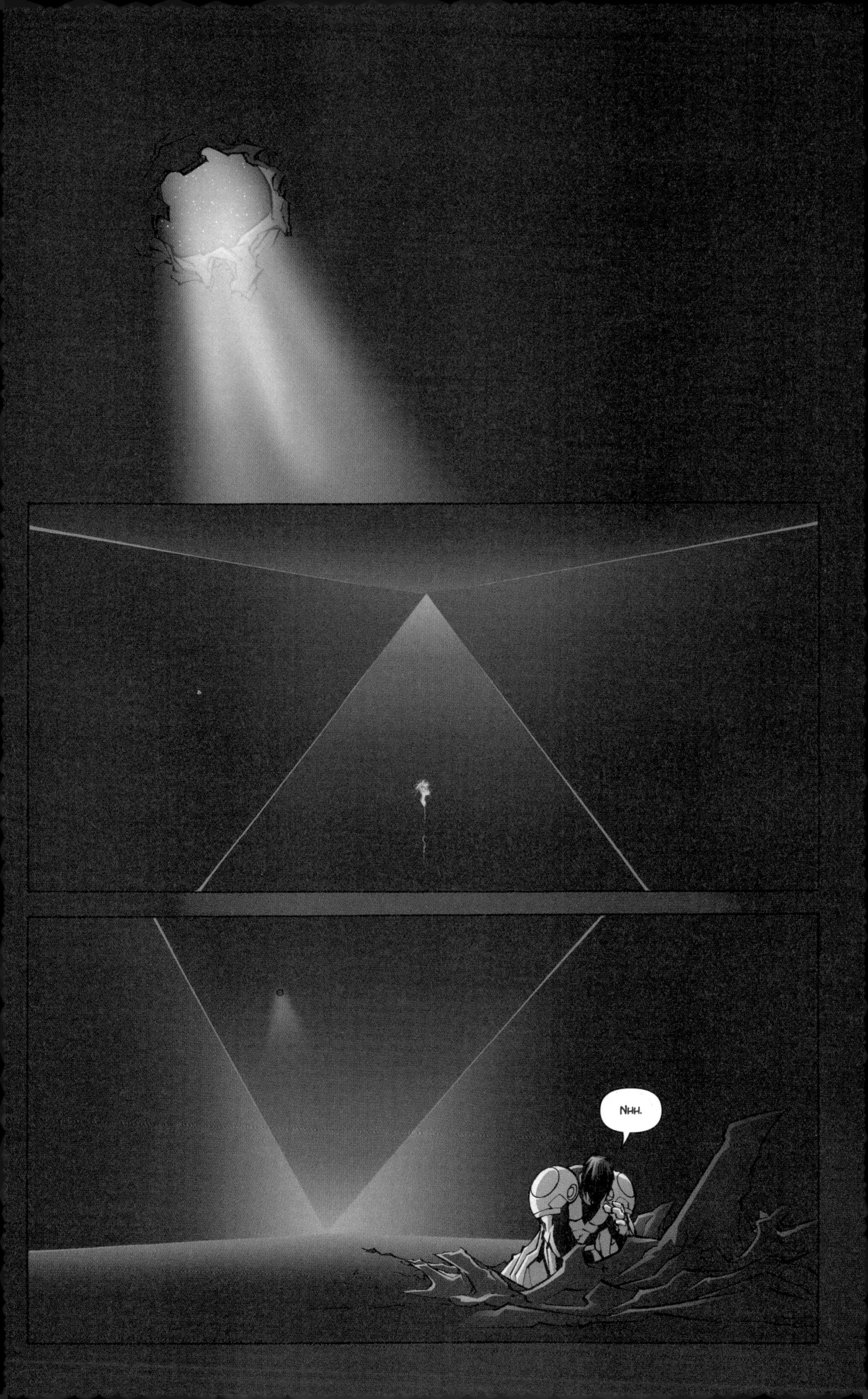
NHH.

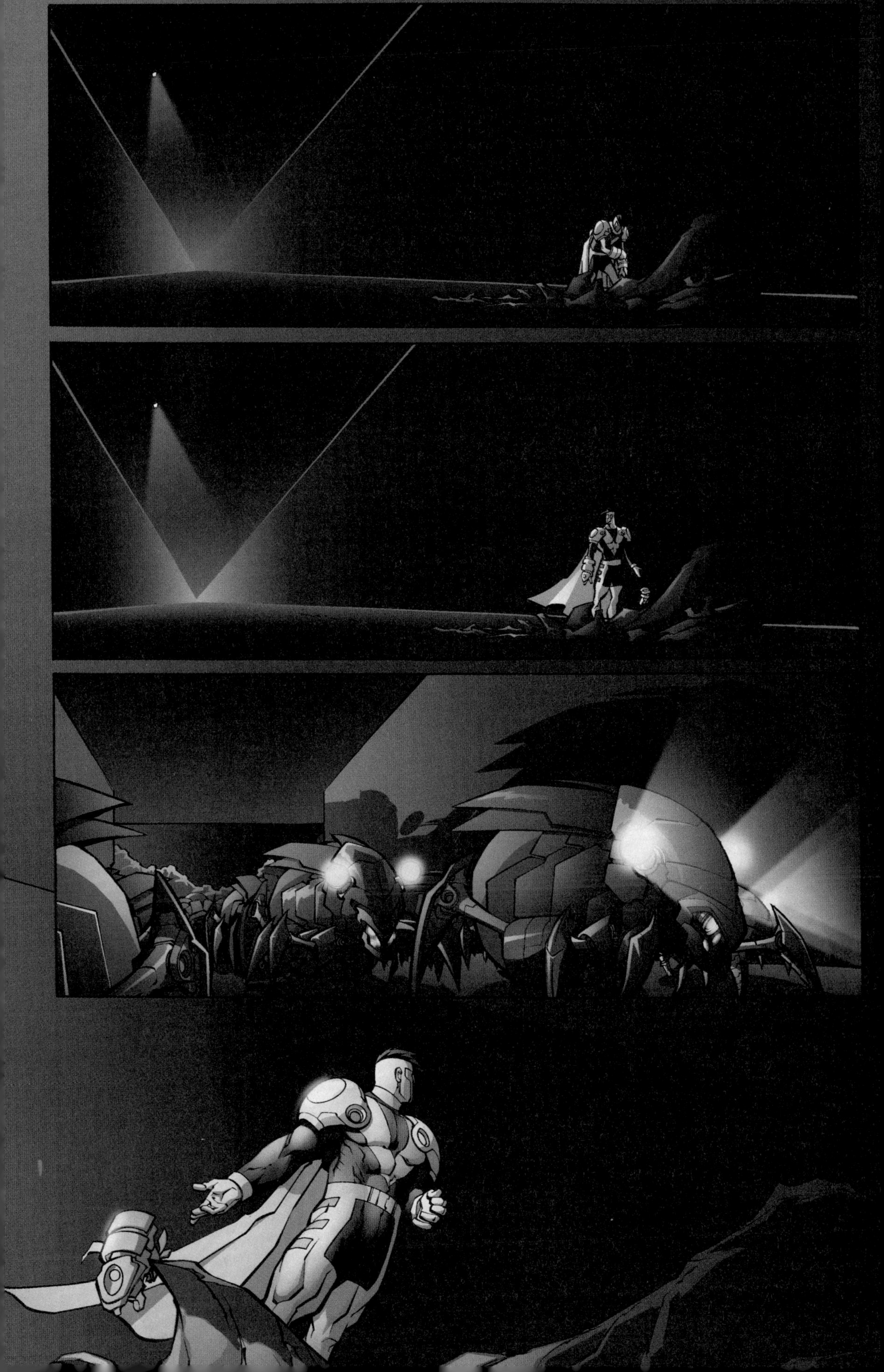

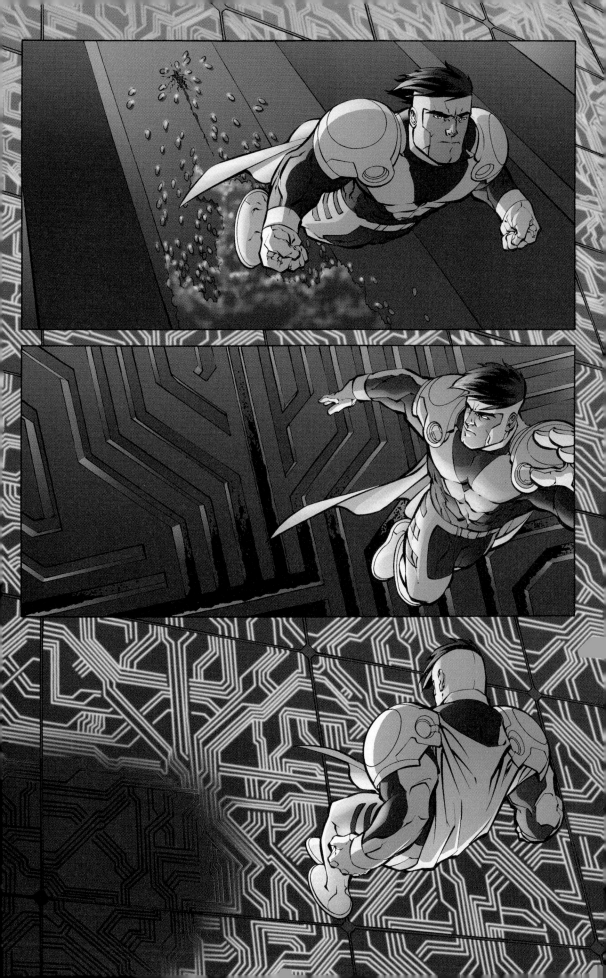

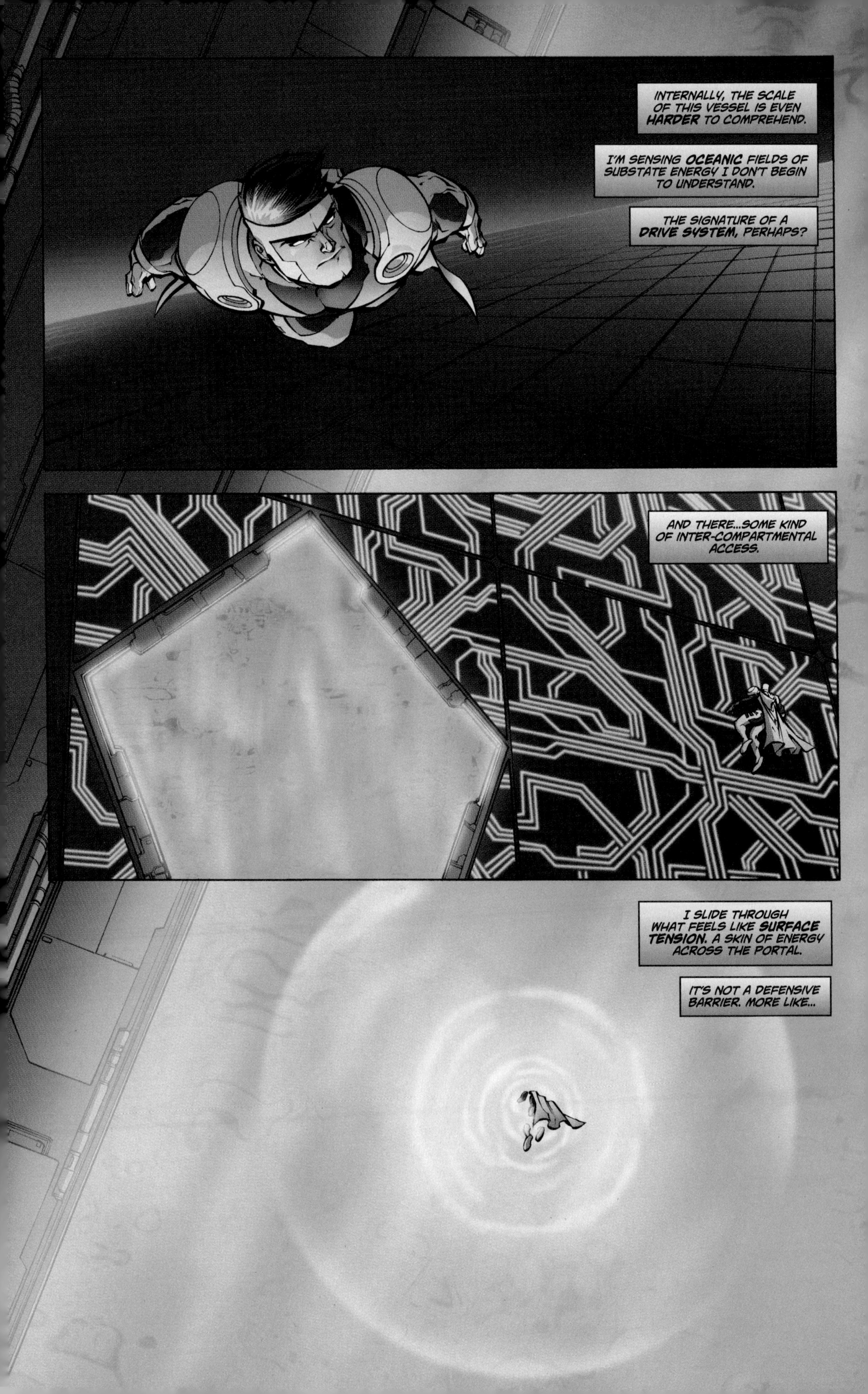
INTERNALLY, THE SCALE OF THIS VESSEL IS EVEN HARDER TO COMPREHEND.
I'M SENSING OCEANIC FIELDS OF SUBSTATE ENERGY I DON'T BEGIN TO UNDERSTAND.
THE SIGNATURE OF A DRIVE SYSTEM, PERHAPS?
AND THERE...SOME KIND OF INTER-COMPARTMENTAL ACCESS.
I SLIDE THROUGH WHAT FEELS LIKE SURFACE TENSION. A SKIN OF ENERGY ACROSS THE PORTAL.
IT'S NOT A DEFENSIVE BARRIER. MORE LIKE...

YES, I GUESSED RIGHT. IT'S TO KEEP THIS COMPARTMENT'S ATMOSPHERE INTACT.

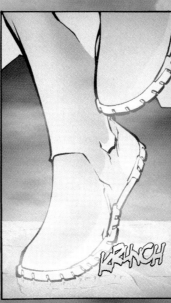

KRUNCH

KHERA'S SKIES!

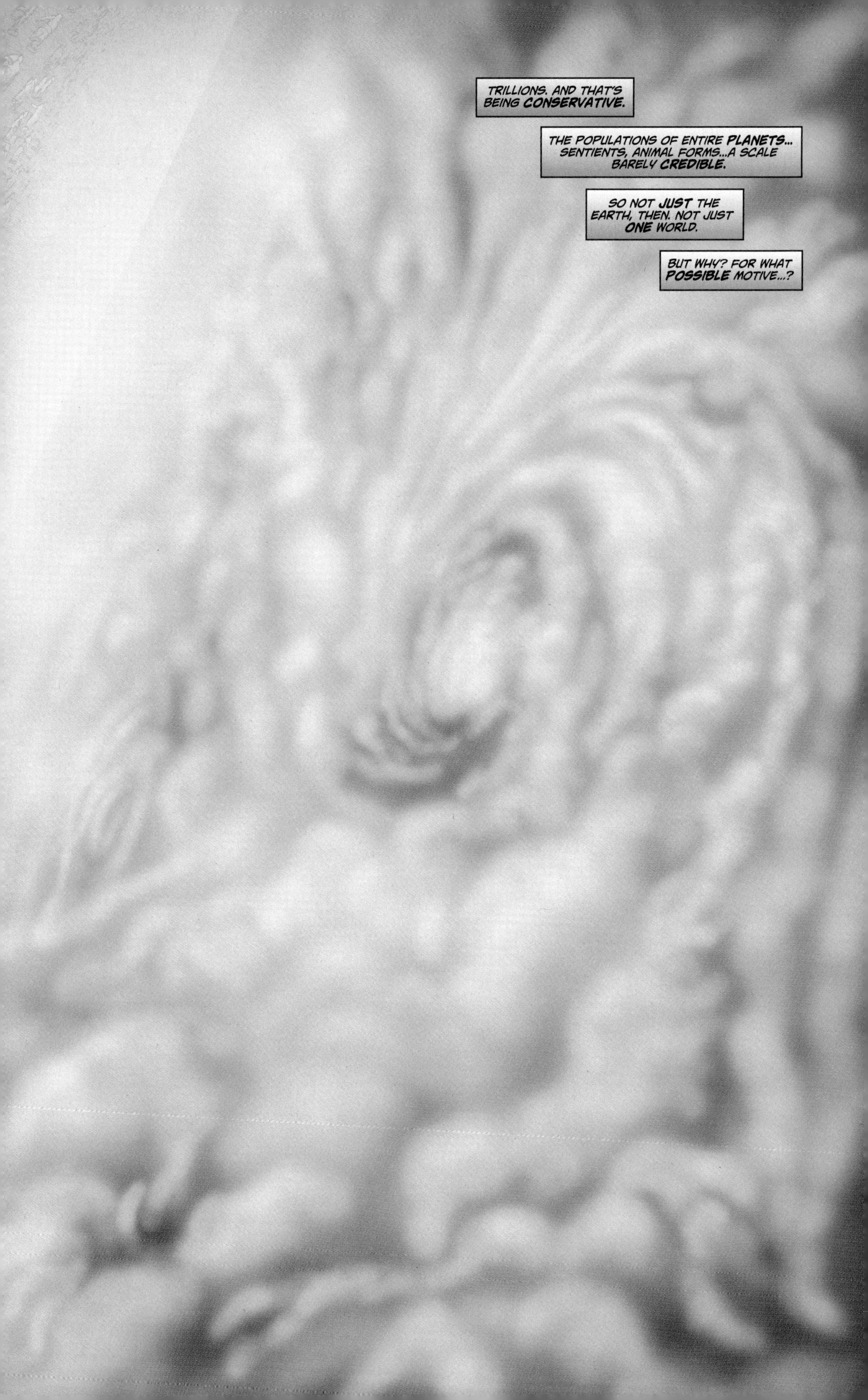
TRILLIONS. AND THAT'S BEING CONSERVATIVE.
THE POPULATIONS OF ENTIRE PLANETS... SENTIENTS, ANIMAL FORMS...A SCALE BARELY CREDIBLE.
SO NOT JUST THE EARTH, THEN. NOT JUST ONE WORLD.
BUT WHY? FOR WHAT POSSIBLE MOTIVE...?

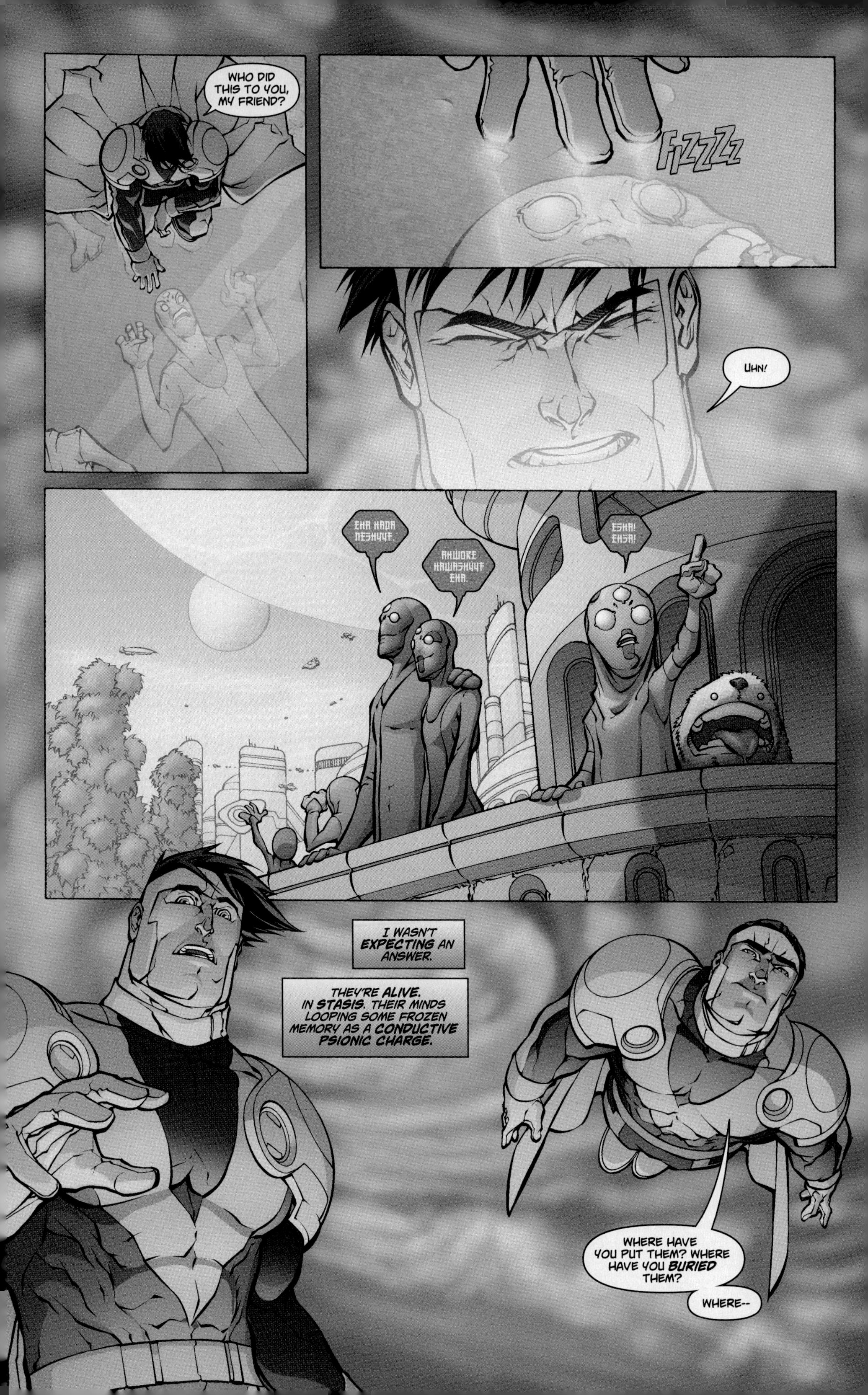
WHO DID THIS TO YOU, MY FRIEND?
FZZZZ
UHN!
EHA HADA NESHUUF.
ANWORE HAWASHUUF EHA.
ESHA! EHSA!
I WASN'T EXPECTING AN ANSWER.
THEY'RE ALIVE. IN STASIS. THEIR MINDS LOOPING SOME FROZEN MEMORY AS A CONDUCTIVE PSIONIC CHARGE.
WHERE HAVE YOU PUT THEM? WHERE HAVE YOU BURIED THEM?
WHERE--

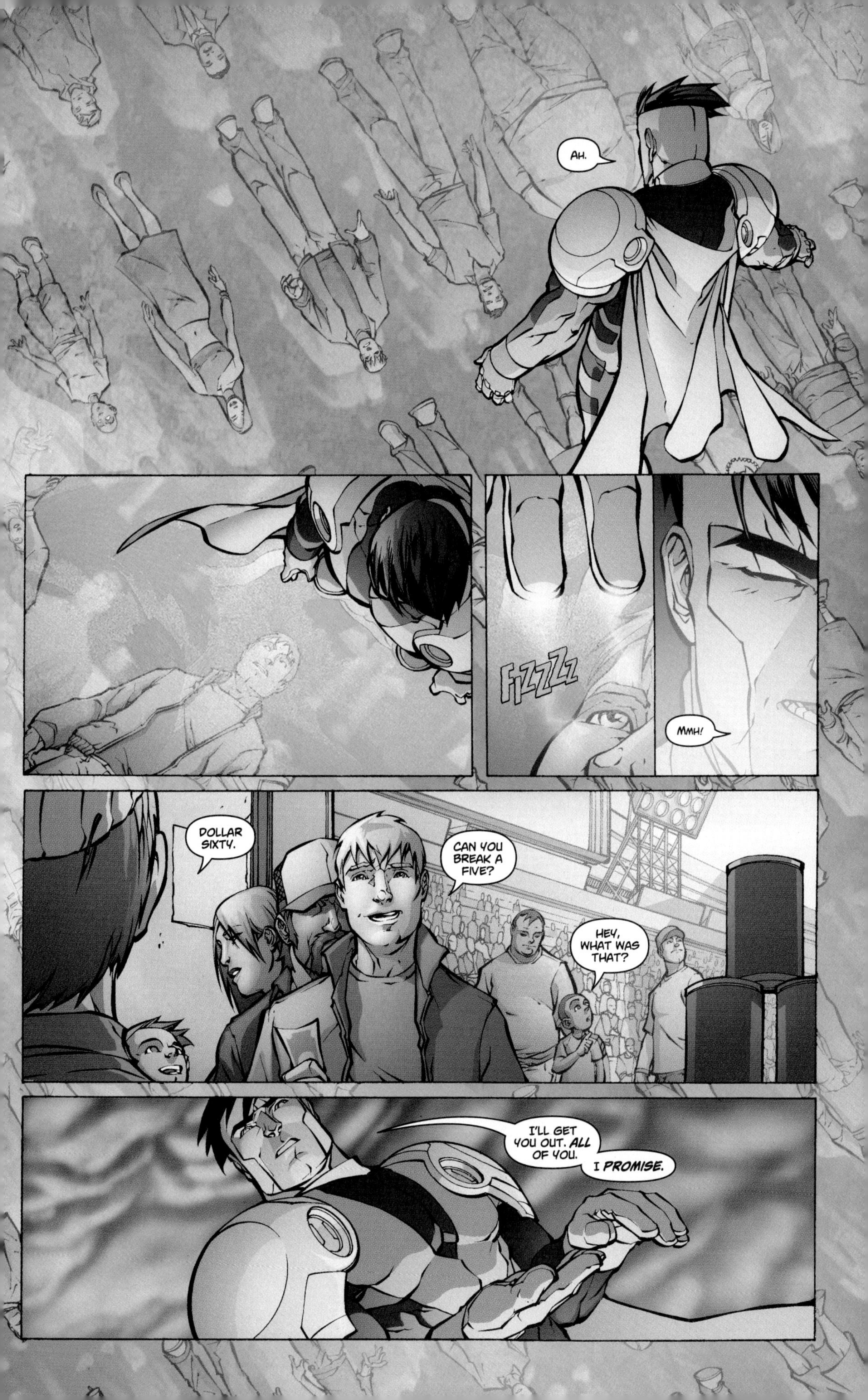
AH.
FIZZZZ
MMH!
DOLLAR SIXTY.
CAN YOU BREAK A FIVE?
HEY, WHAT WAS THAT?
I'LL GET YOU OUT. ALL OF YOU.
I PROMISE.

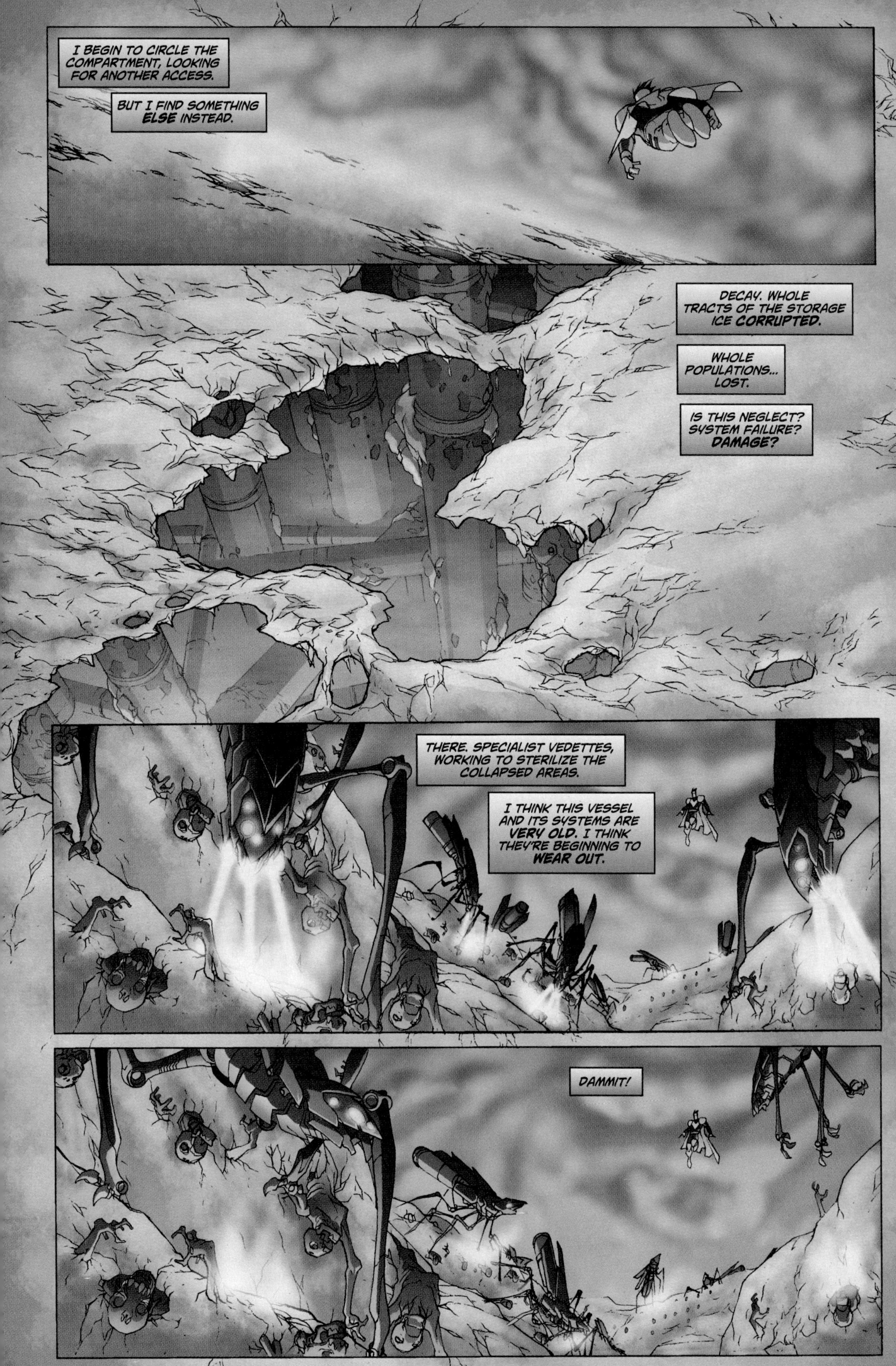
I BEGIN TO CIRCLE THE COMPARTMENT, LOOKING FOR ANOTHER ACCESS.
BUT I FIND SOMETHING ELSE INSTEAD.
DECAY. WHOLE TRACTS OF THE STORAGE ICE CORRUPTED.
WHOLE POPULATIONS... LOST.
IS THIS NEGLECT? SYSTEM FAILURE? DAMAGE?
THERE. SPECIALIST VEDETTES, WORKING TO STERILIZE THE COLLAPSED AREAS.
I THINK THIS VESSEL AND ITS SYSTEMS ARE VERY OLD. I THINK THEY'RE BEGINNING TO WEAR OUT.
DAMMIT!

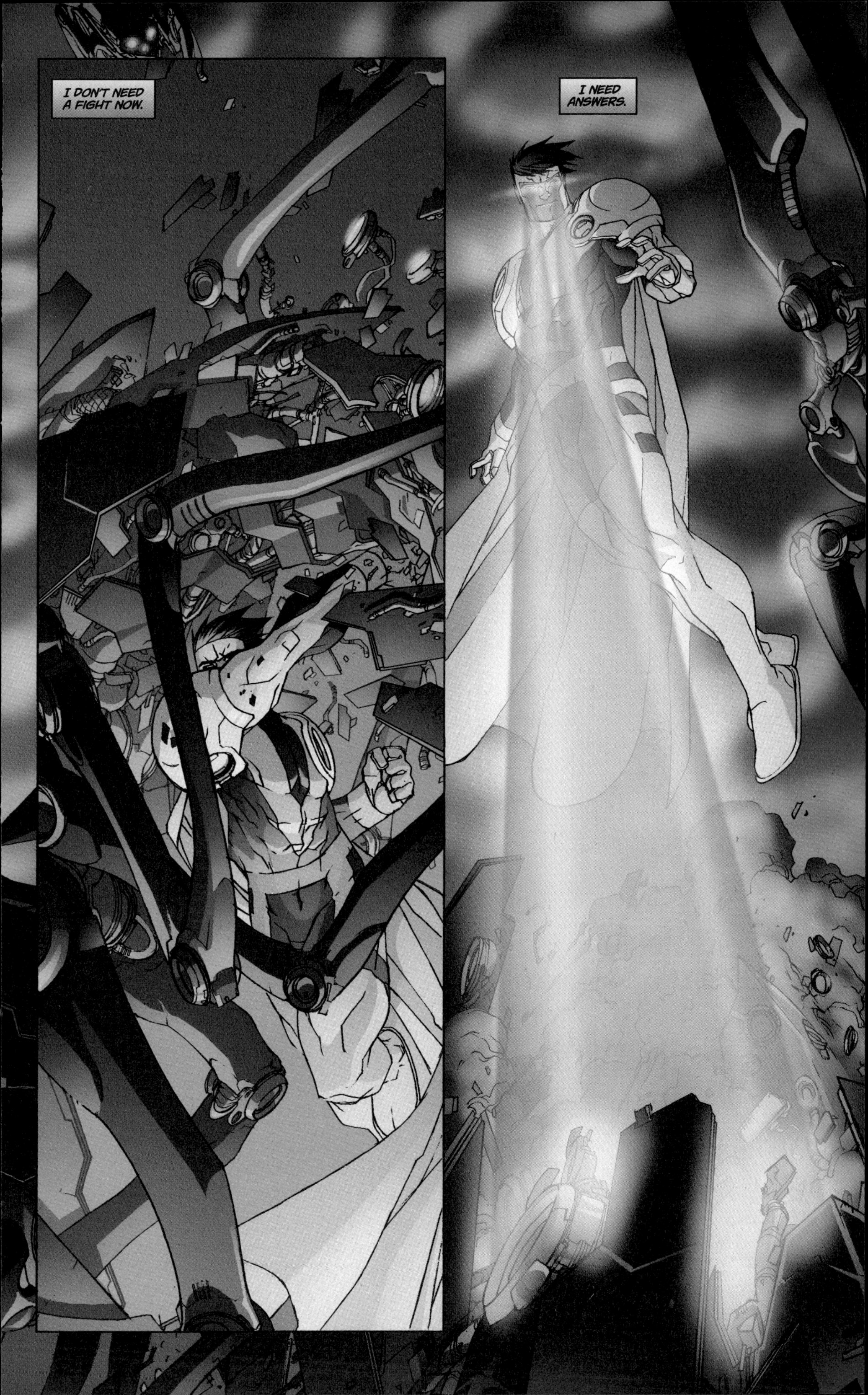
I DON'T NEED A FIGHT NOW.
I NEED ANSWERS.

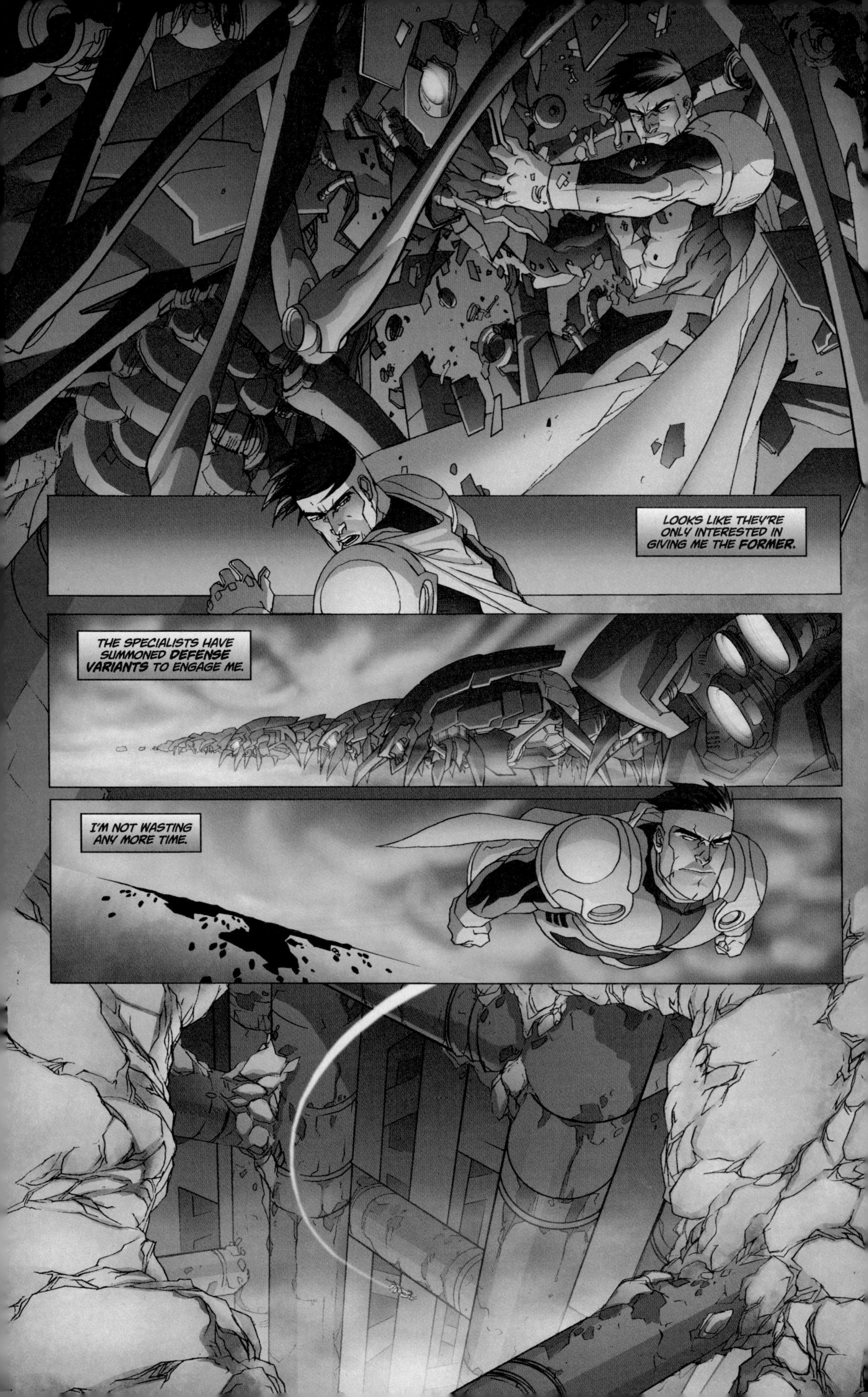
LOOKS LIKE THEY'RE ONLY INTERESTED IN GIVING ME THE FORMER.
THE SPECIALISTS HAVE SUMMONED DEFENSE VARIANTS TO ENGAGE ME.
I'M NOT WASTING ANY MORE TIME.

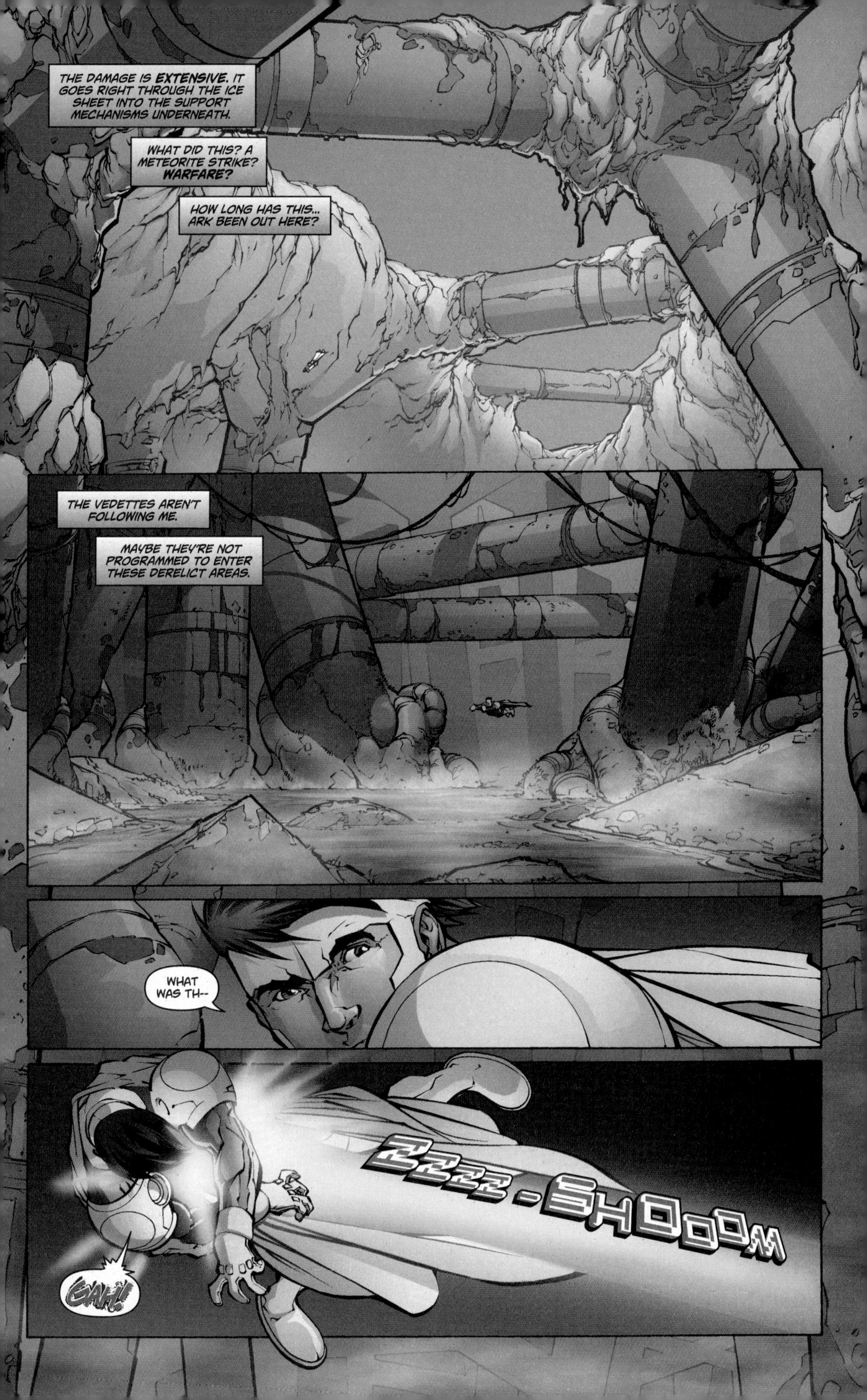
THE DAMAGE IS EXTENSIVE. IT GOES RIGHT THROUGH THE ICE SHEET INTO THE SUPPORT MECHANISMS UNDERNEATH.
WHAT DID THIS? A METEORITE STRIKE? WARFARE?
HOW LONG HAS THIS... ARK BEEN OUT HERE?
THE VEDETTES AREN'T FOLLOWING ME.
MAYBE THEY'RE NOT PROGRAMMED TO ENTER THESE DERELICT AREAS.
WHAT WAS TH--
ZZZZ-SHOOOOM
GAH!

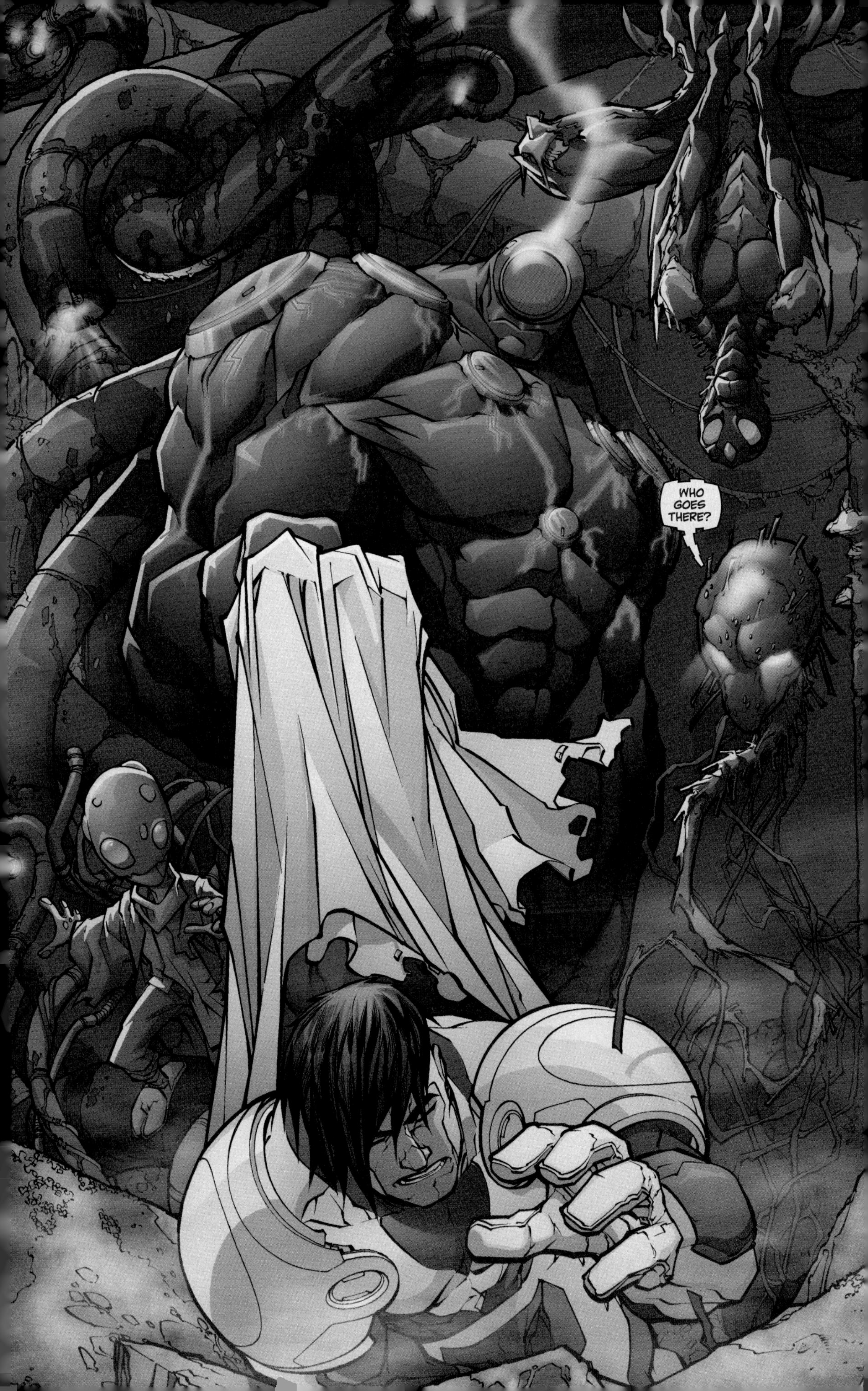
WHO GOES THERE?

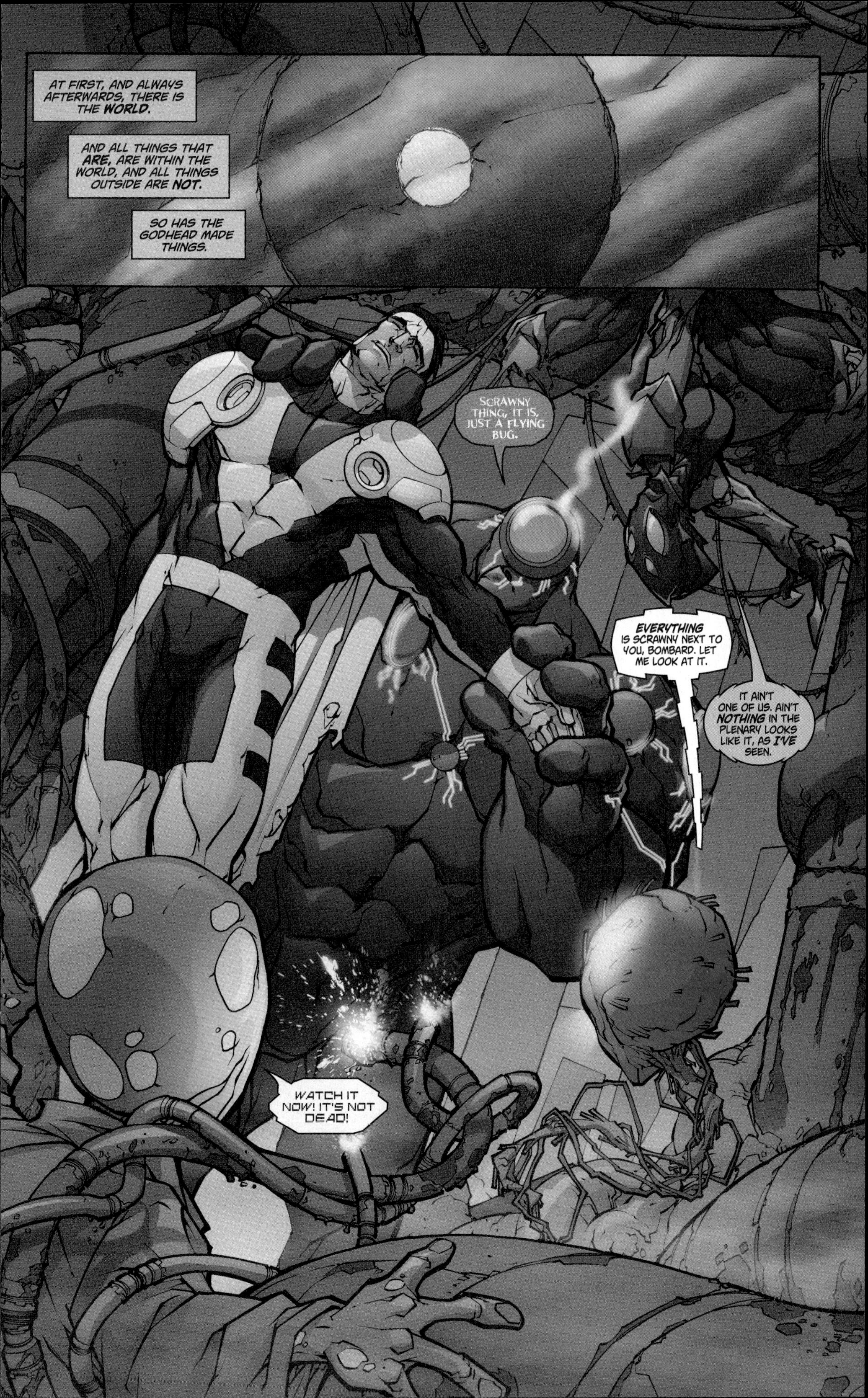
AT FIRST, AND ALWAYS AFTERWARDS, THERE IS THE WORLD.
AND ALL THINGS THAT ARE, ARE WITHIN THE WORLD, AND ALL THINGS OUTSIDE ARE NOT.
SO HAS THE GODHEAD MADE THINGS.
SCRAWNY THING, IT IS, JUST A FLYING BUG.
EVERYTHING IS SCRAWNY NEXT TO YOU, BOMBARD. LET ME LOOK AT IT.
IT AIN'T ONE OF US. AIN'T NOTHING IN THE PLENARY LOOKS LIKE IT, AS I'VE SEEN.
WATCH IT NOW! IT'S NOT DEAD!

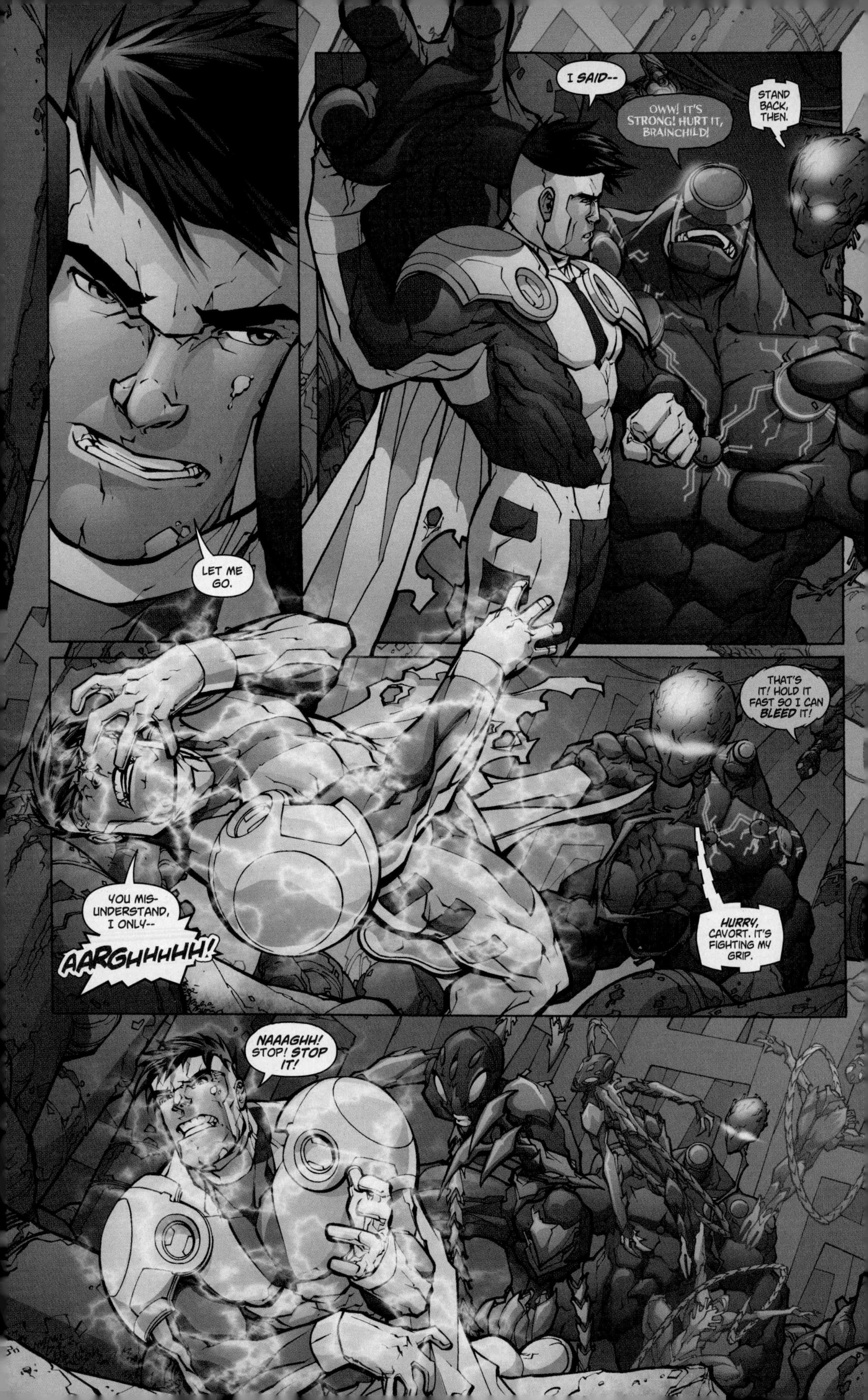
I SAID--
OWW! IT'S STRONG! HURT IT, BRAINCHILD!
STAND BACK, THEN.
LET ME GO.
THAT'S IT! HOLD IT FAST SO I CAN BLEED IT!
YOU MIS-UNDERSTAND, I ONLY--
AARGHHHHH!
HURRY, CAVORT. IT'S FIGHTING MY GRIP.
NAAAGHH! STOP! STOP IT!

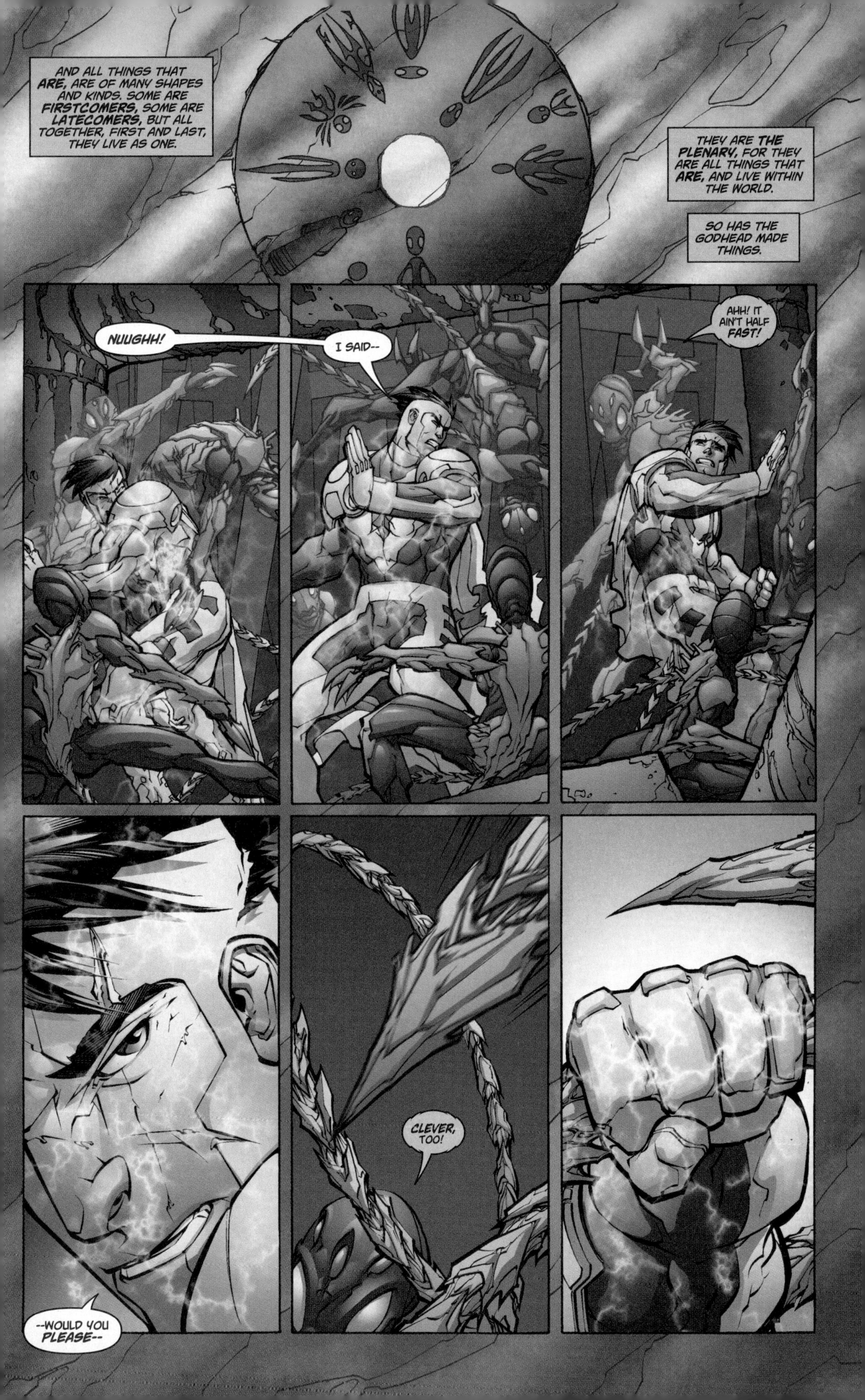
AND ALL THINGS THAT ARE, ARE OF MANY SHAPES AND KINDS. SOME ARE FIRSTCOMERS, SOME ARE LATECOMERS, BUT ALL TOGETHER, FIRST AND LAST, THEY LIVE AS ONE.
THEY ARE THE PLENARY, FOR THEY ARE ALL THINGS THAT ARE, AND LIVE WITHIN THE WORLD.
SO HAS THE GODHEAD MADE THINGS.
NUUGHH!
I SAID--
AHH! IT AIN'T HALF FAST!
CLEVER, TOO!
--WOULD YOU PLEASE--

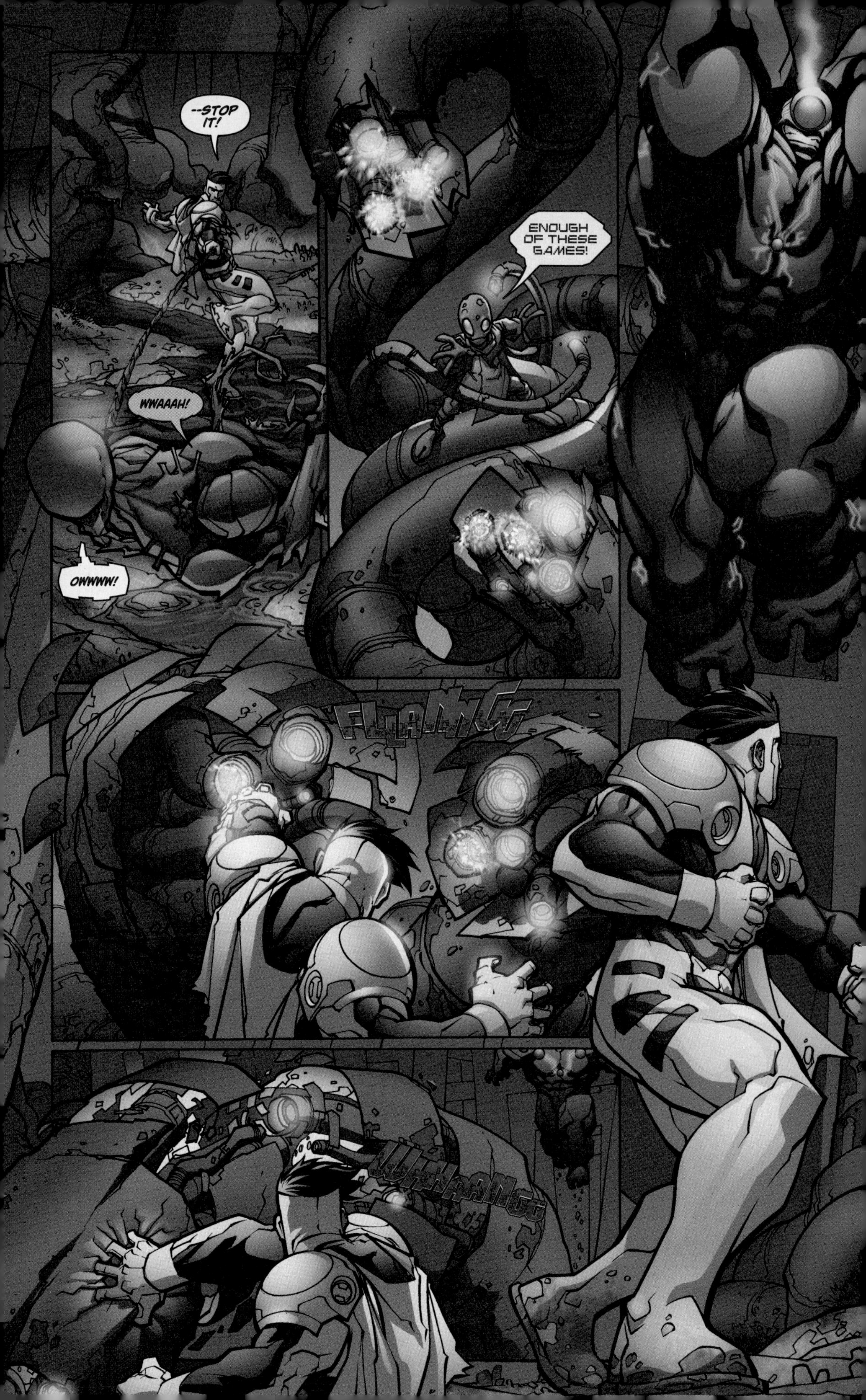
--STOP IT!
WWAAAH!
OWWWW!
ENOUGH OF THESE GAMES!
FLAANG
WHAANG

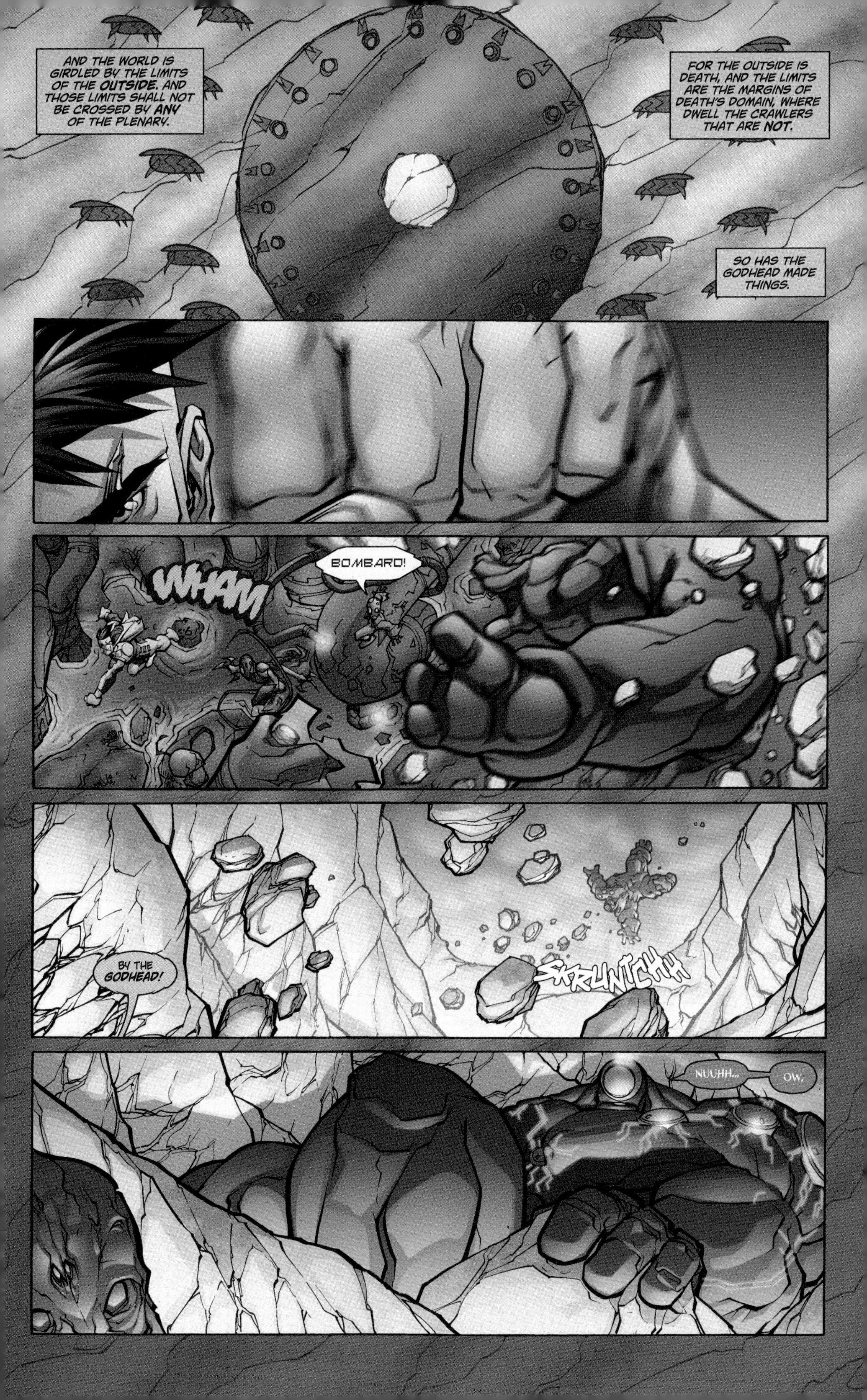
AND THE WORLD IS GIRDLED BY THE LIMITS OF THE OUTSIDE. AND THOSE LIMITS SHALL NOT BE CROSSED BY ANY OF THE PLENARY.
FOR THE OUTSIDE IS DEATH, AND THE LIMITS ARE THE MARGINS OF DEATH'S DOMAIN, WHERE DWELL THE CRAWLERS THAT ARE NOT.
SO HAS THE GODHEAD MADE THINGS.
WHAM
BOMBARD!
BY THE GODHEAD!
SKRUNTCHH
NUUHH...
OW.

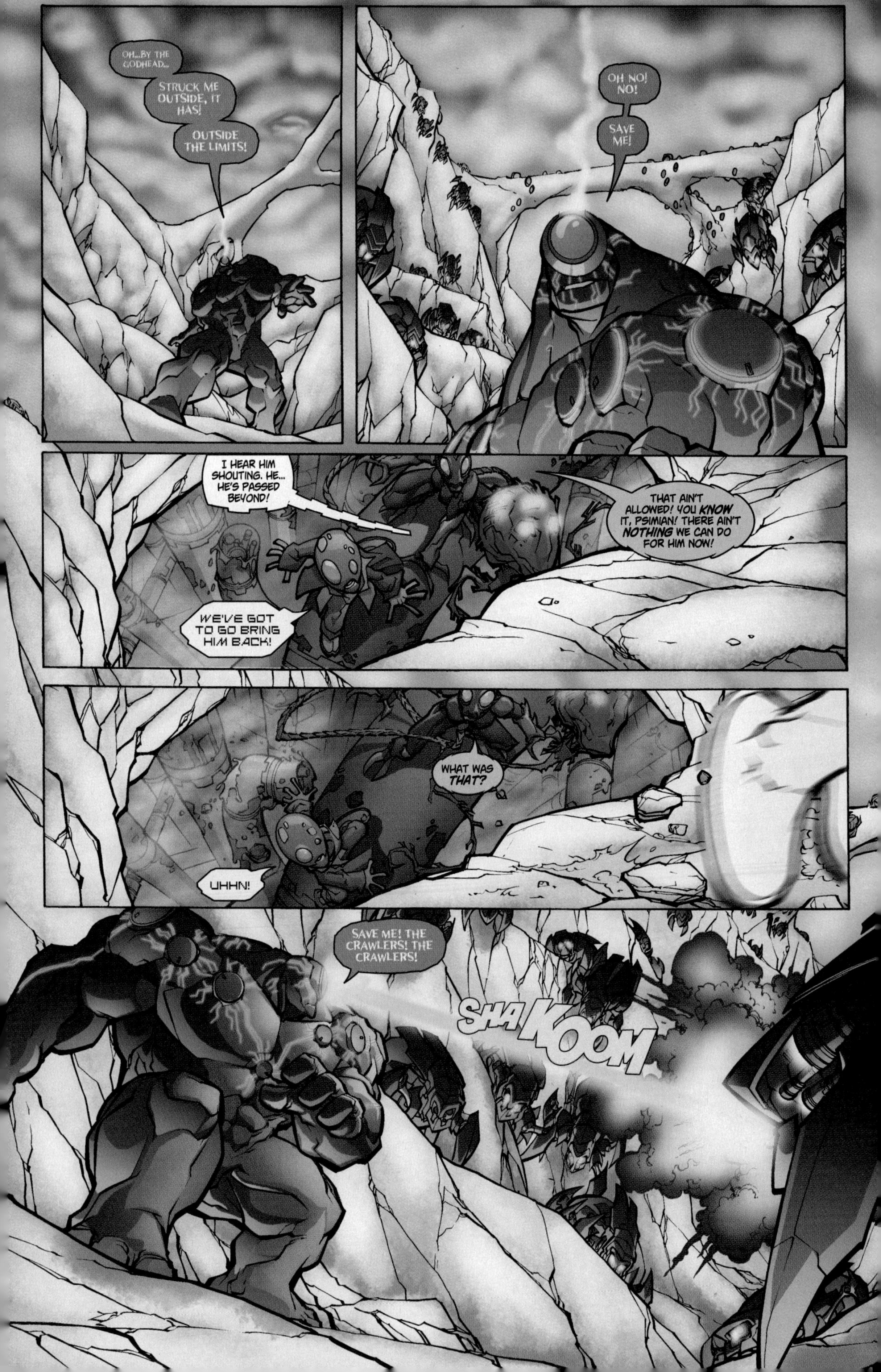
OH...BY THE GODHEAD...
STRUCK ME OUTSIDE, IT HAS!
OUTSIDE THE LIMITS!
OH NO! NO!
SAVE ME!
I HEAR HIM SHOUTING. HE... HE'S PASSED BEYOND!
THAT AIN'T ALLOWED! YOU KNOW IT, PSIMIAN! THERE AIN'T NOTHING WE CAN DO FOR HIM NOW!
WE'VE GOT TO GO BRING HIM BACK!
WHAT WAS THAT?
UHHN!
SAVE ME! THE CRAWLERS! THE CRAWLERS!
SHAKOOM

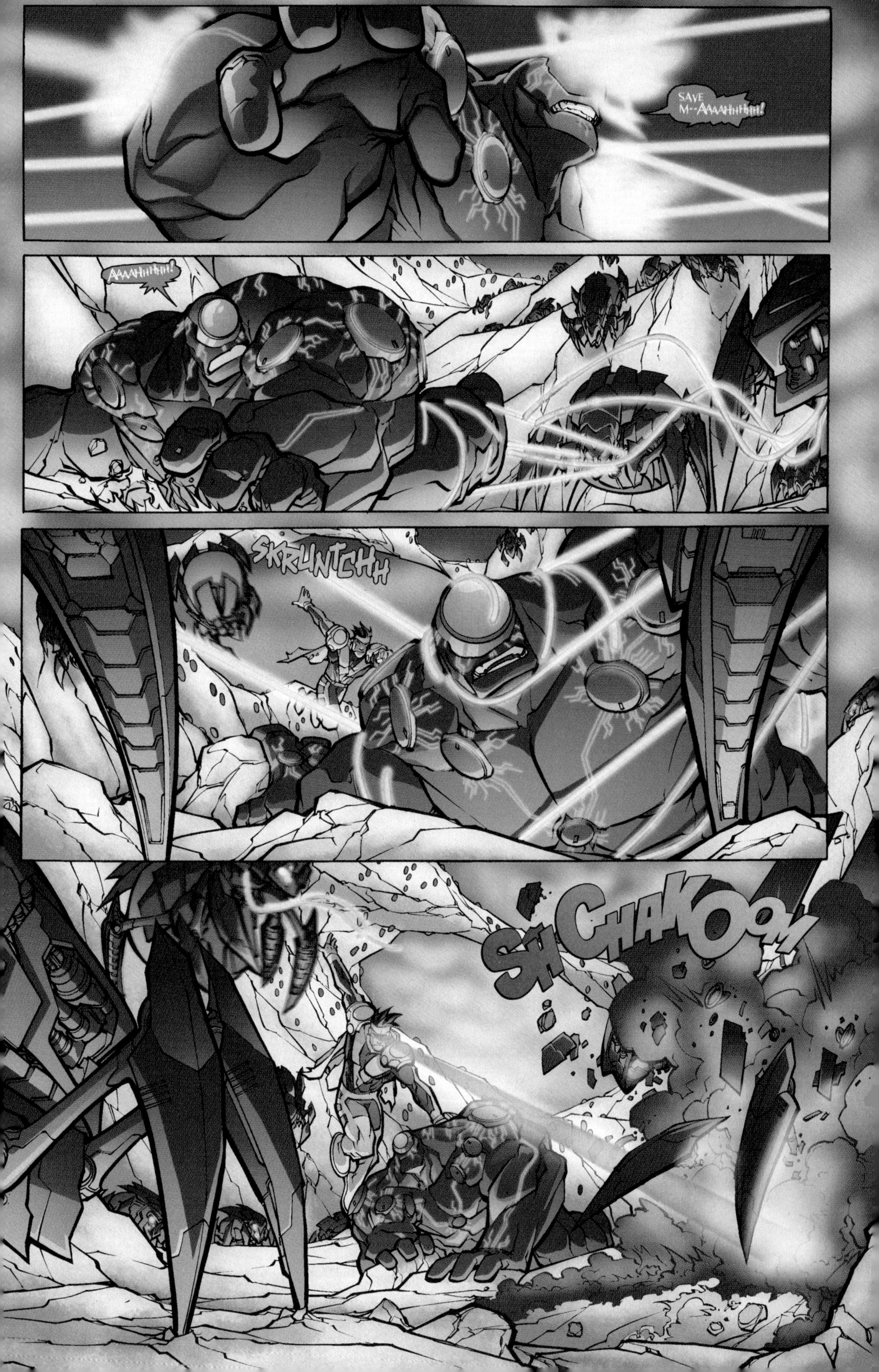
SAVE M--AAAAHHHHH!
AAAAHHHHH!
SKRUNTCHH
SHCHAKOOM

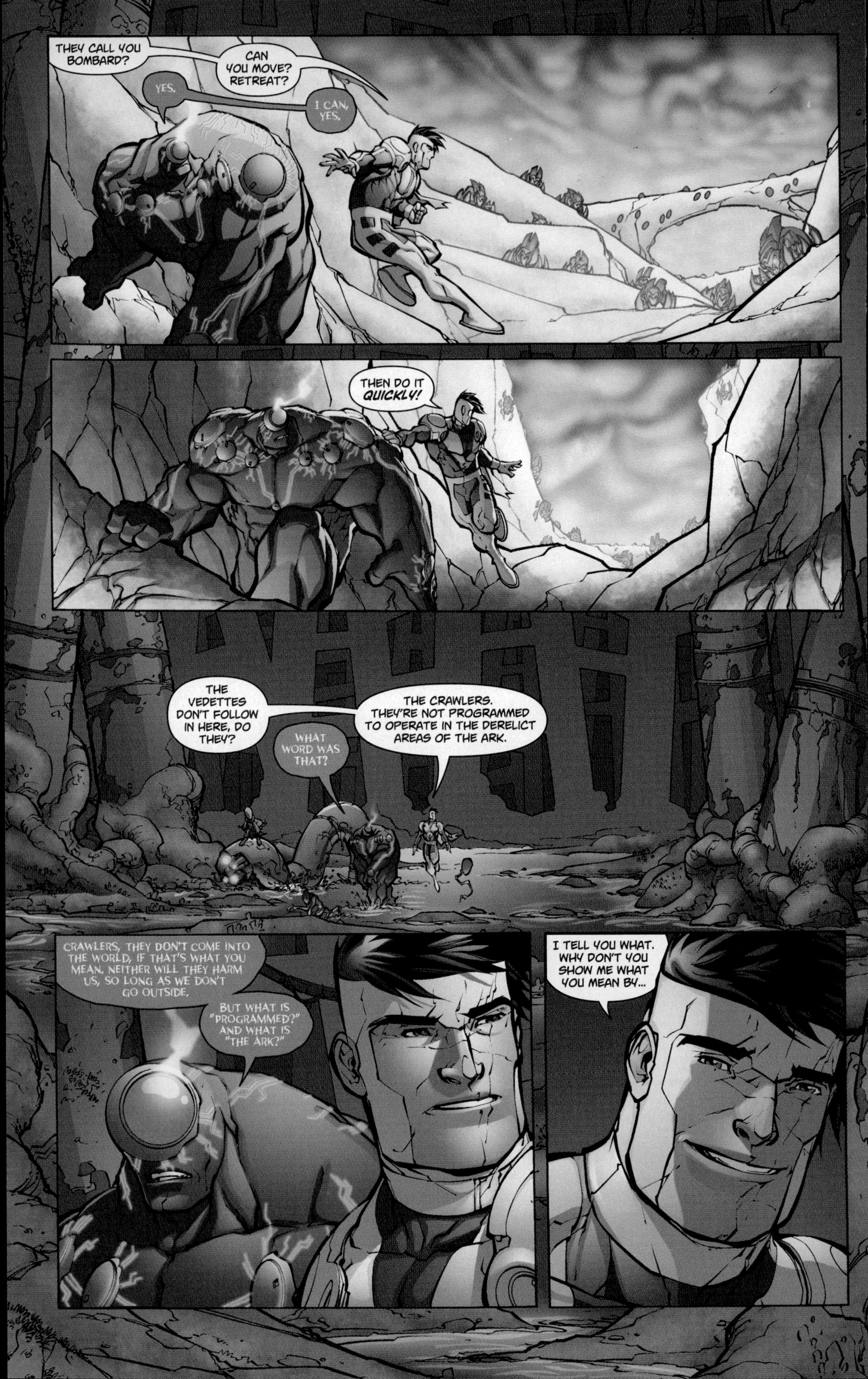
THEY CALL YOU BOMBARD?
CAN YOU MOVE? RETREAT?
YES.
I CAN, YES.
THEN DO IT QUICKLY!
THE VEDETTES DON'T FOLLOW IN HERE, DO THEY?
THE CRAWLERS. THEY'RE NOT PROGRAMMED TO OPERATE IN THE DERELICT AREAS OF THE ARK.
WHAT WORD WAS THAT?
CRAWLERS, THEY DON'T COME INTO THE WORLD, IF THAT'S WHAT YOU MEAN. NEITHER WILL THEY HARM US, SO LONG AS WE DON'T GO OUTSIDE.
BUT WHAT IS "PROGRAMMED?" AND WHAT IS "THE ARK?"
I TELL YOU WHAT. WHY DON'T YOU SHOW ME WHAT YOU MEAN BY...

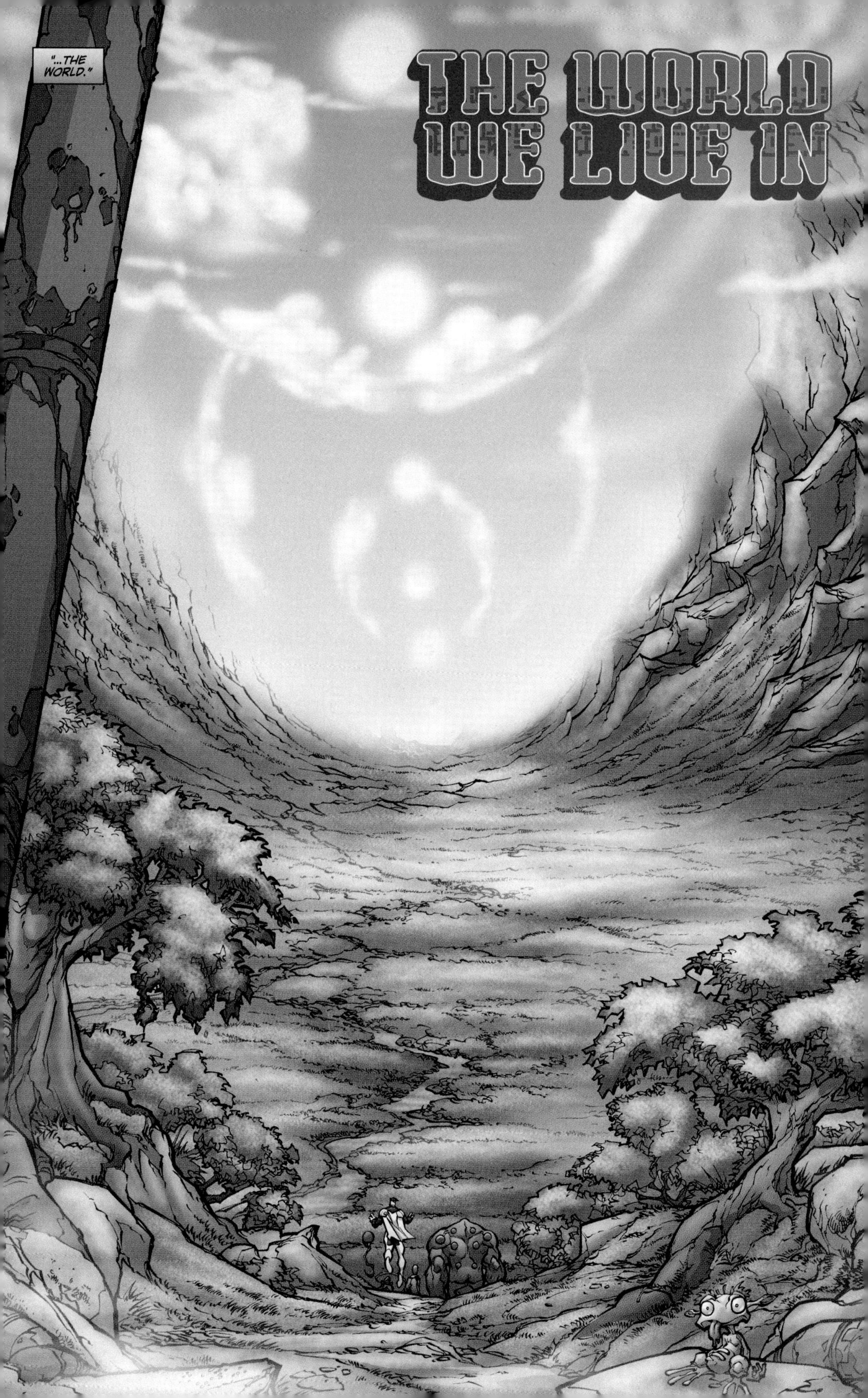
"...THE WORLD."
THE WORLD WE LIVE IN

I SEE A CULTIVATION ZONE, DESIGNED TO YIELD NUTRIENTS FOR THE POPULATIONS IN STASIS.

PHOTOVOLTAIC ENERGY SOURCES, THOUSANDS OF KILOMETERS ABOVE, BURN LIKE SUNS.

BUT THE LAND GOES UP THE WALLS OF THE WORLD AND MEETS ON THE OTHER SIDE OF THOSE SUNS.

VAST, BECAUSE THE NUTRIENT DEMANDS ARE VAST. BUT STILL JUST ANOTHER SECTION OF THE ARK.

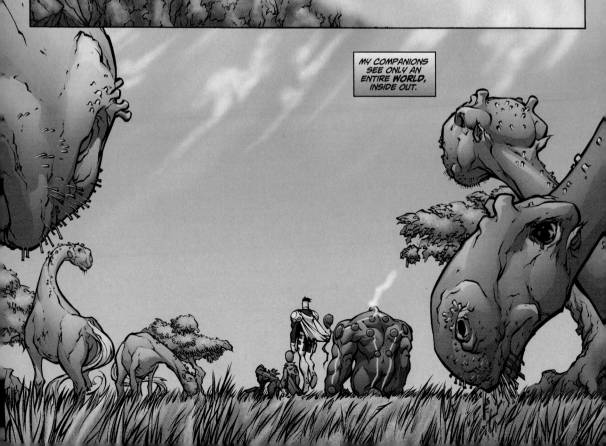

MY COMPANIONS SEE ONLY AN ENTIRE WORLD, INSIDE OUT.

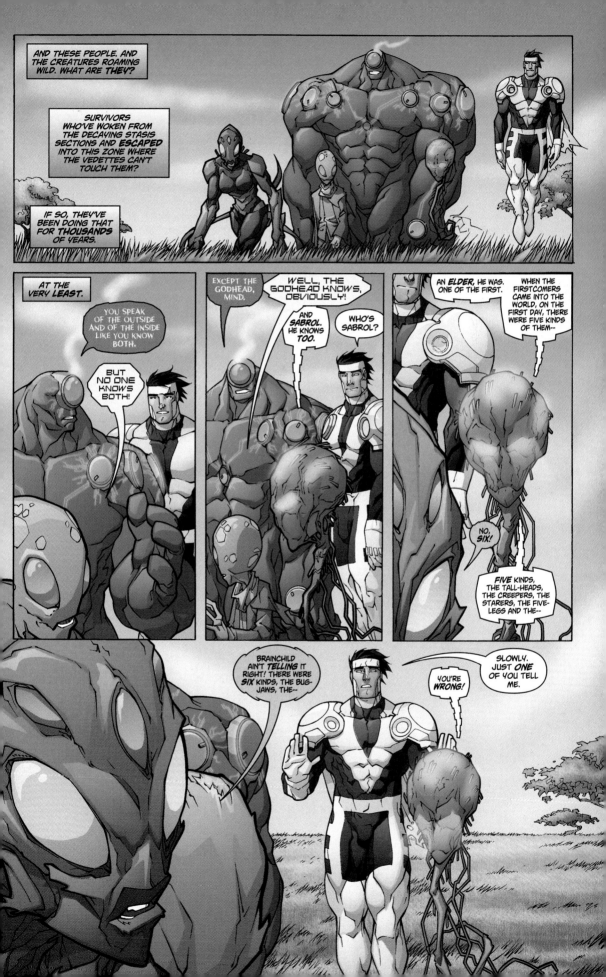

AND THESE PEOPLE. AND THE CREATURES ROAMING WILD. WHAT ARE *THEY*?

SURVIVORS WHO'VE WOKEN FROM THE DECAYING STASIS SECTIONS AND *ESCAPED* INTO THIS ZONE WHERE THE VEDETTES CAN'T TOUCH THEM?

IF SO, THEY'VE BEEN DOING THAT FOR *THOUSANDS* OF YEARS.

AT THE VERY *LEAST*.

YOU SPEAK OF THE OUTSIDE AND OF THE INSIDE LIKE YOU KNOW BOTH.

BUT NO ONE KNOWS BOTH!

EXCEPT THE GODHEAD, MIND.

WELL, THE GODHEAD KNOWS, OBVIOUSLY!

AND *SABROL*. HE KNOWS TOO.

WHO'S SABROL?

AN *ELDER*, HE WAS. ONE OF THE FIRST.

WHEN THE FIRSTCOMERS CAME INTO THE WORLD, ON THE FIRST DAY, THERE WERE FIVE KINDS OF THEM--

NO, *SIX*!

FIVE KINDS, THE TALL-HEADS, THE CREEPERS, THE STARERS, THE FIVE-LEGS AND THE--

BRAINCHILD AIN'T *TELLING* IT RIGHT! THERE WERE *SIX* KINDS, THE BUG-JAWS, THE--

YOU'RE *WRONG*!

SLOWLY. JUST *ONE* OF YOU TELL ME.

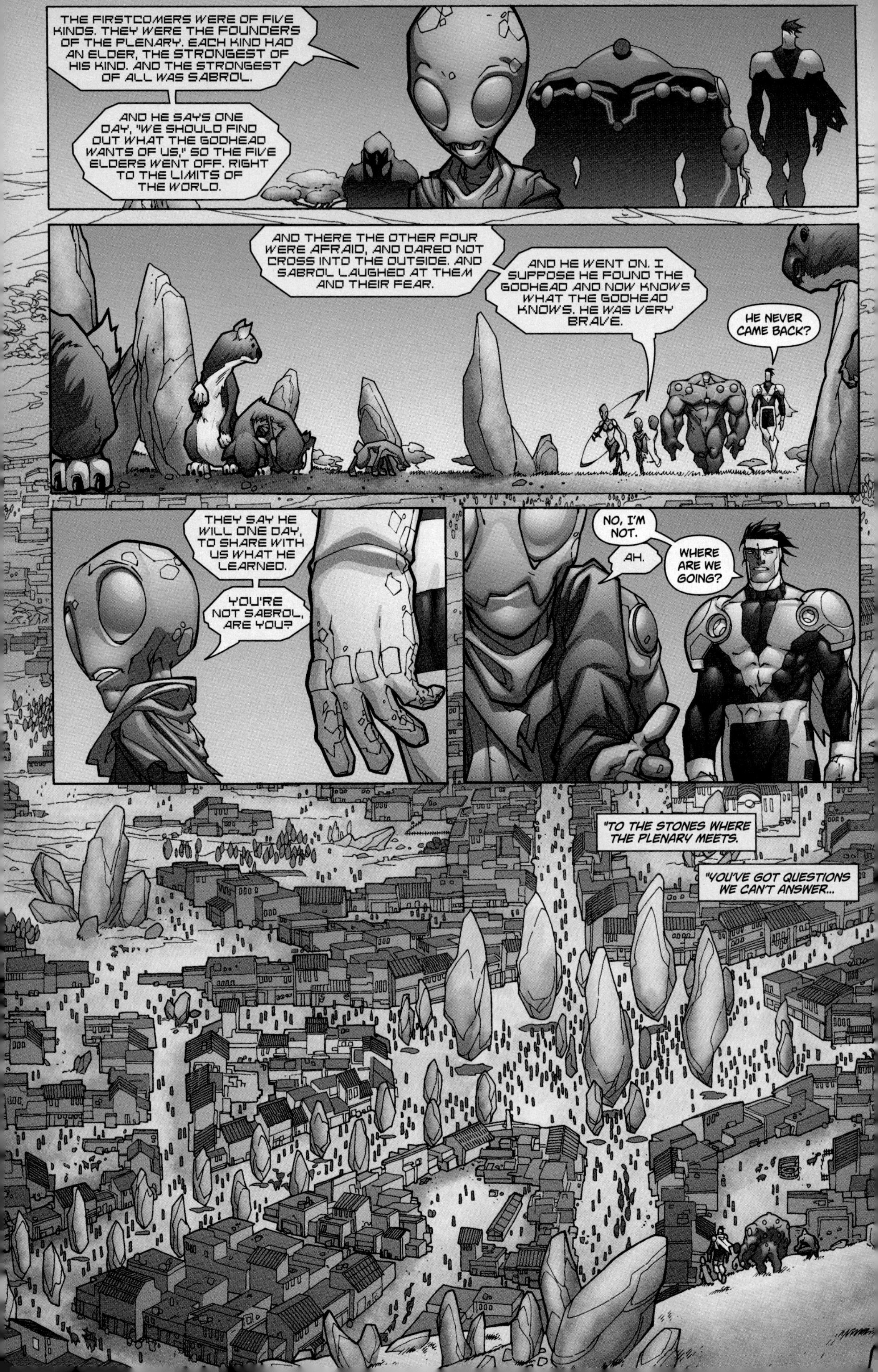
THE FIRSTCOMERS WERE OF FIVE KINDS. THEY WERE THE FOUNDERS OF THE PLENARY. EACH KIND HAD AN ELDER, THE STRONGEST OF HIS KIND. AND THE STRONGEST OF ALL WAS SABROL.
AND HE SAYS ONE DAY, "WE SHOULD FIND OUT WHAT THE GODHEAD WANTS OF US," SO THE FIVE ELDERS WENT OFF. RIGHT TO THE LIMITS OF THE WORLD.
AND THERE THE OTHER FOUR WERE AFRAID, AND DARED NOT CROSS INTO THE OUTSIDE. AND SABROL LAUGHED AT THEM AND THEIR FEAR.
AND HE WENT ON. I SUPPOSE HE FOUND THE GODHEAD AND NOW KNOWS WHAT THE GODHEAD KNOWS. HE WAS VERY BRAVE.
HE NEVER CAME BACK?
THEY SAY HE WILL ONE DAY, TO SHARE WITH US WHAT HE LEARNED.
YOU'RE NOT SABROL, ARE YOU?
NO, I'M NOT.
AH.
WHERE ARE WE GOING?
"TO THE STONES WHERE THE PLENARY MEETS.
"YOU'VE GOT QUESTIONS WE CAN'T ANSWER...

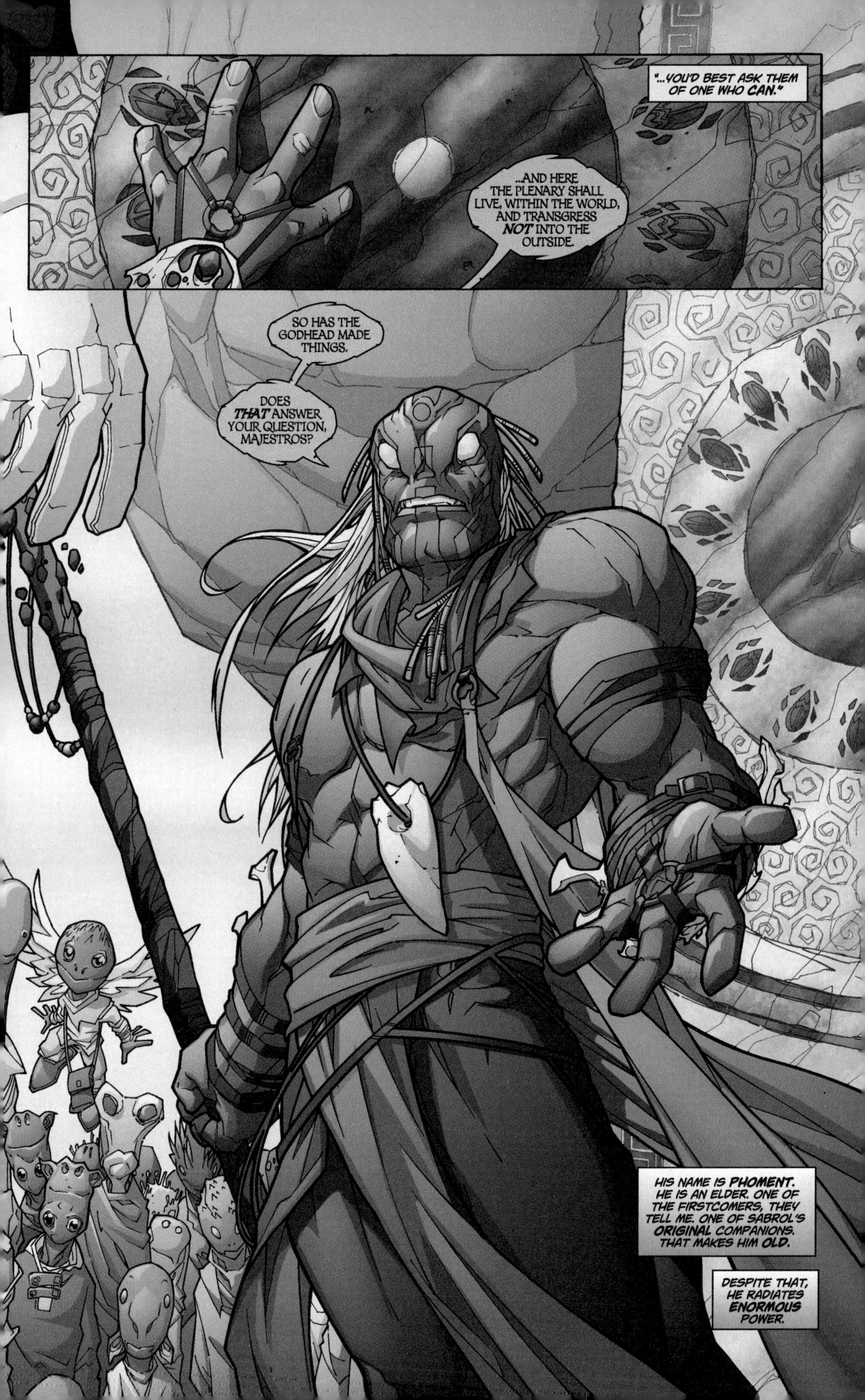
"...YOU'D BEST ASK THEM OF ONE WHO CAN."
...AND HERE THE PLENARY SHALL LIVE, WITHIN THE WORLD, AND TRANSGRESS NOT INTO THE OUTSIDE.
SO HAS THE GODHEAD MADE THINGS.
DOES THAT ANSWER YOUR QUESTION, MAJESTROS?
HIS NAME IS PHOMENT. HE IS AN ELDER. ONE OF THE FIRSTCOMERS, THEY TELL ME. ONE OF SABROL'S ORIGINAL COMPANIONS. THAT MAKES HIM OLD.
DESPITE THAT, HE RADIATES ENORMOUS POWER.

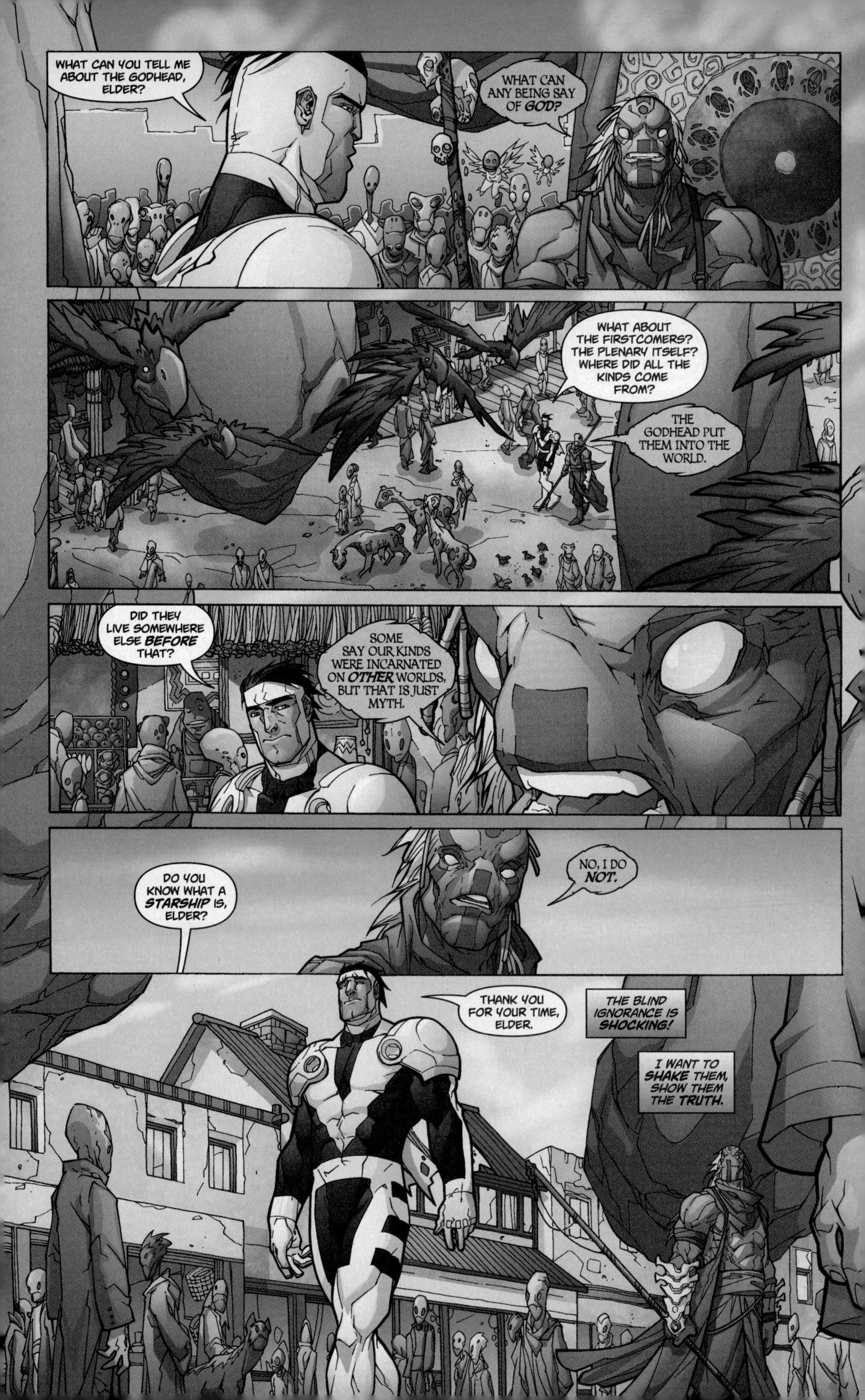
WHAT CAN YOU TELL ME ABOUT THE GODHEAD, ELDER?
WHAT CAN ANY BEING SAY OF GOD?
WHAT ABOUT THE FIRSTCOMERS? THE PLENARY ITSELF? WHERE DID ALL THE KINDS COME FROM?
THE GODHEAD PUT THEM INTO THE WORLD.
DID THEY LIVE SOMEWHERE ELSE BEFORE THAT?
SOME SAY OUR KINDS WERE INCARNATED ON OTHER WORLDS, BUT THAT IS JUST MYTH.
DO YOU KNOW WHAT A STARSHIP IS, ELDER?
NO, I DO NOT.
THANK YOU FOR YOUR TIME, ELDER.
THE BLIND IGNORANCE IS SHOCKING!
I WANT TO SHAKE THEM, SHOW THEM THE TRUTH.

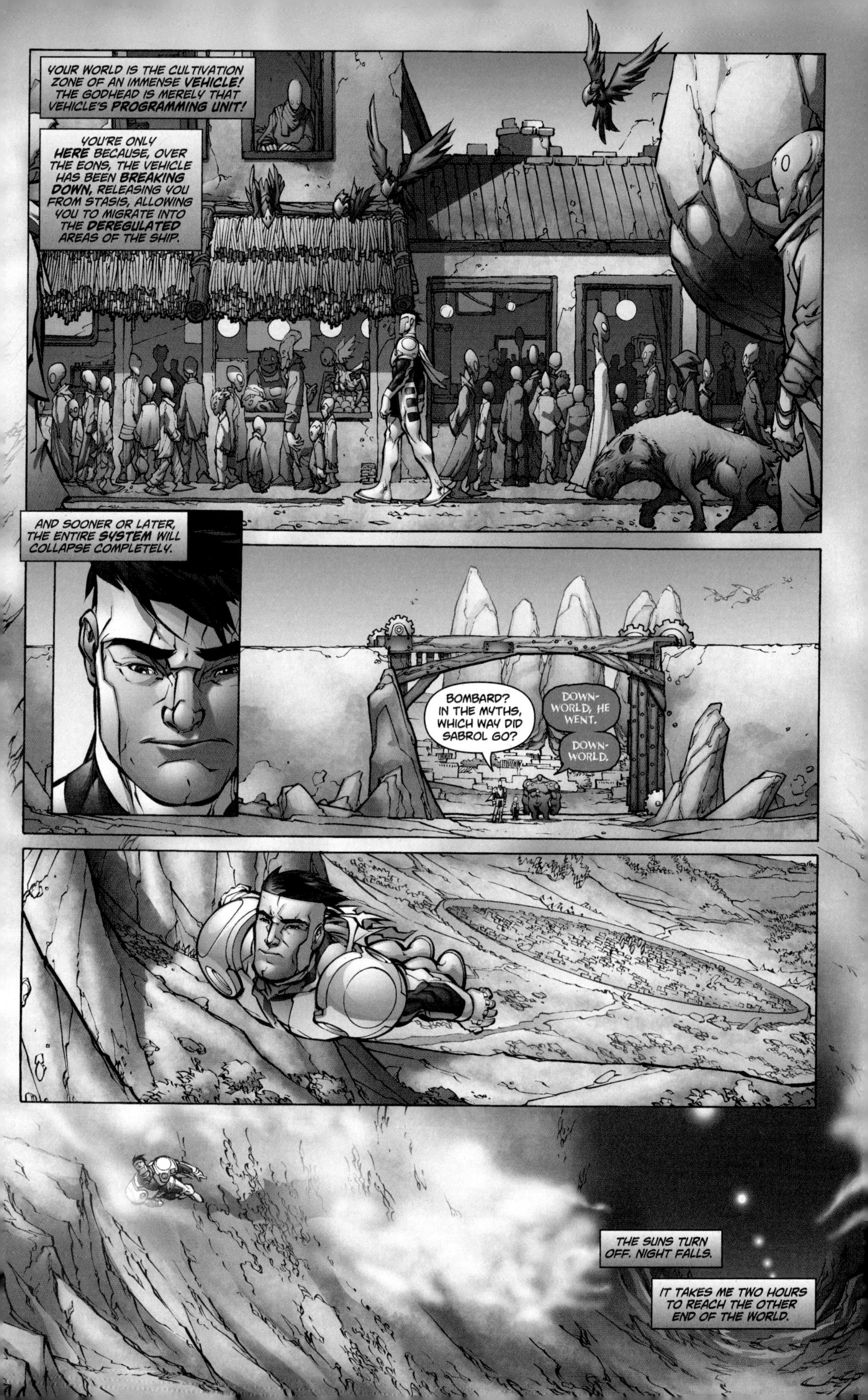
YOUR WORLD IS THE CULTIVATION ZONE OF AN IMMENSE VEHICLE! THE GODHEAD IS MERELY THAT VEHICLE'S PROGRAMMING UNIT!
YOU'RE ONLY HERE BECAUSE, OVER THE EONS, THE VEHICLE HAS BEEN BREAKING DOWN, RELEASING YOU FROM STASIS, ALLOWING YOU TO MIGRATE INTO THE DEREGULATED AREAS OF THE SHIP.
AND SOONER OR LATER, THE ENTIRE SYSTEM WILL COLLAPSE COMPLETELY.
BOMBARD? IN THE MYTHS, WHICH WAY DID SABROL GO?
DOWN-WORLD, HE WENT.
DOWN-WORLD.
THE SUNS TURN OFF. NIGHT FALLS.
IT TAKES ME TWO HOURS TO REACH THE OTHER END OF THE WORLD.

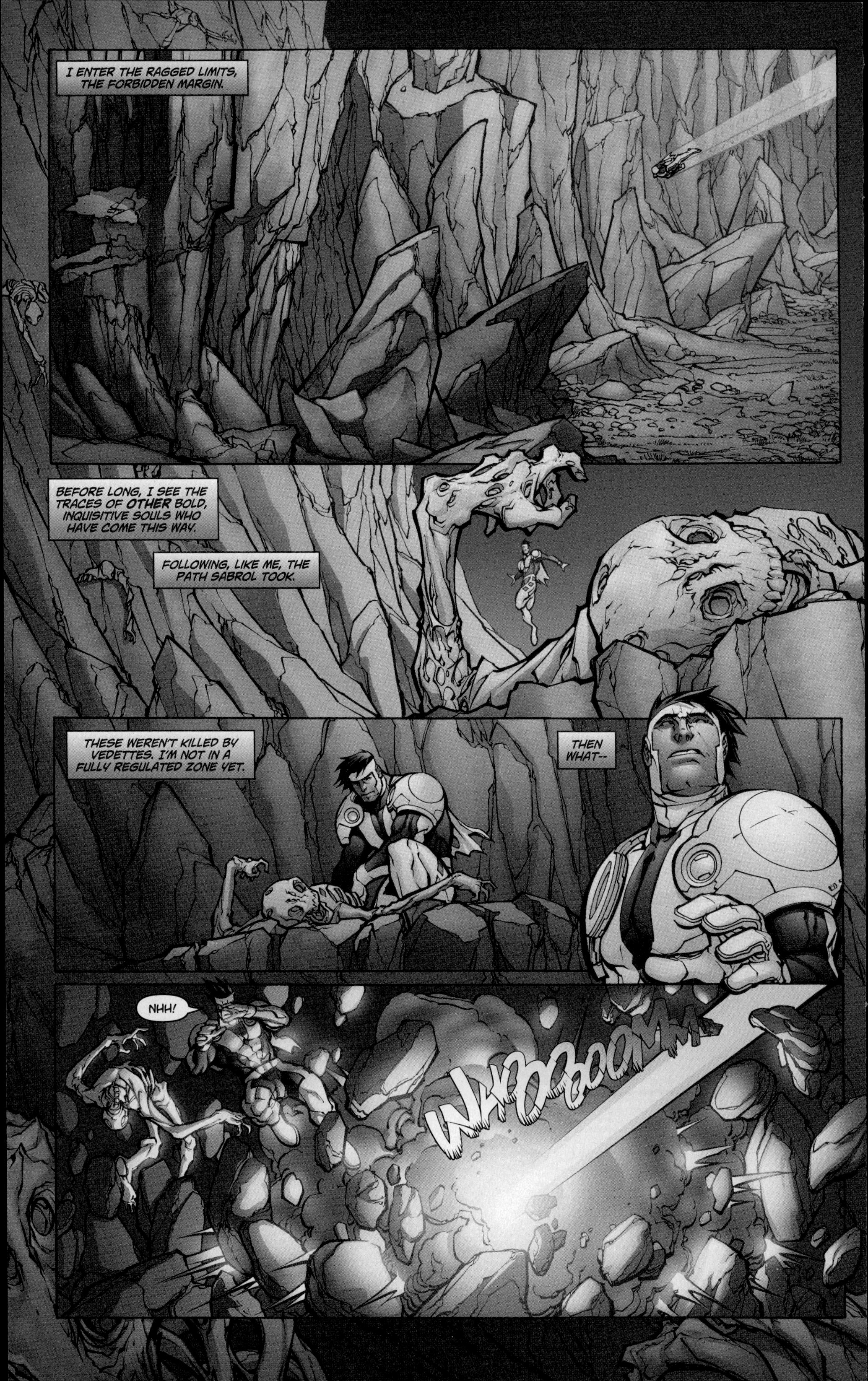
I ENTER THE RAGGED LIMITS, THE FORBIDDEN MARGIN.
BEFORE LONG, I SEE THE TRACES OF OTHER BOLD, INQUISITIVE SOULS WHO HAVE COME THIS WAY.
FOLLOWING, LIKE ME, THE PATH SABROL TOOK.
THESE WEREN'T KILLED BY VEDETTES. I'M NOT IN A FULLY REGULATED ZONE YET.
THEN WHAT--
NHH!
WHOOOOOMM

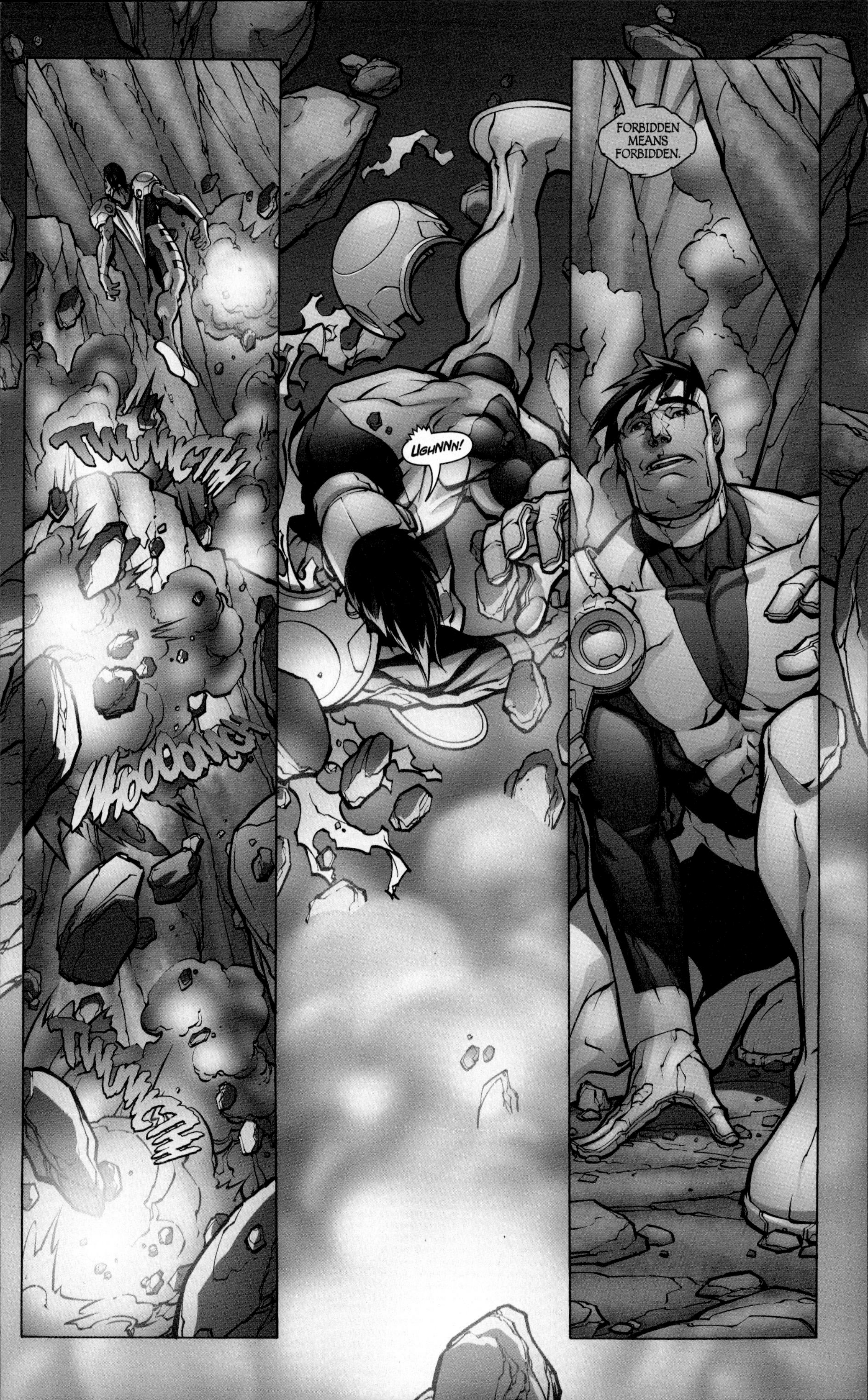
TWUNCTH
WHOOOMCH
TWUNCTH
UGHNNN!
FORBIDDEN MEANS FORBIDDEN.

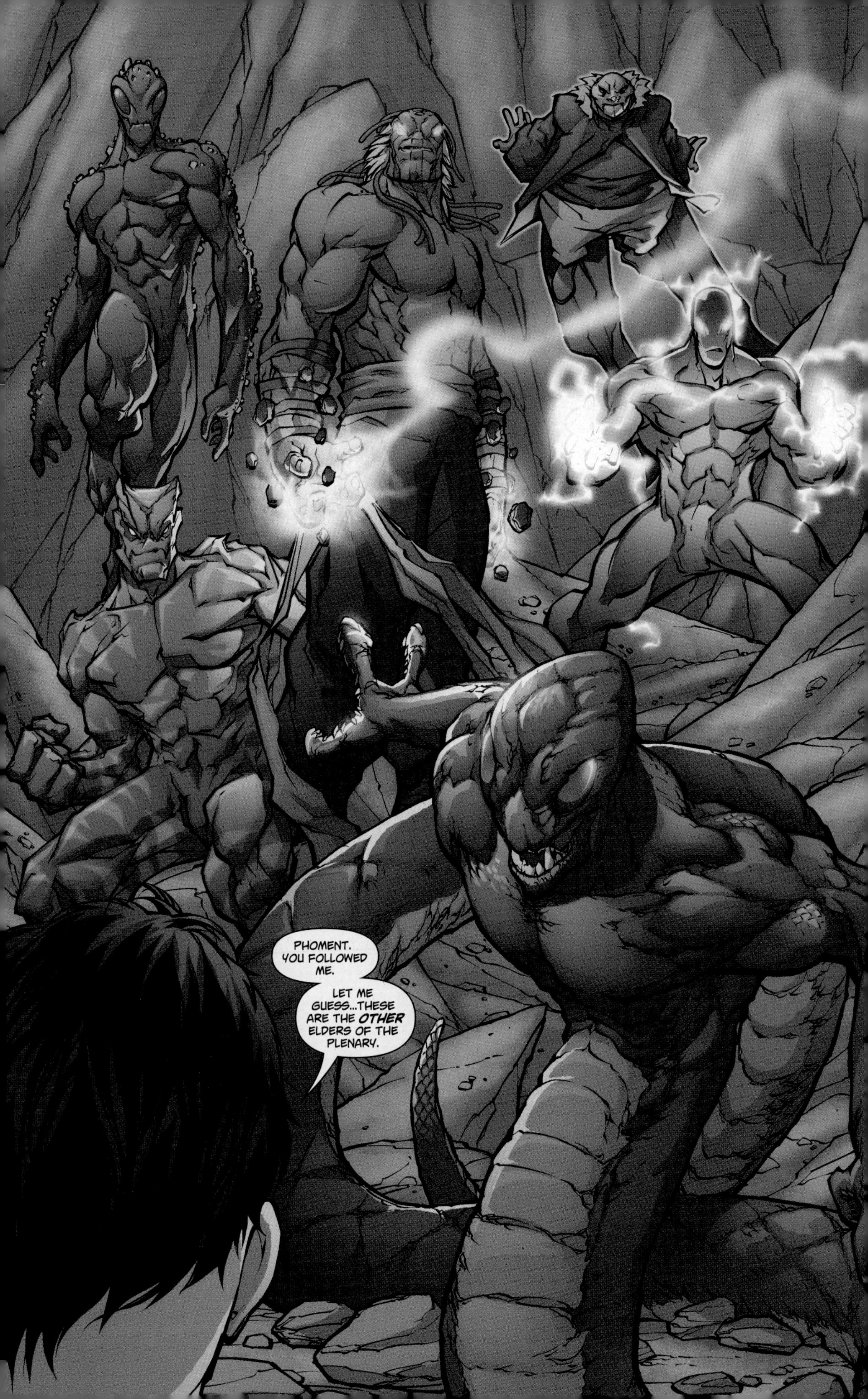
PHOMENT. YOU FOLLOWED ME.
LET ME GUESS...THESE ARE THE *OTHER* ELDERS OF THE PLENARY.

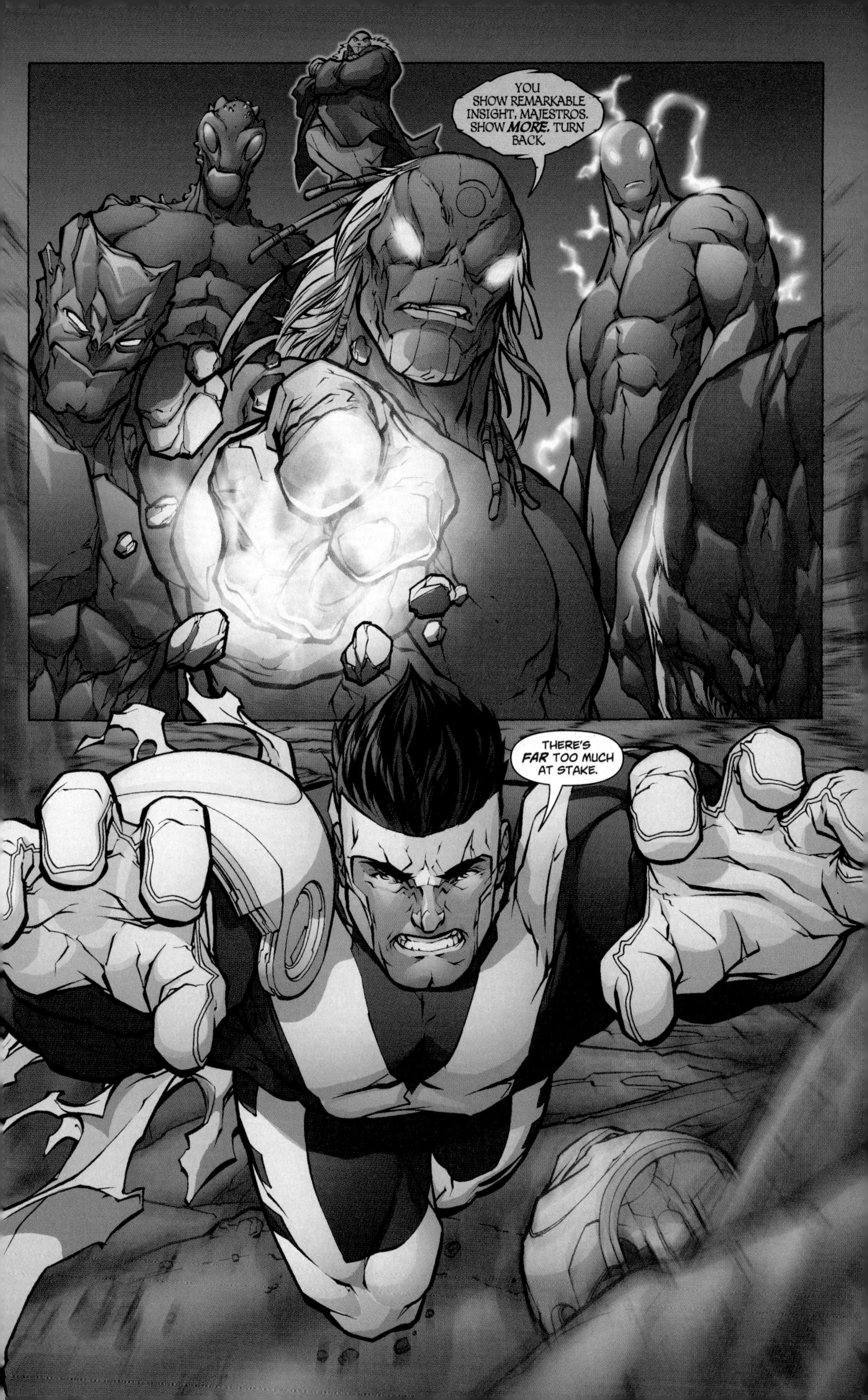
YOU SHOW REMARKABLE INSIGHT, MAJESTROS. SHOW MORE. TURN BACK.
THERE'S FAR TOO MUCH AT STAKE.

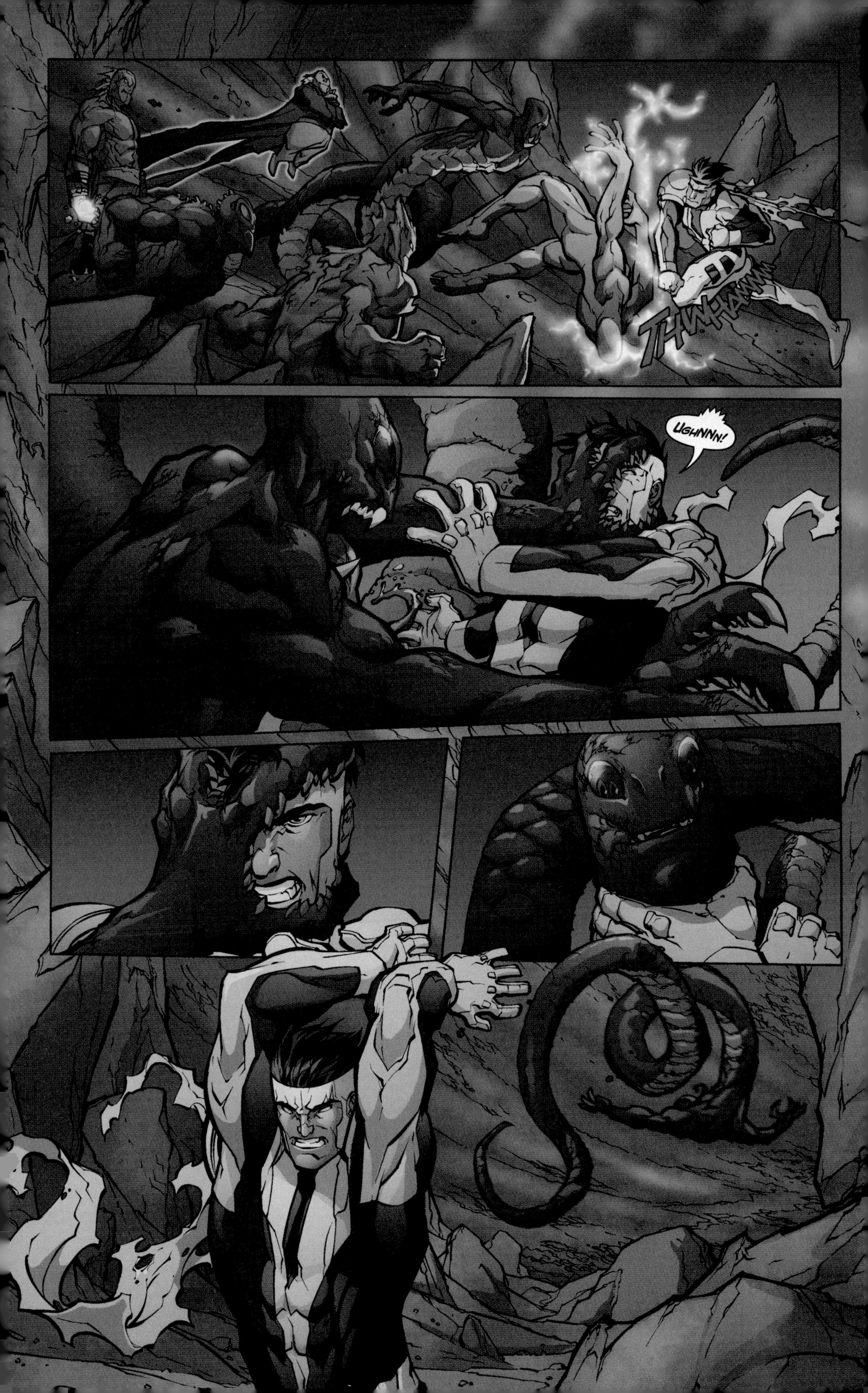
THWHAMM
UGHNNN!

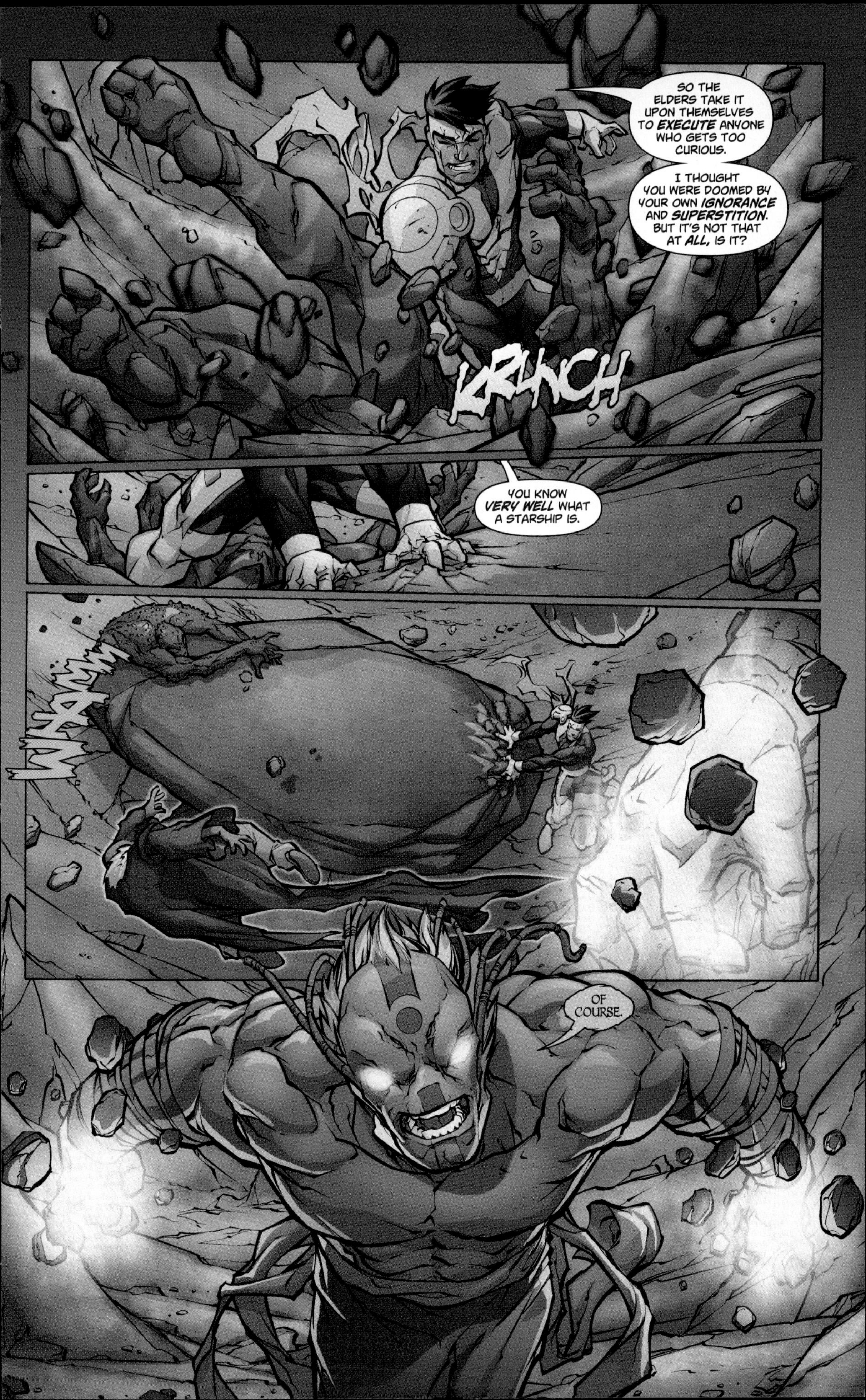
SO THE ELDERS TAKE IT UPON THEMSELVES TO EXECUTE ANYONE WHO GETS TOO CURIOUS.
I THOUGHT YOU WERE DOOMED BY YOUR OWN IGNORANCE AND SUPERSTITION. BUT IT'S NOT THAT AT ALL, IS IT?
KRUNCH
YOU KNOW VERY WELL WHAT A STARSHIP IS.
WHAMM
OF COURSE.

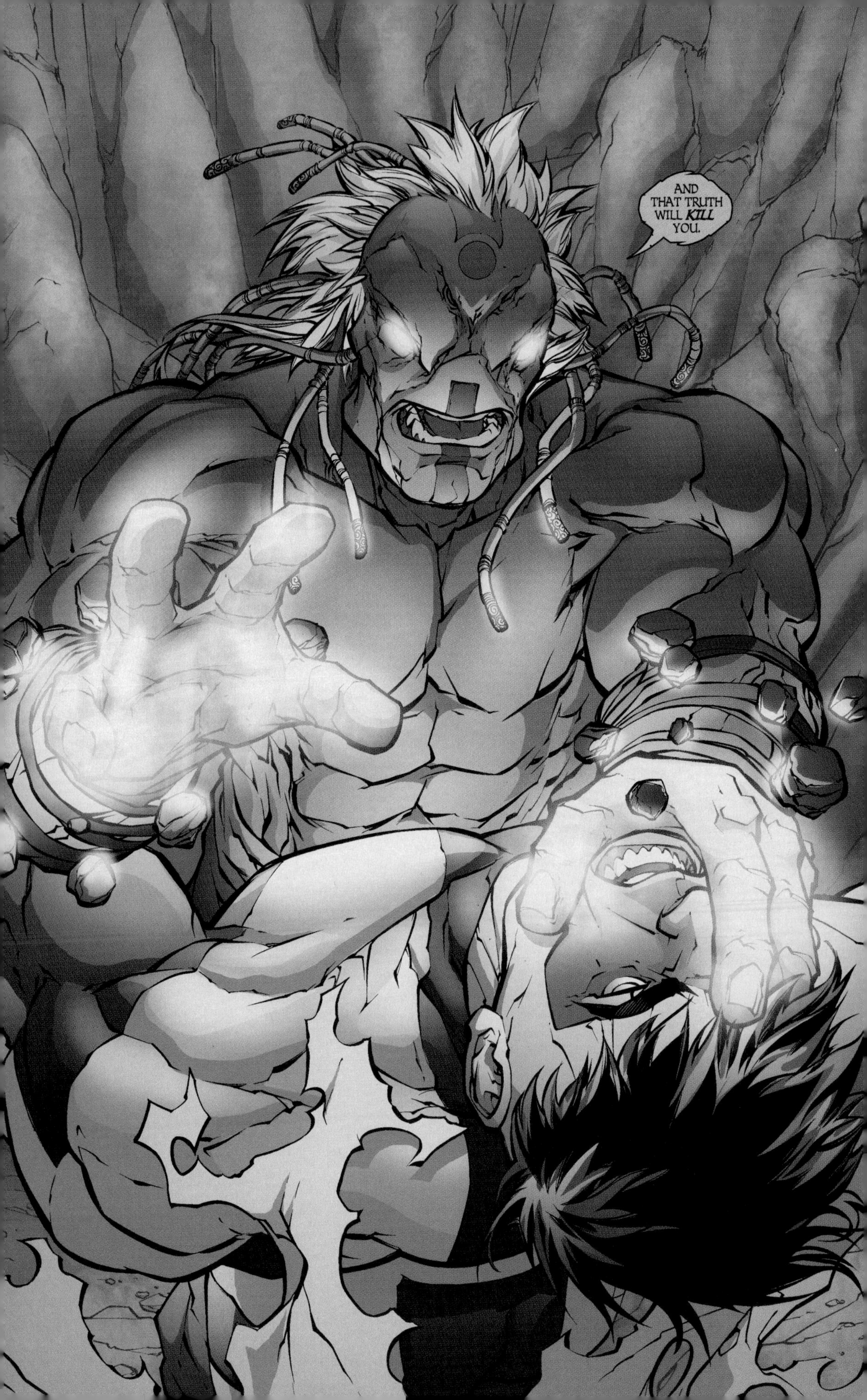
AND THAT TRUTH WILL KILL YOU.

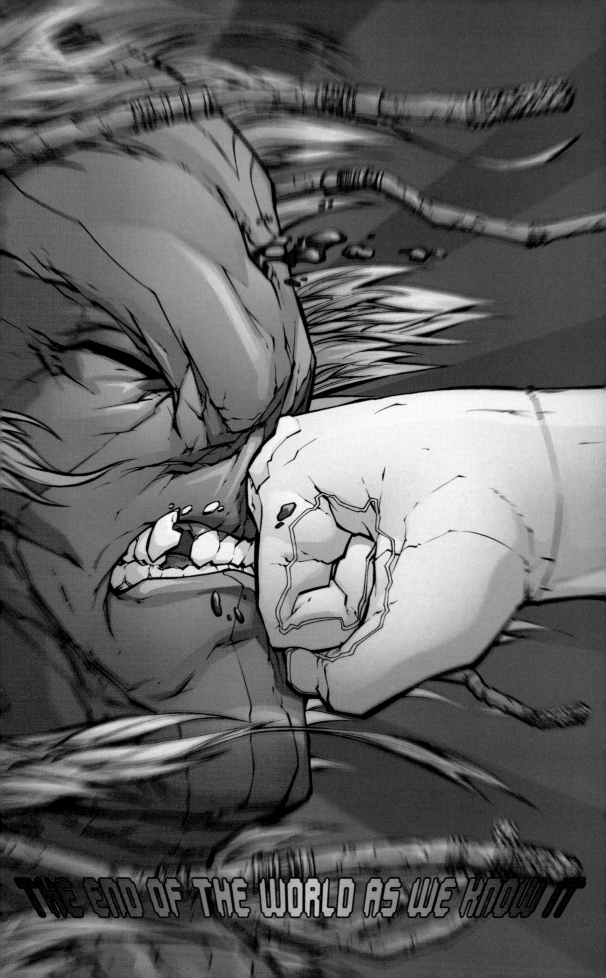

THE END OF THE WORLD AS WE KNOW IT

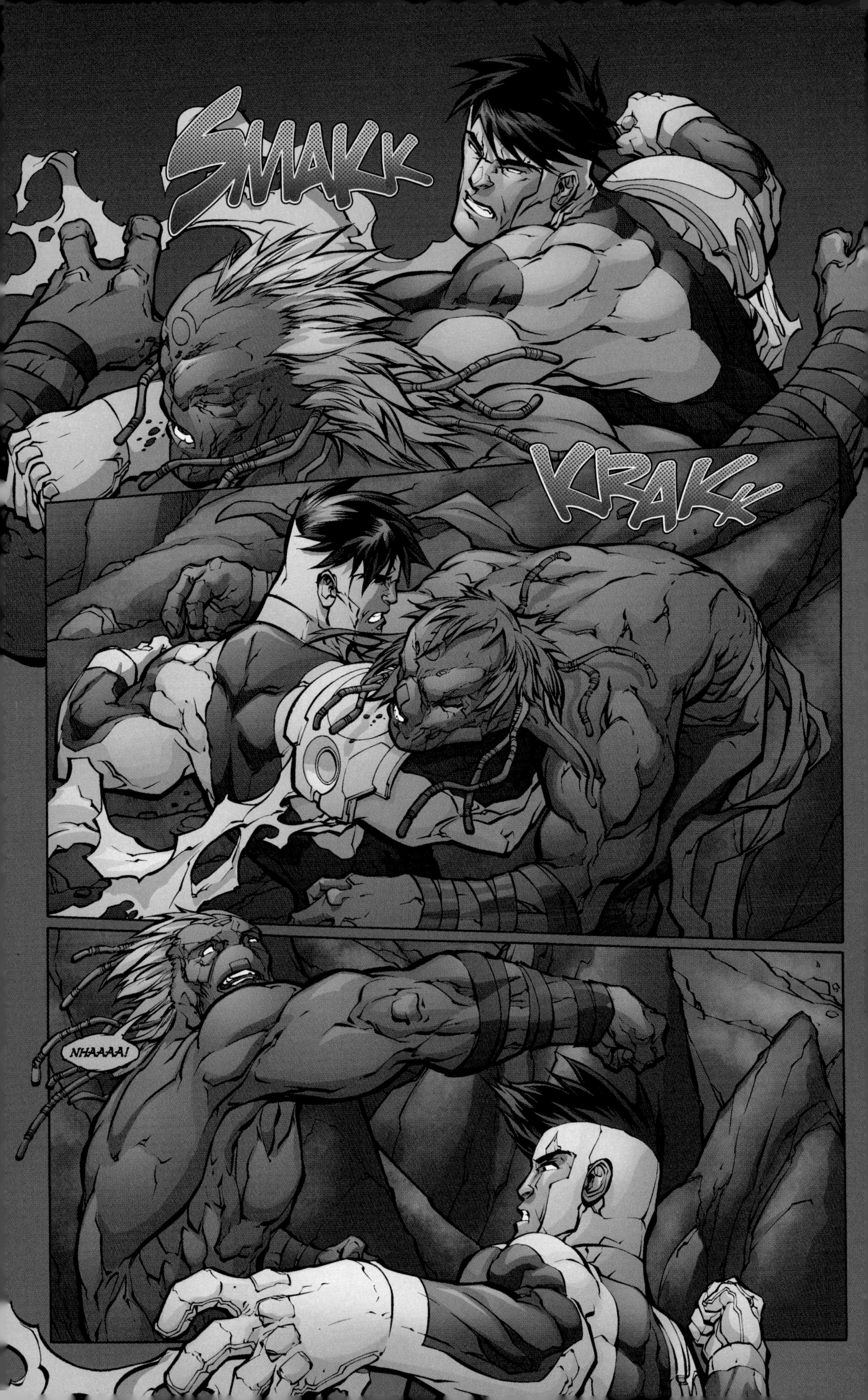
SMAKK
KRAKK
NHAAAA!

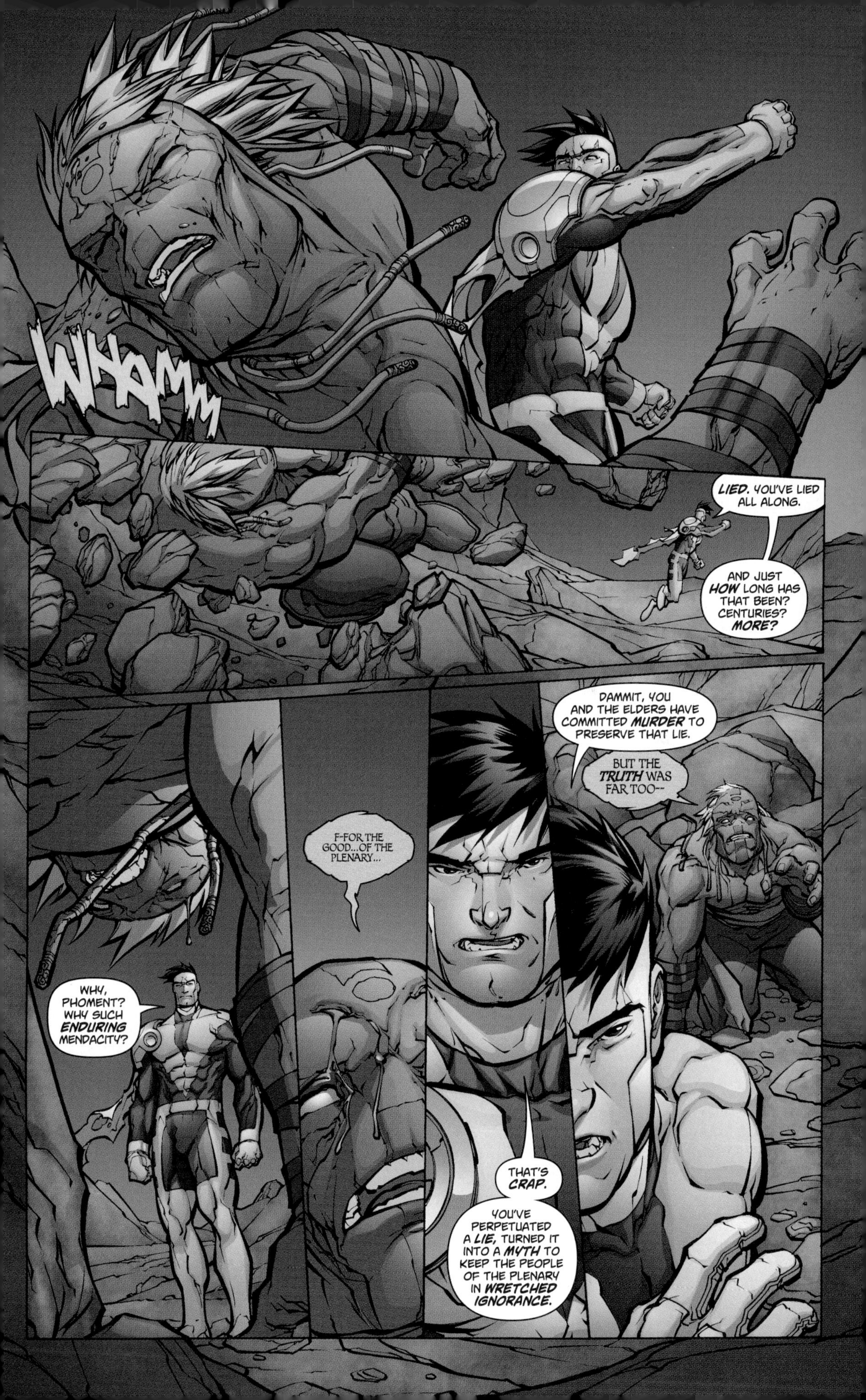
WHAMM
LIED. YOU'VE LIED ALL ALONG.
AND JUST HOW LONG HAS THAT BEEN? CENTURIES? MORE?
WHY, PHOMENT? WHY SUCH ENDURING MENDACITY?
F-FOR THE GOOD...OF THE PLENARY...
THAT'S CRAP.
YOU'VE PERPETUATED A LIE, TURNED IT INTO A MYTH TO KEEP THE PEOPLE OF THE PLENARY IN WRETCHED IGNORANCE.
DAMMIT, YOU AND THE ELDERS HAVE COMMITTED MURDER TO PRESERVE THAT LIE.
BUT THE TRUTH WAS FAR TOO--

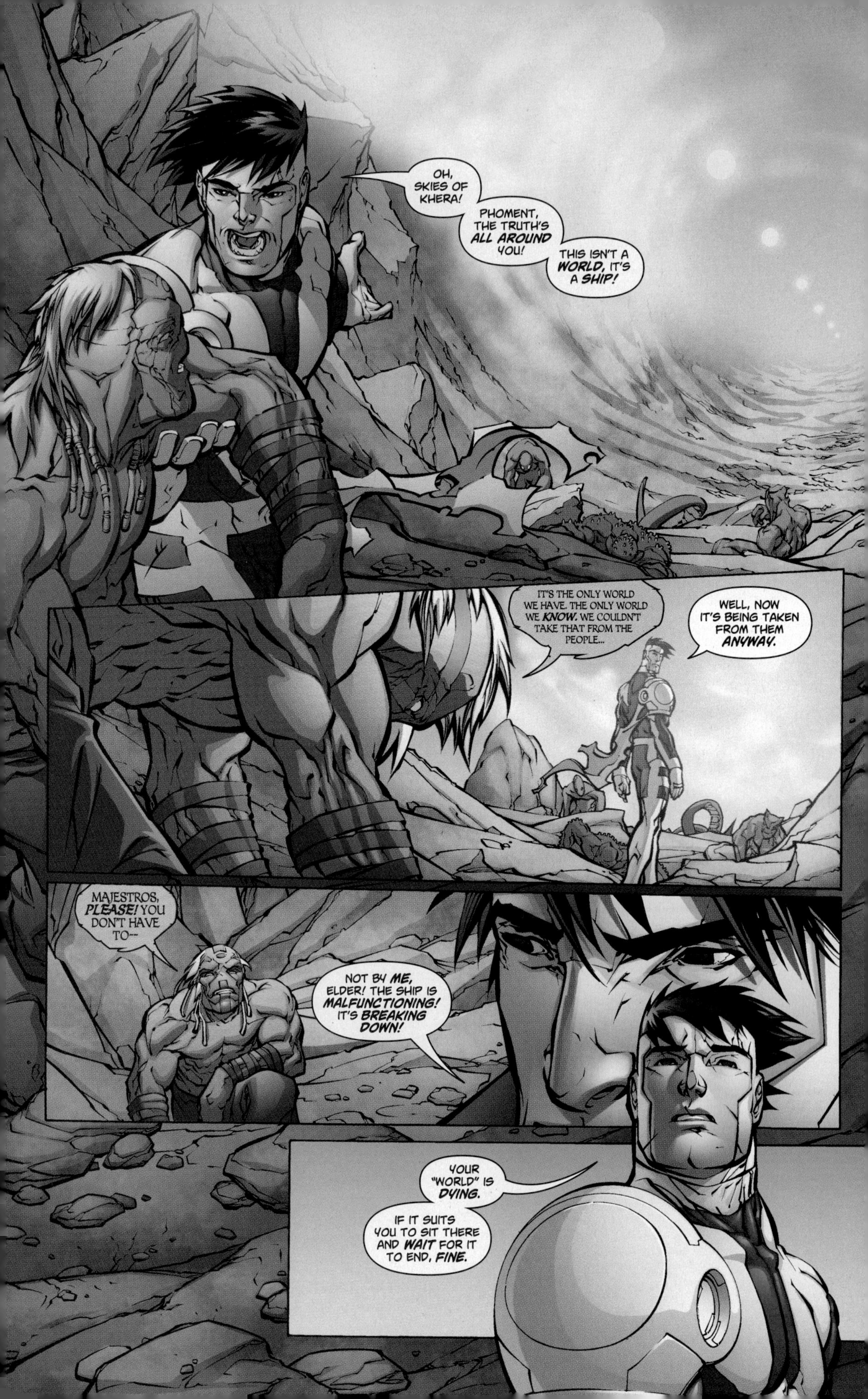
OH, SKIES OF KHERA!
PHOMENT, THE TRUTH'S ALL AROUND YOU!
THIS ISN'T A WORLD, IT'S A SHIP!
IT'S THE ONLY WORLD WE HAVE. THE ONLY WORLD WE KNOW. WE COULDN'T TAKE THAT FROM THE PEOPLE...
WELL, NOW IT'S BEING TAKEN FROM THEM ANYWAY.
MAJESTROS, PLEASE! YOU DON'T HAVE TO--
NOT BY ME, ELDER! THE SHIP IS MALFUNCTIONING! IT'S BREAKING DOWN!
YOUR "WORLD" IS DYING.
IF IT SUITS YOU TO SIT THERE AND WAIT FOR IT TO END, FINE.

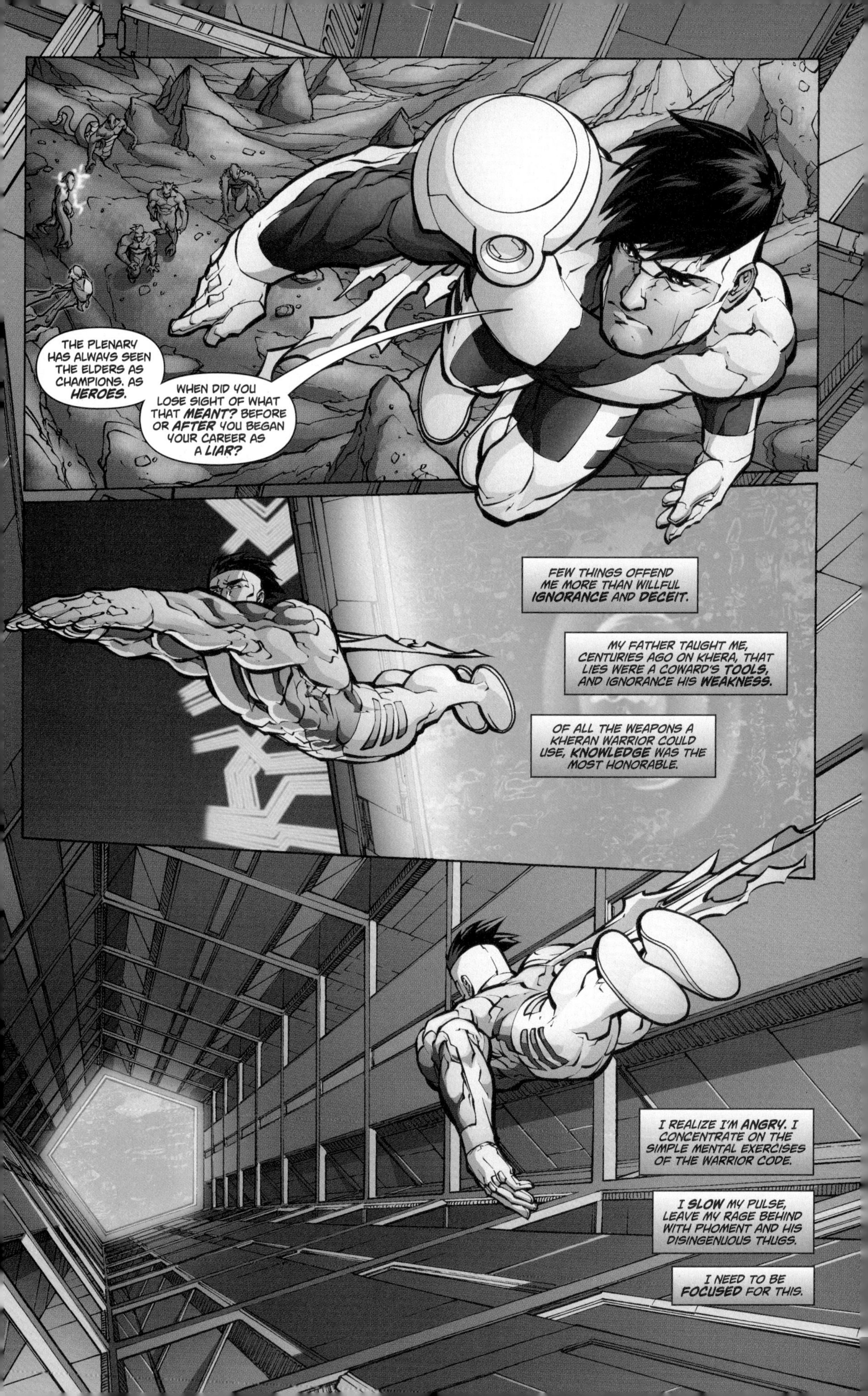
THE PLENARY HAS ALWAYS SEEN THE ELDERS AS CHAMPIONS. AS **HEROES**.
WHEN DID YOU LOSE SIGHT OF WHAT THAT **MEANT?** BEFORE OR **AFTER** YOU BEGAN YOUR CAREER AS A **LIAR?**
FEW THINGS OFFEND ME MORE THAN WILLFUL **IGNORANCE** AND **DECEIT**.
MY FATHER TAUGHT ME, CENTURIES AGO ON KHERA, THAT LIES WERE A COWARD'S **TOOLS**, AND IGNORANCE HIS **WEAKNESS**.
OF ALL THE WEAPONS A KHERAN WARRIOR COULD USE, **KNOWLEDGE** WAS THE MOST HONORABLE.
I REALIZE I'M **ANGRY**. I CONCENTRATE ON THE SIMPLE MENTAL EXERCISES OF THE WARRIOR CODE.
I **SLOW** MY PULSE, LEAVE MY RAGE BEHIND WITH PHOMENT AND HIS DISINGENUOUS THUGS.
I NEED TO BE **FOCUSED** FOR THIS.

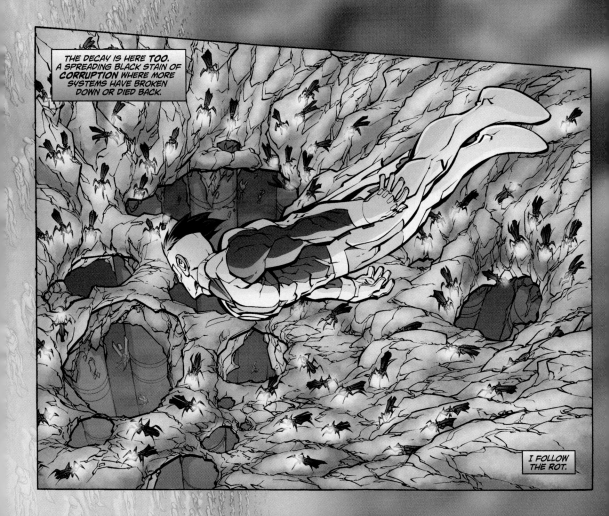

I PASS THROUGH ANOTHER *STASIS CHAMBER.* THE LIFE FORMS OF ANOTHER *HUNDRED WORLDS* FROZEN IN SUSPENSION.

THE DECAY IS HERE *TOO.* A SPREADING BLACK STAIN OF *CORRUPTION* WHERE MORE SYSTEMS HAVE BROKEN DOWN OR DIED BACK.

I FOLLOW THE ROT.

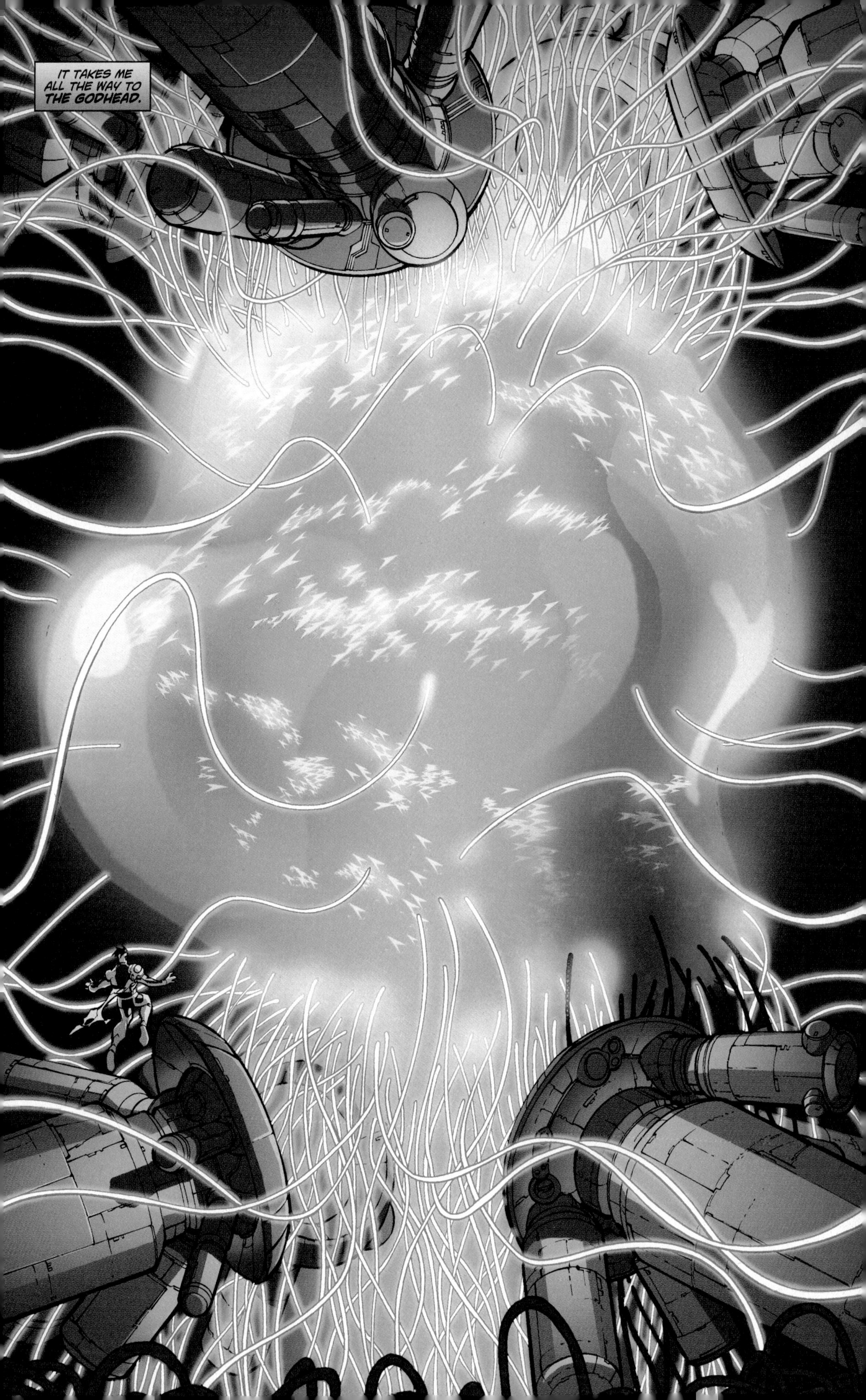
IT TAKES ME ALL THE WAY TO THE GODHEAD.

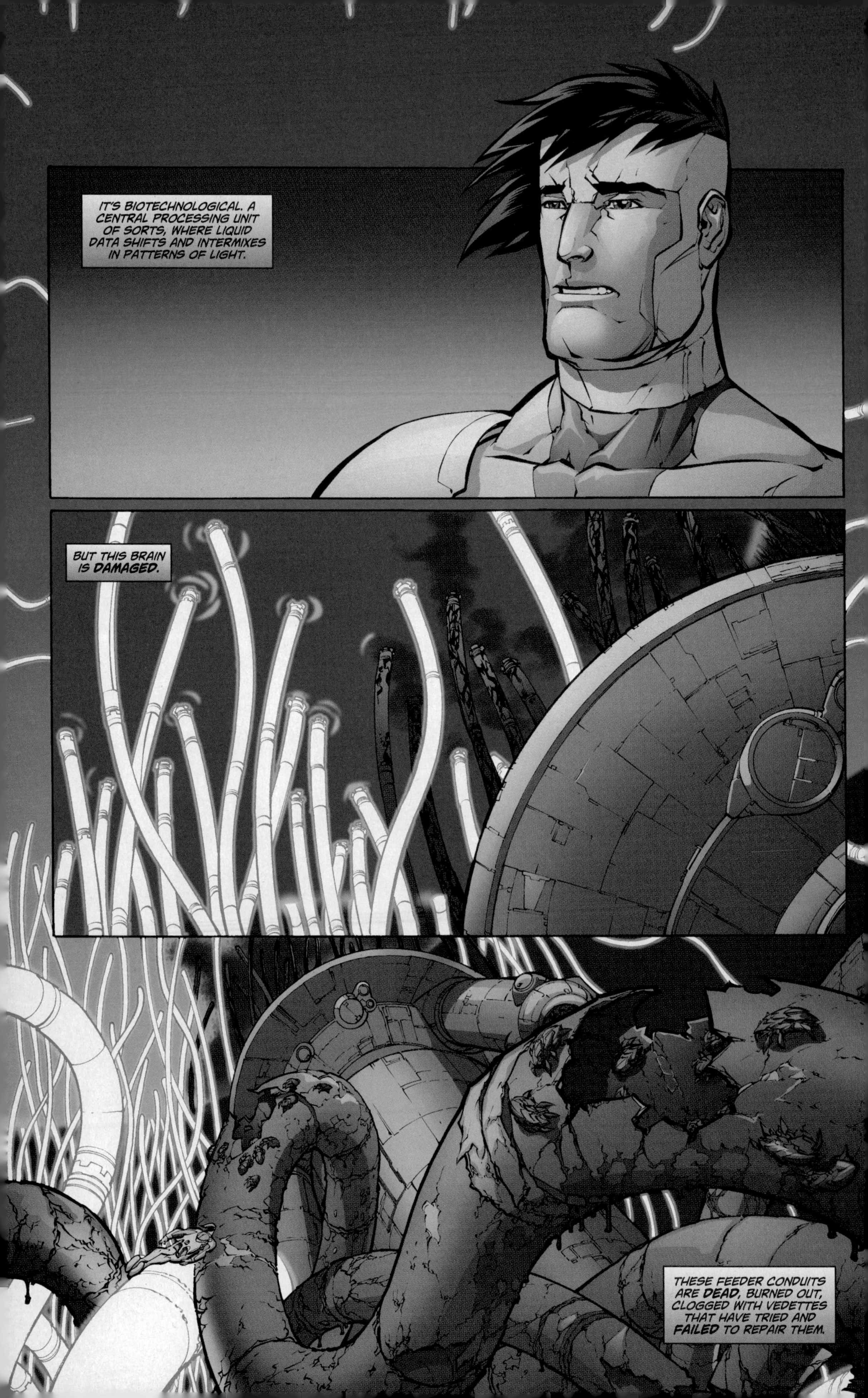
IT'S BIOTECHNOLOGICAL. A CENTRAL PROCESSING UNIT OF SORTS, WHERE LIQUID DATA SHIFTS AND INTERMIXES IN PATTERNS OF LIGHT.
BUT THIS BRAIN IS DAMAGED.
THESE FEEDER CONDUITS ARE DEAD, BURNED OUT, CLOGGED WITH VEDETTES THAT HAVE TRIED AND FAILED TO REPAIR THEM.

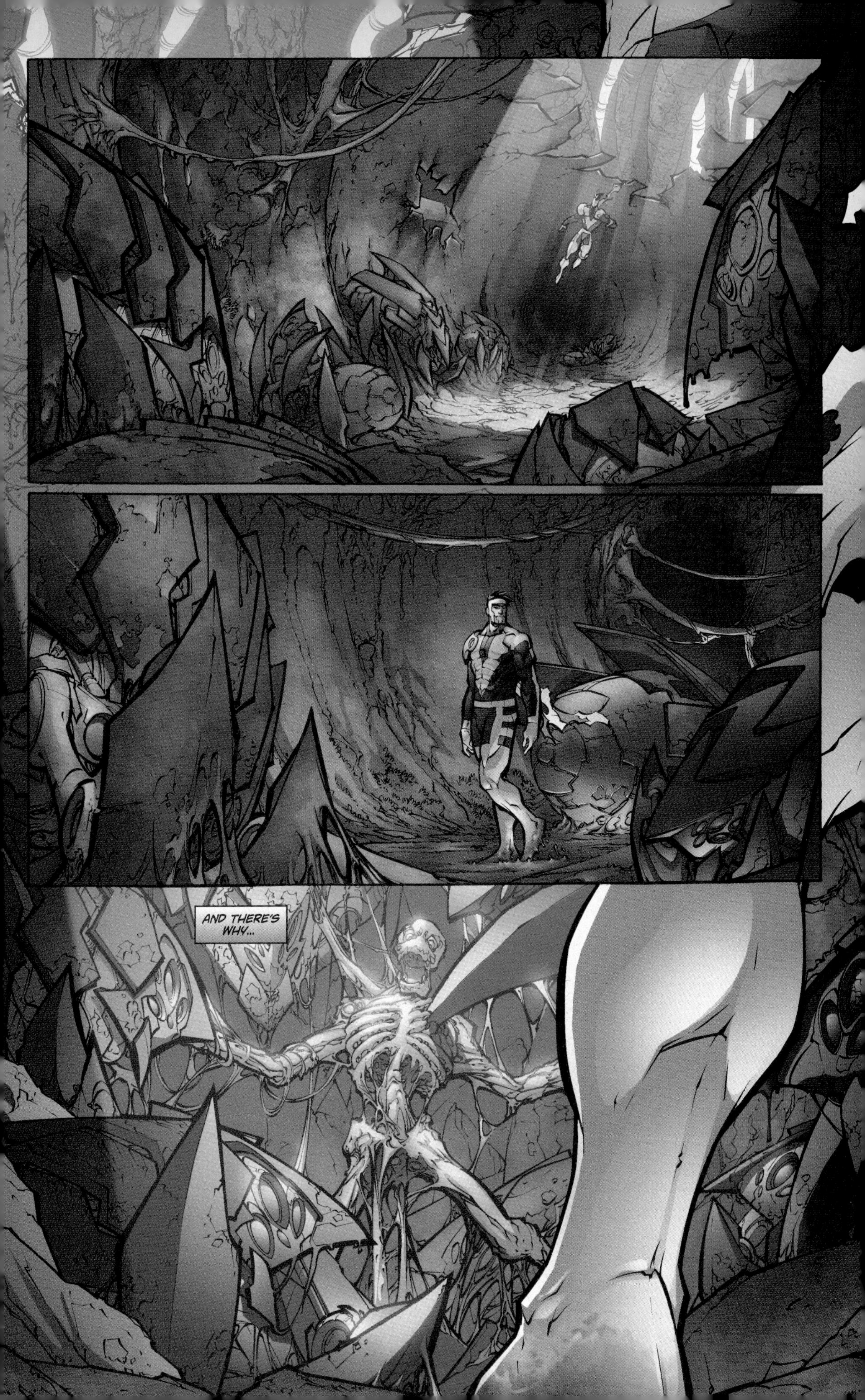
AND THERE'S WHY...

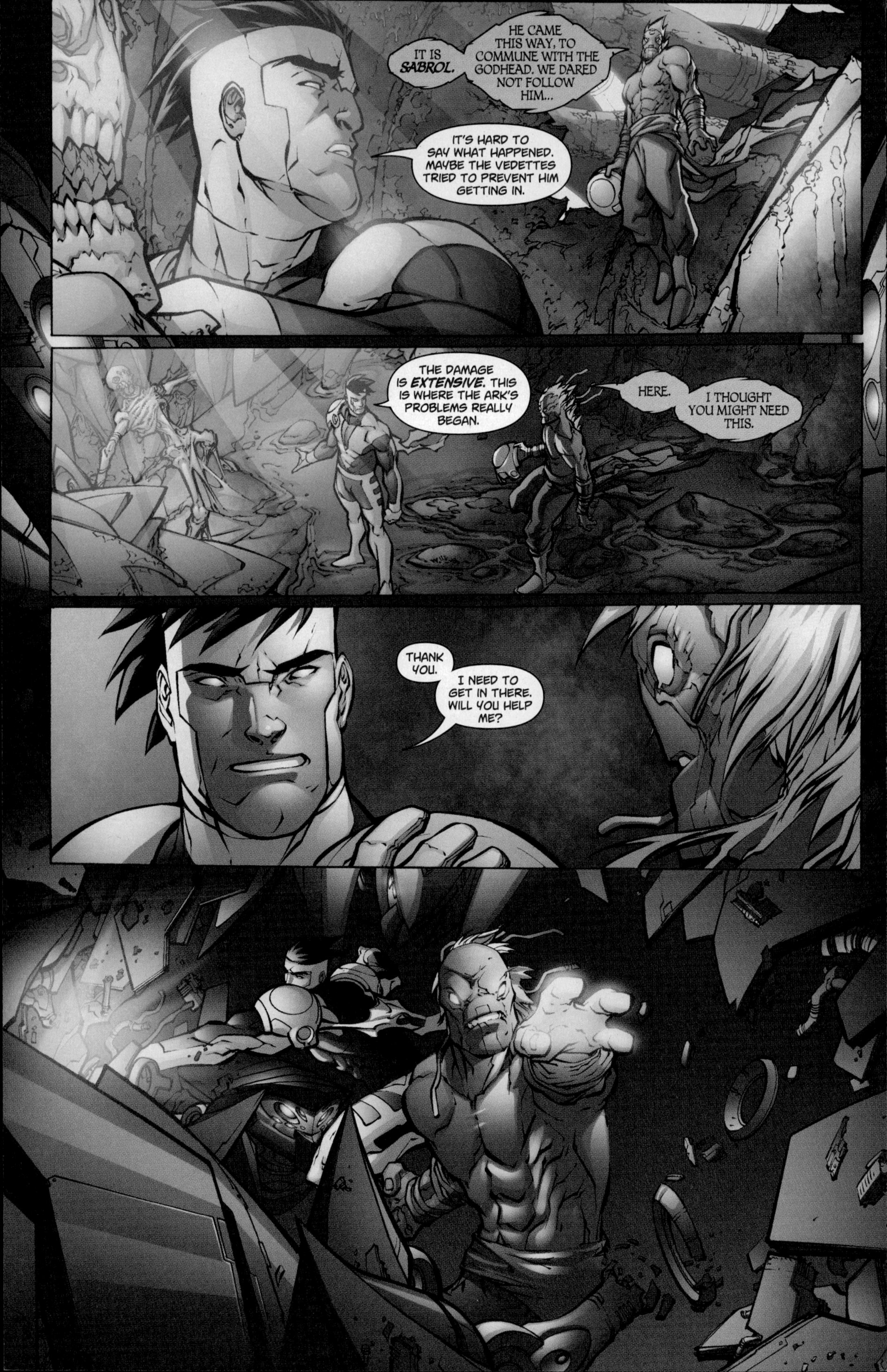
IT IS SABROL.
HE CAME THIS WAY, TO COMMUNE WITH THE GODHEAD. WE DARED NOT FOLLOW HIM...
IT'S HARD TO SAY WHAT HAPPENED. MAYBE THE VEDETTES TRIED TO PREVENT HIM GETTING IN.
THE DAMAGE IS EXTENSIVE. THIS IS WHERE THE ARK'S PROBLEMS REALLY BEGAN.
HERE.
I THOUGHT YOU MIGHT NEED THIS.
THANK YOU.
I NEED TO GET IN THERE. WILL YOU HELP ME?

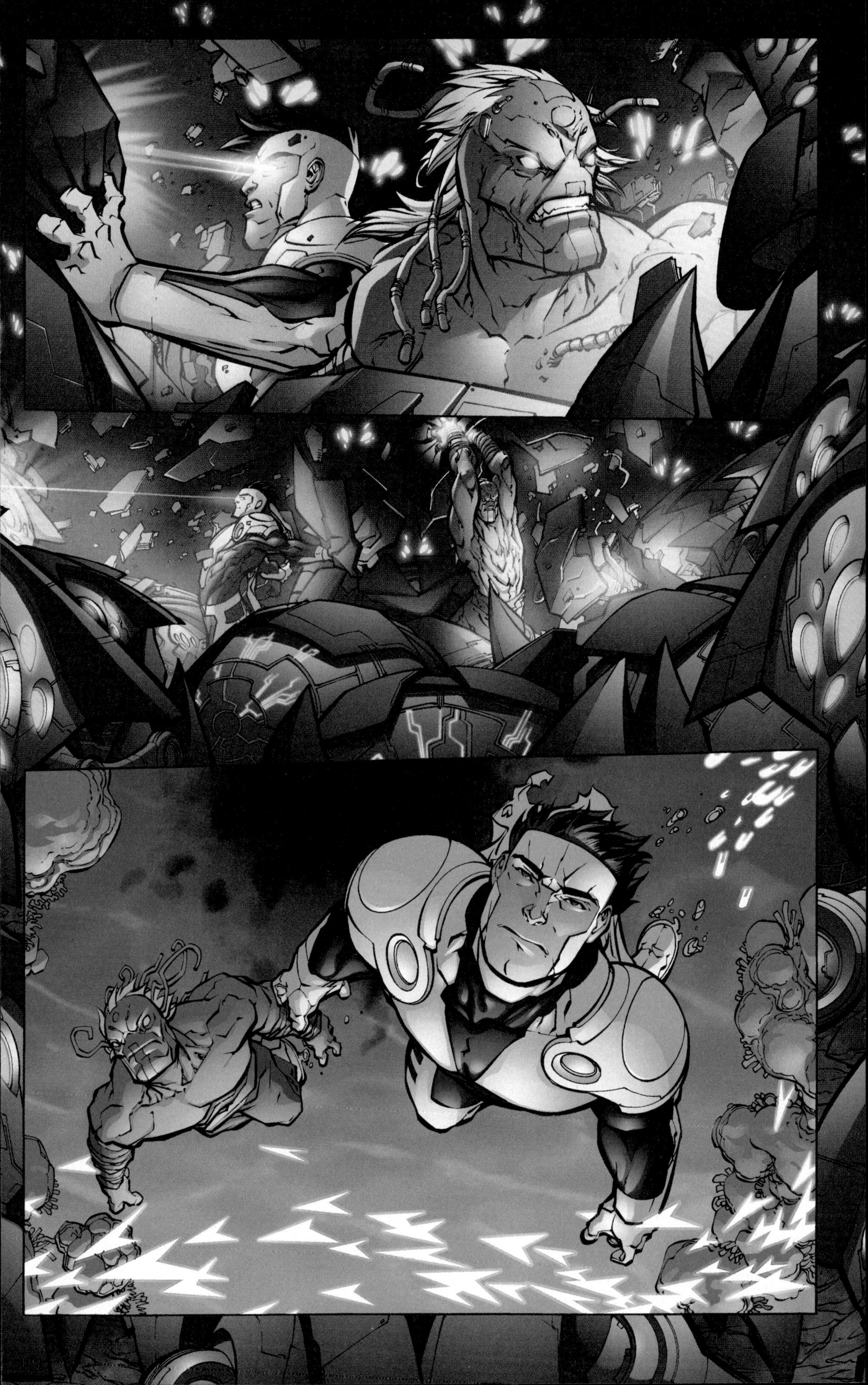

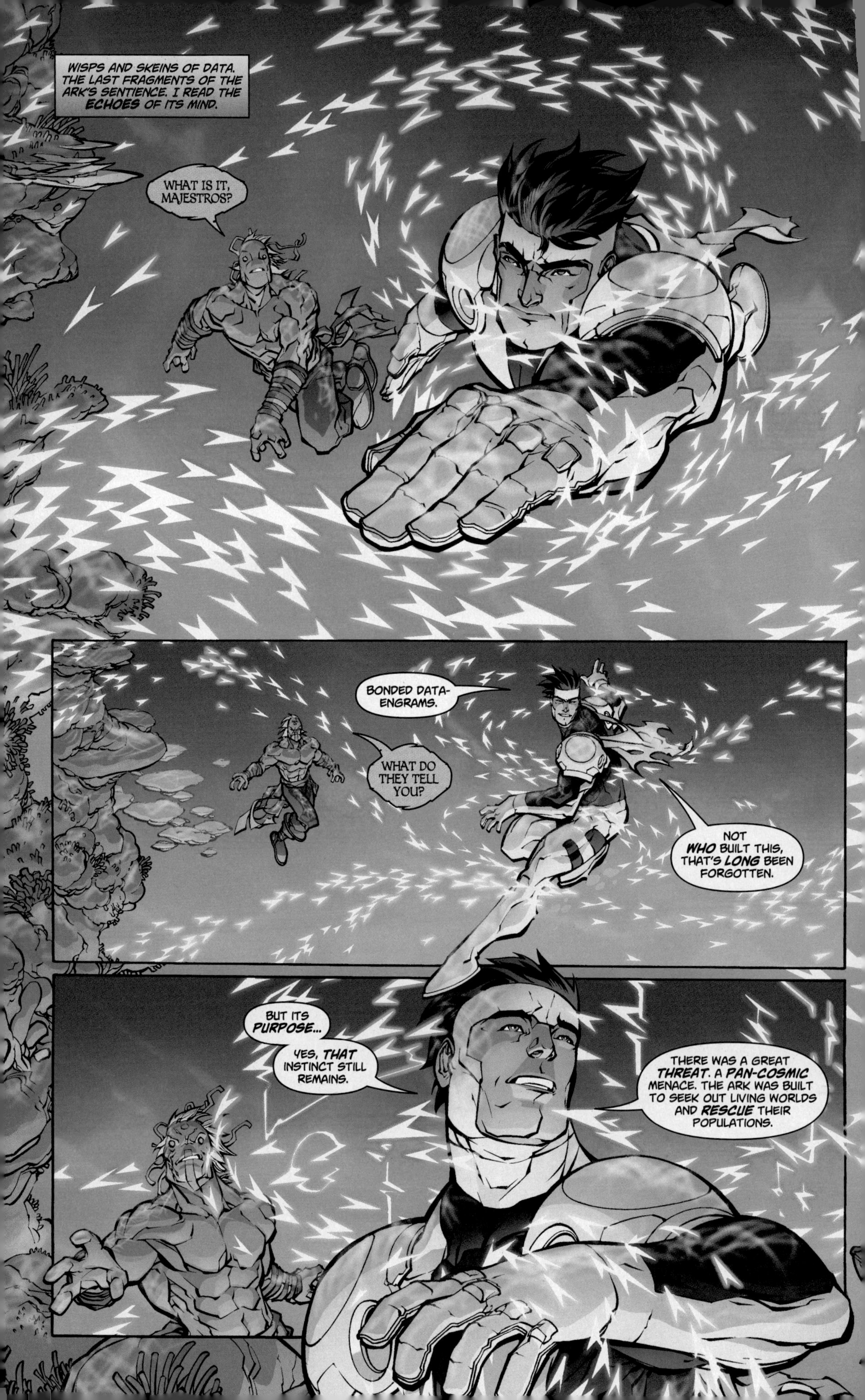
WISPS AND SKEINS OF DATA. THE LAST FRAGMENTS OF THE ARK'S SENTIENCE. I READ THE ECHOES OF ITS MIND.
WHAT IS IT, MAJESTROS?
BONDED DATA-ENGRAMS.
WHAT DO THEY TELL YOU?
NOT WHO BUILT THIS, THAT'S LONG BEEN FORGOTTEN.
BUT ITS PURPOSE...
YES, THAT INSTINCT STILL REMAINS.
THERE WAS A GREAT THREAT. A PAN-COSMIC MENACE. THE ARK WAS BUILT TO SEEK OUT LIVING WORLDS AND RESCUE THEIR POPULATIONS.

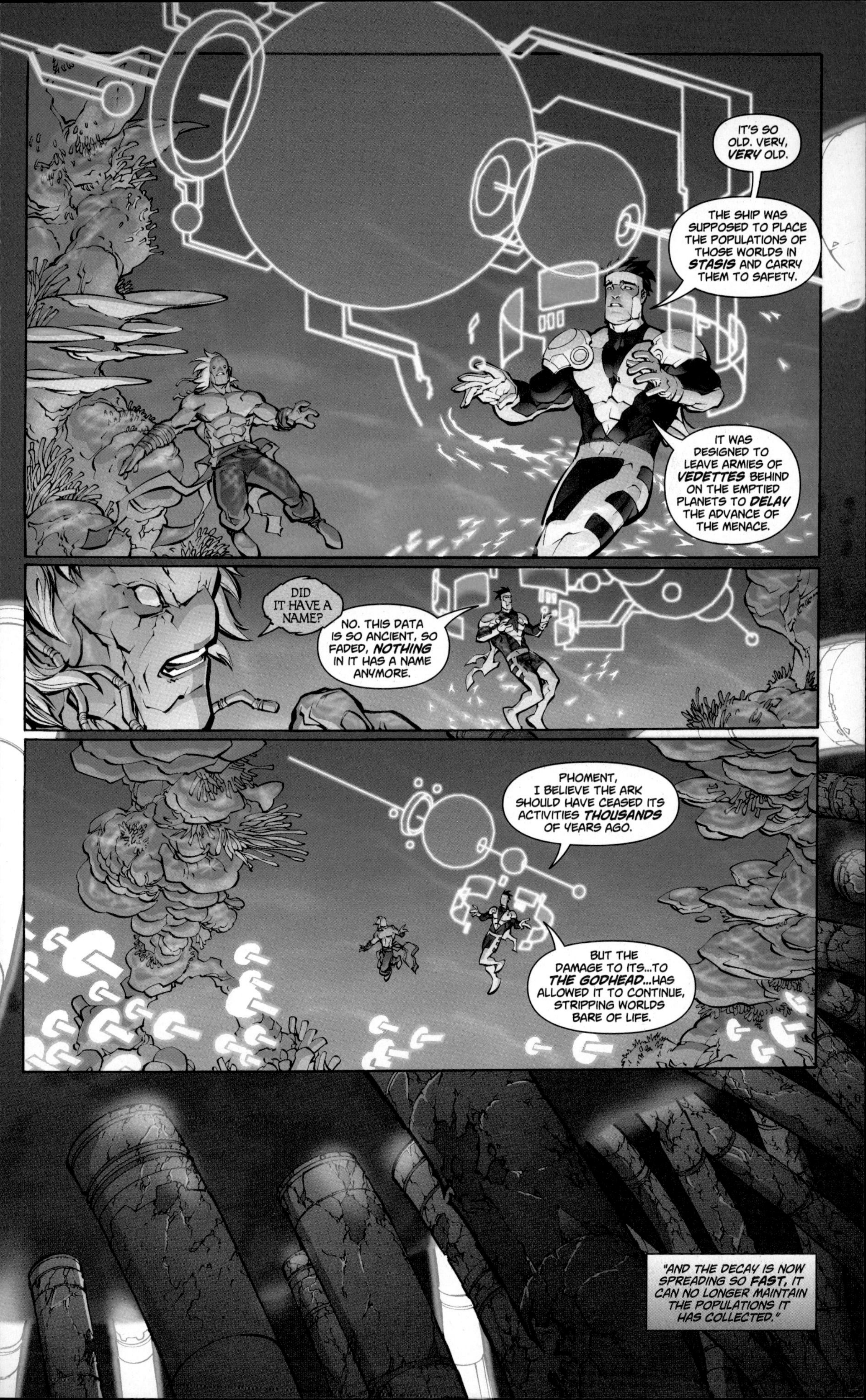
IT'S SO OLD. VERY, VERY OLD.
THE SHIP WAS SUPPOSED TO PLACE THE POPULATIONS OF THOSE WORLDS IN STASIS AND CARRY THEM TO SAFETY.
IT WAS DESIGNED TO LEAVE ARMIES OF VEDETTES BEHIND ON THE EMPTIED PLANETS TO DELAY THE ADVANCE OF THE MENACE.
DID IT HAVE A NAME?
NO. THIS DATA IS SO ANCIENT, SO FADED, NOTHING IN IT HAS A NAME ANYMORE.
PHOMENT, I BELIEVE THE ARK SHOULD HAVE CEASED ITS ACTIVITIES THOUSANDS OF YEARS AGO.
BUT THE DAMAGE TO ITS...TO THE GODHEAD...HAS ALLOWED IT TO CONTINUE, STRIPPING WORLDS BARE OF LIFE.
"AND THE DECAY IS NOW SPREADING SO FAST, IT CAN NO LONGER MAINTAIN THE POPULATIONS IT HAS COLLECTED."

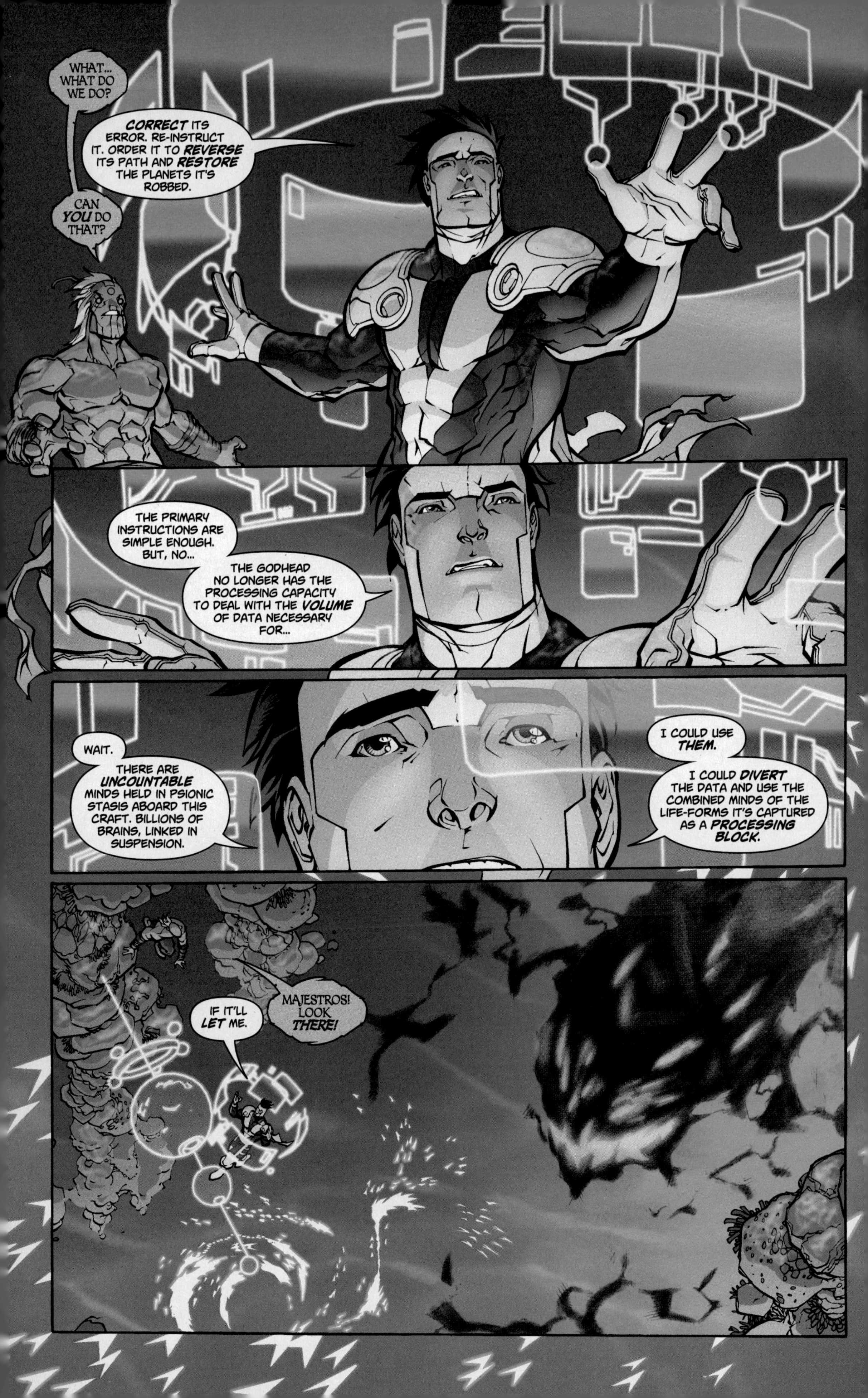
WHAT... WHAT DO WE DO?
CORRECT ITS ERROR. RE-INSTRUCT IT. ORDER IT TO REVERSE ITS PATH AND RESTORE THE PLANETS IT'S ROBBED.
CAN YOU DO THAT?
THE PRIMARY INSTRUCTIONS ARE SIMPLE ENOUGH. BUT, NO...
THE GODHEAD NO LONGER HAS THE PROCESSING CAPACITY TO DEAL WITH THE VOLUME OF DATA NECESSARY FOR...
WAIT.
THERE ARE UNCOUNTABLE MINDS HELD IN PSIONIC STASIS ABOARD THIS CRAFT. BILLIONS OF BRAINS, LINKED IN SUSPENSION.
I COULD USE THEM.
I COULD DIVERT THE DATA AND USE THE COMBINED MINDS OF THE LIFE-FORMS IT'S CAPTURED AS A PROCESSING BLOCK.
IF IT'LL LET ME.
MAJESTROS! LOOK THERE!

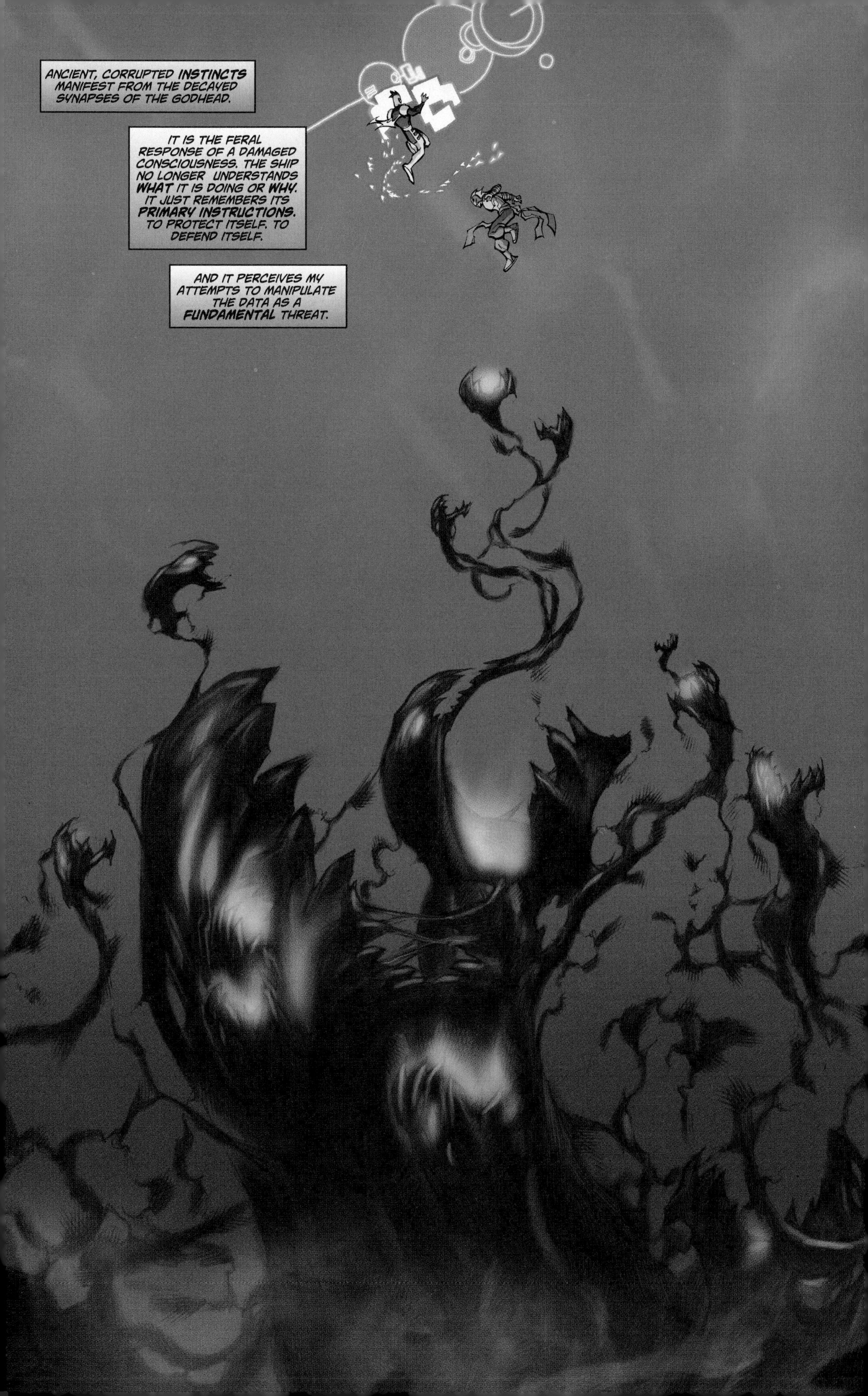
ANCIENT, CORRUPTED INSTINCTS MANIFEST FROM THE DECAYED SYNAPSES OF THE GODHEAD.
IT IS THE FERAL RESPONSE OF A DAMAGED CONSCIOUSNESS. THE SHIP NO LONGER UNDERSTANDS WHAT IT IS DOING OR WHY. IT JUST REMEMBERS ITS PRIMARY INSTRUCTIONS. TO PROTECT ITSELF. TO DEFEND ITSELF.
AND IT PERCEIVES MY ATTEMPTS TO MANIPULATE THE DATA AS A FUNDAMENTAL THREAT.

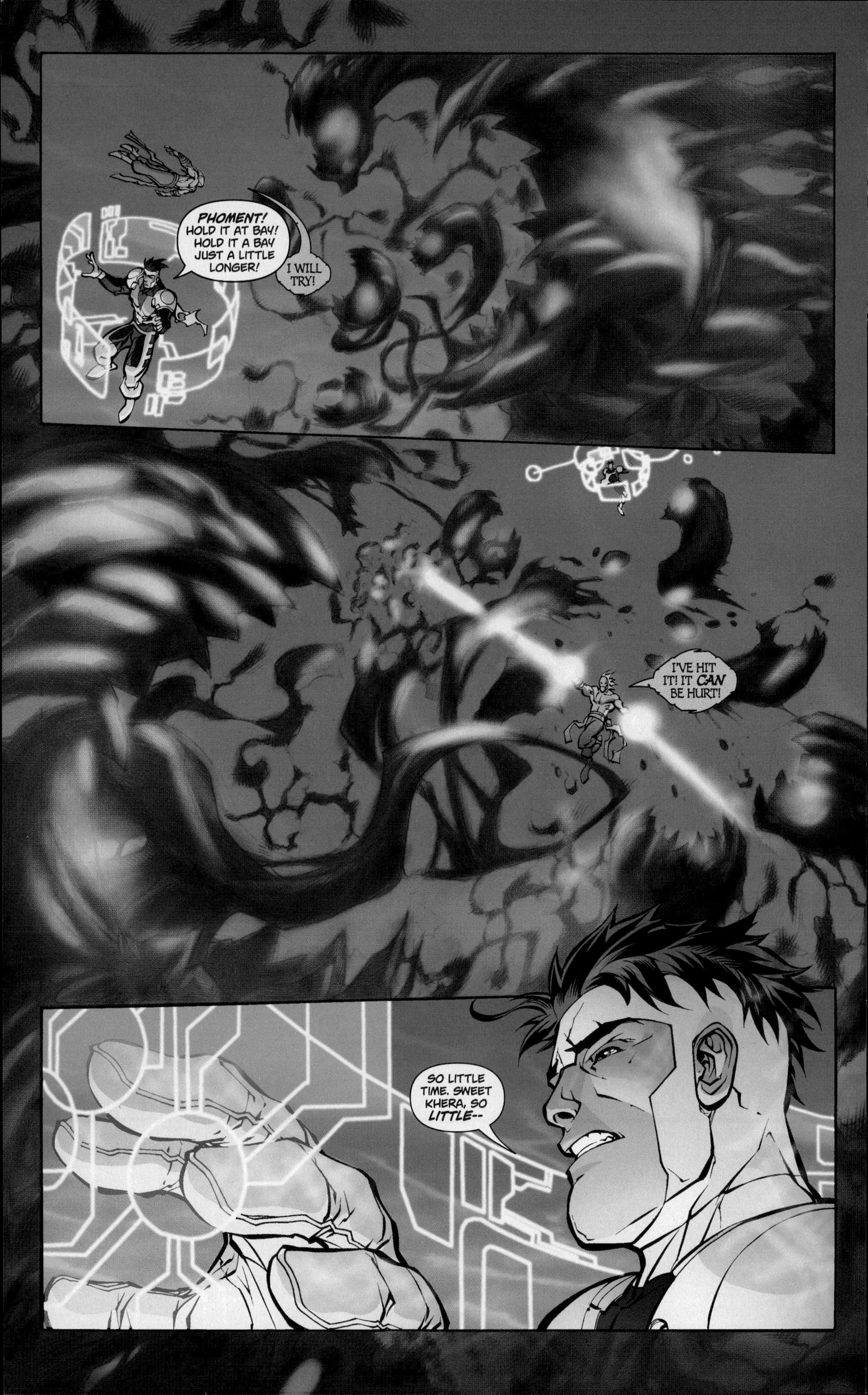
PHOMENT! HOLD IT AT BAY! HOLD IT A BAY JUST A LITTLE LONGER!
I WILL TRY!
I'VE HIT IT! IT CAN BE HURT!
SO LITTLE TIME. SWEET KHERA, SO LITTLE--

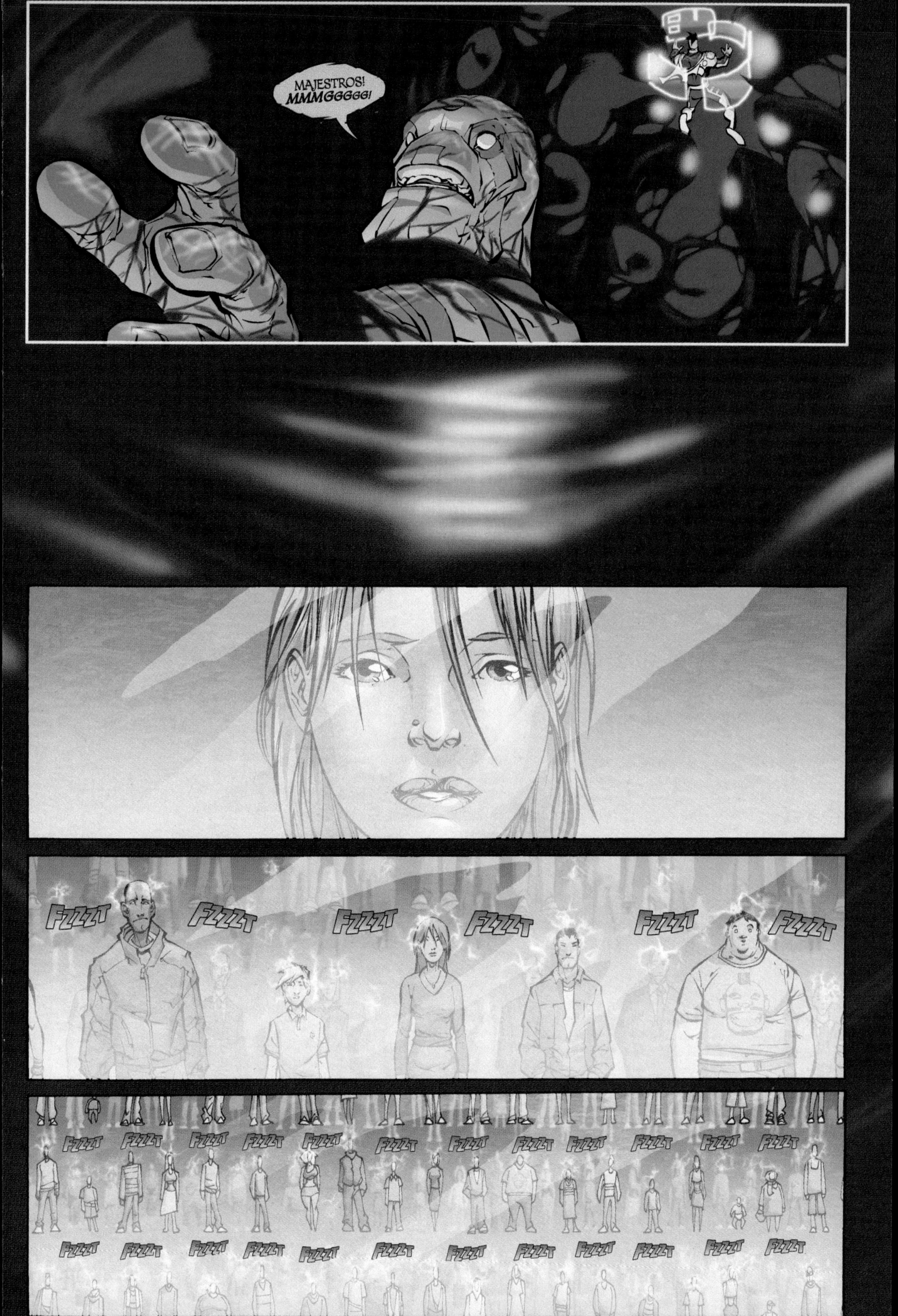

MAJESTROS! MMMGGGGG!
FZZZZT
FZZZZT
FZZZZT
FZZZZT
FZZZZT
FZZZZT

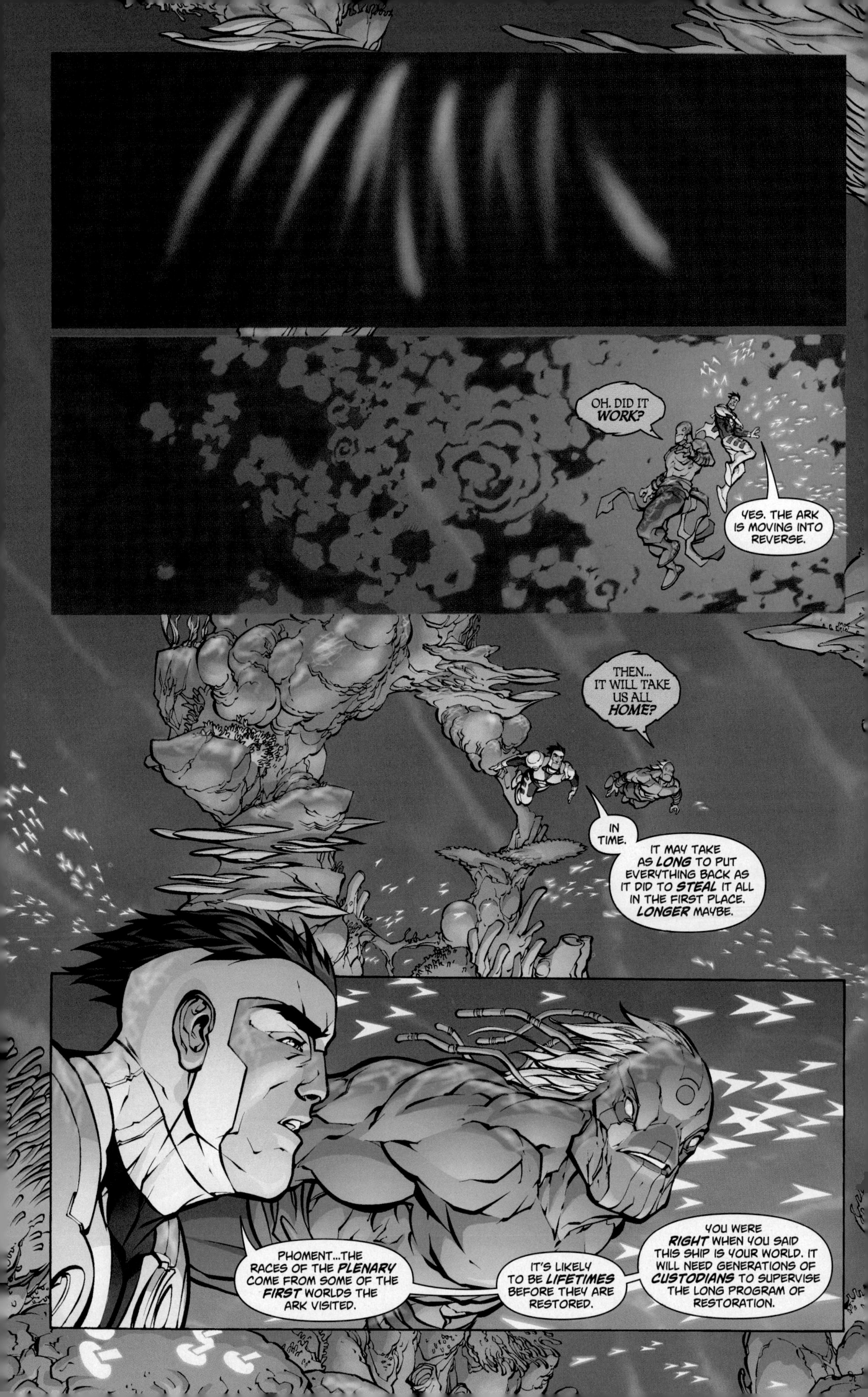
OH. DID IT WORK?
YES. THE ARK IS MOVING INTO REVERSE.
THEN... IT WILL TAKE US ALL HOME?
IN TIME.
IT MAY TAKE AS LONG TO PUT EVERYTHING BACK AS IT DID TO STEAL IT ALL IN THE FIRST PLACE. LONGER MAYBE.
PHOMENT...THE RACES OF THE PLENARY COME FROM SOME OF THE FIRST WORLDS THE ARK VISITED.
IT'S LIKELY TO BE LIFETIMES BEFORE THEY ARE RESTORED.
YOU WERE RIGHT WHEN YOU SAID THIS SHIP IS YOUR WORLD. IT WILL NEED GENERATIONS OF CUSTODIANS TO SUPERVISE THE LONG PROGRAM OF RESTORATION.

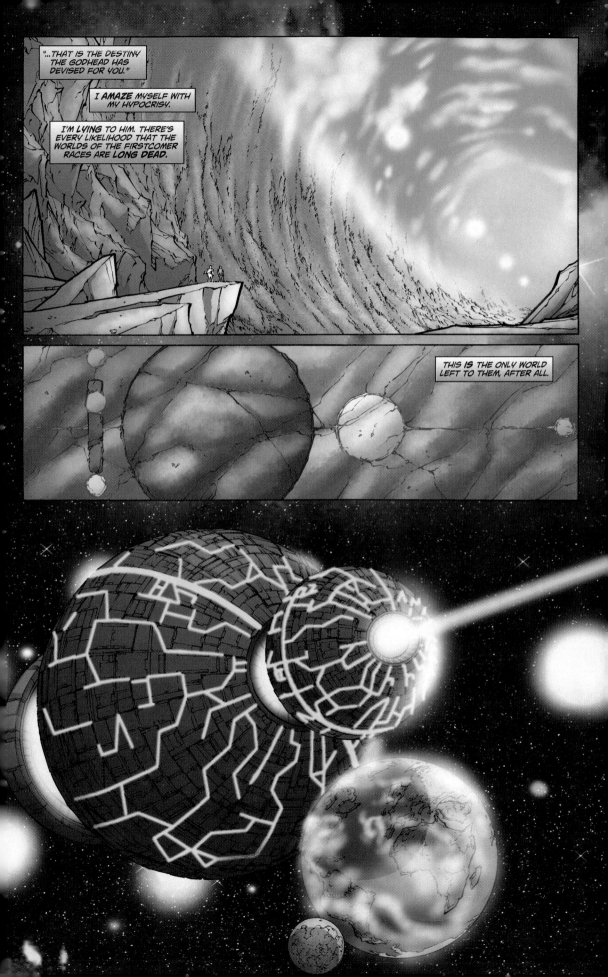

"...THAT IS THE DESTINY THE GODHEAD HAS DEVISED FOR YOU."

I AMAZE MYSELF WITH MY HYPOCRISY.

I'M LYING TO HIM. THERE'S EVERY LIKELIHOOD THAT THE WORLDS OF THE FIRSTCOMER RACES ARE LONG DEAD.

THIS IS THE ONLY WORLD LEFT TO THEM, AFTER ALL.

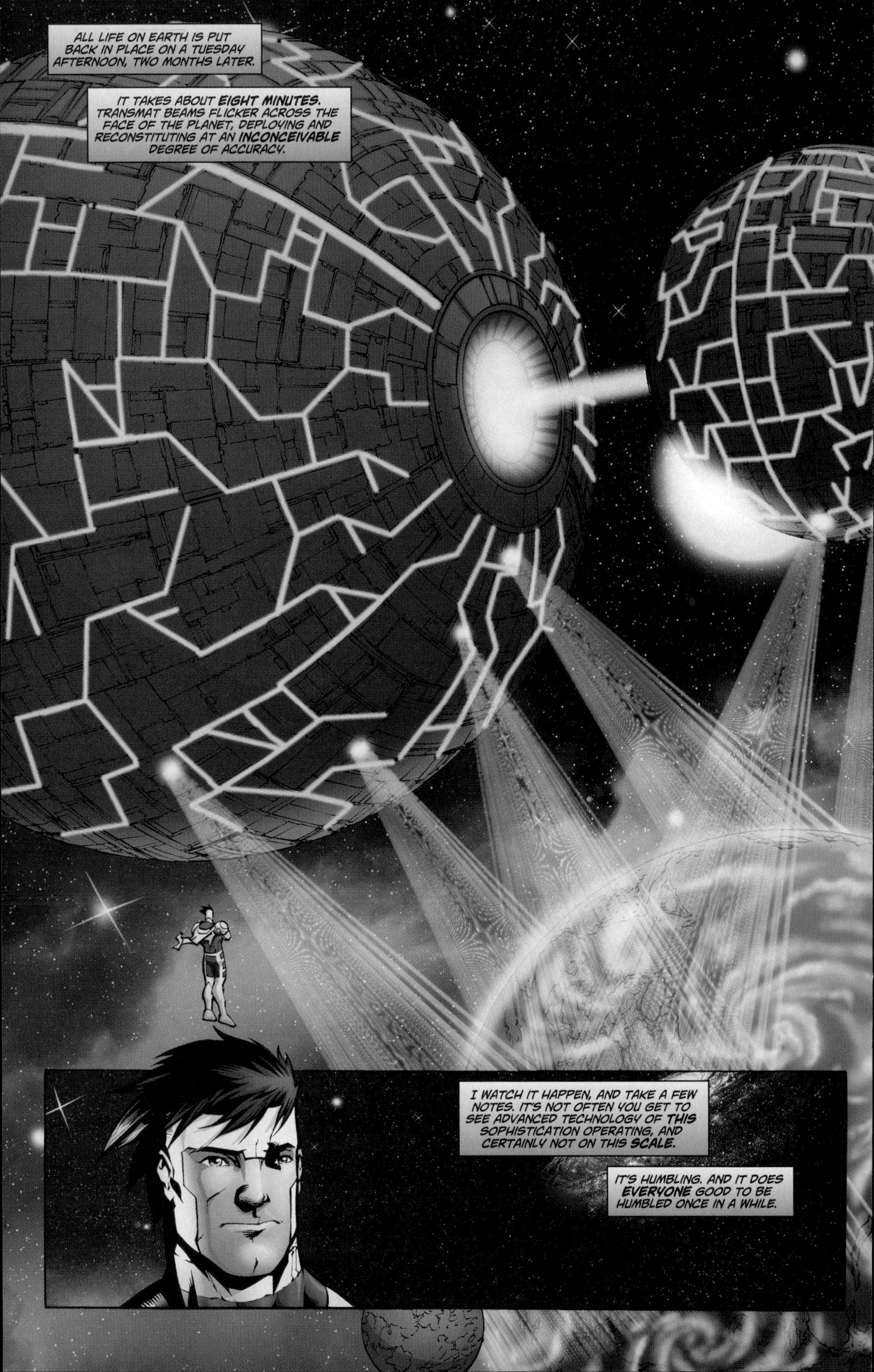
ALL LIFE ON EARTH IS PUT BACK IN PLACE ON A TUESDAY AFTERNOON, TWO MONTHS LATER.
IT TAKES ABOUT EIGHT MINUTES. TRANSMAT BEAMS FLICKER ACROSS THE FACE OF THE PLANET, DEPLOYING AND RECONSTITUTING AT AN INCONCEIVABLE DEGREE OF ACCURACY.
I WATCH IT HAPPEN, AND TAKE A FEW NOTES. IT'S NOT OFTEN YOU GET TO SEE ADVANCED TECHNOLOGY OF THIS SOPHISTICATION OPERATING, AND CERTAINLY NOT ON THIS SCALE.
IT'S HUMBLING. AND IT DOES EVERYONE GOOD TO BE HUMBLED ONCE IN A WHILE.

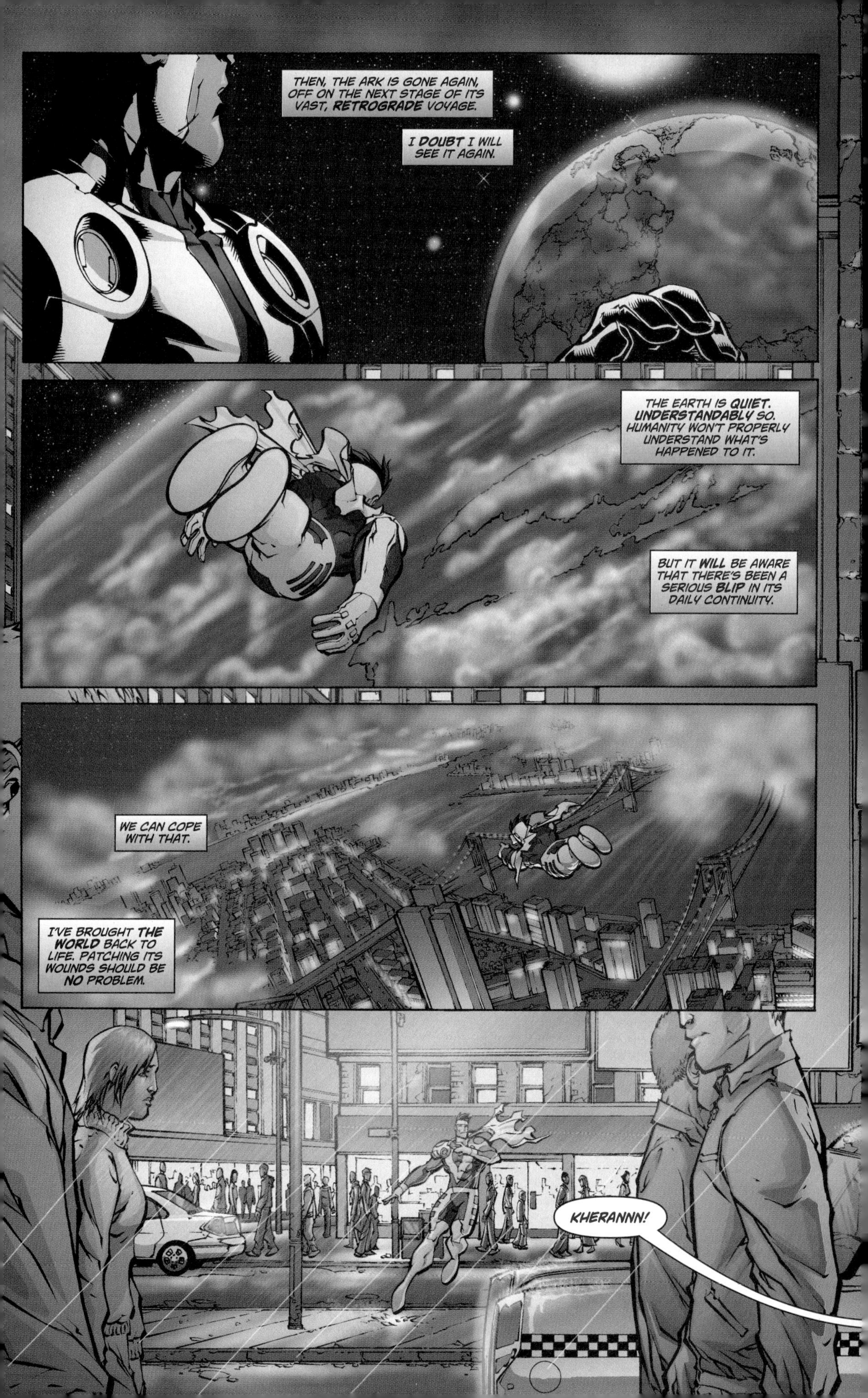

THEN, THE ARK IS GONE AGAIN, OFF ON THE NEXT STAGE OF ITS VAST, RETROGRADE VOYAGE.
I DOUBT I WILL SEE IT AGAIN.
THE EARTH IS QUIET. UNDERSTANDABLY SO. HUMANITY WON'T PROPERLY UNDERSTAND WHAT'S HAPPENED TO IT.
BUT IT WILL BE AWARE THAT THERE'S BEEN A SERIOUS BLIP IN ITS DAILY CONTINUITY.
WE CAN COPE WITH THAT.
I'VE BROUGHT THE WORLD BACK TO LIFE. PATCHING ITS WOUNDS SHOULD BE NO PROBLEM.
KHERANNN!

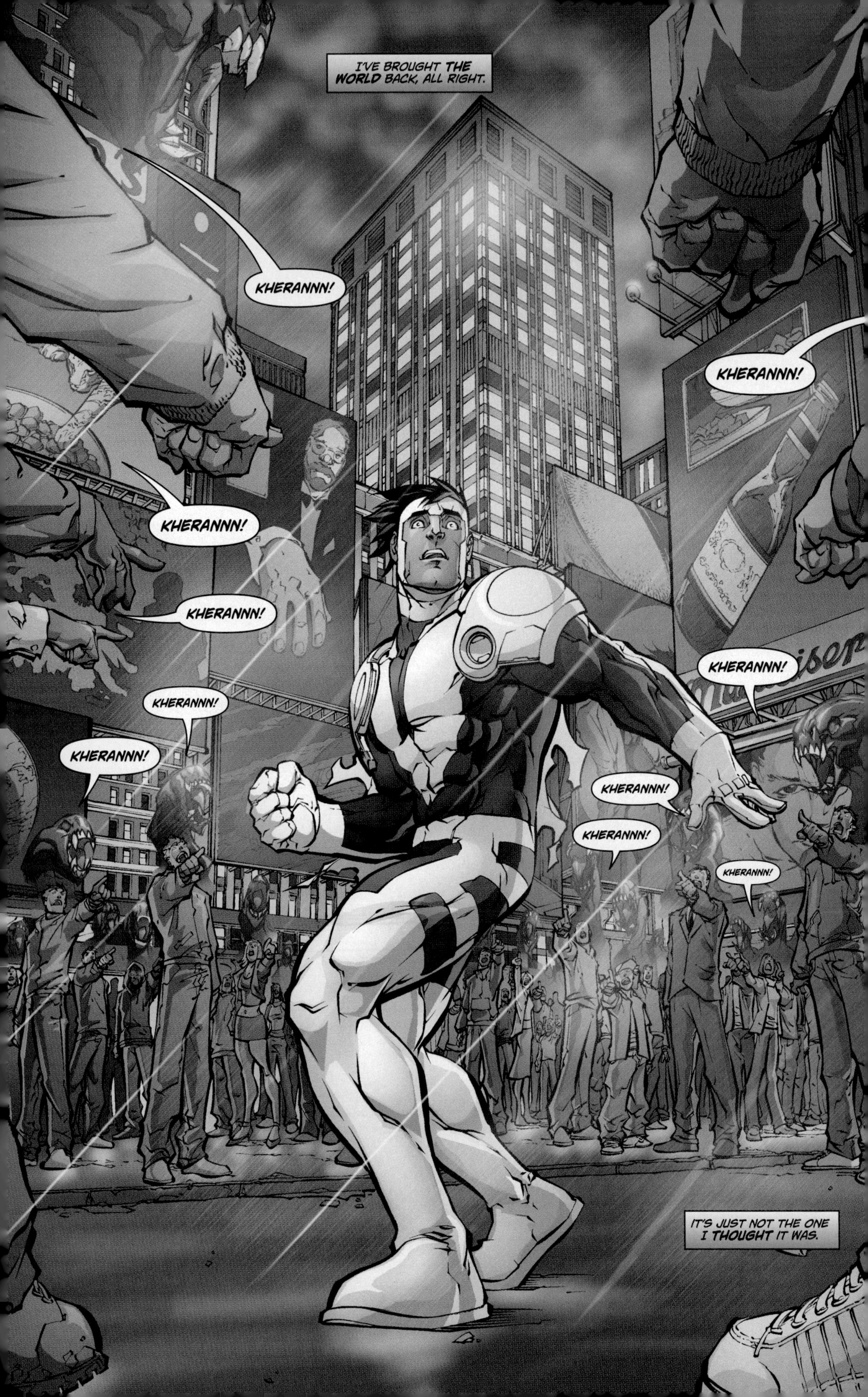
I'VE BROUGHT THE WORLD BACK, ALL RIGHT.
KHERANNN!
KHERANNN!
KHERANNN!
KHERANNN!
KHERANNN!
KHERANNN!
KHERANNN!
KHERANNN!
KHERANNN!
KHERANNN!
KHERANNN!
IT'S JUST NOT THE ONE I THOUGHT IT WAS.

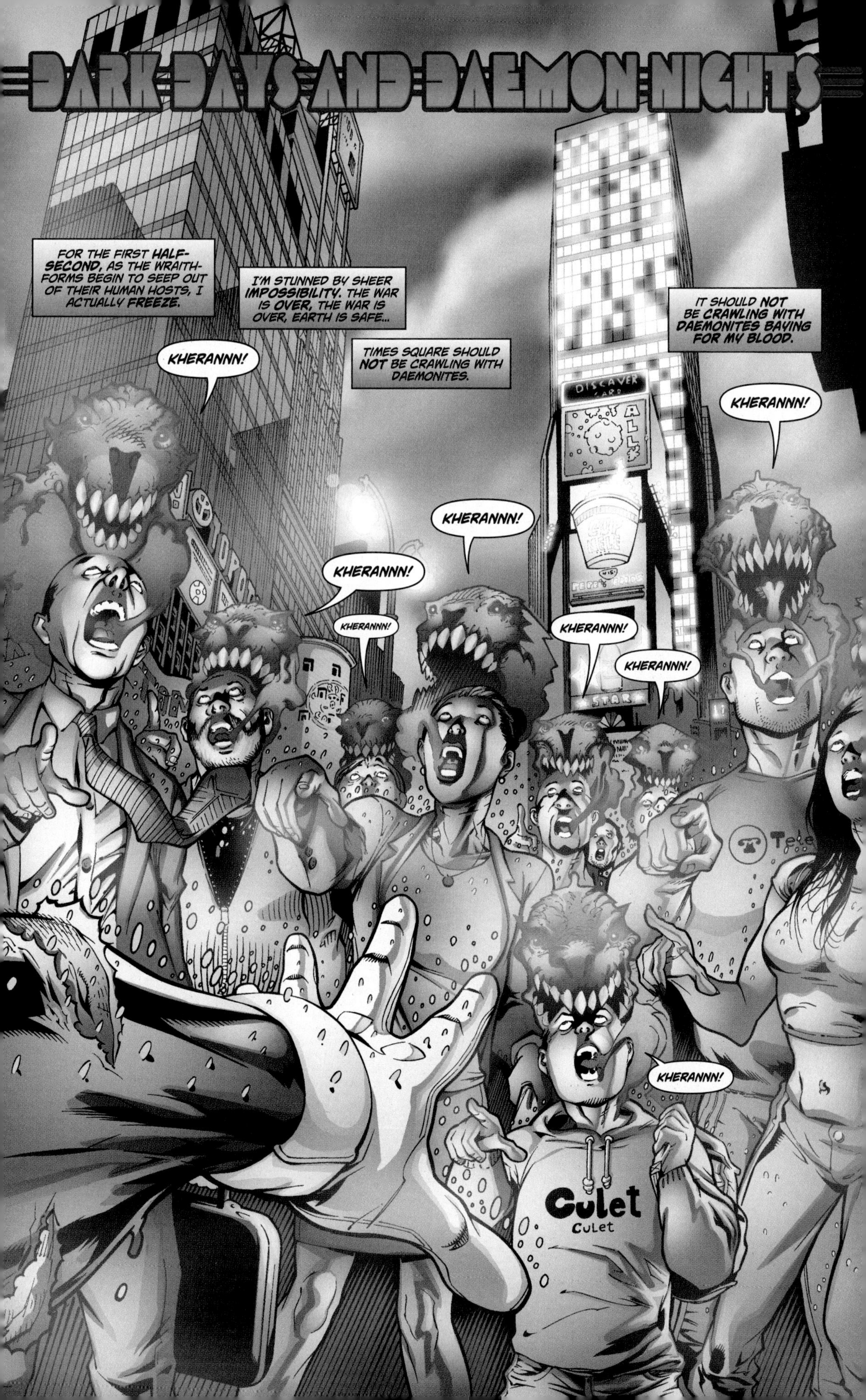
DARK DAYS AND DAEMON NIGHTS
FOR THE FIRST HALF-SECOND, AS THE WRAITH-FORMS BEGIN TO SEEP OUT OF THEIR HUMAN HOSTS, I ACTUALLY FREEZE.
I'M STUNNED BY SHEER IMPOSSIBILITY. THE WAR IS OVER, THE WAR IS OVER, EARTH IS SAFE...
TIMES SQUARE SHOULD NOT BE CRAWLING WITH DAEMONITES.
IT SHOULD NOT BE CRAWLING WITH DAEMONITES BAYING FOR MY BLOOD.
KHERANNN!
KHERANNN!
KHERANNN!
KHERANNN!
KHERANNN!
KHERANNN!
KHERANNN!
KHERANNN!
KHERANNN!
DISCOVER
STAR
Culet
Culet

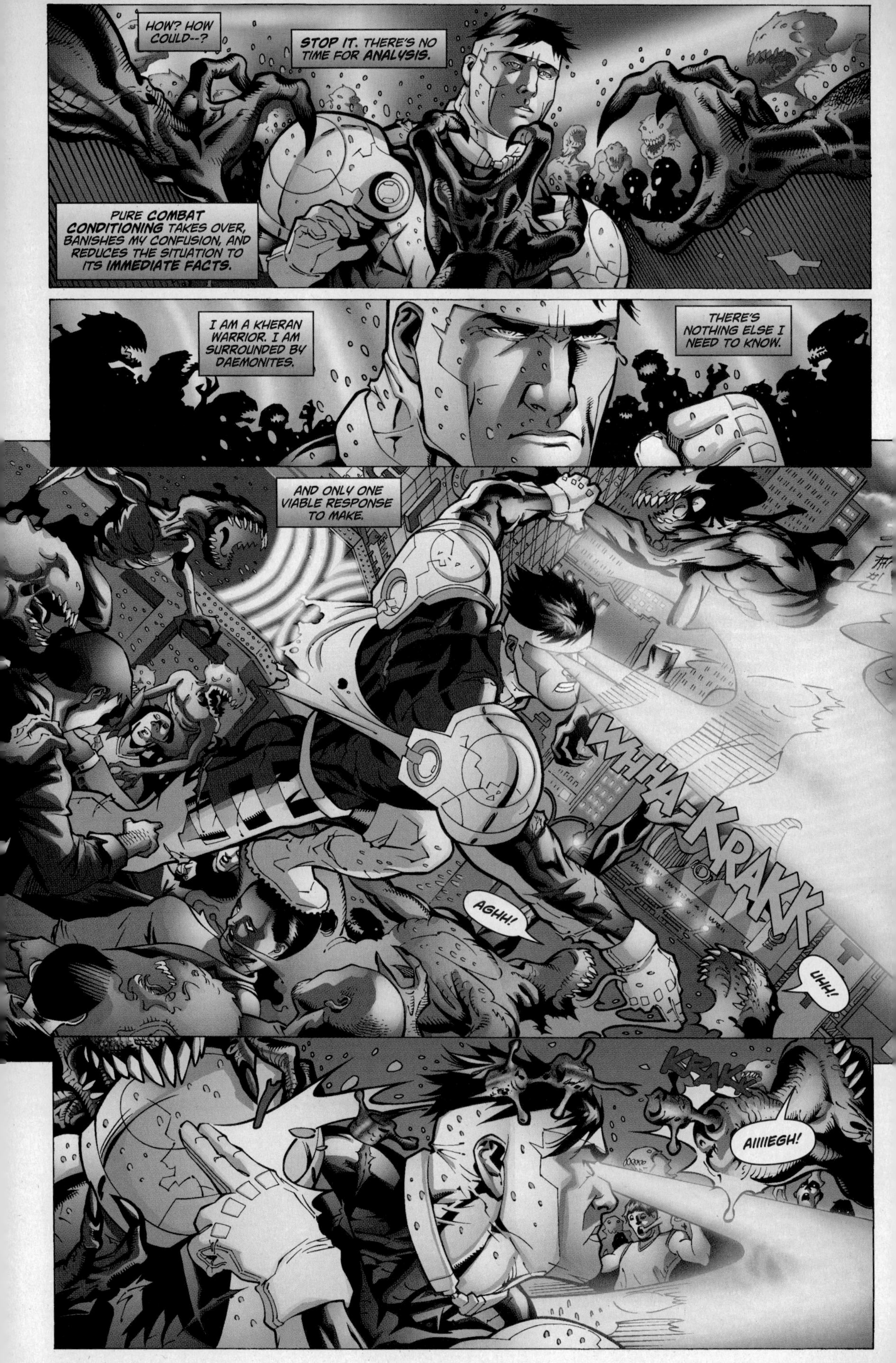
HOW? HOW COULD--?
STOP IT. THERE'S NO TIME FOR ANALYSIS.
PURE COMBAT CONDITIONING TAKES OVER, BANISHES MY CONFUSION, AND REDUCES THE SITUATION TO ITS IMMEDIATE FACTS.
I AM A KHERAN WARRIOR. I AM SURROUNDED BY DAEMONITES.
THERE'S NOTHING ELSE I NEED TO KNOW.
AND ONLY ONE VIABLE RESPONSE TO MAKE.
WHA-KRAKK
AGHH!
UHH!
KRAKK
AIIIIEGH!

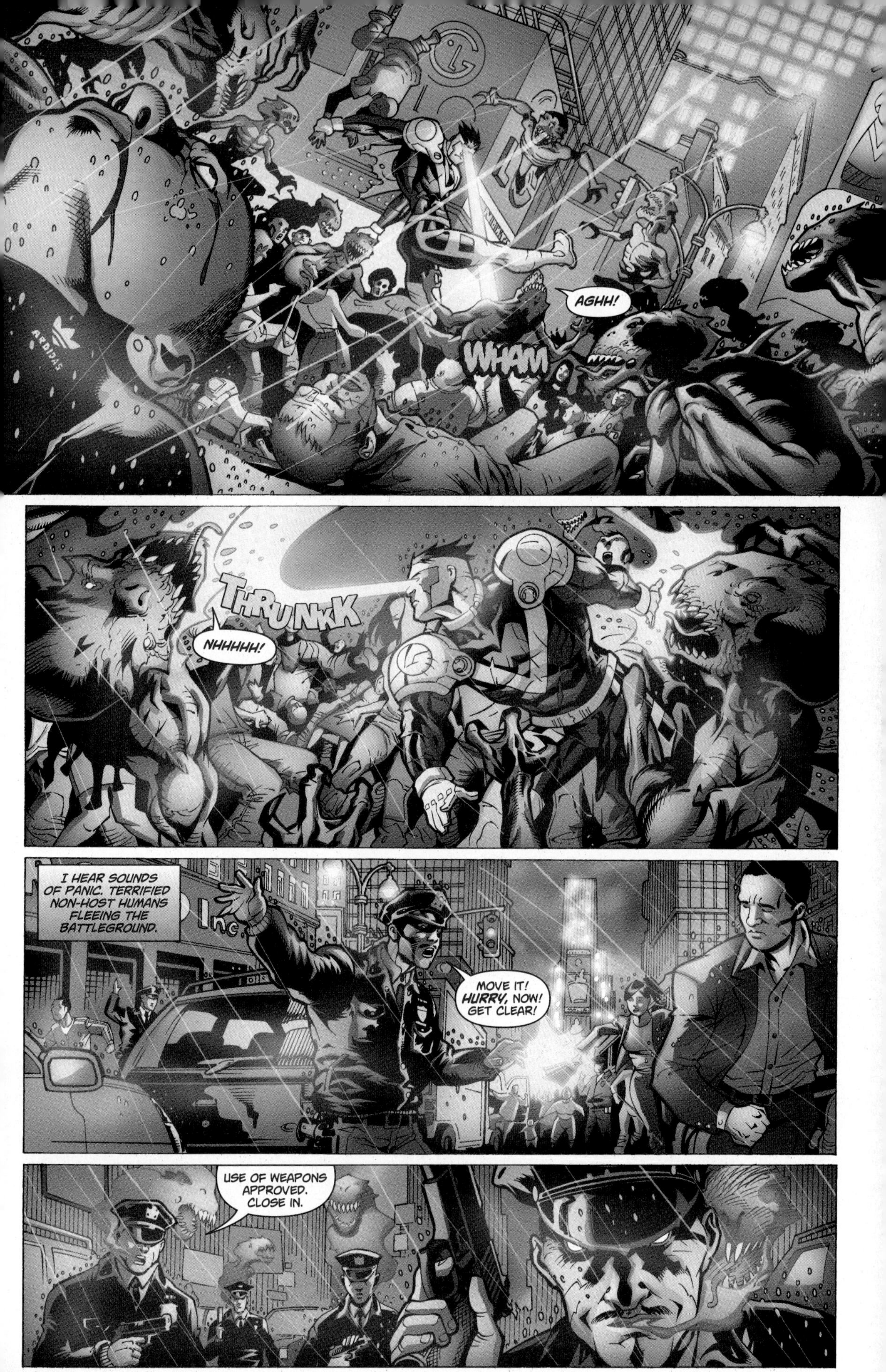
AGHH!
WHAM
THRUNKK
NHHHHH!
I HEAR SOUNDS OF PANIC. TERRIFIED NON-HOST HUMANS FLEEING THE BATTLEGROUND.
MOVE IT! HURRY, NOW! GET CLEAR!
USE OF WEAPONS APPROVED. CLOSE IN.

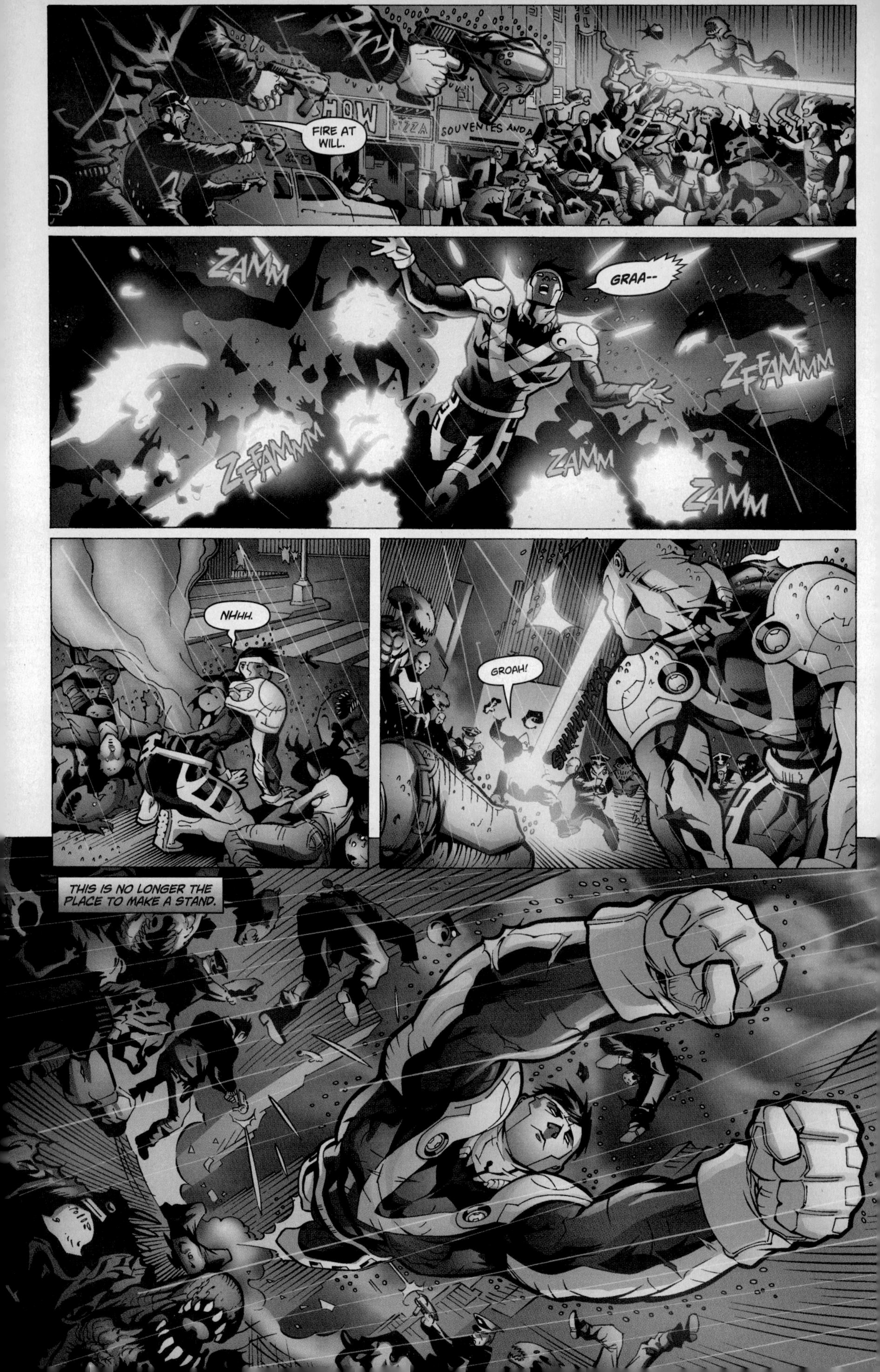
SHOW
PIZZA
SOUVENTES ANDA
FIRE AT WILL.
ZAMM
GRAA--
ZFAMMM
ZFAMMM
ZAMM
ZAMM
NHHH.
GROAH!
THIS IS NO LONGER THE PLACE TO MAKE A STAND.

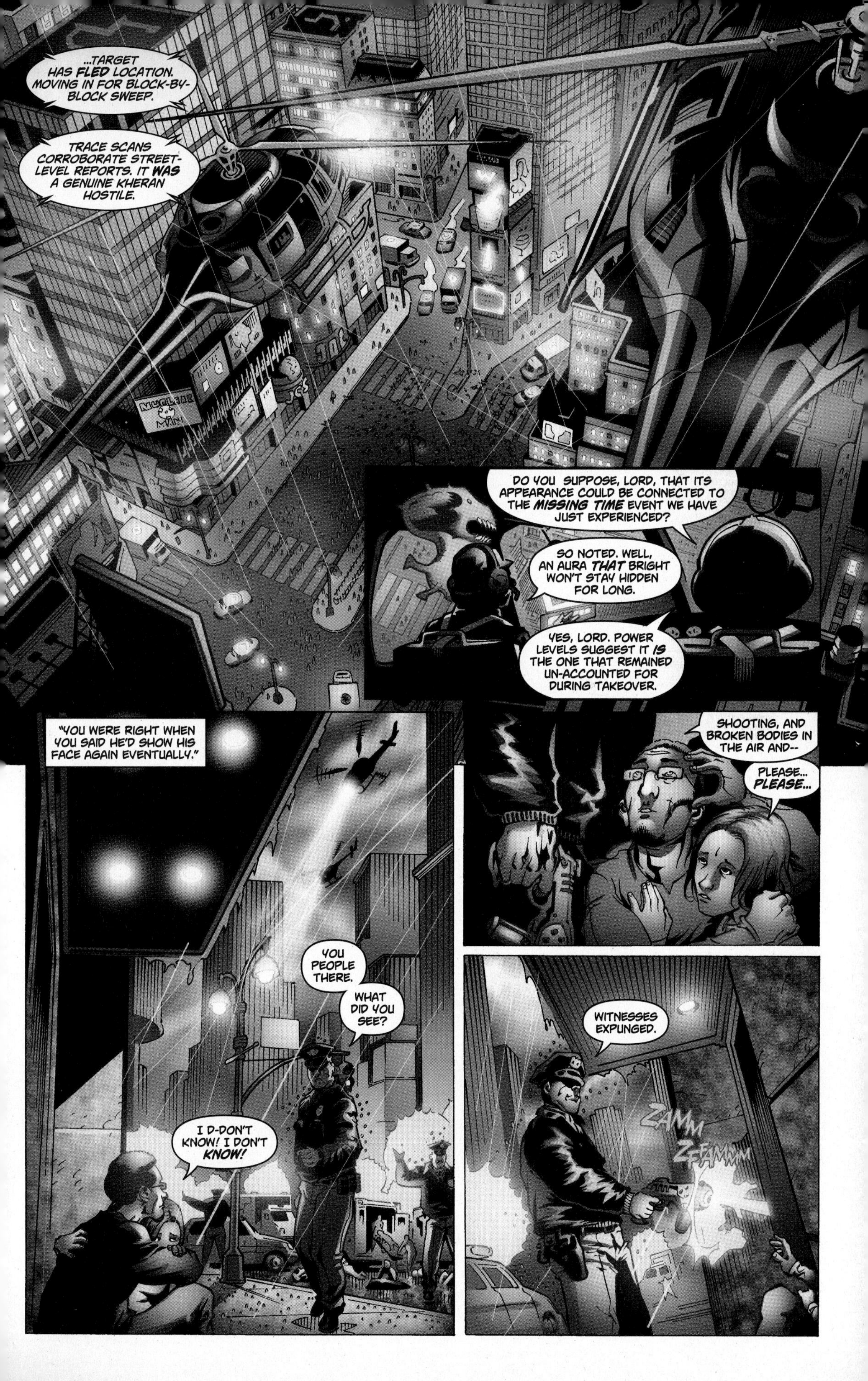
...TARGET HAS FLED LOCATION. MOVING IN FOR BLOCK-BY-BLOCK SWEEP.
TRACE SCANS CORROBORATE STREET-LEVEL REPORTS. IT WAS A GENUINE KHERAN HOSTILE.
DO YOU SUPPOSE, LORD, THAT ITS APPEARANCE COULD BE CONNECTED TO THE MISSING TIME EVENT WE HAVE JUST EXPERIENCED?
SO NOTED. WELL, AN AURA THAT BRIGHT WON'T STAY HIDDEN FOR LONG.
YES, LORD. POWER LEVELS SUGGEST IT IS THE ONE THAT REMAINED UN-ACCOUNTED FOR DURING TAKEOVER.
"YOU WERE RIGHT WHEN YOU SAID HE'D SHOW HIS FACE AGAIN EVENTUALLY."
YOU PEOPLE THERE.
WHAT DID YOU SEE?
I D-DON'T KNOW! I DON'T KNOW!
SHOOTING, AND BROKEN BODIES IN THE AIR AND--
PLEASE... PLEASE...
WITNESSES EXPUNGED.
ZAMM
ZFAMMM

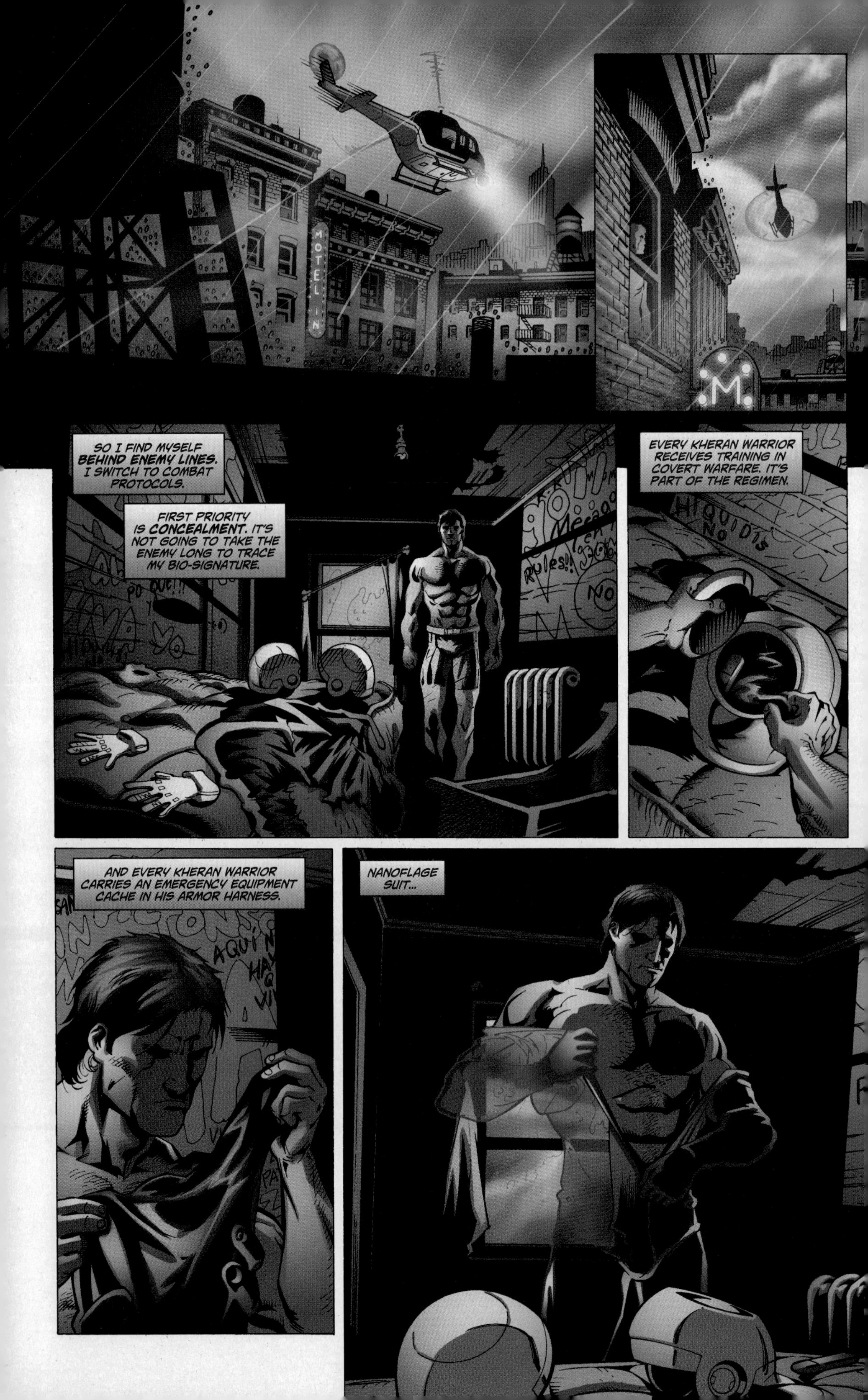
MOTEL INN
SO I FIND MYSELF BEHIND ENEMY LINES. I SWITCH TO COMBAT PROTOCOLS.
FIRST PRIORITY IS CONCEALMENT. IT'S NOT GOING TO TAKE THE ENEMY LONG TO TRACE MY BIO-SIGNATURE.
EVERY KHERAN WARRIOR RECEIVES TRAINING IN COVERT WARFARE. IT'S PART OF THE REGIMEN.
AND EVERY KHERAN WARRIOR CARRIES AN EMERGENCY EQUIPMENT CACHE IN HIS ARMOR HARNESS.
NANOFLAGE SUIT...

QUANTUM-FOLDED COMBAT BLADE...

...COURTESY OF THE SHAPERS' GUILD...

TCHSSHNNG

...AND ONE HIGH-DOSE DAMPER CAPSULE.

ONCE INGESTED, IT WILL MASK MY NATURAL KHERAN AURA FOR THREE HOURS.

OF COURSE, THAT'LL ALSO MEAN I'LL HAVE NO POWERS FOR THREE HOURS EITHER.

UNTIL THE EFFECTS WEAR OFF, I'LL JUST BE A REGULAR MORTAL.

SO I NEED TO BE IN THE RIGHT PLACE BEFORE I TAKE IT.

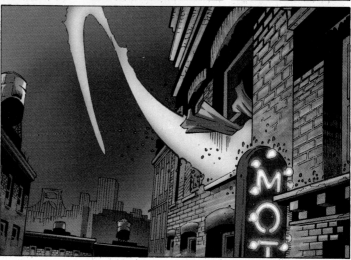

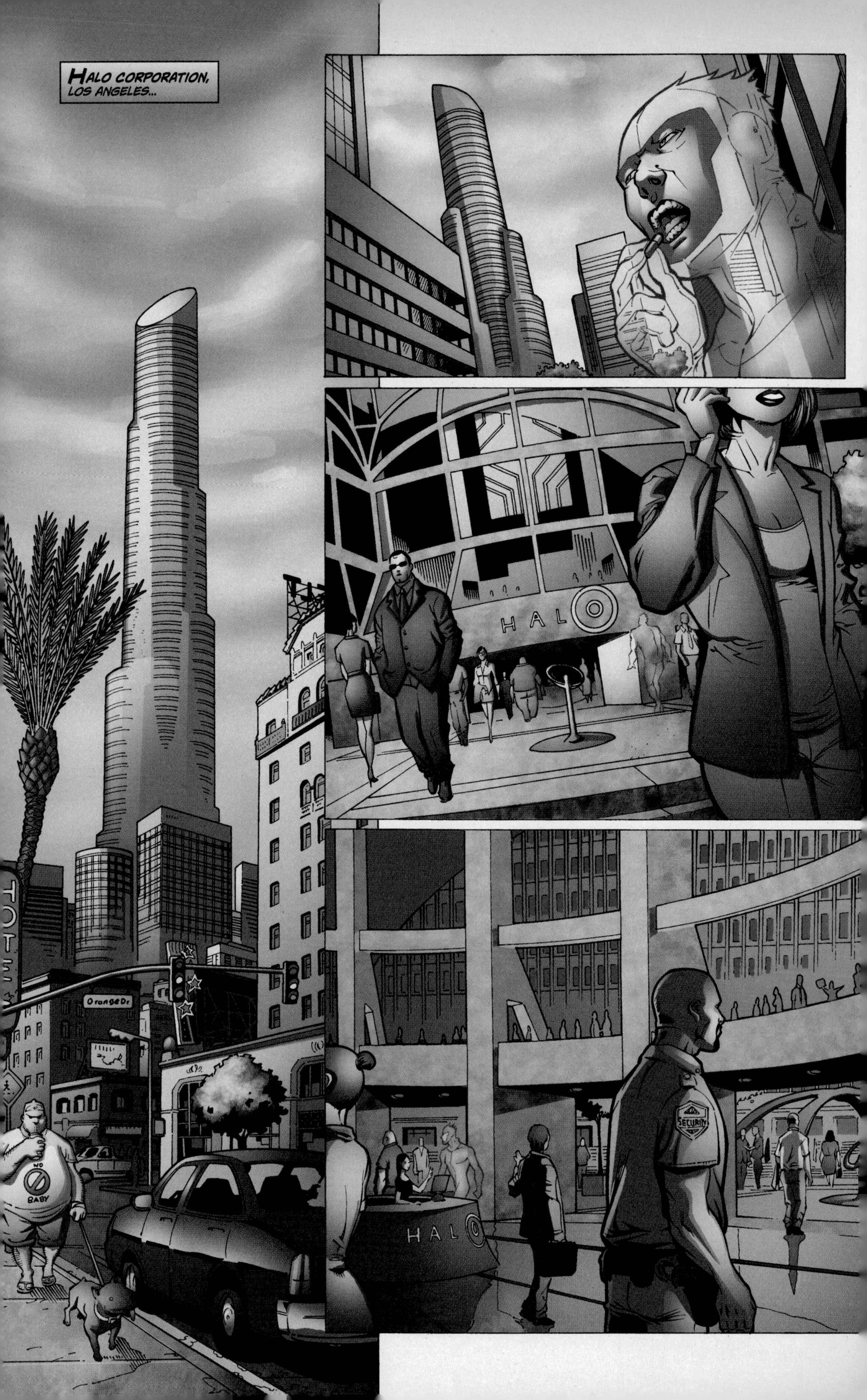
HALO CORPORATION, LOS ANGELES...
HALO
Orange Dr
NO
BABY
HALO
SECURITY

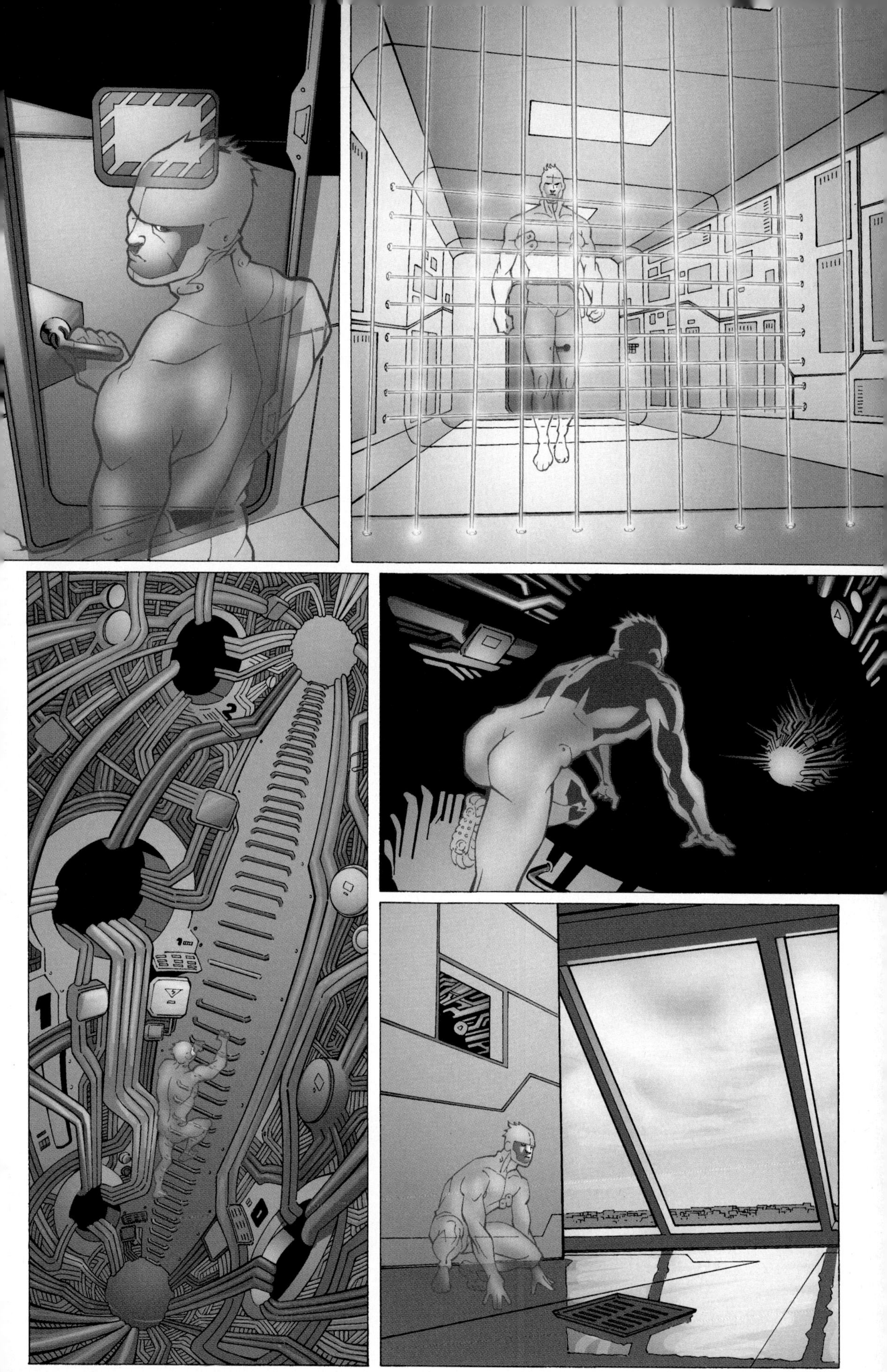

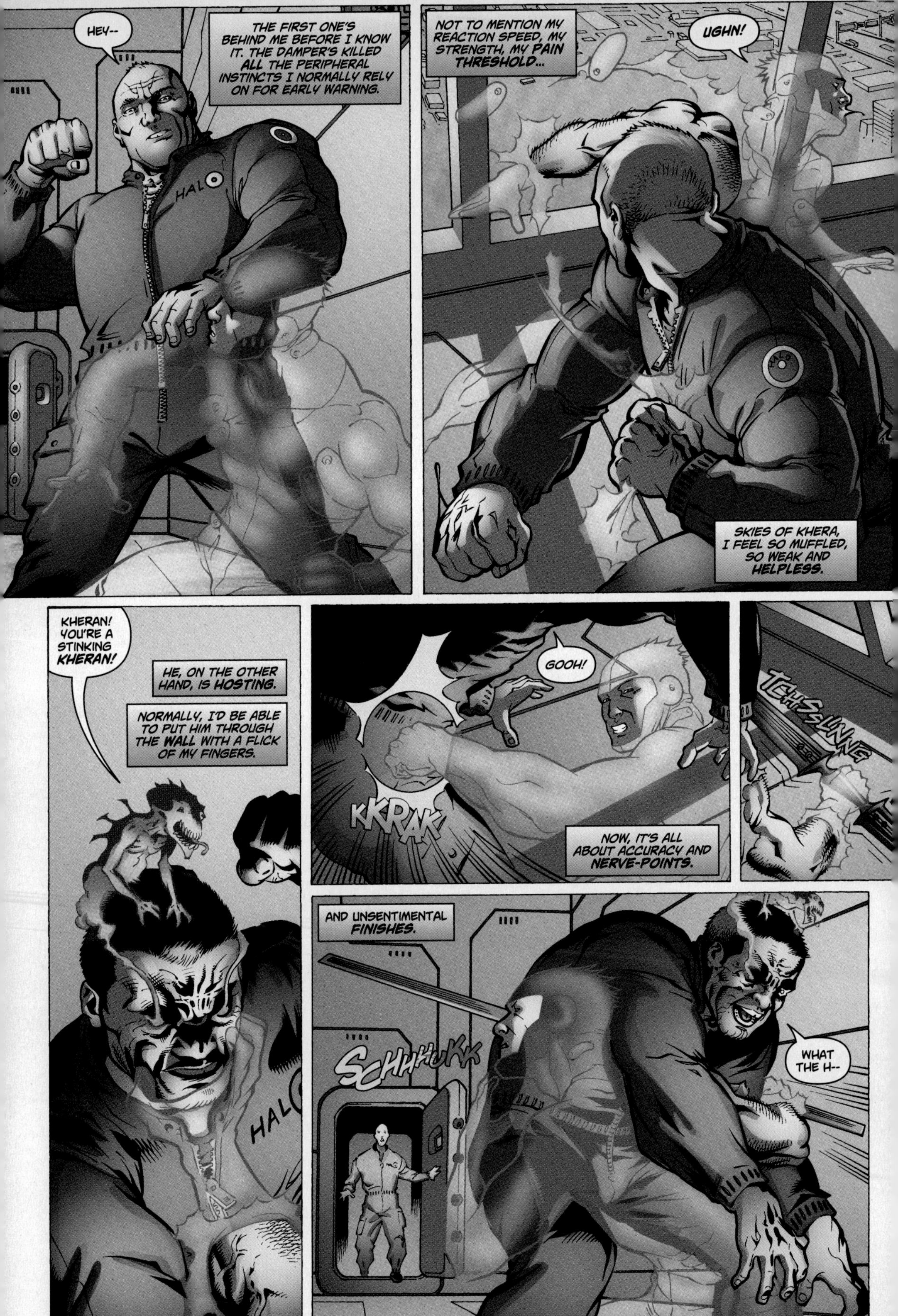
HEY--
THE FIRST ONE'S BEHIND ME BEFORE I KNOW IT. THE DAMPER'S KILLED ALL THE PERIPHERAL INSTINCTS I NORMALLY RELY ON FOR EARLY WARNING.
NOT TO MENTION MY REACTION SPEED, MY STRENGTH, MY PAIN THRESHOLD...
UGHN!
HALO
SKIES OF KHERA, I FEEL SO MUFFLED, SO WEAK AND HELPLESS.
KHERAN! YOU'RE A STINKING KHERAN!
HE, ON THE OTHER HAND, IS HOSTING.
NORMALLY, I'D BE ABLE TO PUT HIM THROUGH THE WALL WITH A FLICK OF MY FINGERS.
HAL
GOOH!
KKRAK!
NOW, IT'S ALL ABOUT ACCURACY AND NERVE-POINTS.
TCHSSLNNG
AND UNSENTIMENTAL FINISHES.
SCHHHUKK
WHAT THE H--

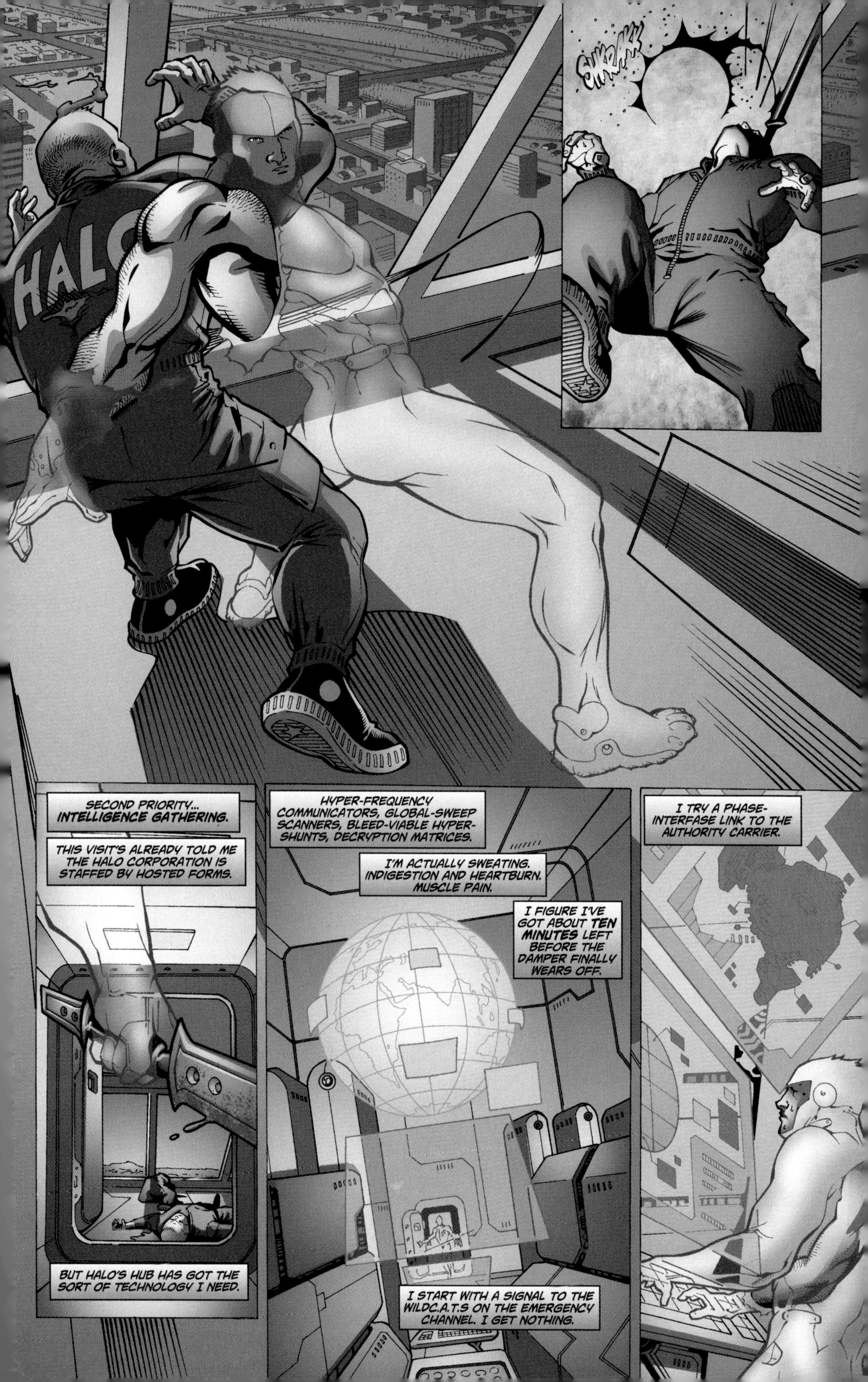
HALO
SHRAKK
HAL
SECOND PRIORITY... INTELLIGENCE GATHERING.
THIS VISIT'S ALREADY TOLD ME THE HALO CORPORATION IS STAFFED BY HOSTED FORMS.
BUT HALO'S HUB HAS GOT THE SORT OF TECHNOLOGY I NEED.
HYPER-FREQUENCY COMMUNICATORS, GLOBAL-SWEEP SCANNERS, BLEED-VIABLE HYPER-SHUNTS, DECRYPTION MATRICES.
I'M ACTUALLY SWEATING. INDIGESTION AND HEARTBURN. MUSCLE PAIN.
I FIGURE I'VE GOT ABOUT TEN MINUTES LEFT BEFORE THE DAMPER FINALLY WEARS OFF.
I START WITH A SIGNAL TO THE WILDC.A.T.S ON THE EMERGENCY CHANNEL. I GET NOTHING.
I TRY A PHASE-INTERFASE LINK TO THE AUTHORITY CARRIER.

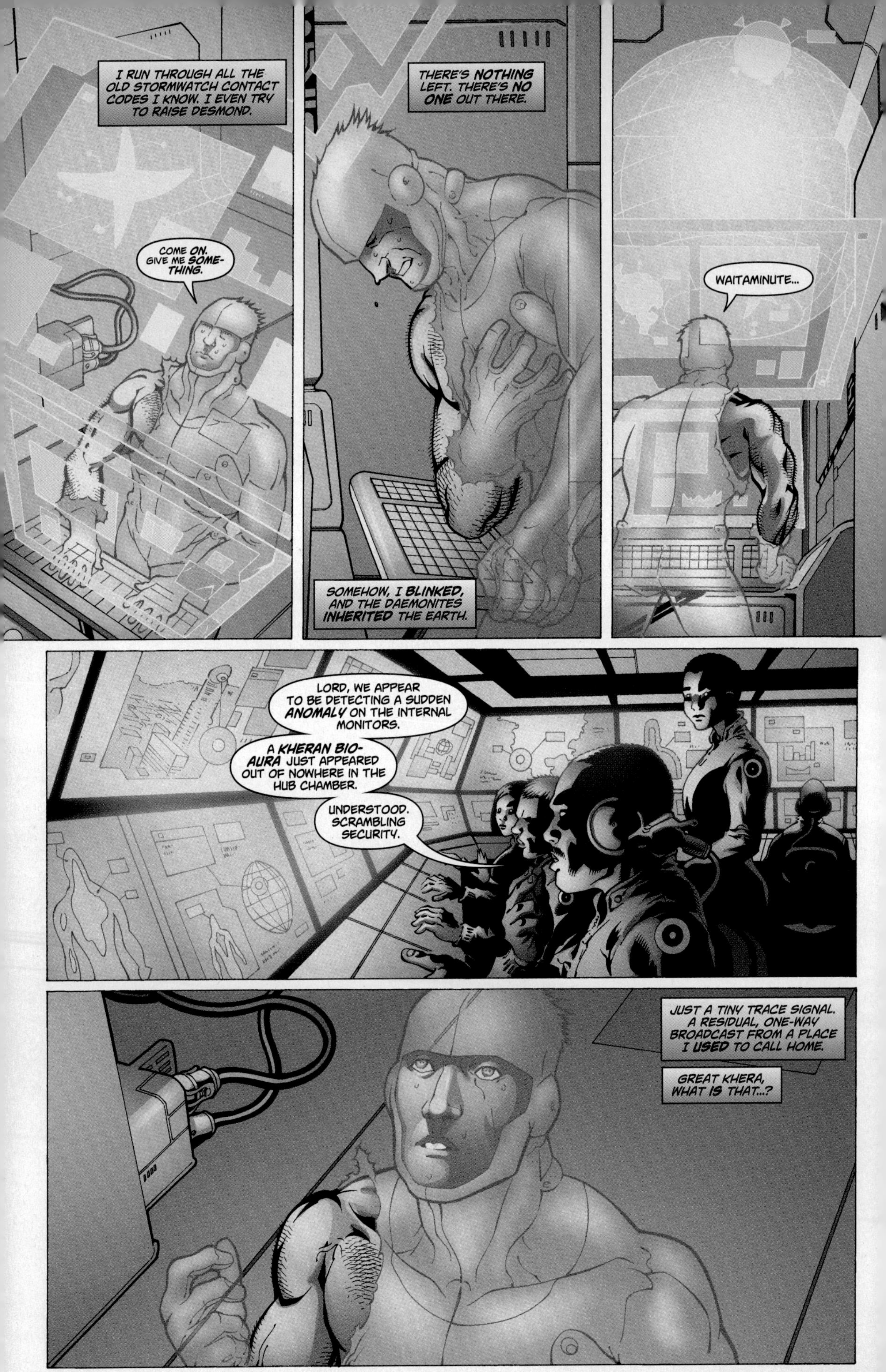
I RUN THROUGH ALL THE OLD STORMWATCH CONTACT CODES I KNOW. I EVEN TRY TO RAISE DESMOND.
COME ON. GIVE ME SOME-THING.
THERE'S NOTHING LEFT. THERE'S NO ONE OUT THERE.
SOMEHOW, I BLINKED, AND THE DAEMONITES INHERITED THE EARTH.
WAITAMINUTE...
LORD, WE APPEAR TO BE DETECTING A SUDDEN ANOMALY ON THE INTERNAL MONITORS.
A KHERAN BIO-AURA JUST APPEARED OUT OF NOWHERE IN THE HUB CHAMBER.
UNDERSTOOD. SCRAMBLING SECURITY.
JUST A TINY TRACE SIGNAL. A RESIDUAL, ONE-WAY BROADCAST FROM A PLACE I USED TO CALL HOME.
GREAT KHERA, WHAT IS THAT...?

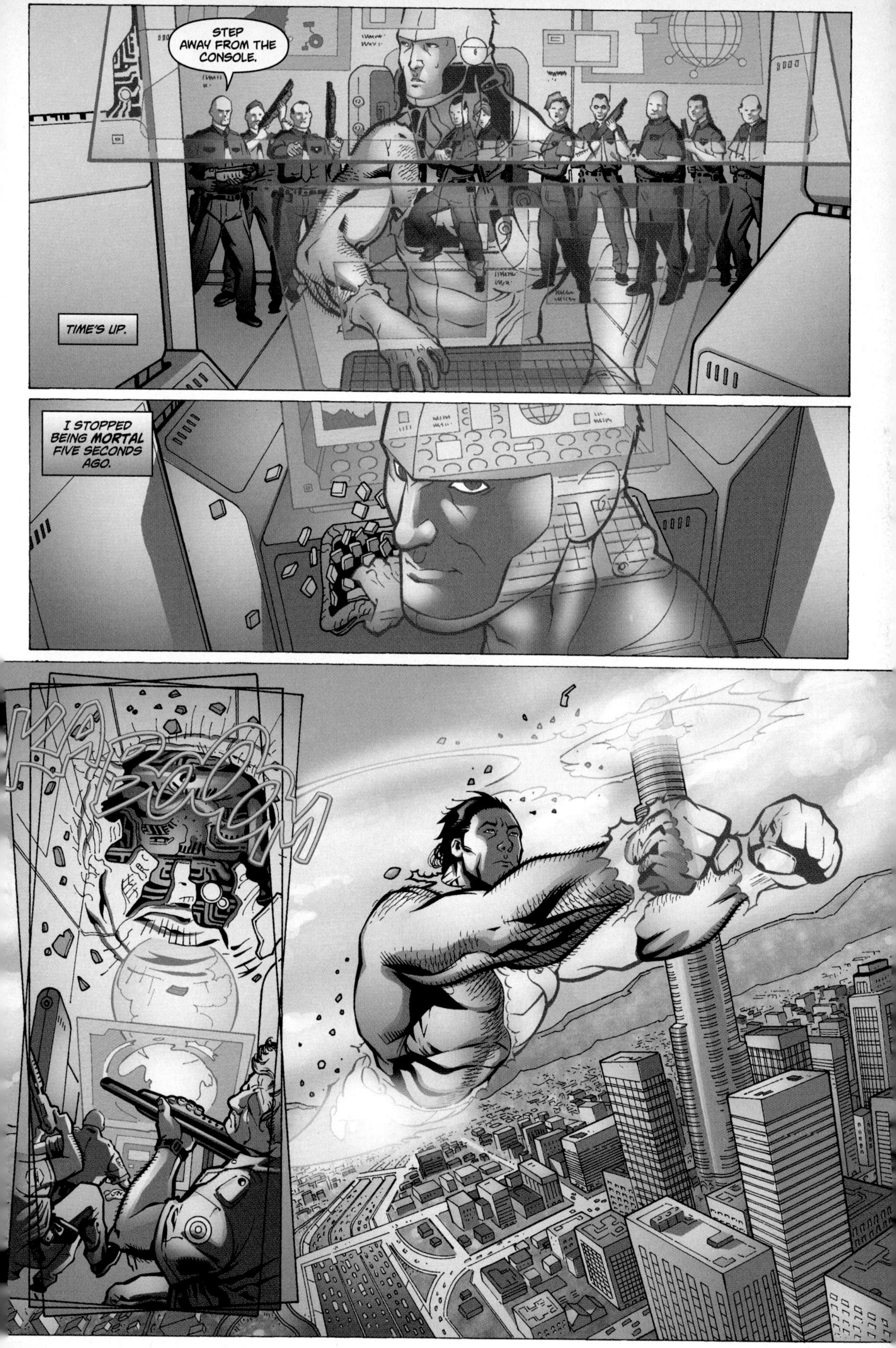

STEP AWAY FROM THE CONSOLE.
TIME'S UP.
I STOPPED BEING MORTAL FIVE SECONDS AGO.
KABOOM

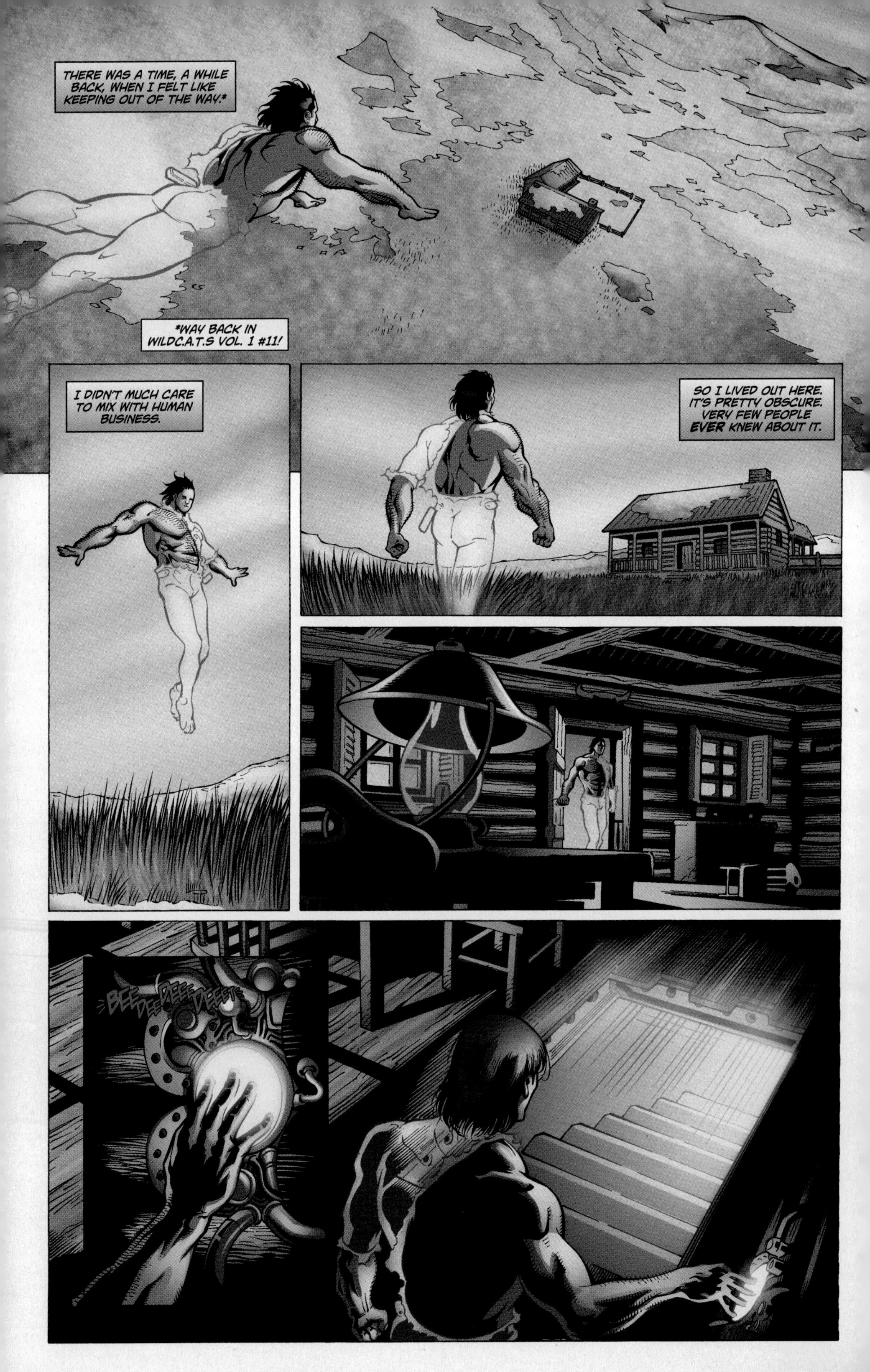
THERE WAS A TIME, A WHILE BACK, WHEN I FELT LIKE KEEPING OUT OF THE WAY.*
*WAY BACK IN WILDC.A.T.S VOL. 1 #11!
I DIDN'T MUCH CARE TO MIX WITH HUMAN BUSINESS.
SO I LIVED OUT HERE. IT'S PRETTY OBSCURE. VERY FEW PEOPLE **EVER** KNEW ABOUT IT.
BEE DEE DEEE DEEET

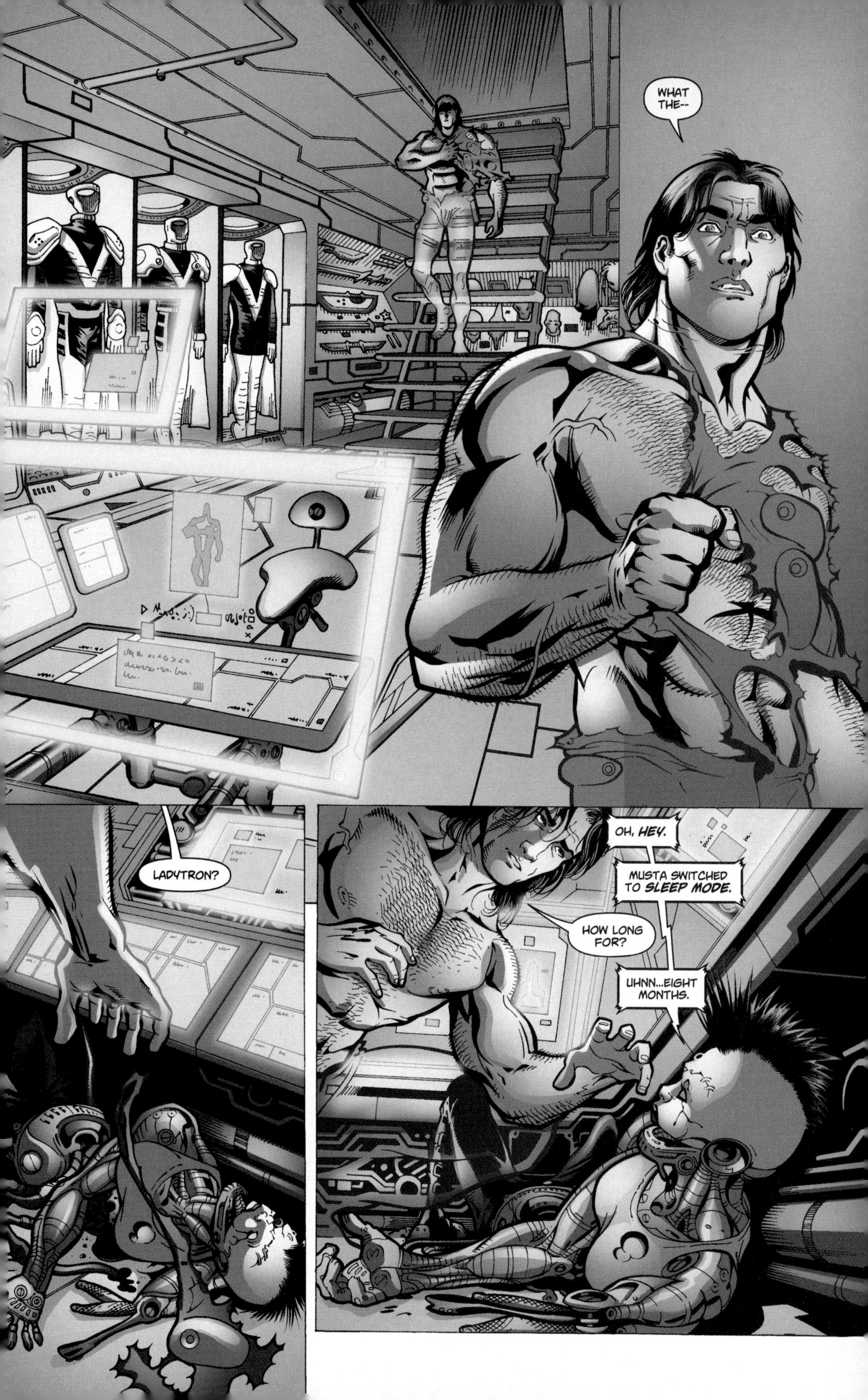
WHAT THE--
LADYTRON?
OH, HEY.
MUSTA SWITCHED TO SLEEP MODE.
HOW LONG FOR?
UHNN...EIGHT MONTHS.

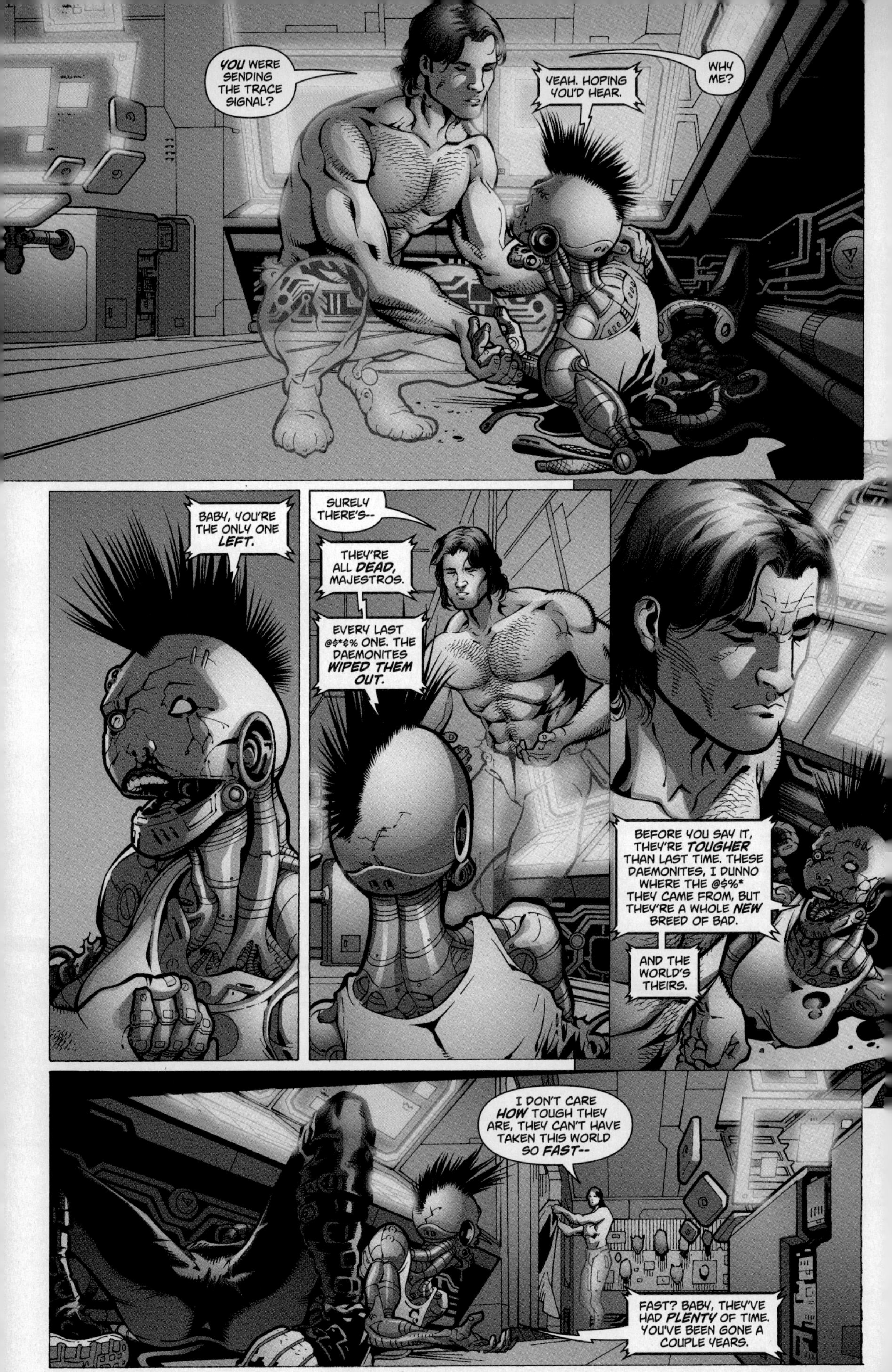

YOU WERE SENDING THE TRACE SIGNAL?
YEAH. HOPING YOU'D HEAR.
WHY ME?
BABY, YOU'RE THE ONLY ONE LEFT.
SURELY THERE'S--
THEY'RE ALL DEAD, MAJESTROS.
EVERY LAST @$*$% ONE. THE DAEMONITES WIPED THEM OUT.
BEFORE YOU SAY IT, THEY'RE TOUGHER THAN LAST TIME. THESE DAEMONITES, I DUNNO WHERE THE @$%* THEY CAME FROM, BUT THEY'RE A WHOLE NEW BREED OF BAD.
AND THE WORLD'S THEIRS.
I DON'T CARE HOW TOUGH THEY ARE, THEY CAN'T HAVE TAKEN THIS WORLD SO FAST--
FAST? BABY, THEY'VE HAD PLENTY OF TIME. YOU'VE BEEN GONE A COUPLE YEARS.

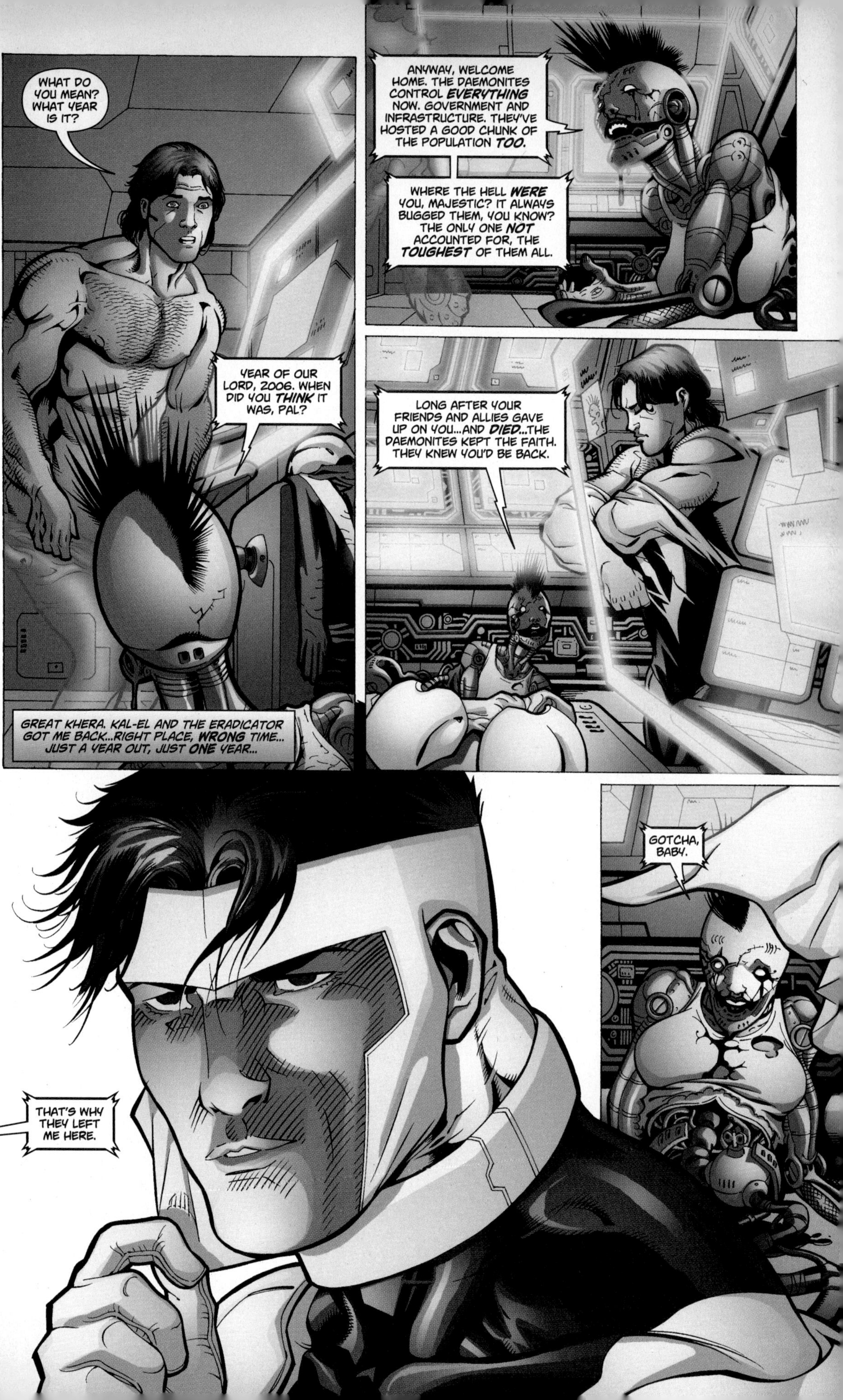
WHAT DO YOU MEAN? WHAT YEAR IS IT?
YEAR OF OUR LORD, 2006. WHEN DID YOU THINK IT WAS, PAL?
GREAT KHERA. KAL-EL AND THE ERADICATOR GOT ME BACK...RIGHT PLACE, WRONG TIME... JUST A YEAR OUT, JUST ONE YEAR...
ANYWAY, WELCOME HOME. THE DAEMONITES CONTROL EVERYTHING NOW. GOVERNMENT AND INFRASTRUCTURE. THEY'VE HOSTED A GOOD CHUNK OF THE POPULATION TOO.
WHERE THE HELL WERE YOU, MAJESTIC? IT ALWAYS BUGGED THEM, YOU KNOW? THE ONLY ONE NOT ACCOUNTED FOR, THE TOUGHEST OF THEM ALL.
LONG AFTER YOUR FRIENDS AND ALLIES GAVE UP ON YOU...AND DIED...THE DAEMONITES KEPT THE FAITH. THEY KNEW YOU'D BE BACK.
THAT'S WHY THEY LEFT ME HERE.
GOTCHA, BABY.

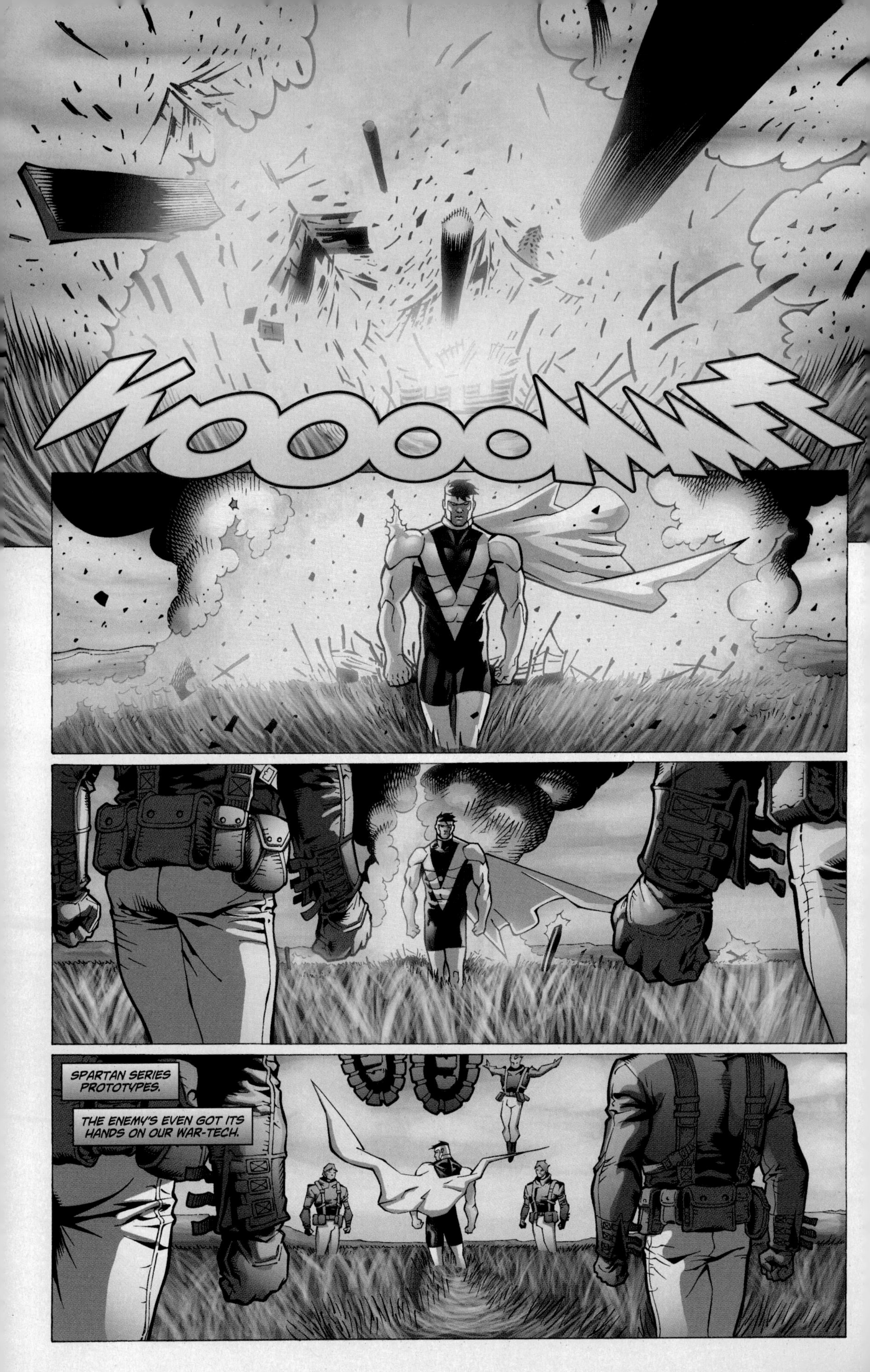
SPARTAN SERIES PROTOTYPES.
THE ENEMY'S EVEN GOT ITS HANDS ON OUR WAR-TECH.

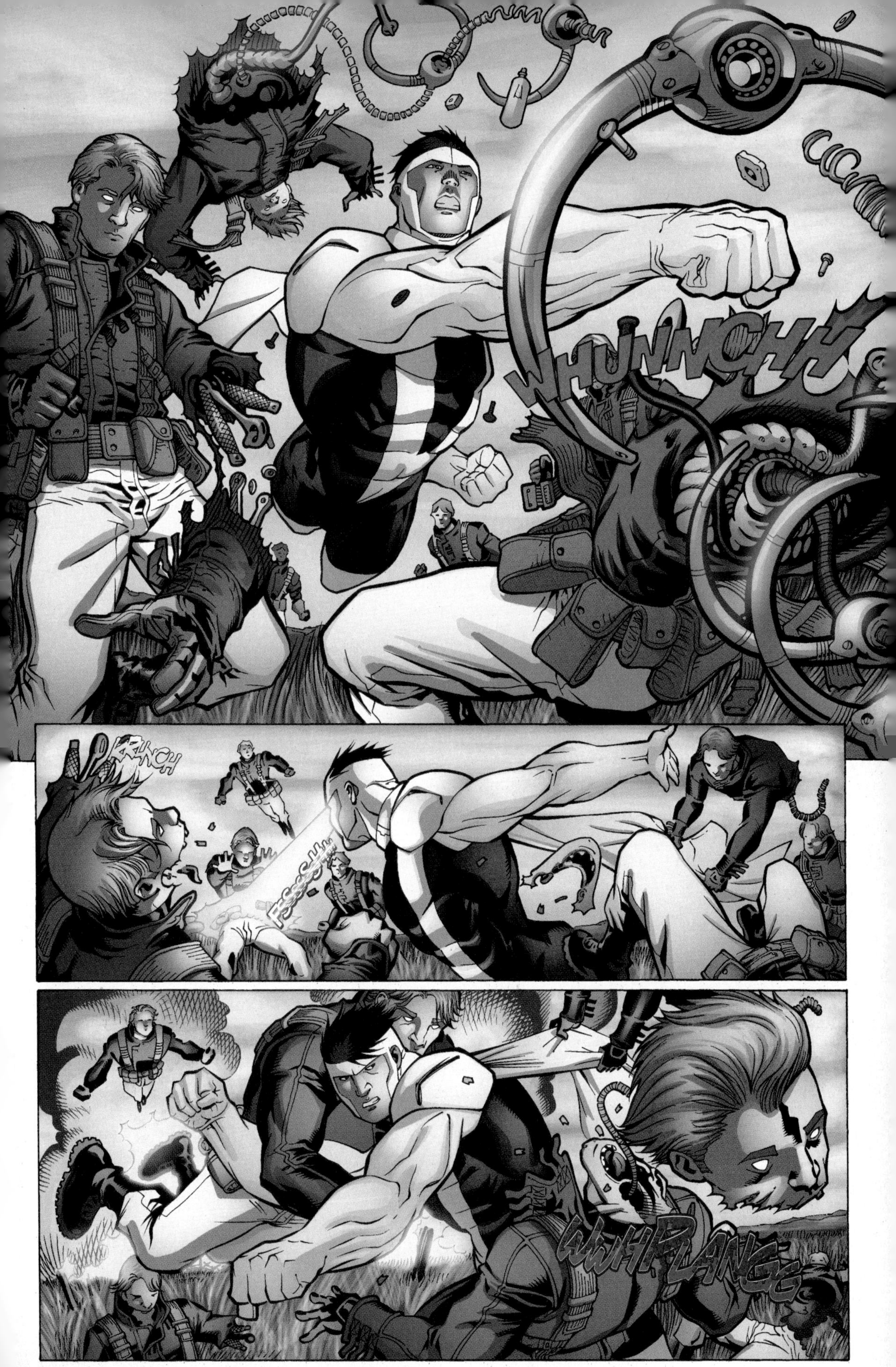
WHUNNCHH
WWHPLANGG

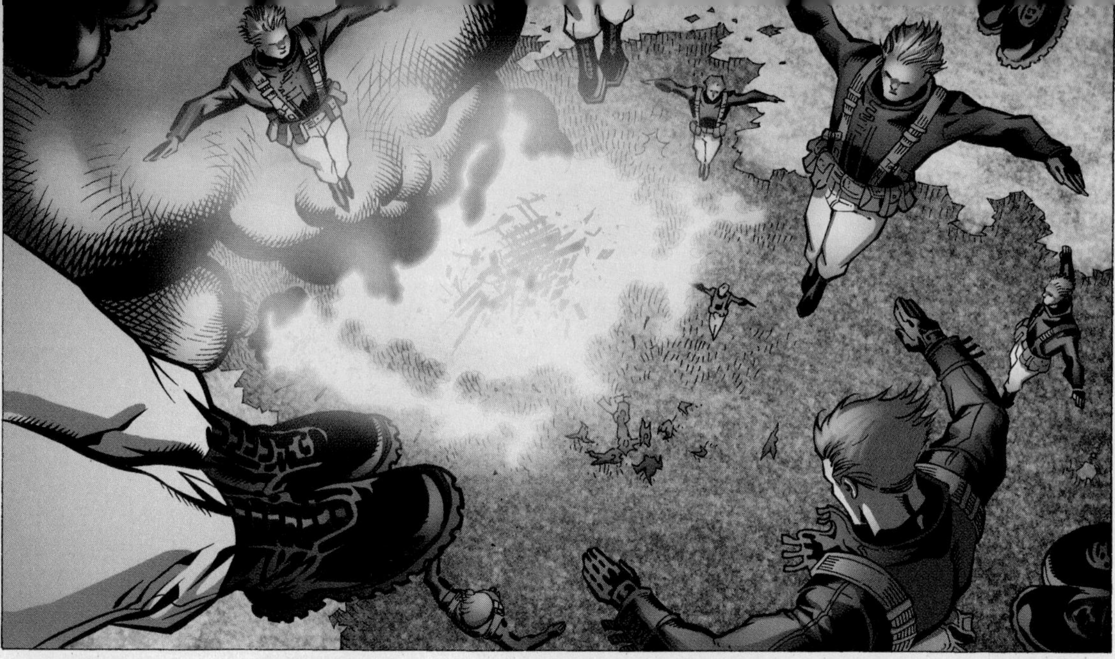

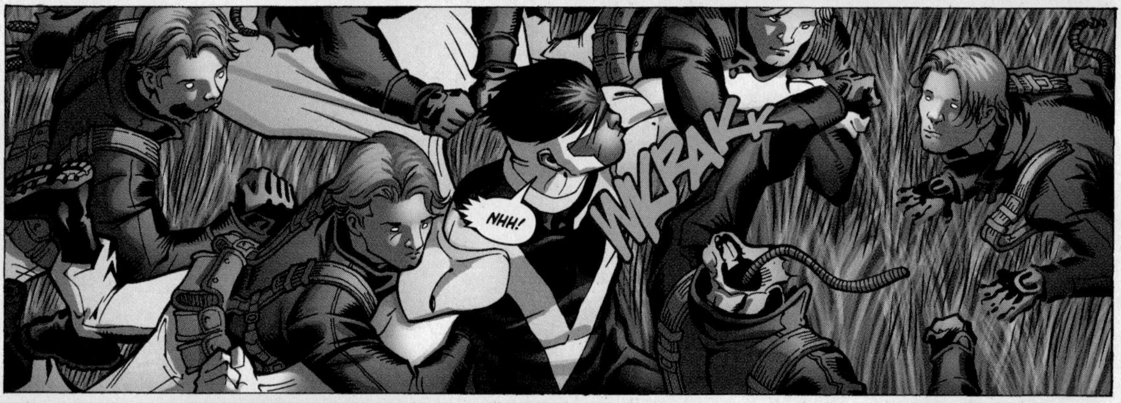
NHH!
WKRAKK

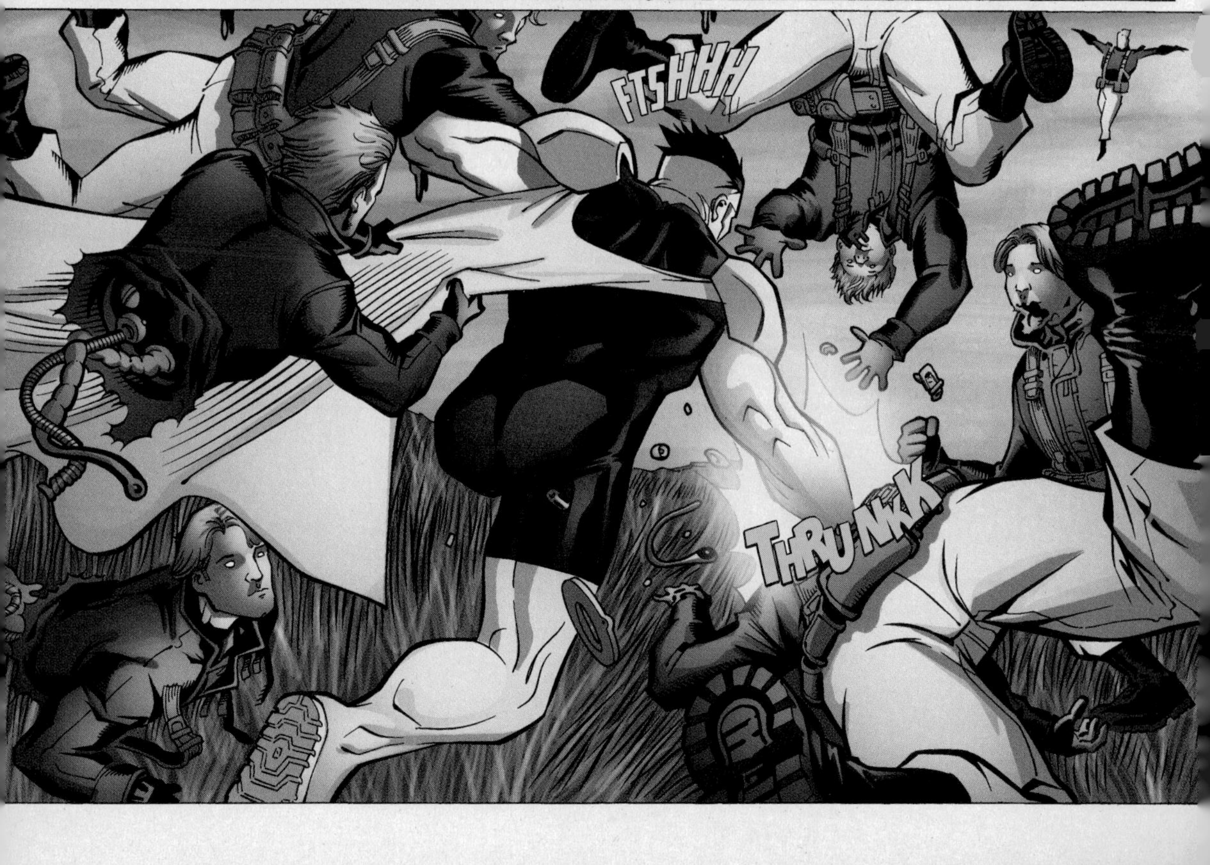
FTSHHH
THRUNKK

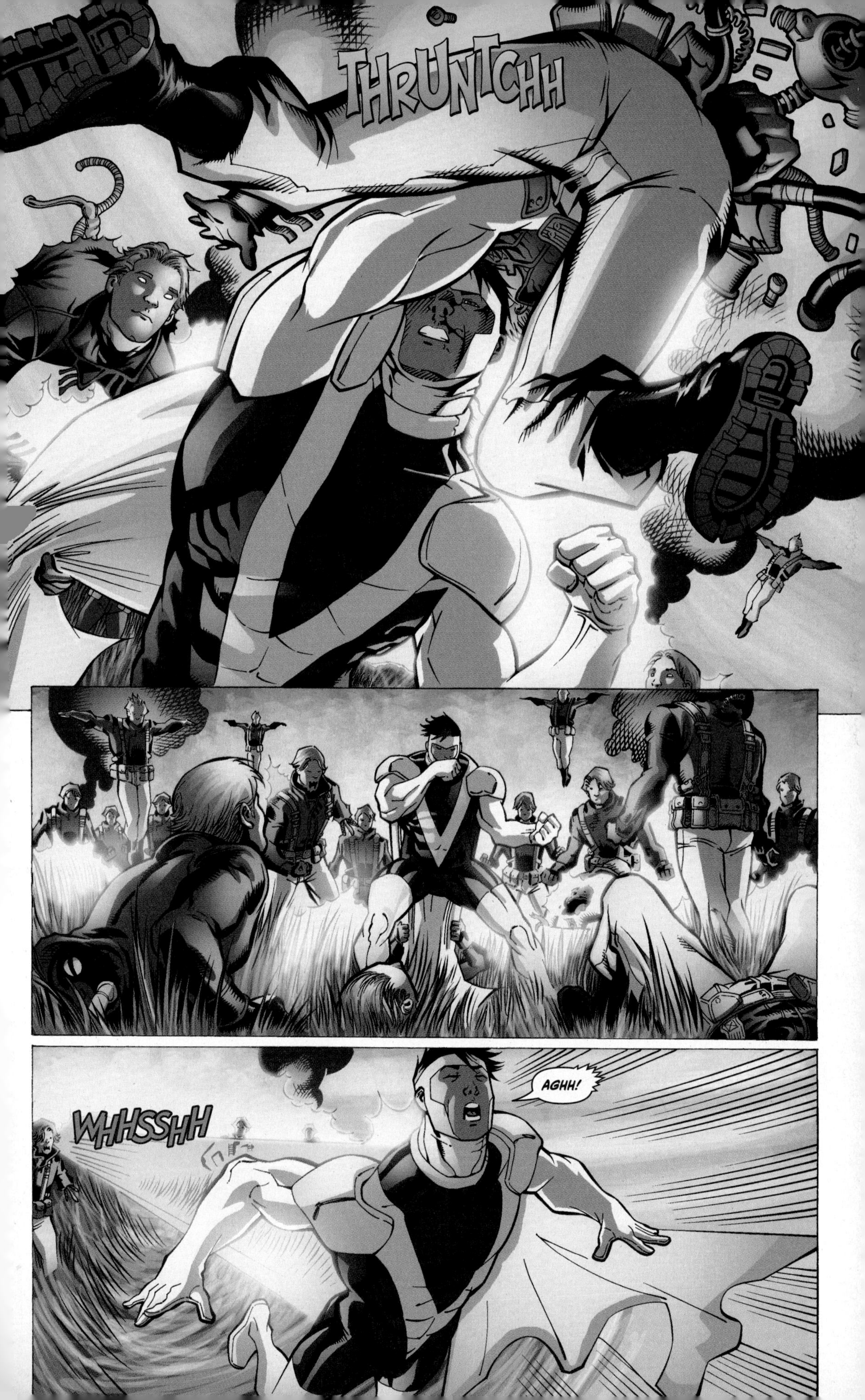
THRUNTCHH
WHHSSHH
AGHH!

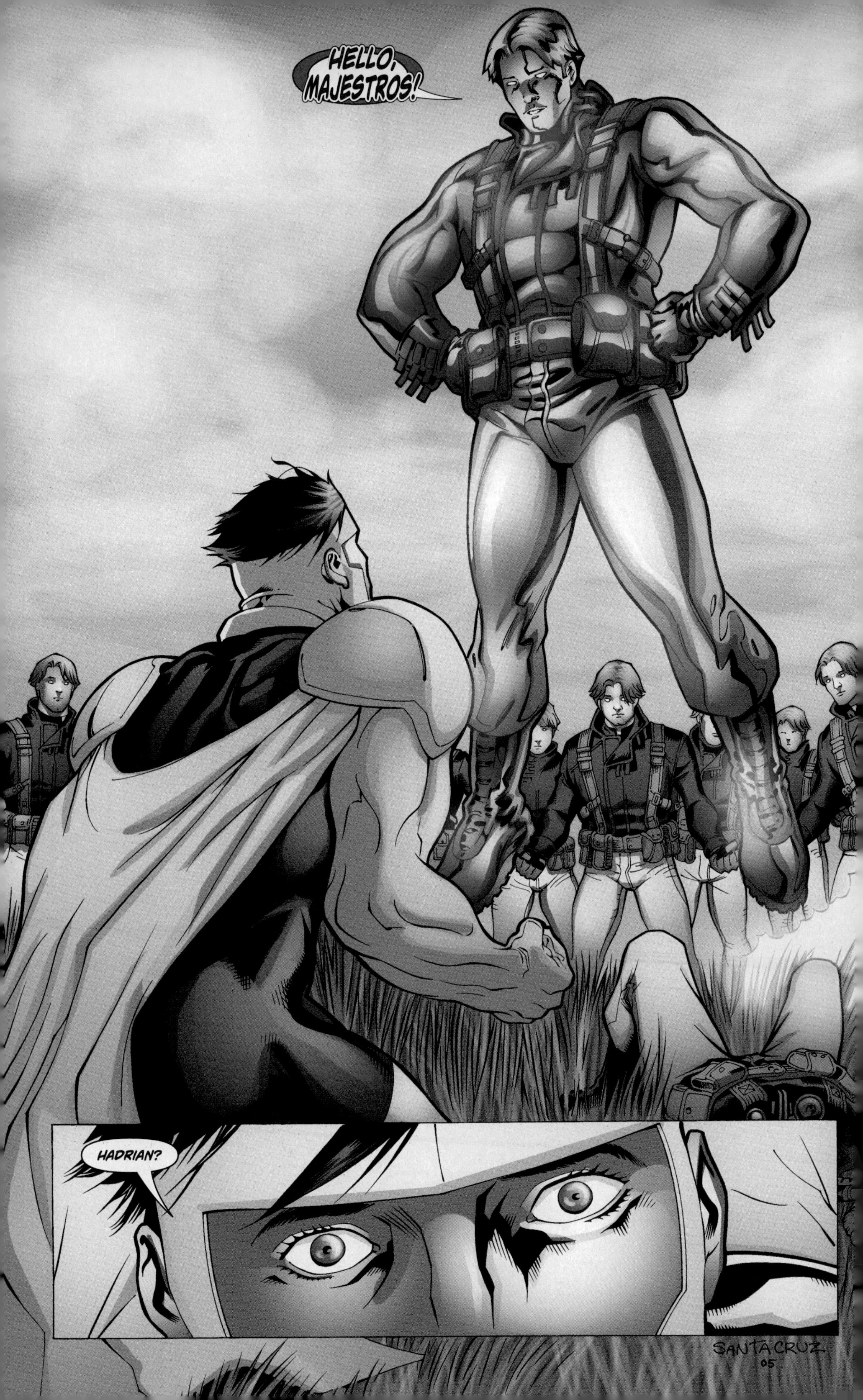
HELLO, MAJESTROS!
HADRIAN?
SANTACRUZ 05

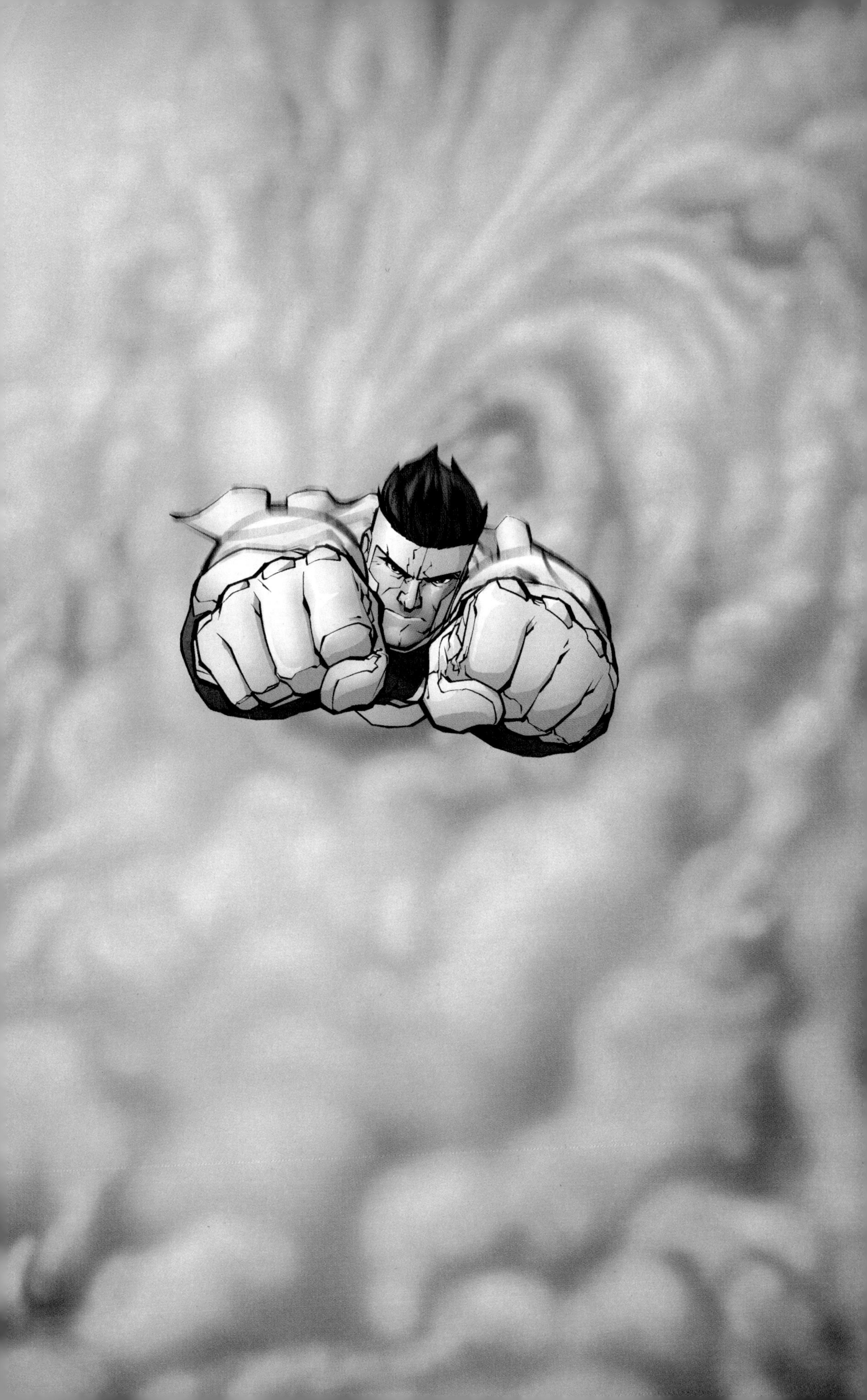

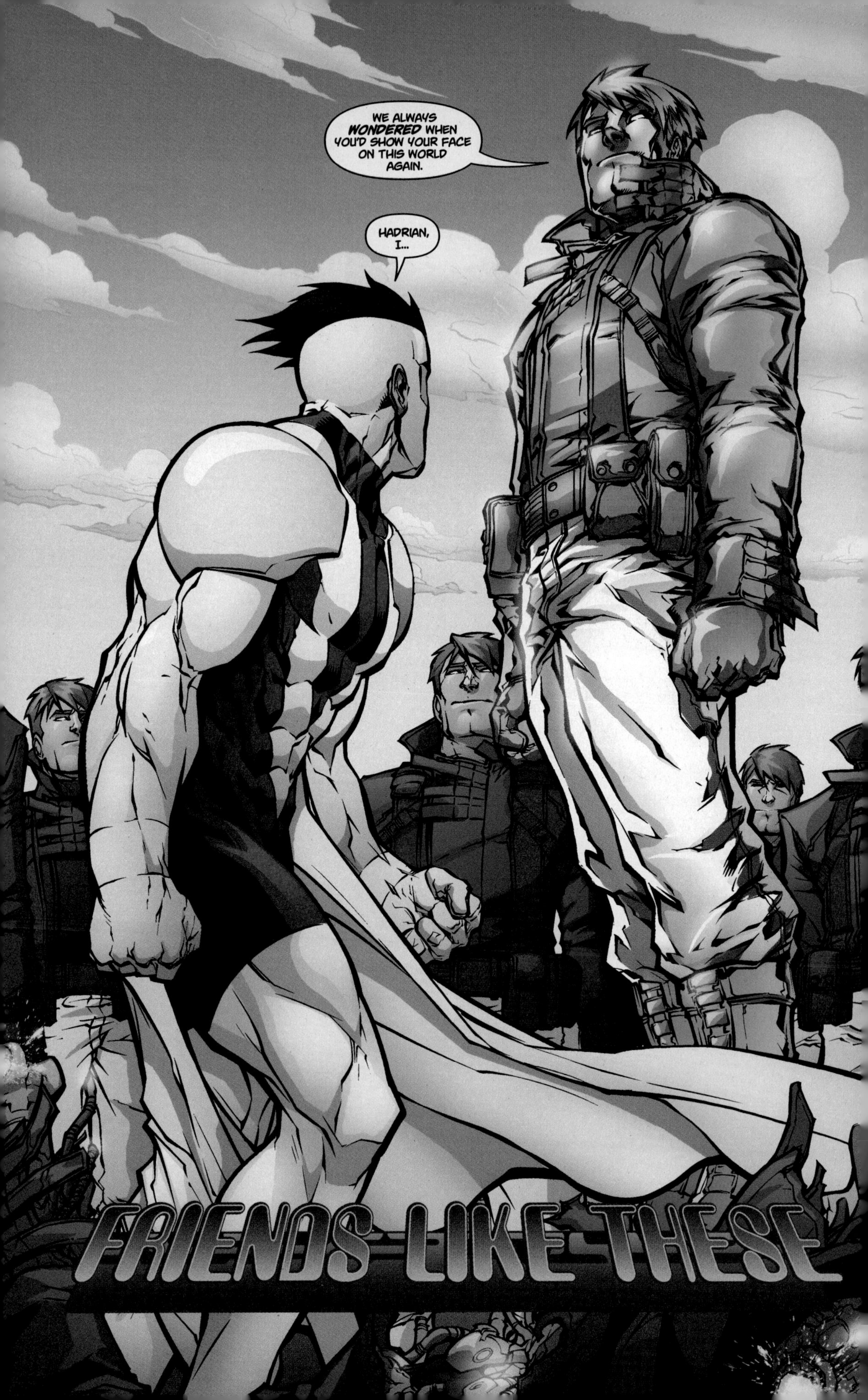
WE ALWAYS WONDERED WHEN YOU'D SHOW YOUR FACE ON THIS WORLD AGAIN.
HADRIAN, I...
FRIENDS LIKE THESE

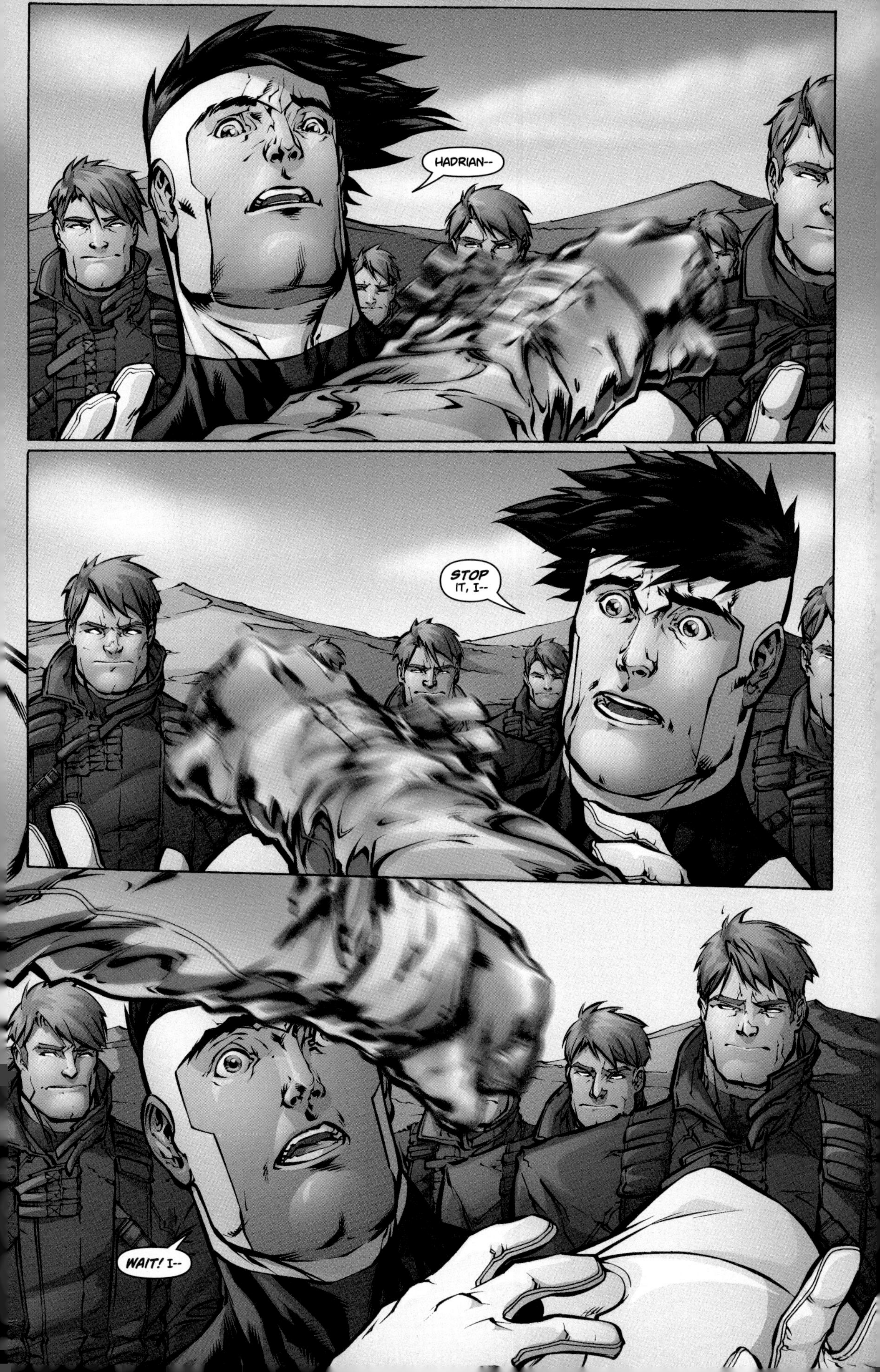
HADRIAN--
STOP IT, I--
WAIT! I--

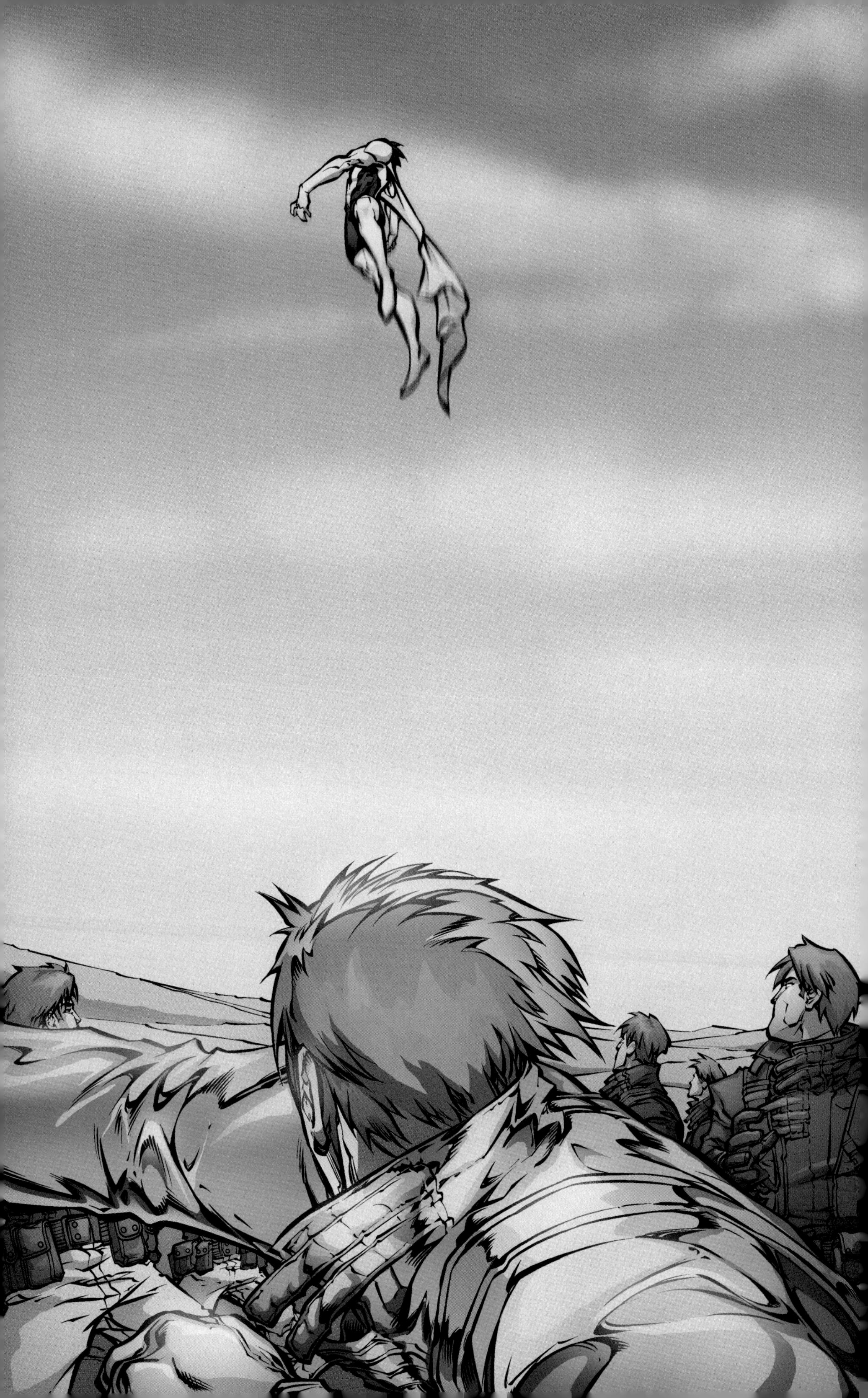

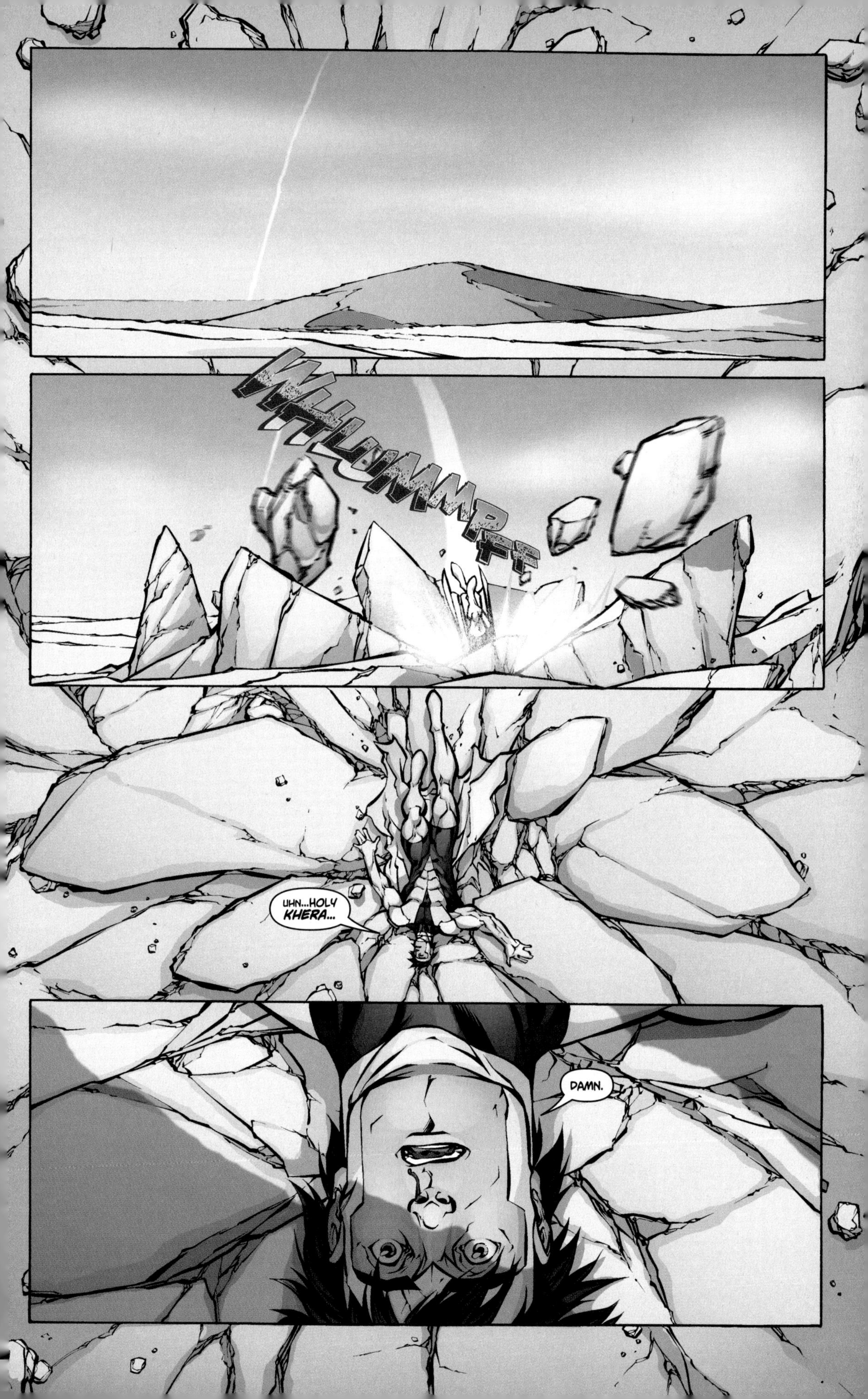
WHUMMPFF
UHN...HOLY KHERA...
DAMN.

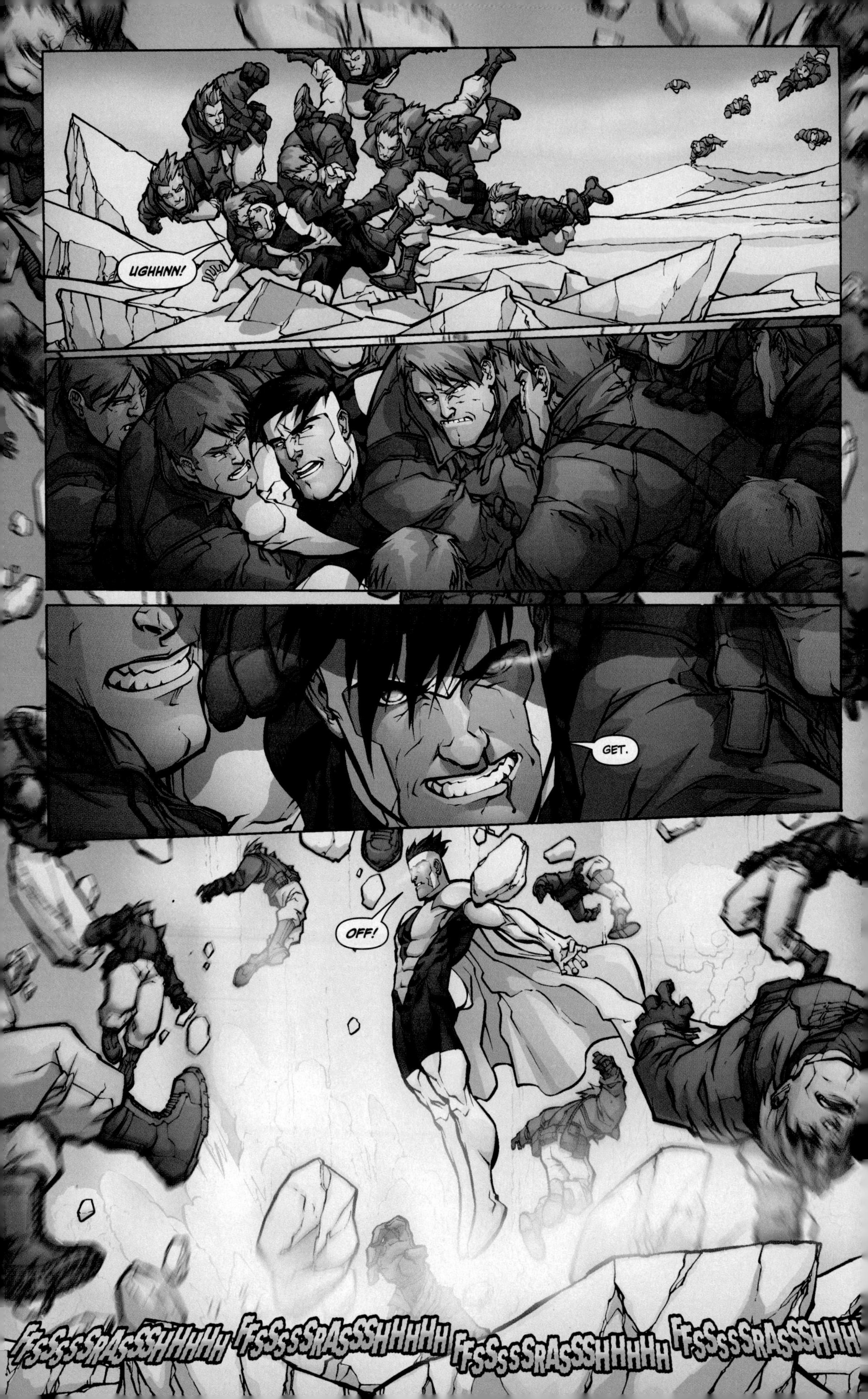
UGHHNN!
GET.
OFF!
FFSSSSSRASSSHHHHH FFSSSSSRASSSHHHHH FFSSSSSRASSSHHHHH FFSSSSSRASSSHHHH

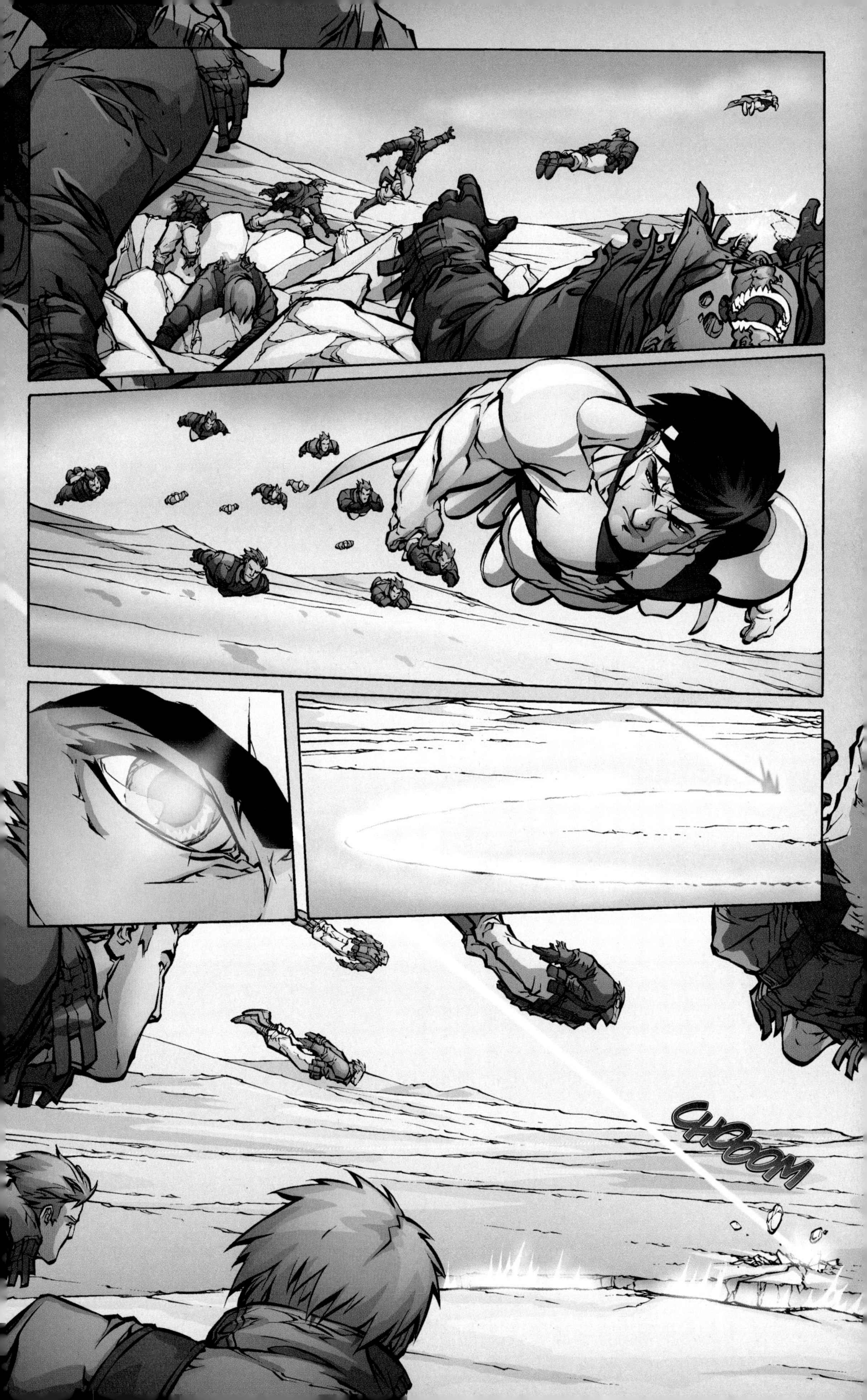
CHOOOM

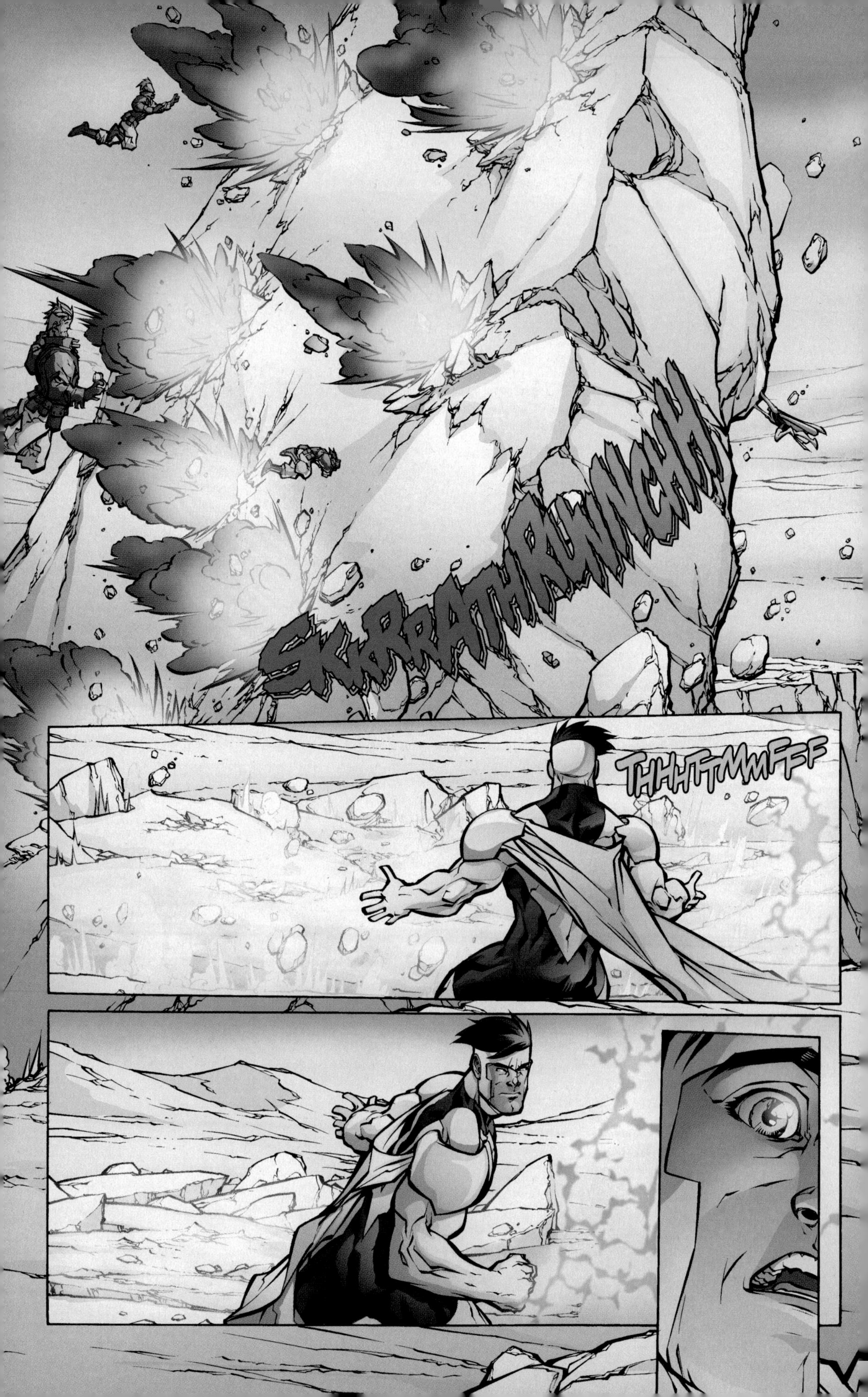
SKRRATHRUNNCH!!
THHTTMMFFF

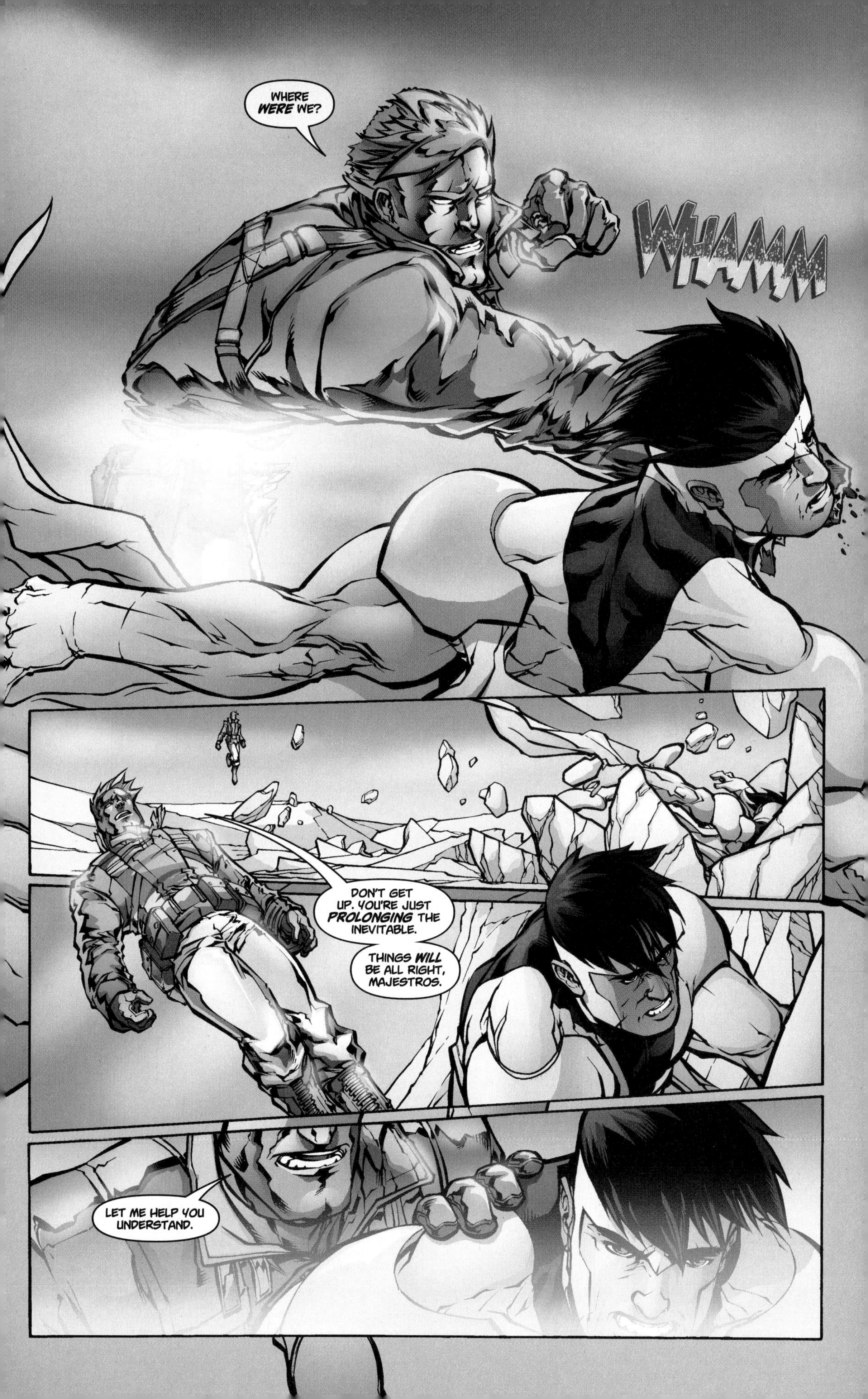
WHERE *WERE* WE?
WHAAAM
DON'T GET UP. YOU'RE JUST *PROLONGING* THE INEVITABLE.
THINGS *WILL* BE ALL RIGHT, MAJESTROS.
LET ME HELP YOU UNDERSTAND.

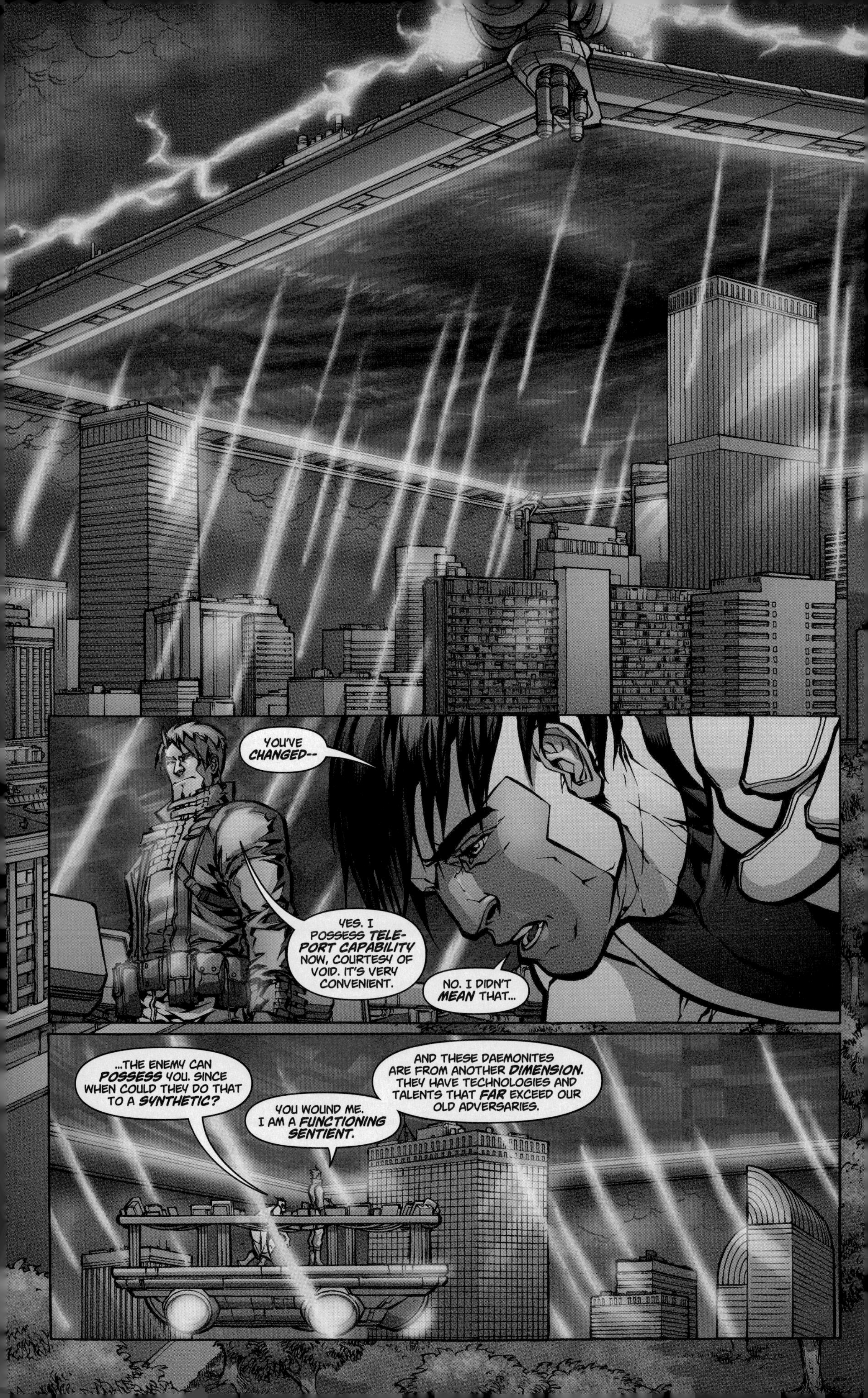
YOU'VE CHANGED--
YES. I POSSESS TELEPORT CAPABILITY NOW, COURTESY OF VOID. IT'S VERY CONVENIENT.
NO. I DIDN'T MEAN THAT...
...THE ENEMY CAN POSSESS YOU. SINCE WHEN COULD THEY DO THAT TO A SYNTHETIC?
YOU WOUND ME. I AM A FUNCTIONING SENTIENT.
AND THESE DAEMONITES ARE FROM ANOTHER DIMENSION. THEY HAVE TECHNOLOGIES AND TALENTS THAT FAR EXCEED OUR OLD ADVERSARIES.

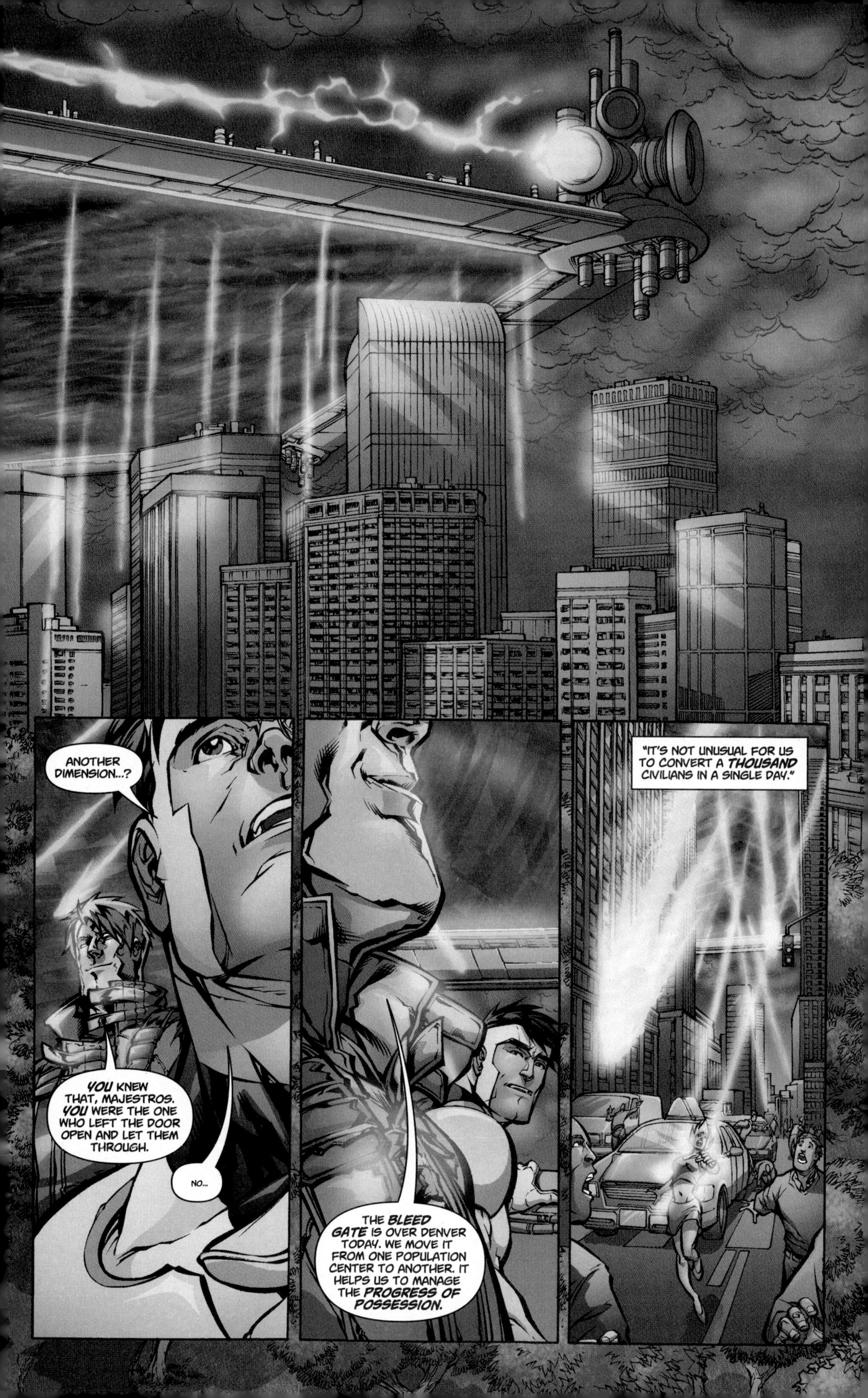
ANOTHER DIMENSION...?
YOU KNEW THAT, MAJESTROS. YOU WERE THE ONE WHO LEFT THE DOOR OPEN AND LET THEM THROUGH.
NO...
THE BLEED GATE IS OVER DENVER TODAY. WE MOVE IT FROM ONE POPULATION CENTER TO ANOTHER. IT HELPS US TO MANAGE THE PROGRESS OF POSSESSION.
"IT'S NOT UNUSUAL FOR US TO CONVERT A THOUSAND CIVILIANS IN A SINGLE DAY."

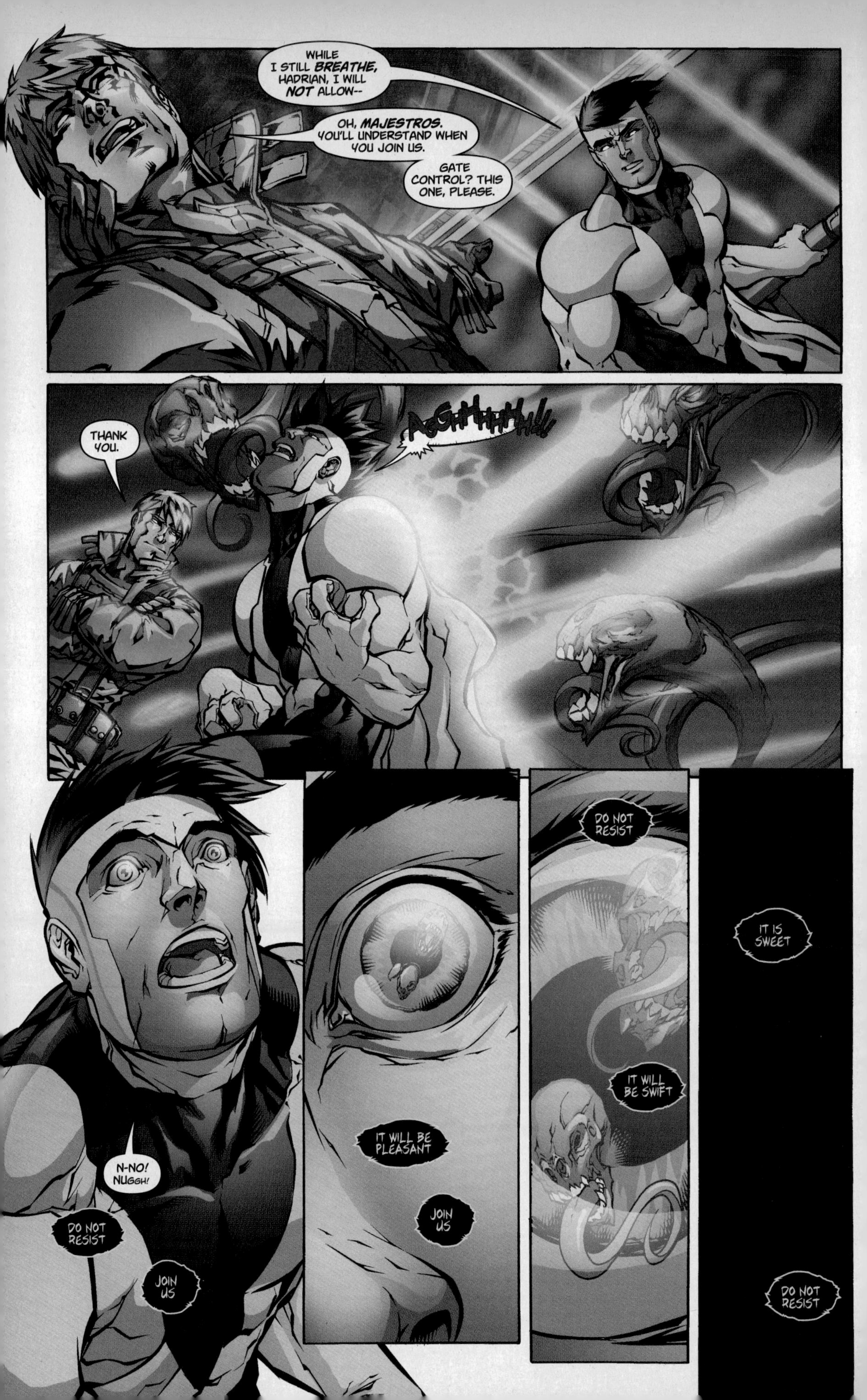
WHILE I STILL BREATHE, HADRIAN, I WILL NOT ALLOW--
OH, MAJESTROS. YOU'LL UNDERSTAND WHEN YOU JOIN US.
GATE CONTROL? THIS ONE, PLEASE.
THANK YOU.
AGHHHHHH!!
N-NO! NUGGH!
DO NOT RESIST
JOIN US
IT WILL BE PLEASANT
JOIN US
DO NOT RESIST
IT WILL BE SWIFT
IT IS SWEET
DO NOT RESIST

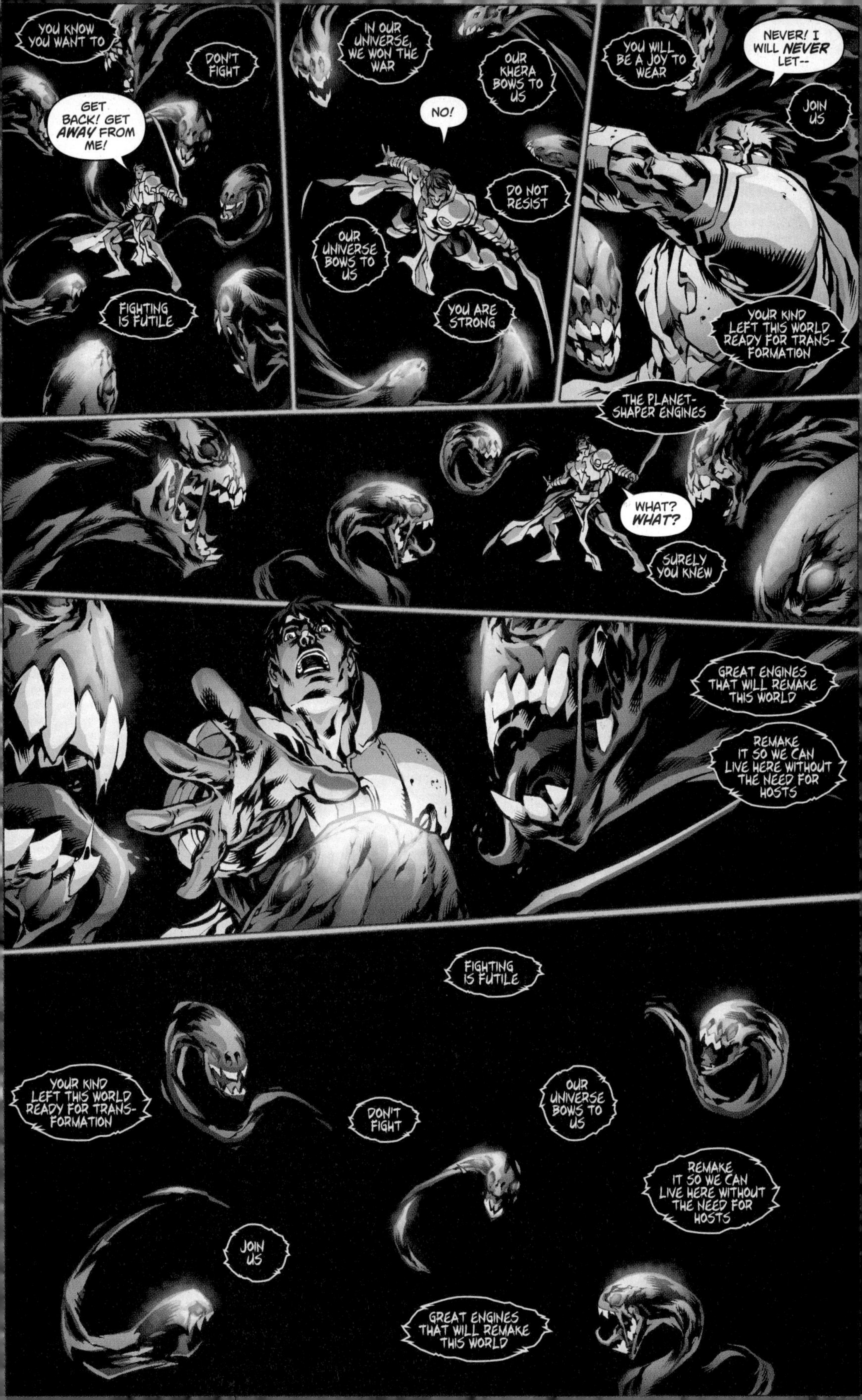

YOU KNOW YOU WANT TO
DON'T FIGHT
GET BACK! GET AWAY FROM ME!
FIGHTING IS FUTILE
IN OUR UNIVERSE, WE WON THE WAR
OUR KHERA BOWS TO US
NO!
DO NOT RESIST
OUR UNIVERSE BOWS TO US
YOU ARE STRONG
YOU WILL BE A JOY TO WEAR
NEVER! I WILL NEVER LET--
JOIN US
YOUR KIND LEFT THIS WORLD READY FOR TRANS-FORMATION
THE PLANET-SHAPER ENGINES
WHAT? WHAT?
SURELY YOU KNEW
GREAT ENGINES THAT WILL REMAKE THIS WORLD
REMAKE IT SO WE CAN LIVE HERE WITHOUT THE NEED FOR HOSTS
FIGHTING IS FUTILE
YOUR KIND LEFT THIS WORLD READY FOR TRANS-FORMATION
DON'T FIGHT
OUR UNIVERSE BOWS TO US
REMAKE IT SO WE CAN LIVE HERE WITHOUT THE NEED FOR HOSTS
JOIN US
GREAT ENGINES THAT WILL REMAKE THIS WORLD

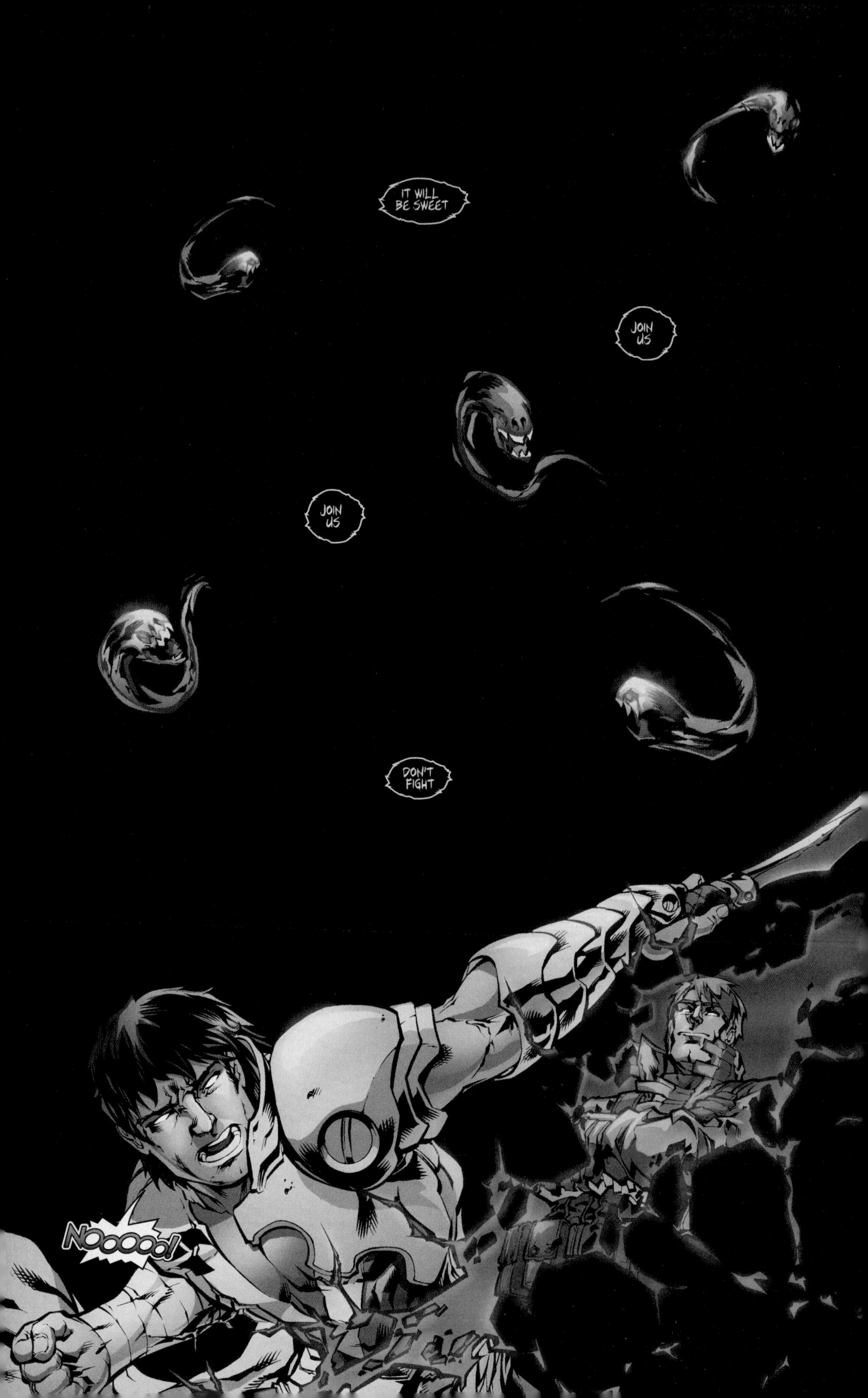
IT WILL BE SWEET
JOIN US
JOIN US
DON'T FIGHT
NOOOOO!

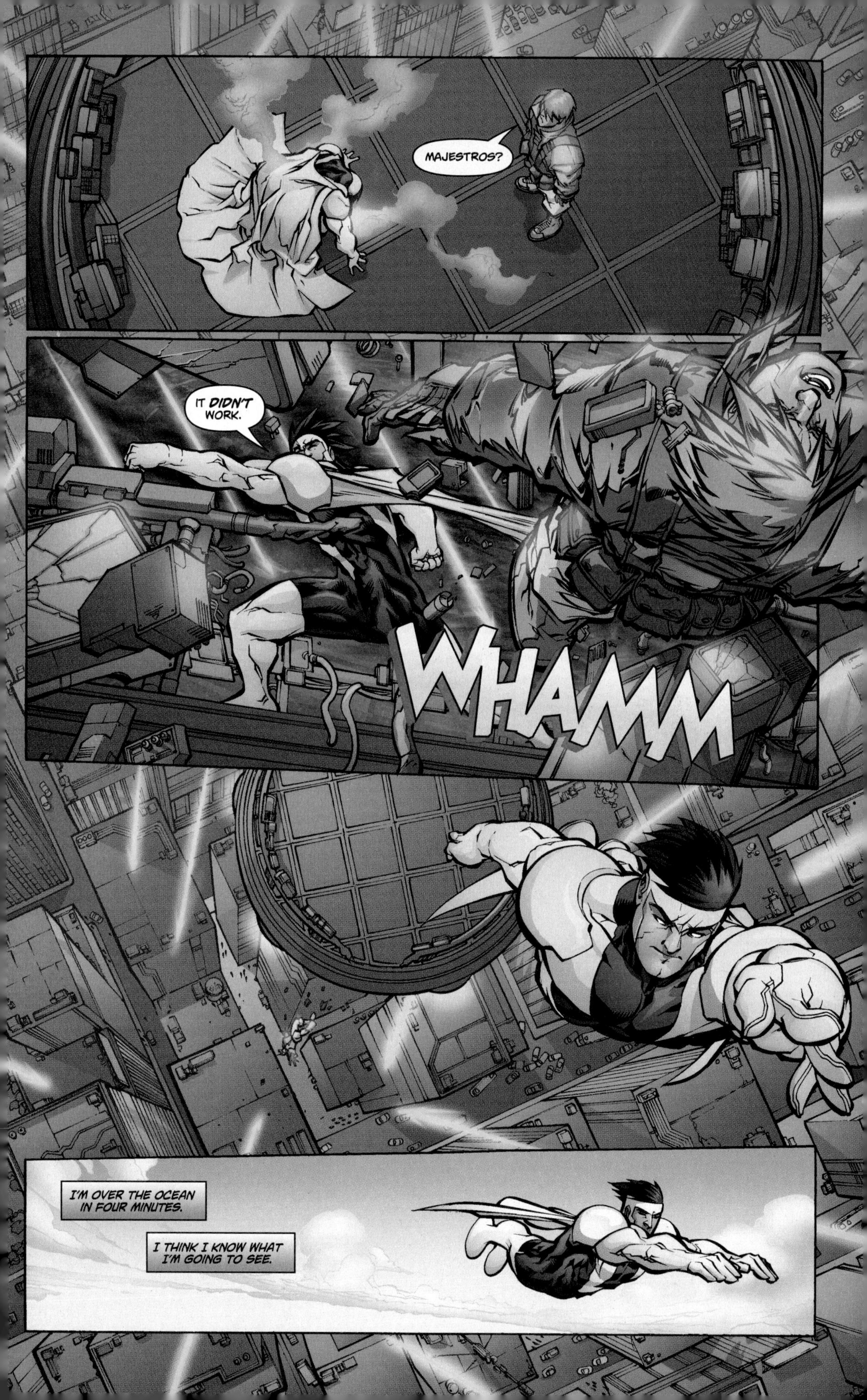
MAJESTROS?
IT DIDN'T WORK.
WHAMM
I'M OVER THE OCEAN IN FOUR MINUTES.
I THINK I KNOW WHAT I'M GOING TO SEE.

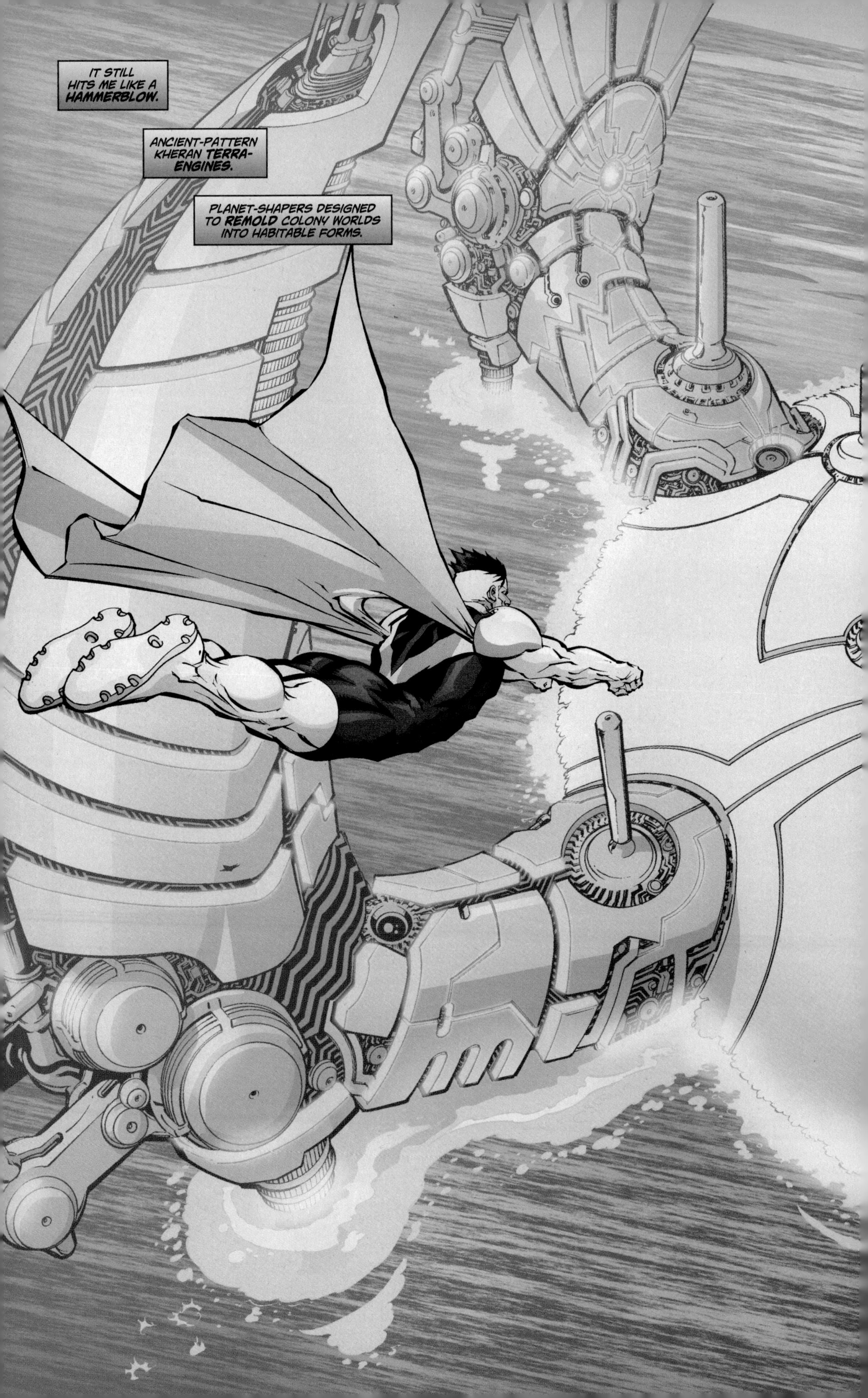
IT STILL HITS ME LIKE A HAMMERBLOW.
ANCIENT-PATTERN KHERAN TERRA-ENGINES.
PLANET-SHAPERS DESIGNED TO REMOLD COLONY WORLDS INTO HABITABLE FORMS.

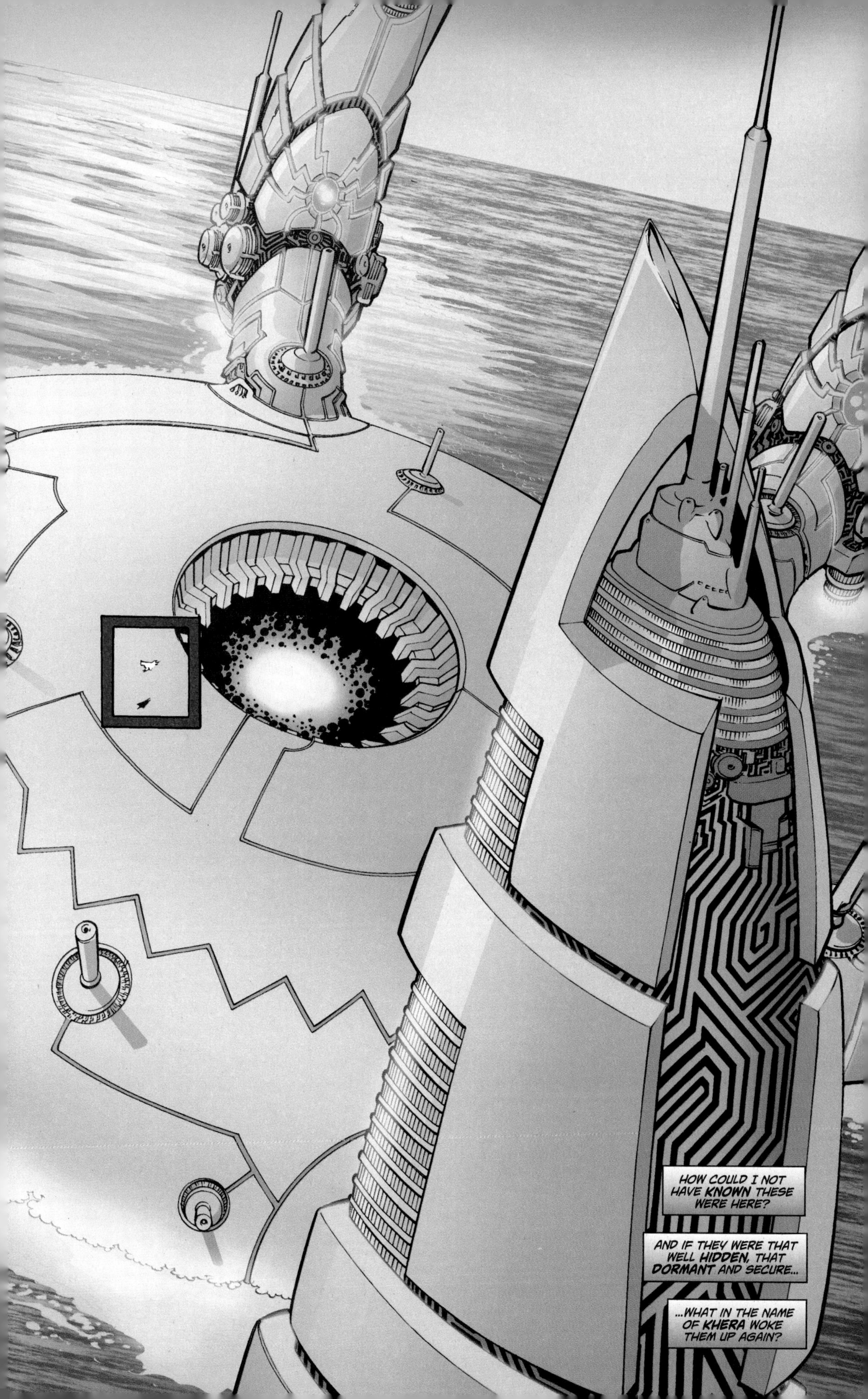
HOW COULD I NOT HAVE KNOWN THESE WERE HERE?
AND IF THEY WERE THAT WELL HIDDEN, THAT DORMANT AND SECURE...
...WHAT IN THE NAME OF KHERA WOKE THEM UP AGAIN?

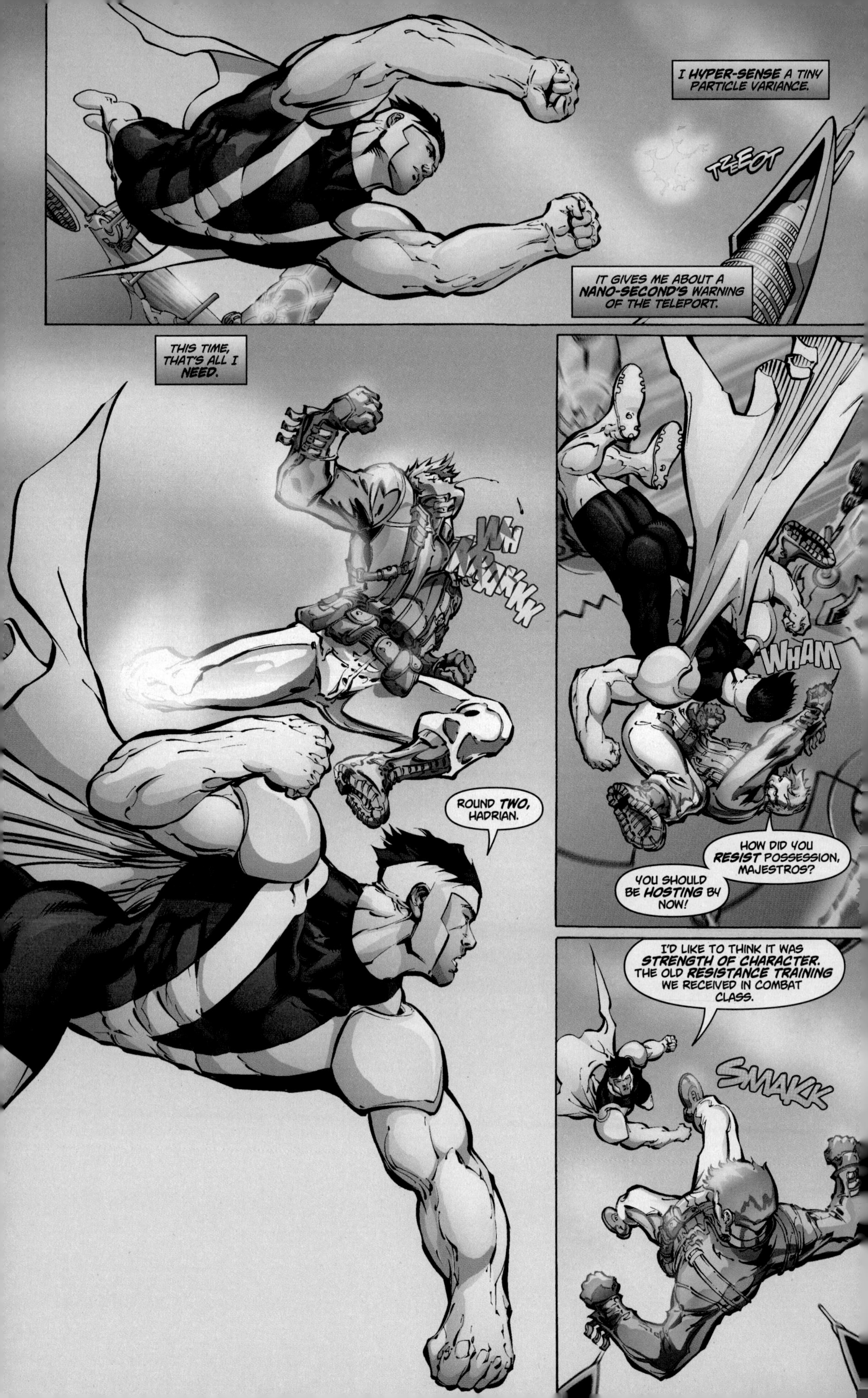
I HYPER-SENSE A TINY PARTICLE VARIANCE.
TZEEOT
IT GIVES ME ABOUT A NANO-SECOND'S WARNING OF THE TELEPORT.
THIS TIME, THAT'S ALL I NEED.
WHKRAKKK
ROUND TWO, HADRIAN.
WHAM
HOW DID YOU RESIST POSSESSION, MAJESTROS?
YOU SHOULD BE HOSTING BY NOW!
I'D LIKE TO THINK IT WAS STRENGTH OF CHARACTER. THE OLD RESISTANCE TRAINING WE RECEIVED IN COMBAT CLASS.
SMAKK

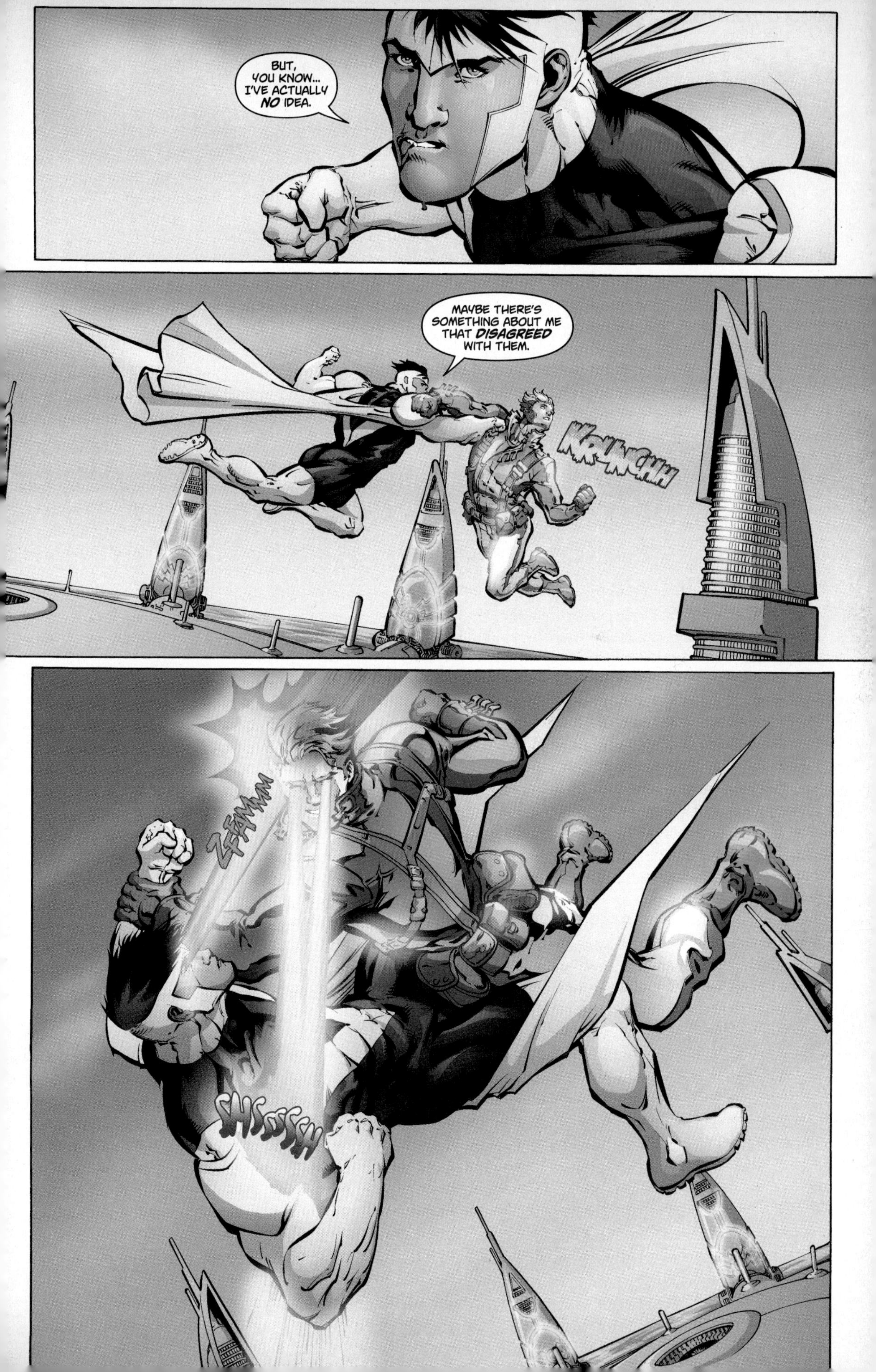
BUT, YOU KNOW... I'VE ACTUALLY NO IDEA.
MAYBE THERE'S SOMETHING ABOUT ME THAT DISAGREED WITH THEM.
KRUNCHH
ZFAMMM
SHSSSSH

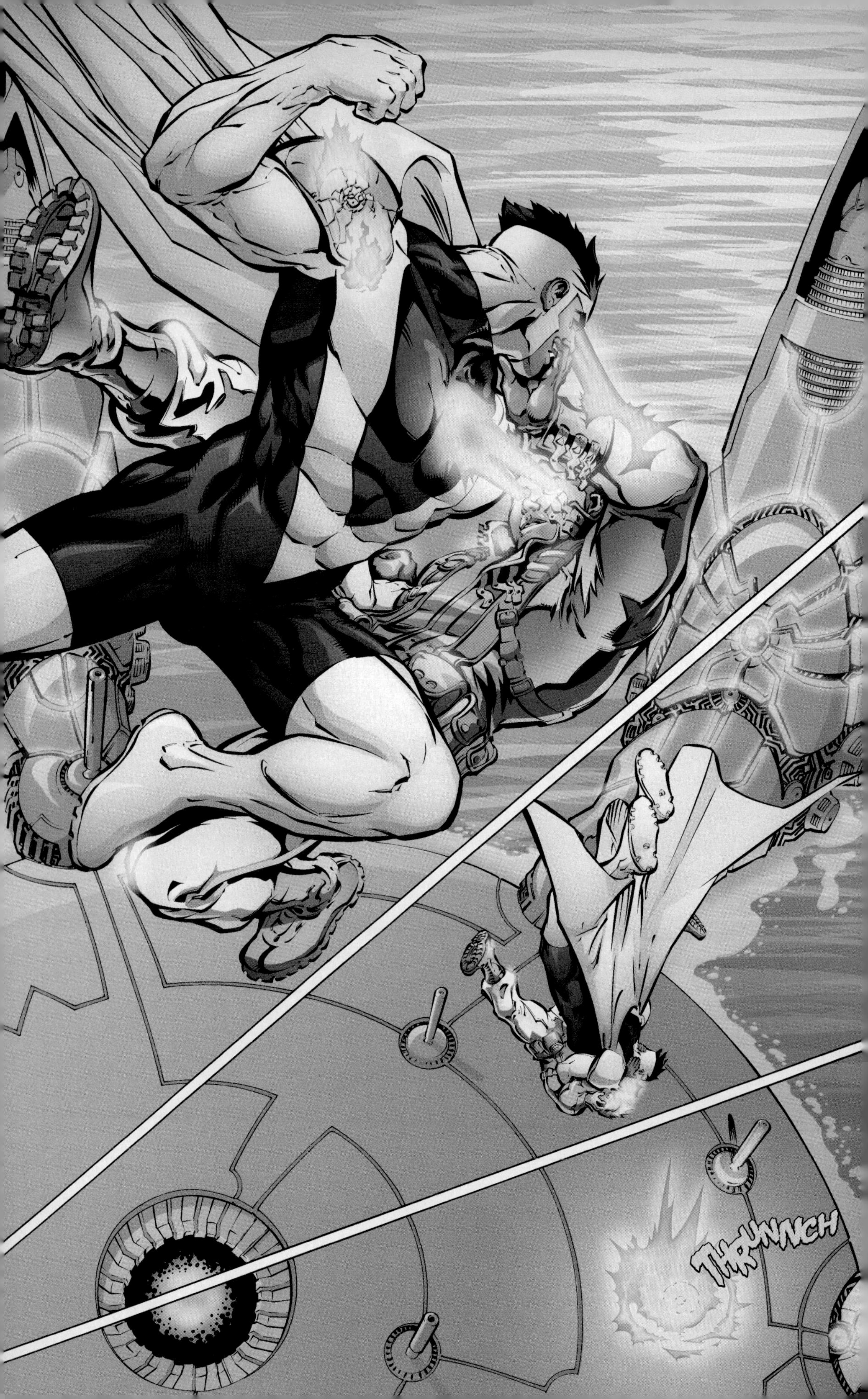
THRUNNCH

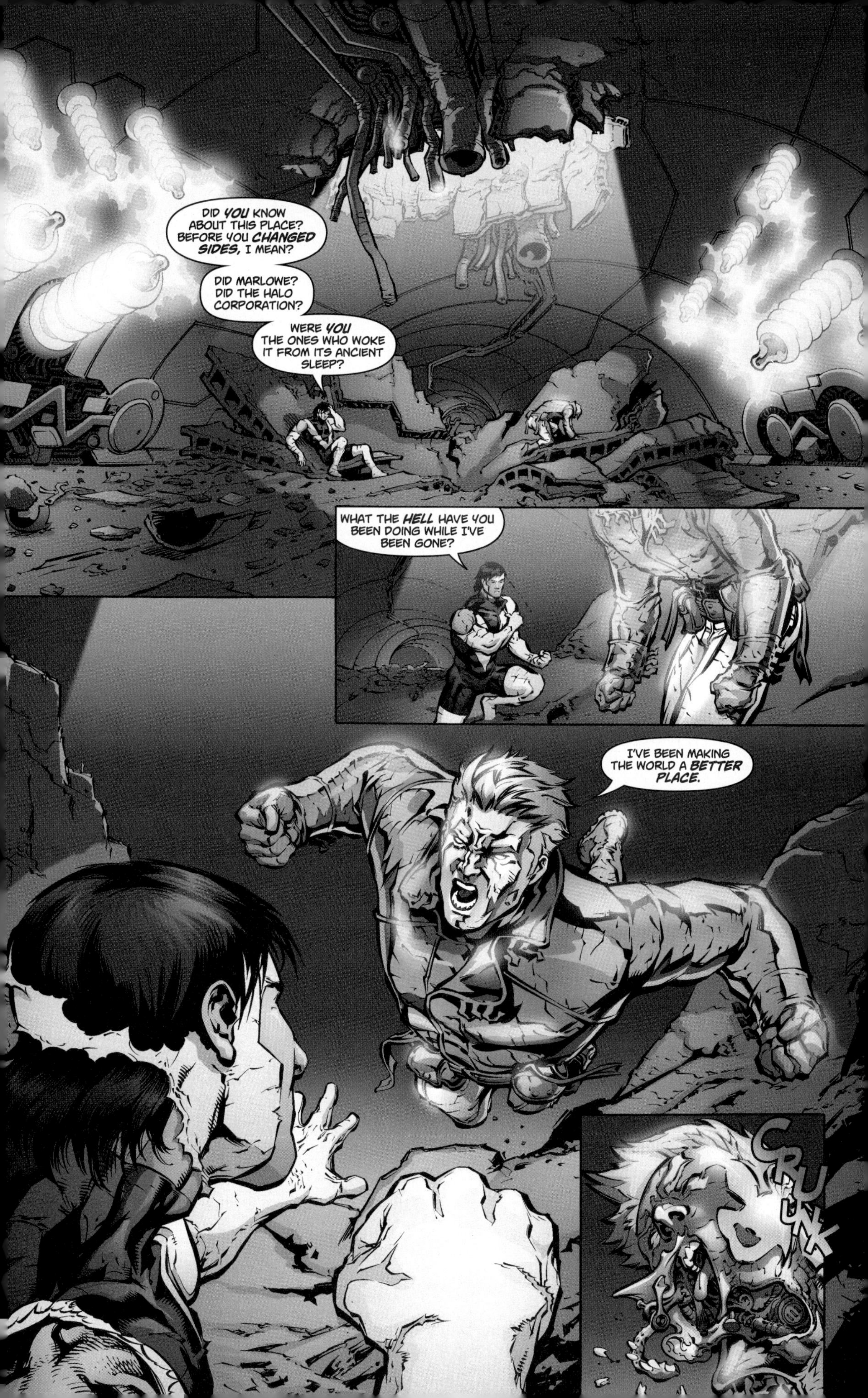
DID YOU KNOW ABOUT THIS PLACE? BEFORE YOU CHANGED SIDES, I MEAN?
DID MARLOWE? DID THE HALO CORPORATION?
WERE YOU THE ONES WHO WOKE IT FROM ITS ANCIENT SLEEP?
WHAT THE HELL HAVE YOU BEEN DOING WHILE I'VE BEEN GONE?
I'VE BEEN MAKING THE WORLD A BETTER PLACE.
CRUNK

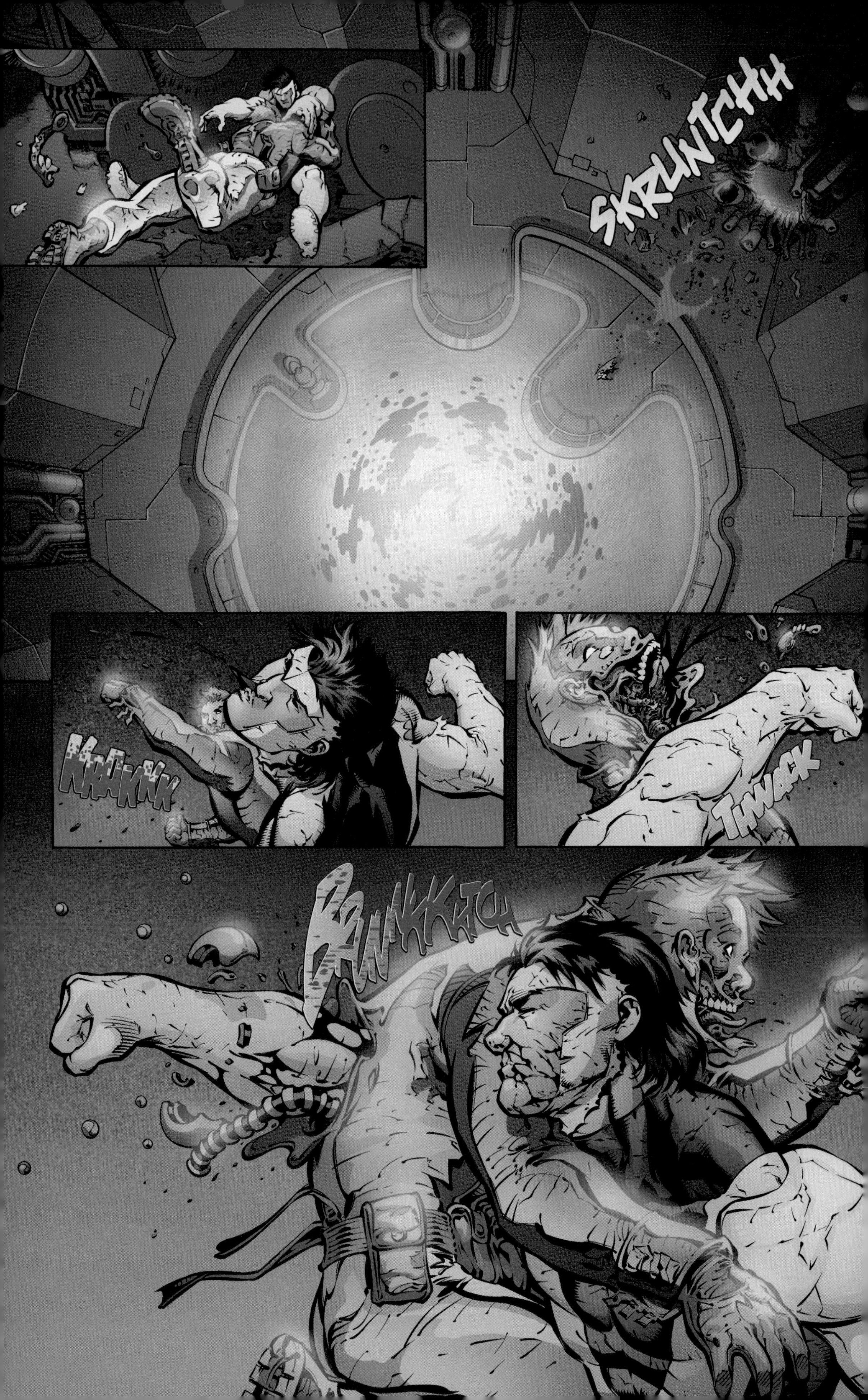
SKRUNTCHH
THWACK

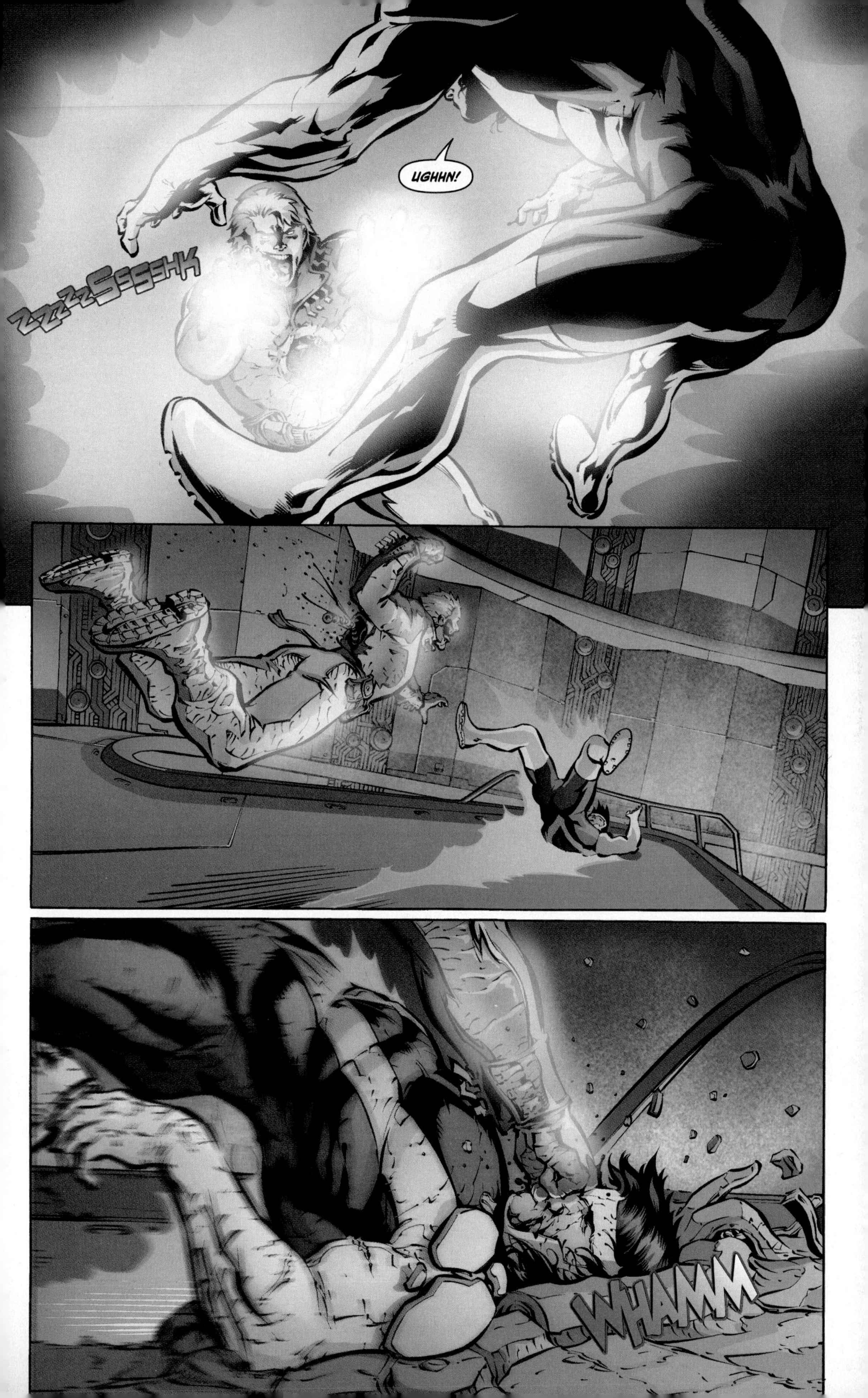
UGHHN!
ZZZZZZSSSSHK
WHAMM

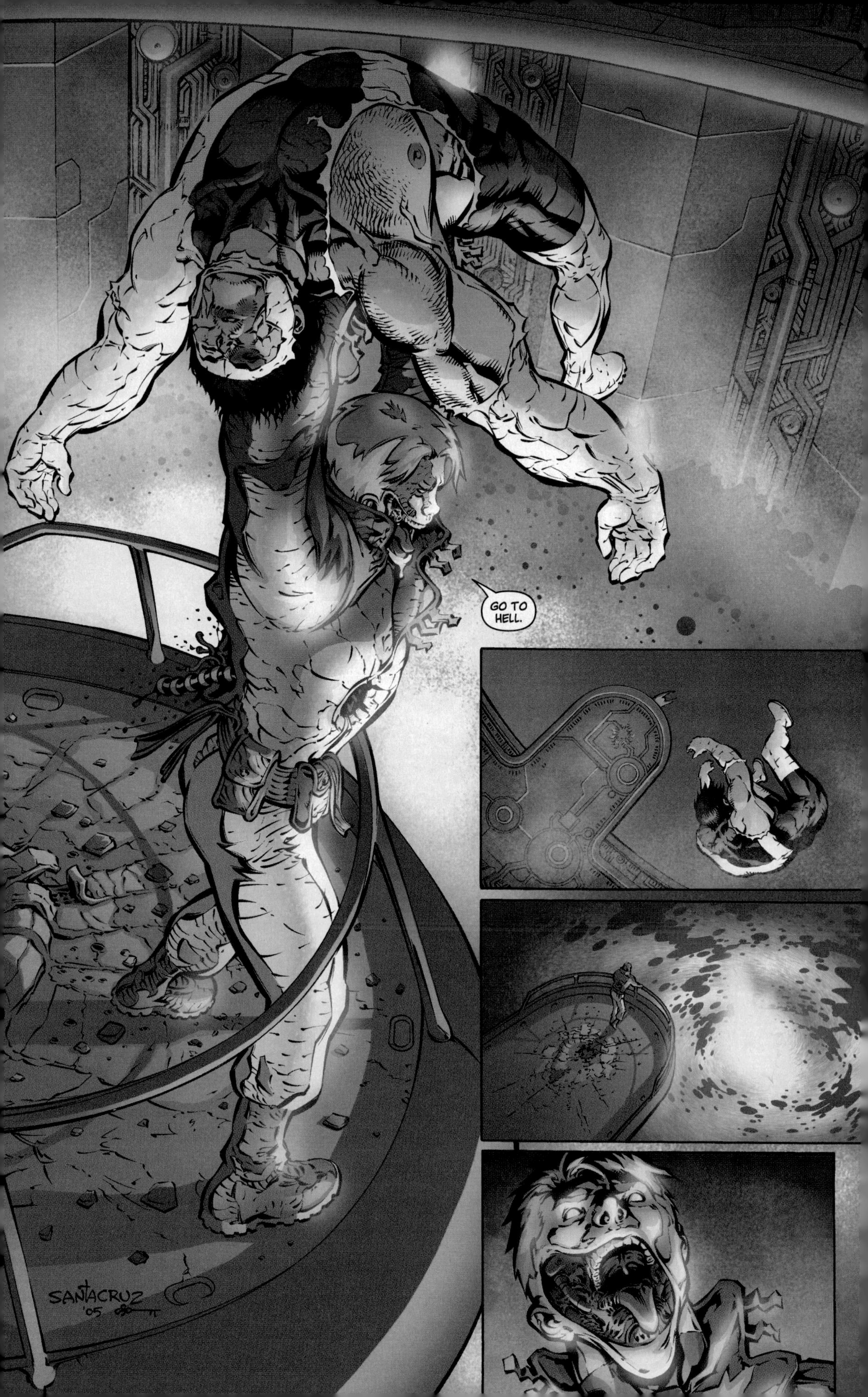
GO TO HELL.
SANTACRUZ '05

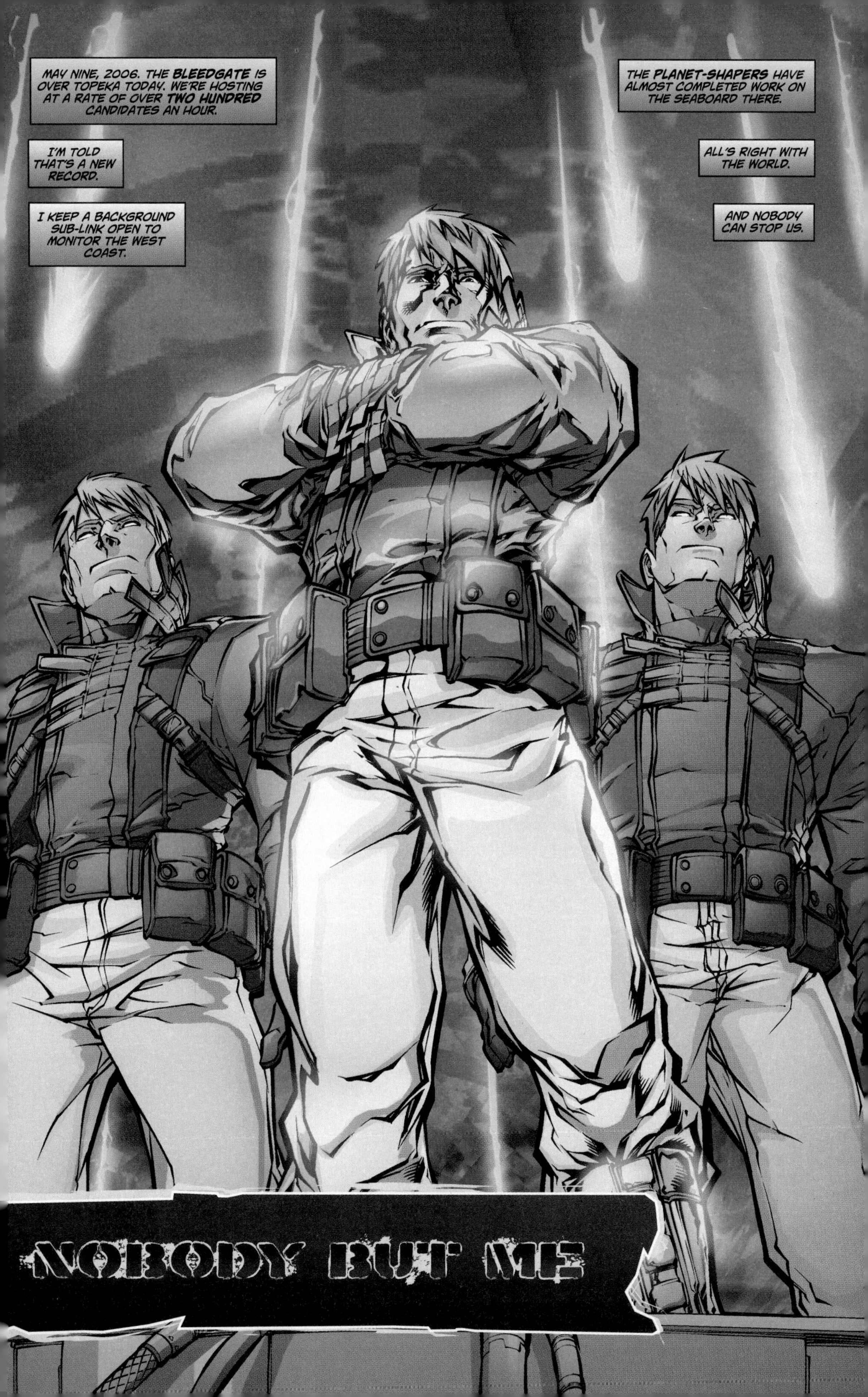
MAY NINE, 2006. THE BLEEDGATE IS OVER TOPEKA TODAY. WE'RE HOSTING AT A RATE OF OVER TWO HUNDRED CANDIDATES AN HOUR.
I'M TOLD THAT'S A NEW RECORD.
I KEEP A BACKGROUND SUB-LINK OPEN TO MONITOR THE WEST COAST.
THE PLANET-SHAPERS HAVE ALMOST COMPLETED WORK ON THE SEABOARD THERE.
ALL'S RIGHT WITH THE WORLD.
AND NOBODY CAN STOP US.
NOBODY BUT ME

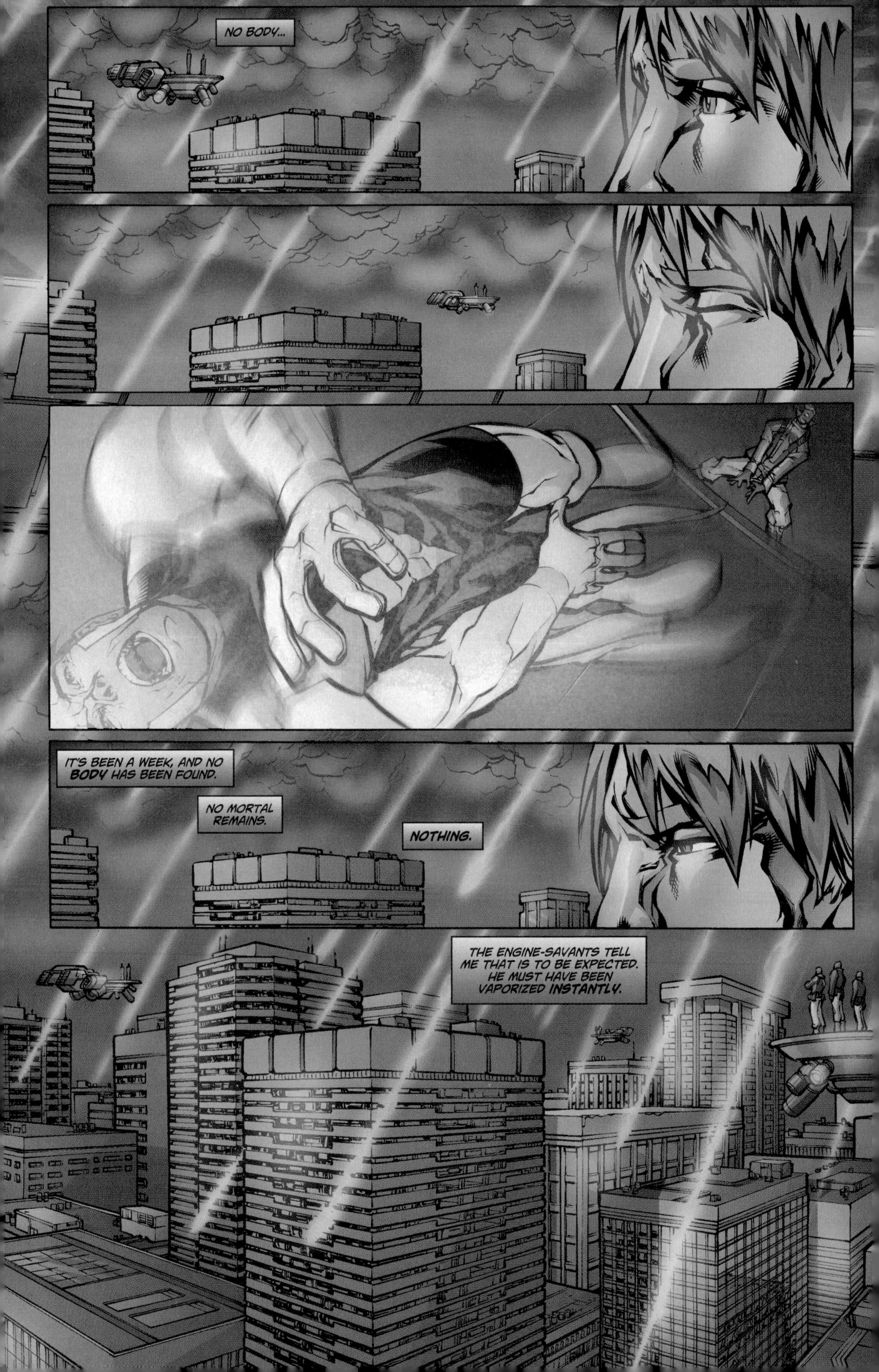
NO BODY...
IT'S BEEN A WEEK, AND NO BODY HAS BEEN FOUND.
NO MORTAL REMAINS.
NOTHING.
THE ENGINE-SAVANTS TELL ME THAT IS TO BE EXPECTED. HE MUST HAVE BEEN VAPORIZED INSTANTLY.

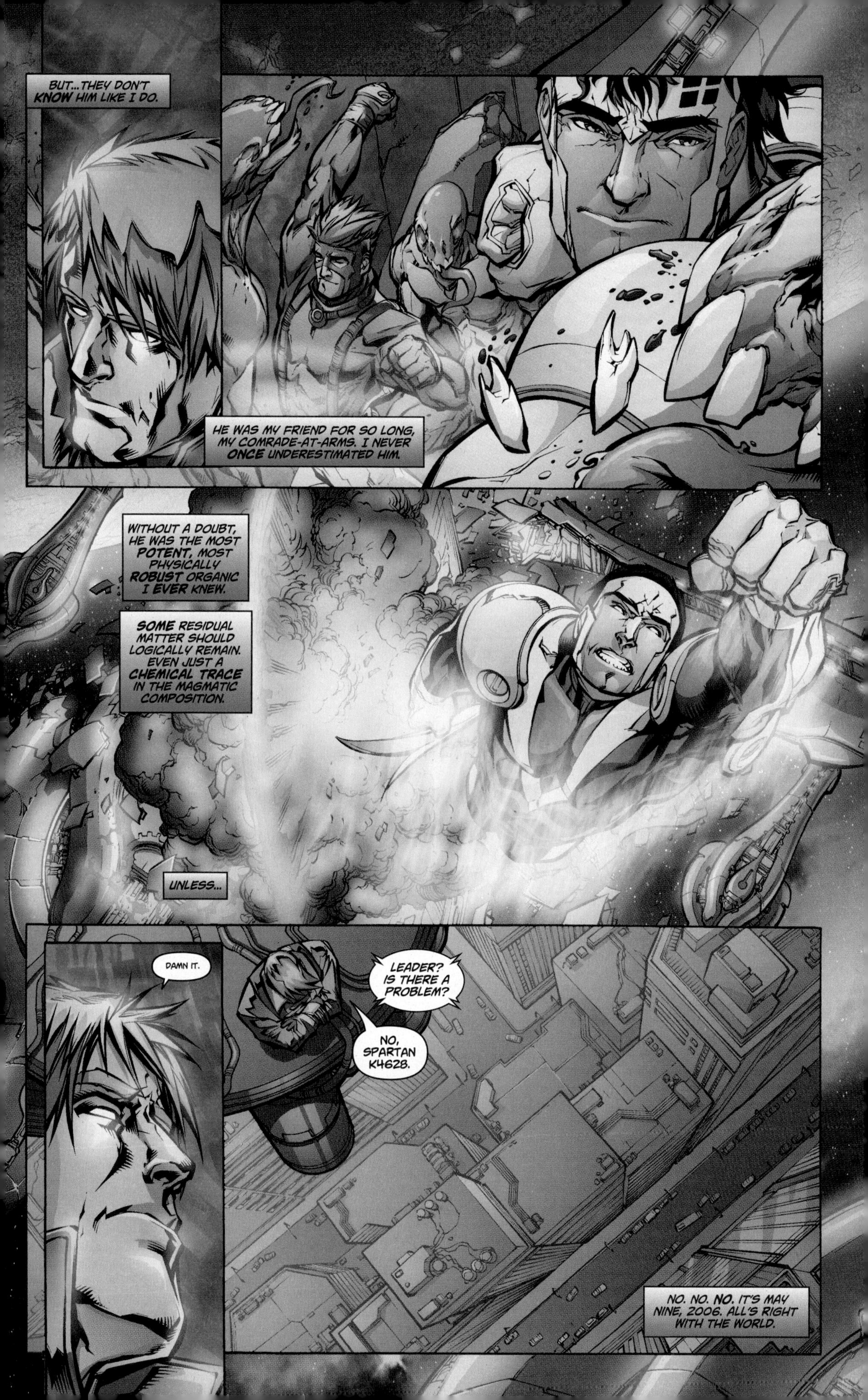
BUT...THEY DON'T KNOW HIM LIKE I DO.
HE WAS MY FRIEND FOR SO LONG, MY COMRADE-AT-ARMS. I NEVER ONCE UNDERESTIMATED HIM.
WITHOUT A DOUBT, HE WAS THE MOST POTENT, MOST PHYSICALLY ROBUST ORGANIC I EVER KNEW.
SOME RESIDUAL MATTER SHOULD LOGICALLY REMAIN. EVEN JUST A CHEMICAL TRACE IN THE MAGMATIC COMPOSITION.
UNLESS...
DAMN IT.
LEADER? IS THERE A PROBLEM?
NO, SPARTAN K4628.
NO. NO. NO. IT'S MAY NINE, 2006. ALL'S RIGHT WITH THE WORLD.

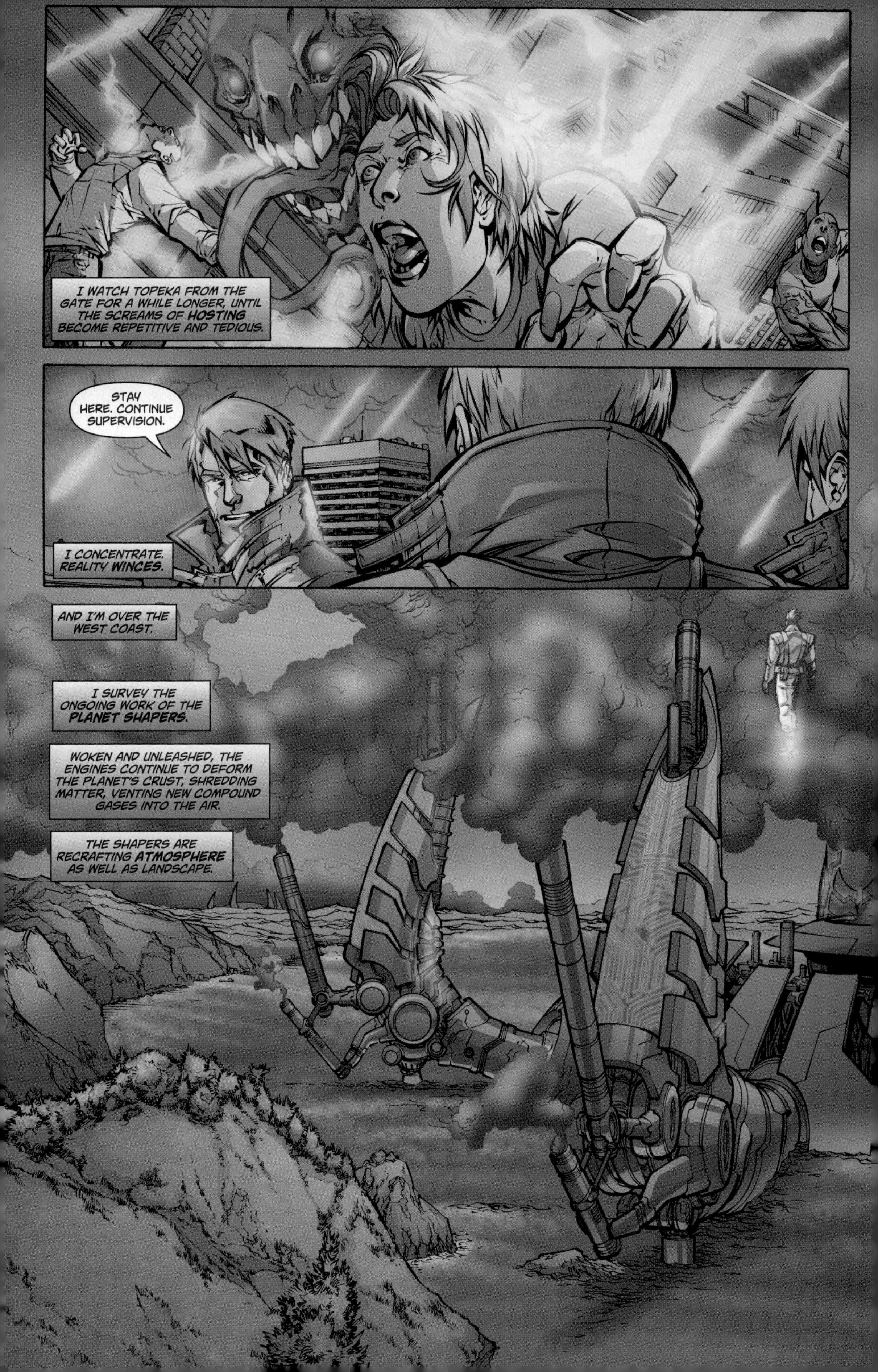

I WATCH TOPEKA FROM THE GATE FOR A WHILE LONGER, UNTIL THE SCREAMS OF HOSTING BECOME REPETITIVE AND TEDIOUS.
STAY HERE. CONTINUE SUPERVISION.
I CONCENTRATE. REALITY WINCES.
AND I'M OVER THE WEST COAST.
I SURVEY THE ONGOING WORK OF THE PLANET SHAPERS.
WOKEN AND UNLEASHED, THE ENGINES CONTINUE TO DEFORM THE PLANET'S CRUST, SHREDDING MATTER, VENTING NEW COMPOUND GASES INTO THE AIR.
THE SHAPERS ARE RECRAFTING ATMOSPHERE AS WELL AS LANDSCAPE.

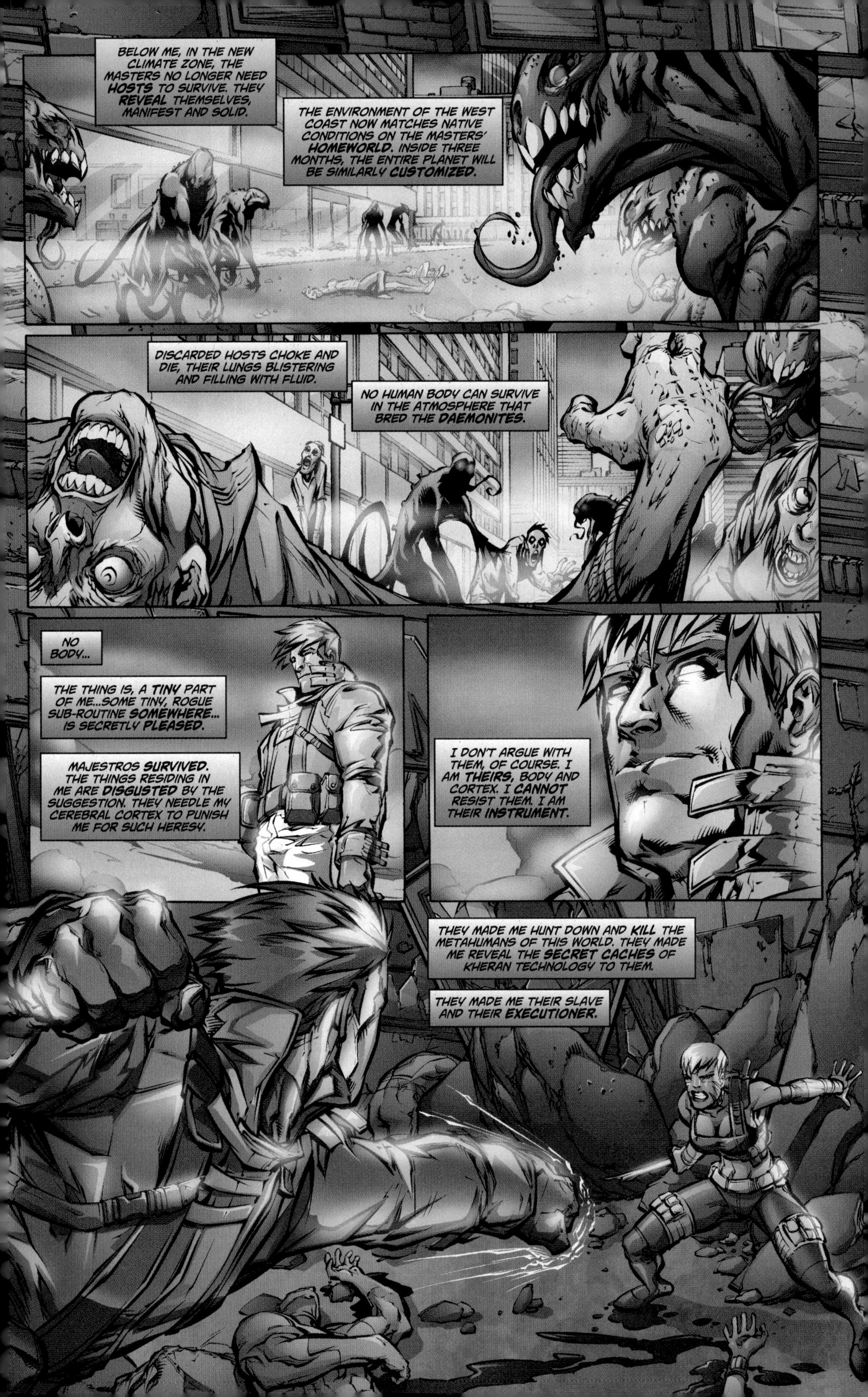
BELOW ME, IN THE NEW CLIMATE ZONE, THE MASTERS NO LONGER NEED HOSTS TO SURVIVE. THEY REVEAL THEMSELVES, MANIFEST AND SOLID.
THE ENVIRONMENT OF THE WEST COAST NOW MATCHES NATIVE CONDITIONS ON THE MASTERS' HOMEWORLD. INSIDE THREE MONTHS, THE ENTIRE PLANET WILL BE SIMILARLY CUSTOMIZED.
DISCARDED HOSTS CHOKE AND DIE, THEIR LUNGS BLISTERING AND FILLING WITH FLUID.
NO HUMAN BODY CAN SURVIVE IN THE ATMOSPHERE THAT BRED THE DAEMONITES.
NO BODY...
THE THING IS, A TINY PART OF ME...SOME TINY, ROGUE SUB-ROUTINE SOMEWHERE... IS SECRETLY PLEASED.
MAJESTROS SURVIVED. THE THINGS RESIDING IN ME ARE DISGUSTED BY THE SUGGESTION. THEY NEEDLE MY CEREBRAL CORTEX TO PUNISH ME FOR SUCH HERESY.
I DON'T ARGUE WITH THEM, OF COURSE. I AM THEIRS, BODY AND CORTEX. I CANNOT RESIST THEM. I AM THEIR INSTRUMENT.
THEY MADE ME HUNT DOWN AND KILL THE METAHUMANS OF THIS WORLD. THEY MADE ME REVEAL THE SECRET CACHES OF KHERAN TECHNOLOGY TO THEM.
THEY MADE ME THEIR SLAVE AND THEIR EXECUTIONER.

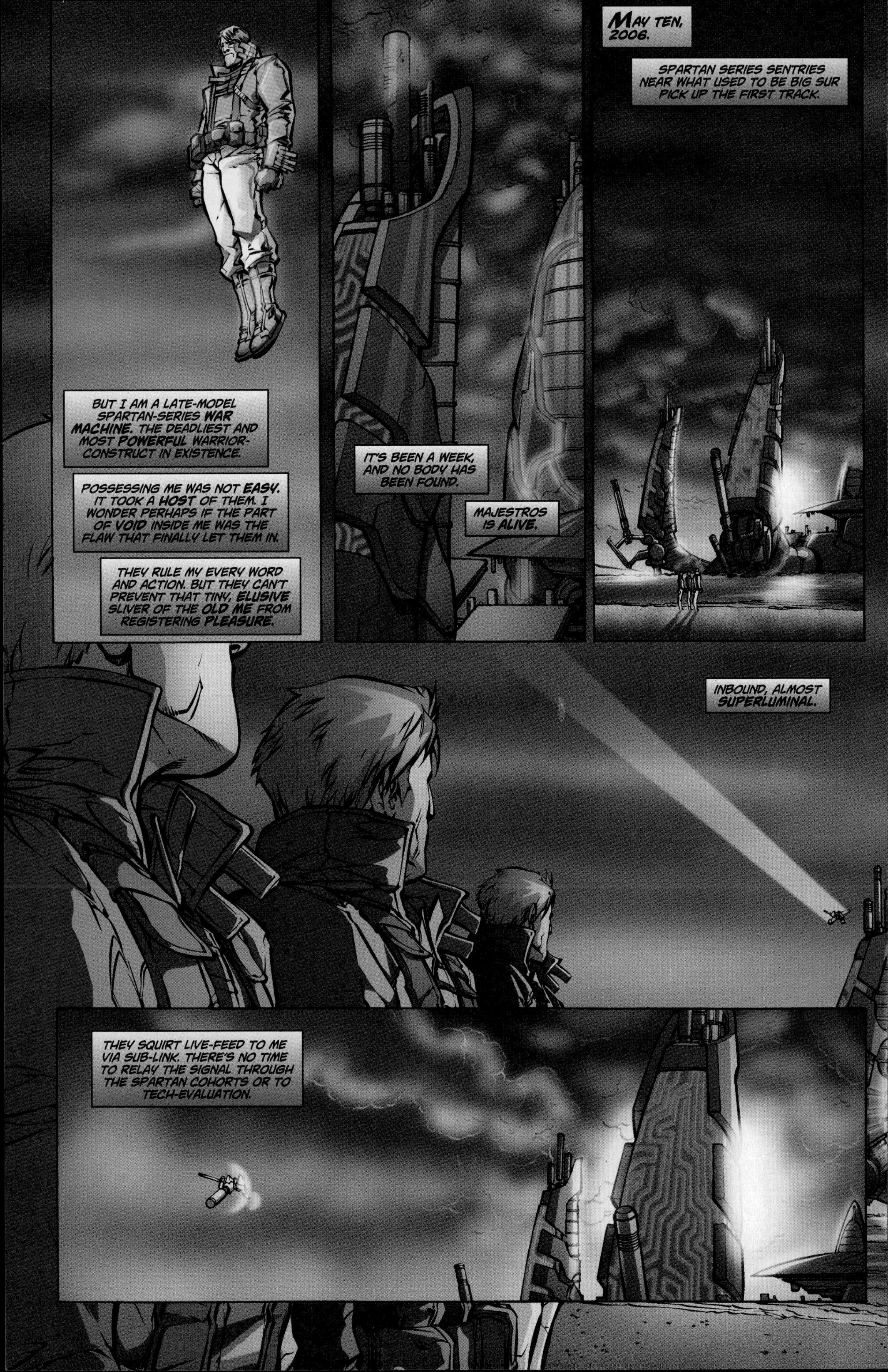
BUT I AM A LATE-MODEL SPARTAN-SERIES WAR MACHINE. THE DEADLIEST AND MOST POWERFUL WARRIOR-CONSTRUCT IN EXISTENCE.
POSSESSING ME WAS NOT EASY. IT TOOK A HOST OF THEM. I WONDER PERHAPS IF THE PART OF VOID INSIDE ME WAS THE FLAW THAT FINALLY LET THEM IN.
THEY RULE MY EVERY WORD AND ACTION. BUT THEY CAN'T PREVENT THAT TINY, ELUSIVE SLIVER OF THE OLD ME FROM REGISTERING PLEASURE.
IT'S BEEN A WEEK, AND NO BODY HAS BEEN FOUND.
MAJESTROS IS ALIVE.
MAY TEN, 2006.
SPARTAN SERIES SENTRIES NEAR WHAT USED TO BE BIG SUR PICK UP THE FIRST TRACK.
INBOUND, ALMOST SUPERLUMINAL.
THEY SQUIRT LIVE-FEED TO ME VIA SUB-LINK. THERE'S NO TIME TO RELAY THE SIGNAL THROUGH THE SPARTAN COHORTS OR TO TECH-EVALUATION.

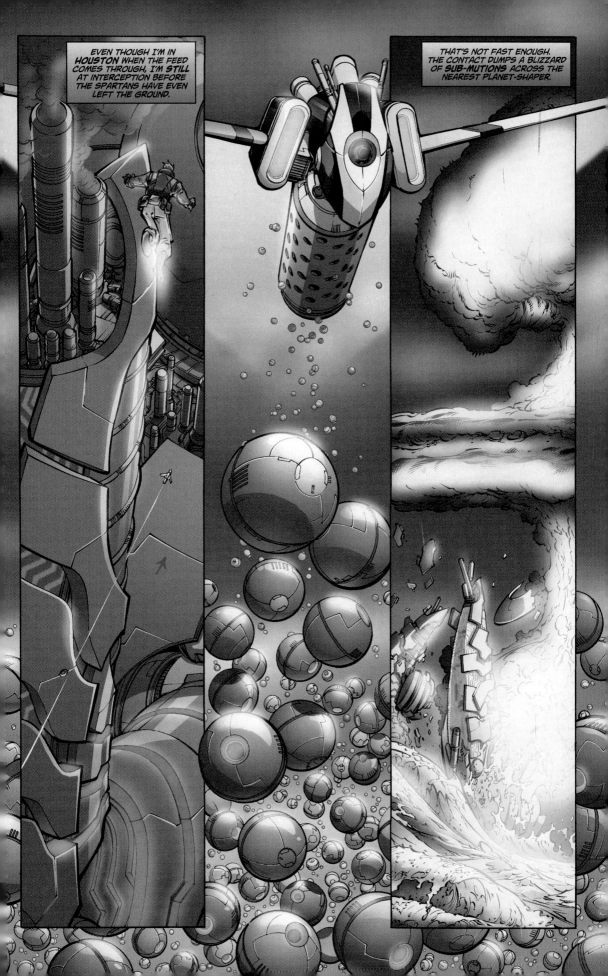

EVEN THOUGH I'M IN HOUSTON WHEN THE FEED COMES THROUGH, I'M STILL AT INTERCEPTION BEFORE THE SPARTANS HAVE EVEN LEFT THE GROUND.

THAT'S NOT FAST ENOUGH. THE CONTACT DUMPS A BLIZZARD OF SUB-MUTIONS ACROSS THE NEAREST PLANET-SHAPER.

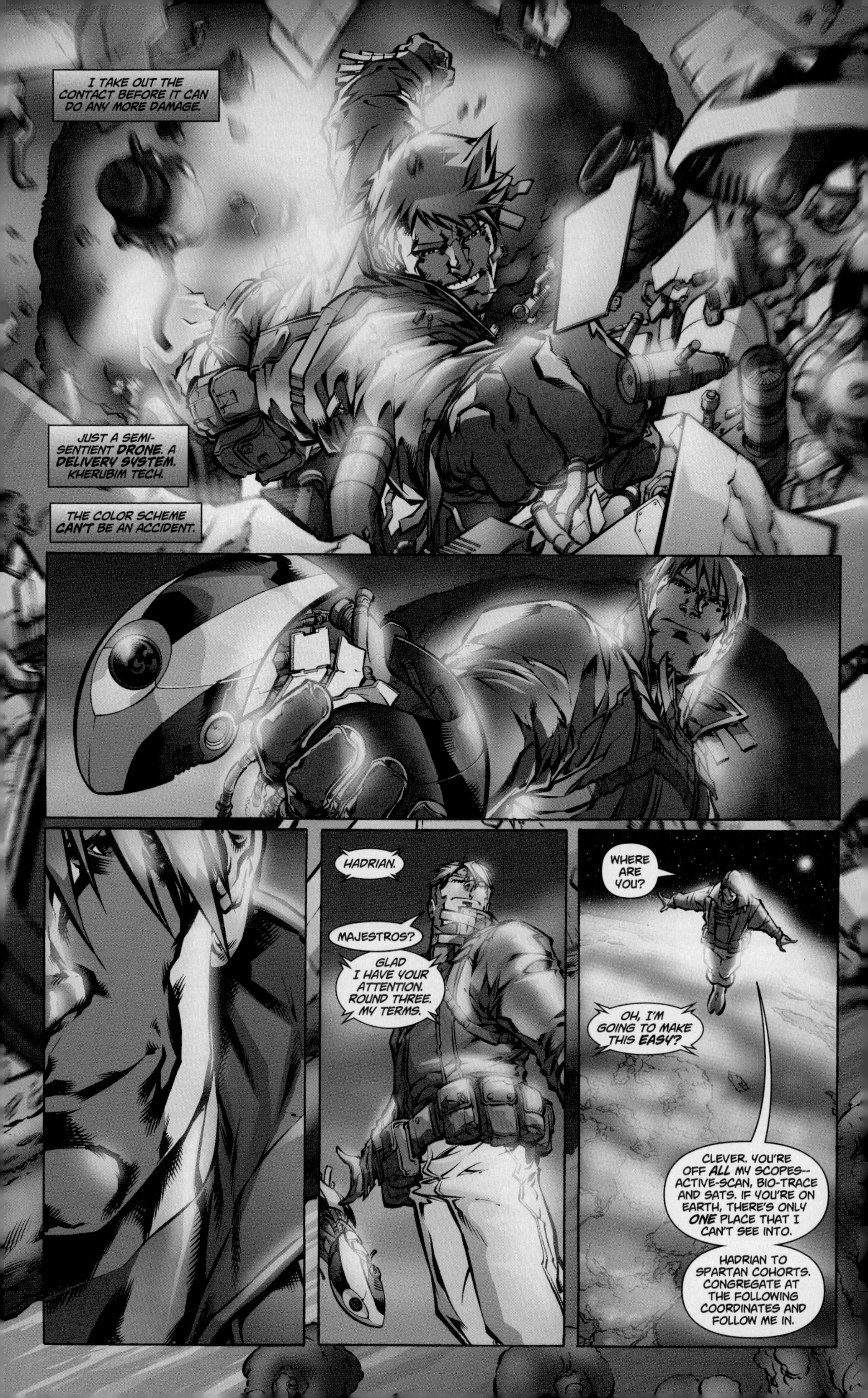
I TAKE OUT THE CONTACT BEFORE IT CAN DO ANY MORE DAMAGE.
JUST A SEMI-SENTIENT DRONE. A DELIVERY SYSTEM. KHERUBIM TECH.
THE COLOR SCHEME CAN'T BE AN ACCIDENT.
HADRIAN.
MAJESTROS?
GLAD I HAVE YOUR ATTENTION. ROUND THREE. MY TERMS.
WHERE ARE YOU?
OH, I'M GOING TO MAKE THIS EASY?
CLEVER. YOU'RE OFF ALL MY SCOPES-- ACTIVE-SCAN, BIO-TRACE AND SATS. IF YOU'RE ON EARTH, THERE'S ONLY ONE PLACE THAT I CAN'T SEE INTO.
HADRIAN TO SPARTAN COHORTS. CONGREGATE AT THE FOLLOWING COORDINATES AND FOLLOW ME IN.

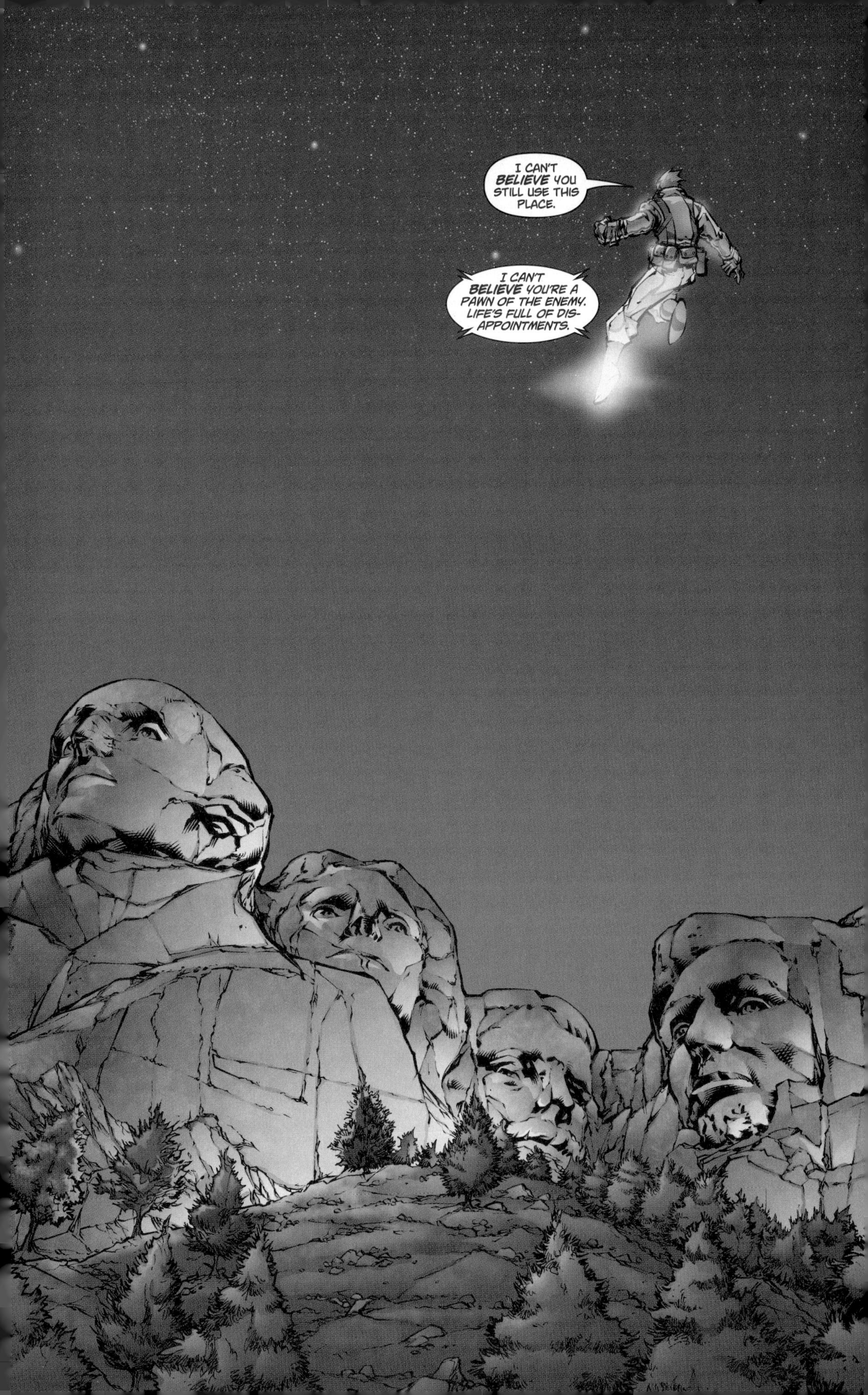
I CAN'T BELIEVE YOU STILL USE THIS PLACE.
I CAN'T BELIEVE YOU'RE A PAWN OF THE ENEMY. LIFE'S FULL OF DIS-APPOINTMENTS.

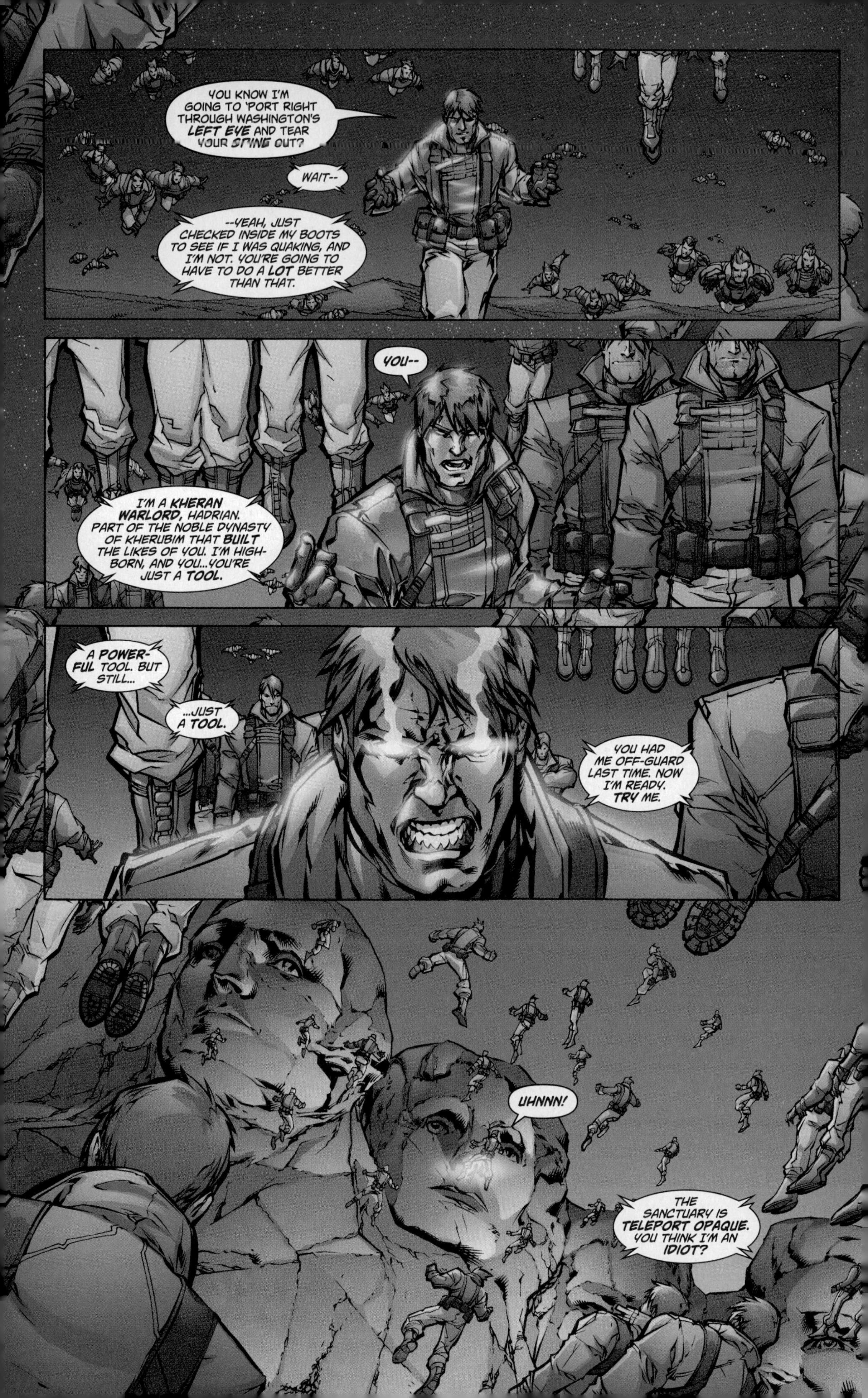
YOU KNOW I'M GOING TO 'PORT RIGHT THROUGH WASHINGTON'S LEFT EYE AND TEAR YOUR SPINE OUT?
WAIT--
--YEAH, JUST CHECKED INSIDE MY BOOTS TO SEE IF I WAS QUAKING, AND I'M NOT. YOU'RE GOING TO HAVE TO DO A LOT BETTER THAN THAT.
YOU--
I'M A KHERAN WARLORD, HADRIAN. PART OF THE NOBLE DYNASTY OF KHERUBIM THAT BUILT THE LIKES OF YOU. I'M HIGH-BORN, AND YOU...YOU'RE JUST A TOOL.
A POWER-FUL TOOL. BUT STILL...
...JUST A TOOL.
YOU HAD ME OFF-GUARD LAST TIME. NOW I'M READY. TRY ME.
UHNNN!
THE SANCTUARY IS TELEPORT OPAQUE. YOU THINK I'M AN IDIOT?

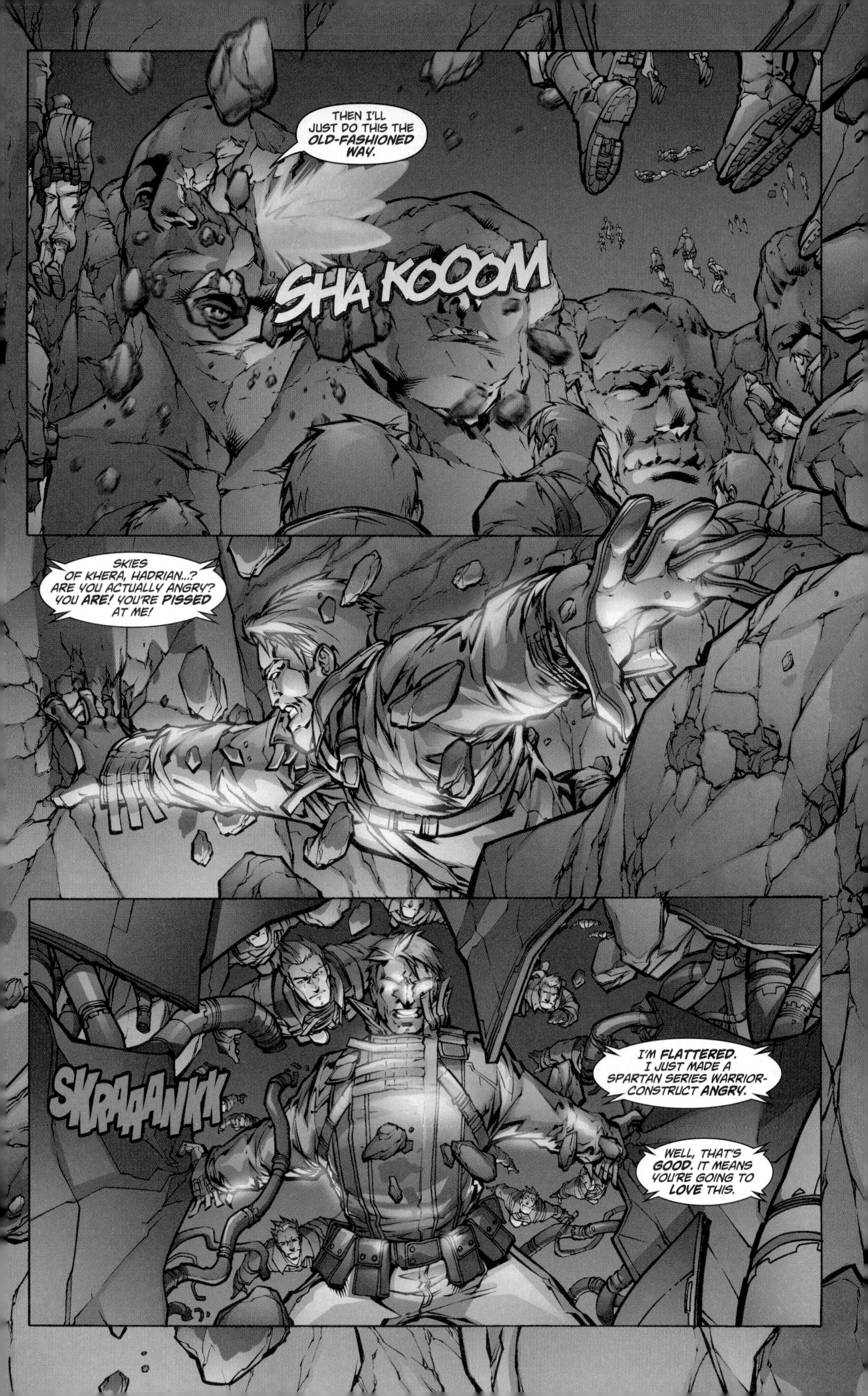
THEN I'LL JUST DO THIS THE OLD-FASHIONED WAY.
SHA KOOOM
SKIES OF KHERA, HADRIAN...? ARE YOU ACTUALLY ANGRY? YOU ARE! YOU'RE PISSED AT ME!
SKRAAAANKK
I'M FLATTERED. I JUST MADE A SPARTAN SERIES WARRIOR-CONSTRUCT ANGRY.
WELL, THAT'S GOOD. IT MEANS YOU'RE GOING TO LOVE THIS.

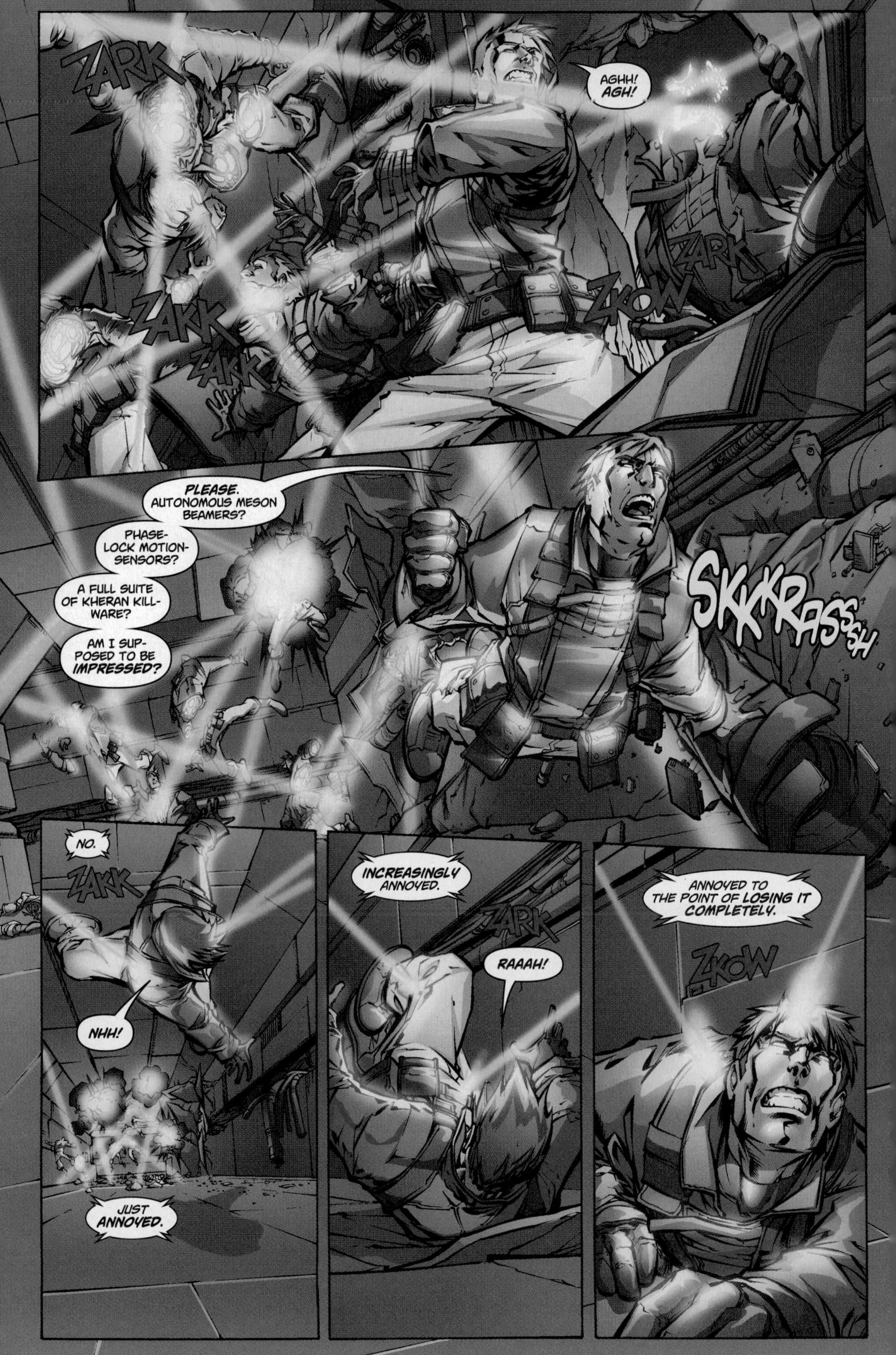
ZARK
AGHH! AGH!
ZARK
ZAKK
ZAKK
ZKOW
PLEASE. AUTONOMOUS MESON BEAMERS?
PHASE-LOCK MOTION-SENSORS?
A FULL SUITE OF KHERAN KILL-WARE?
AM I SUP-POSED TO BE IMPRESSED?
SKKKRASSSH
NO.
ZAKK
NHH!
JUST ANNOYED.
INCREASINGLY ANNOYED.
ZARK
RAAAH!
ANNOYED TO THE POINT OF LOSING IT COMPLETELY.
ZKOW

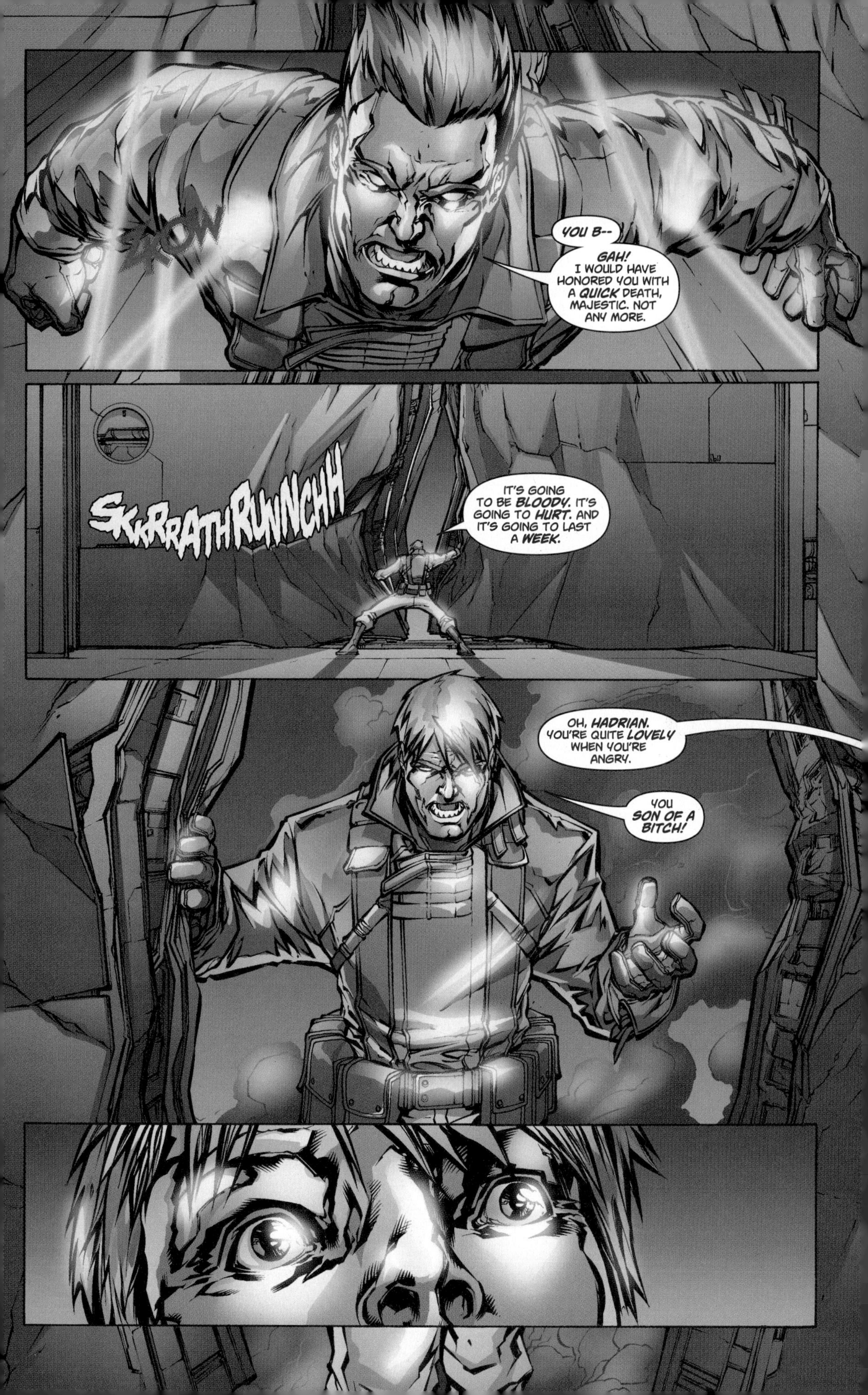

SKKROW
YOU B--
GAH! I WOULD HAVE HONORED YOU WITH A QUICK DEATH, MAJESTIC. NOT ANY MORE.
SKKRRATHRUNNCHH
IT'S GOING TO BE BLOODY. IT'S GOING TO HURT. AND IT'S GOING TO LAST A WEEK.
OH, HADRIAN. YOU'RE QUITE LOVELY WHEN YOU'RE ANGRY.
YOU SON OF A BITCH!

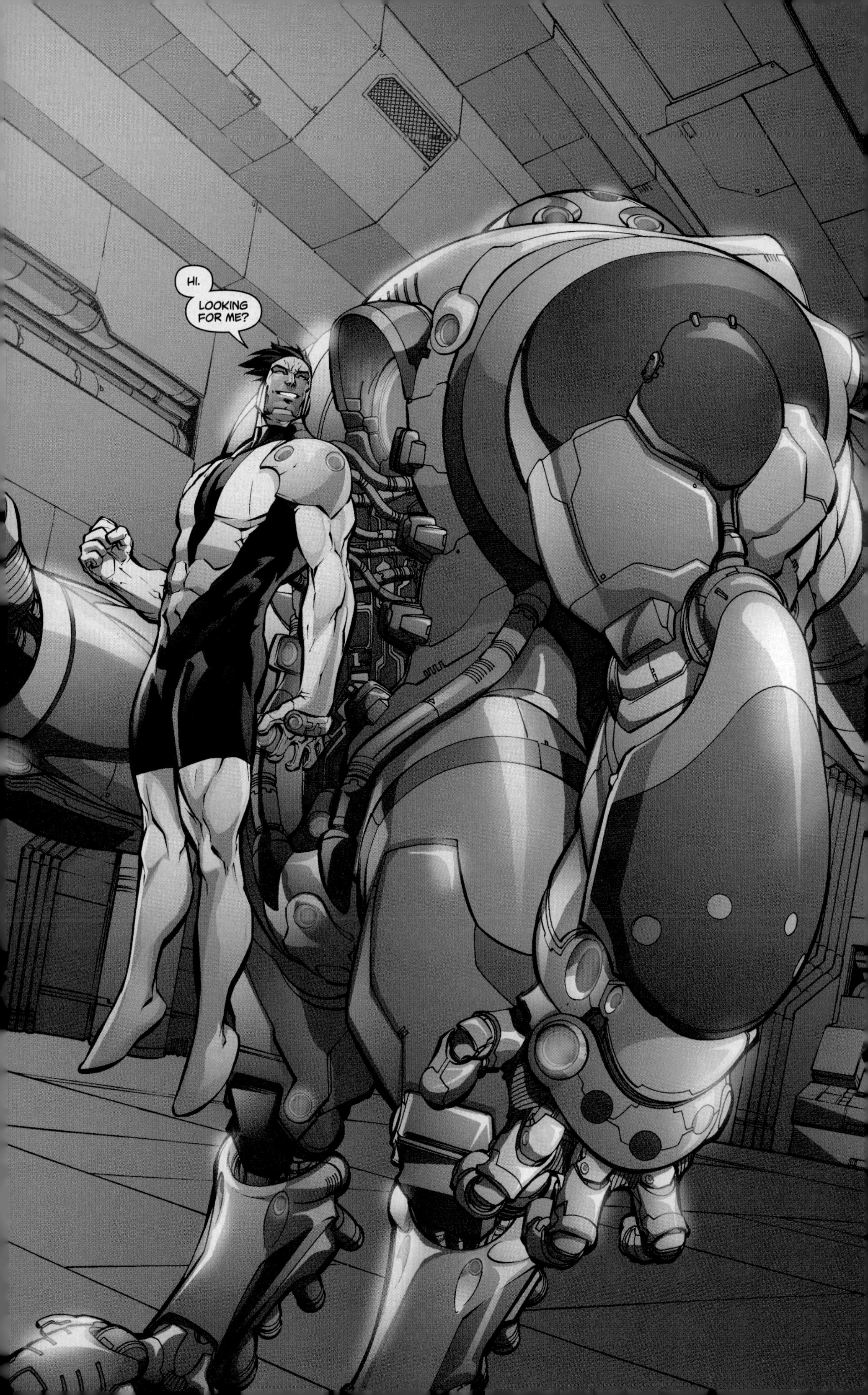
HI.
LOOKING FOR ME?

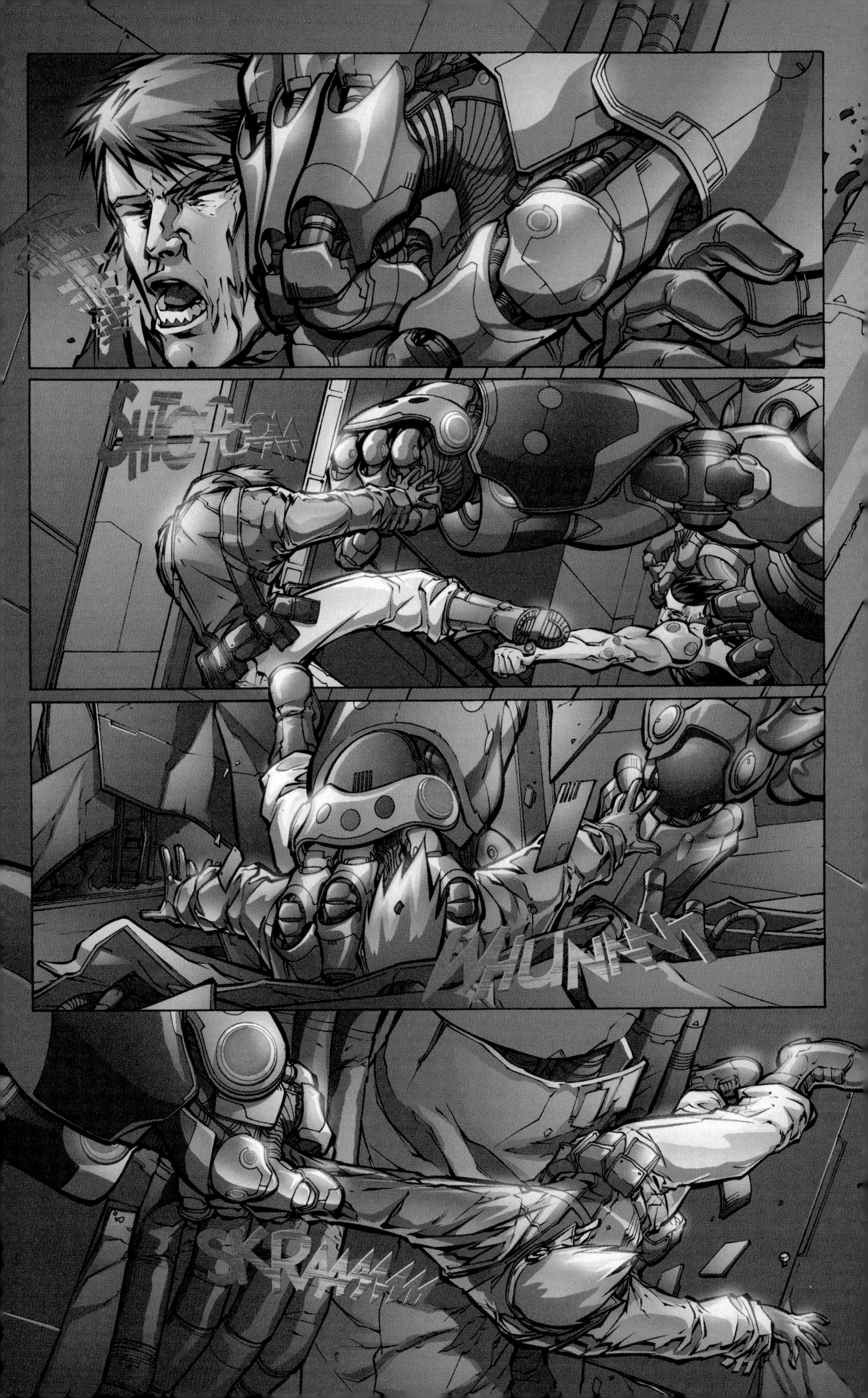
SHTOOM
WHUNNK
SKRAAAAM

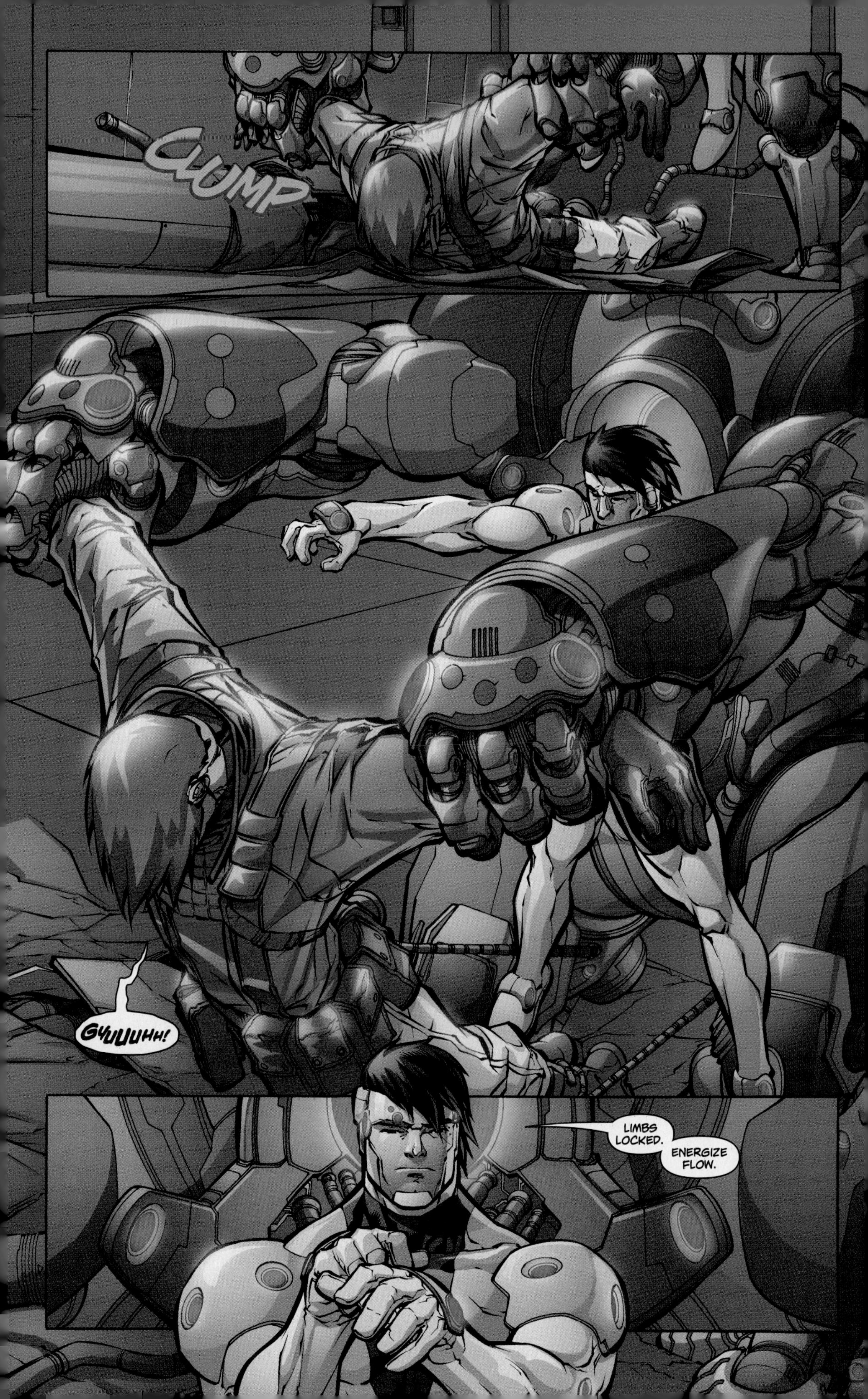
CLUMP
GYUUUHH!
LIMBS LOCKED.
ENERGIZE FLOW.

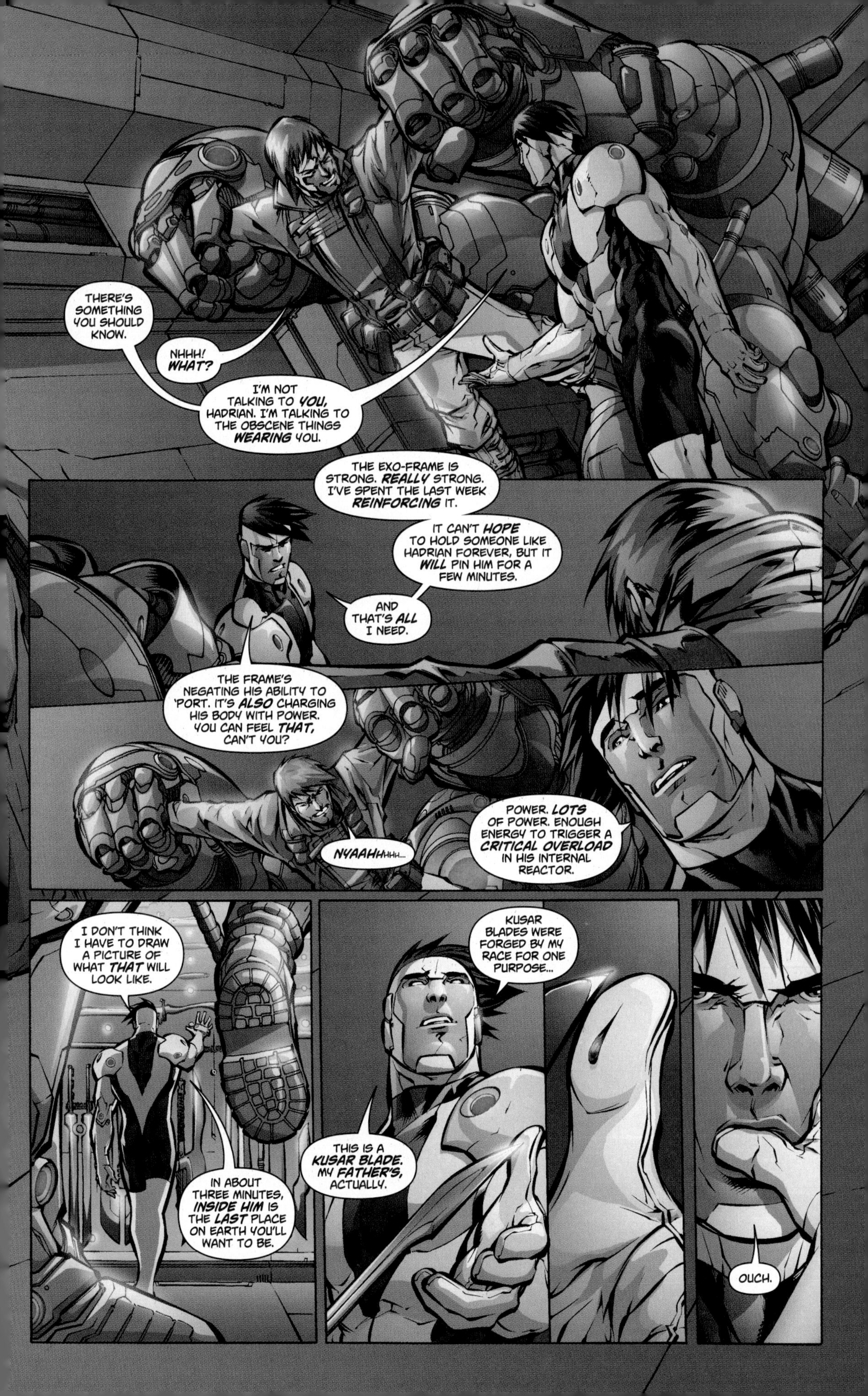
THERE'S SOMETHING YOU SHOULD KNOW.
NHHH! WHAT?
I'M NOT TALKING TO YOU, HADRIAN. I'M TALKING TO THE OBSCENE THINGS WEARING YOU.
THE EXO-FRAME IS STRONG. REALLY STRONG. I'VE SPENT THE LAST WEEK REINFORCING IT.
IT CAN'T HOPE TO HOLD SOMEONE LIKE HADRIAN FOREVER, BUT IT WILL PIN HIM FOR A FEW MINUTES.
AND THAT'S ALL I NEED.
THE FRAME'S NEGATING HIS ABILITY TO 'PORT. IT'S ALSO CHARGING HIS BODY WITH POWER. YOU CAN FEEL THAT, CAN'T YOU?
NYAAHHHHH....
POWER. LOTS OF POWER. ENOUGH ENERGY TO TRIGGER A CRITICAL OVERLOAD IN HIS INTERNAL REACTOR.
I DON'T THINK I HAVE TO DRAW A PICTURE OF WHAT THAT WILL LOOK LIKE.
IN ABOUT THREE MINUTES, INSIDE HIM IS THE LAST PLACE ON EARTH YOU'LL WANT TO BE.
KUSAR BLADES WERE FORGED BY MY RACE FOR ONE PURPOSE...
THIS IS A KUSAR BLADE. MY FATHER'S, ACTUALLY.
OUCH.

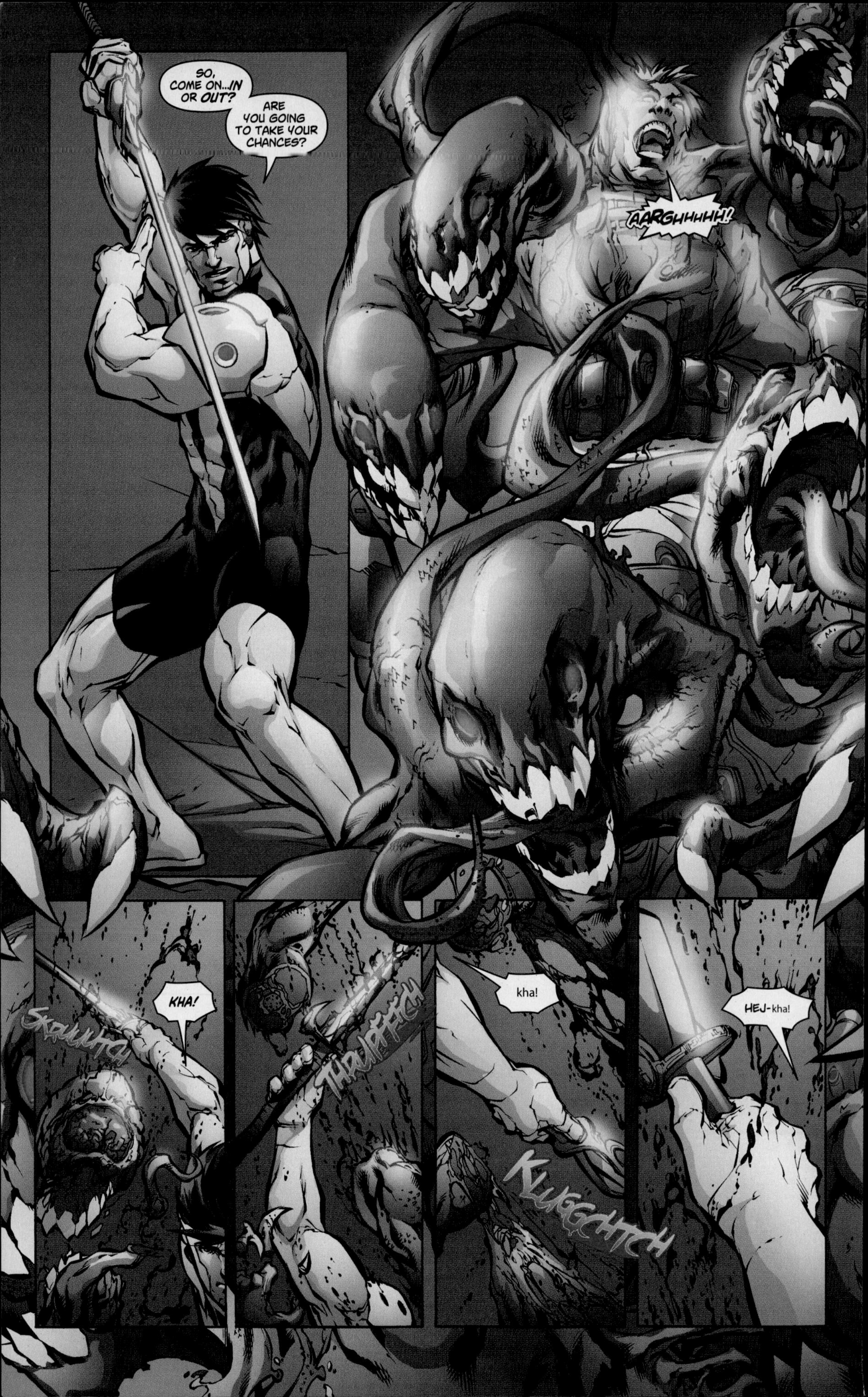
SO, COME ON...IN OR OUT?
ARE YOU GOING TO TAKE YOUR CHANCES?
AARGHHHHH!
SKRUUUTCH
KHA!
THRUPFFCH
kha!
KLUGGCHTCH
HEJ-kha!

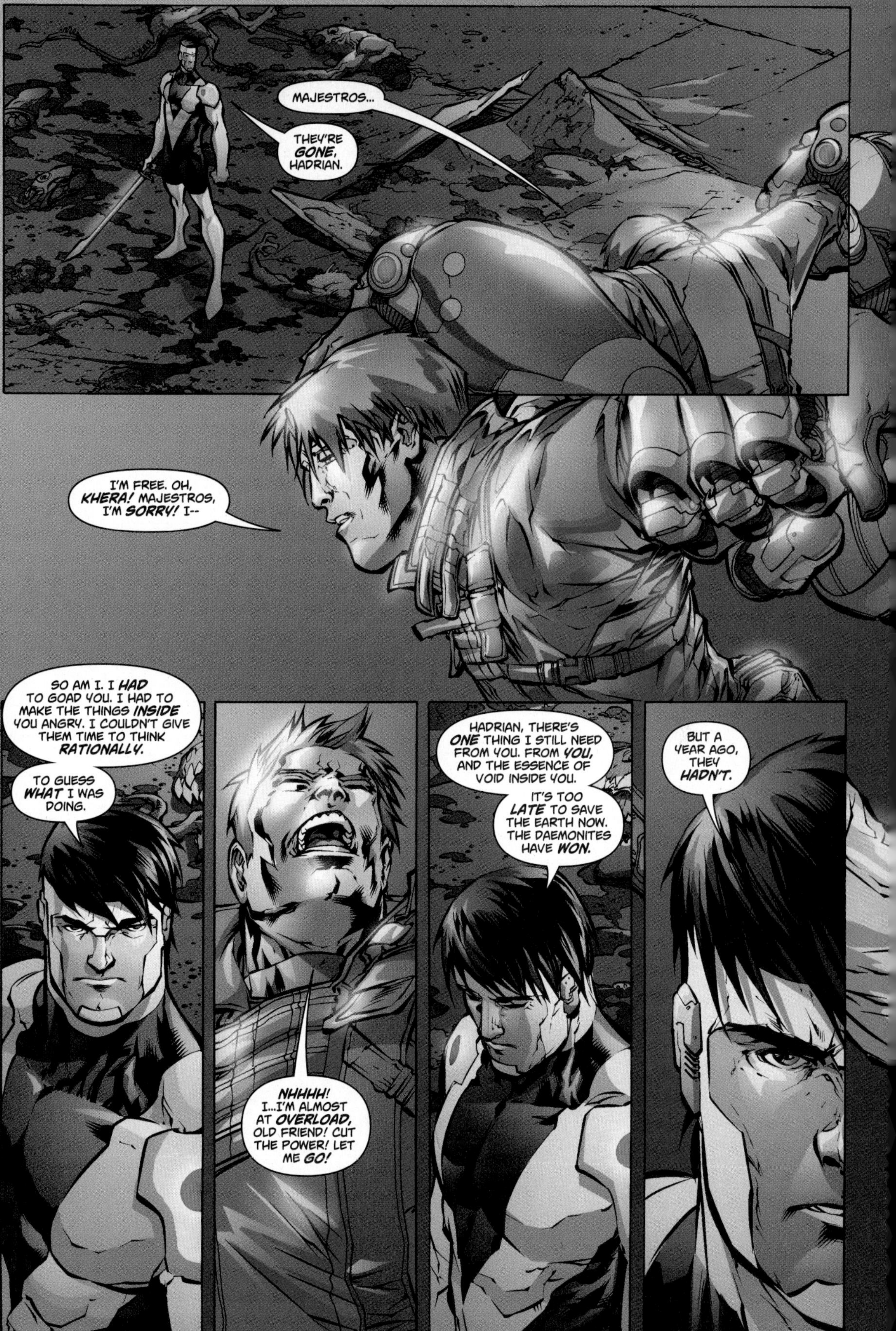
MAJESTROS...
THEY'RE GONE, HADRIAN.
I'M FREE. OH, KHERA! MAJESTROS, I'M SORRY! I--
SO AM I. I HAD TO GOAD YOU. I HAD TO MAKE THE THINGS INSIDE YOU ANGRY. I COULDN'T GIVE THEM TIME TO THINK RATIONALLY.
TO GUESS WHAT I WAS DOING.
NHHHH! I...I'M ALMOST AT OVERLOAD, OLD FRIEND! CUT THE POWER! LET ME GO!
HADRIAN, THERE'S ONE THING I STILL NEED FROM YOU. FROM YOU, AND THE ESSENCE OF VOID INSIDE YOU.
IT'S TOO LATE TO SAVE THE EARTH NOW. THE DAEMONITES HAVE WON.
BUT A YEAR AGO, THEY HADN'T.

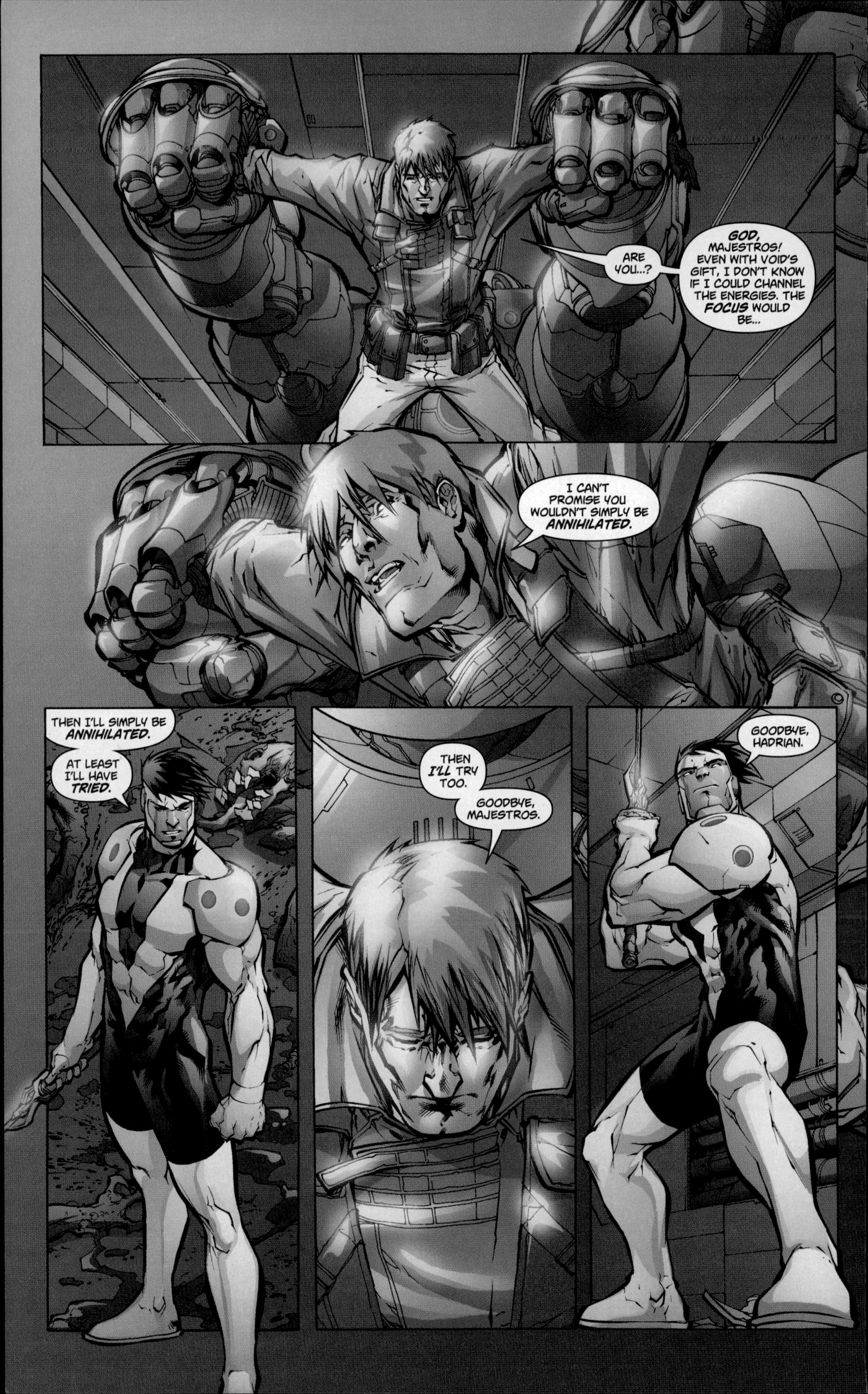
GOD, MAJESTROS! EVEN WITH VOID'S GIFT, I DON'T KNOW IF I COULD CHANNEL THE ENERGIES. THE FOCUS WOULD BE...
ARE YOU...?
I CAN'T PROMISE YOU WOULDN'T SIMPLY BE ANNIHILATED.
THEN I'LL SIMPLY BE ANNIHILATED.
AT LEAST I'LL HAVE TRIED.
THEN I'LL TRY TOO.
GOODBYE, MAJESTROS.
GOODBYE, HADRIAN.

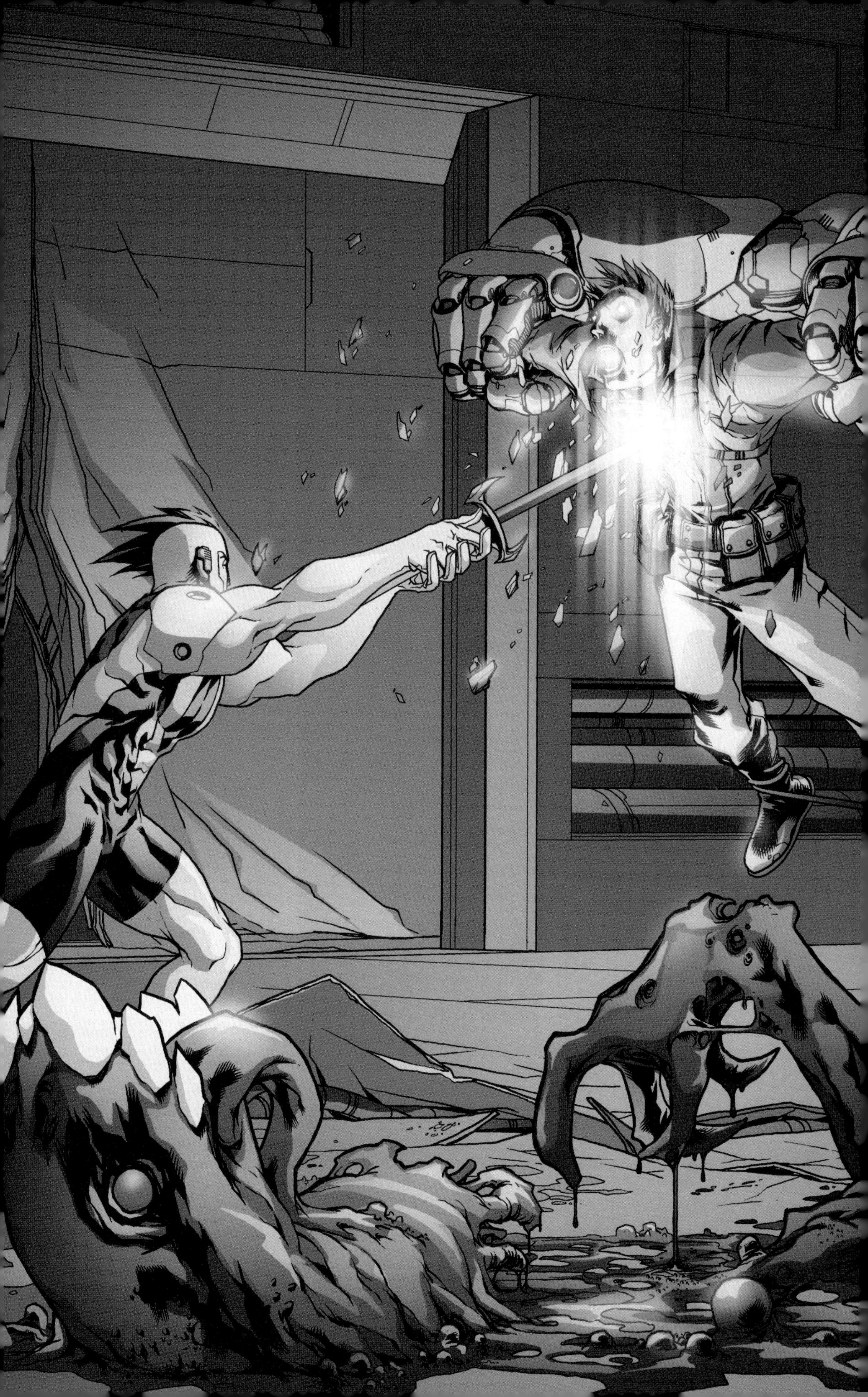

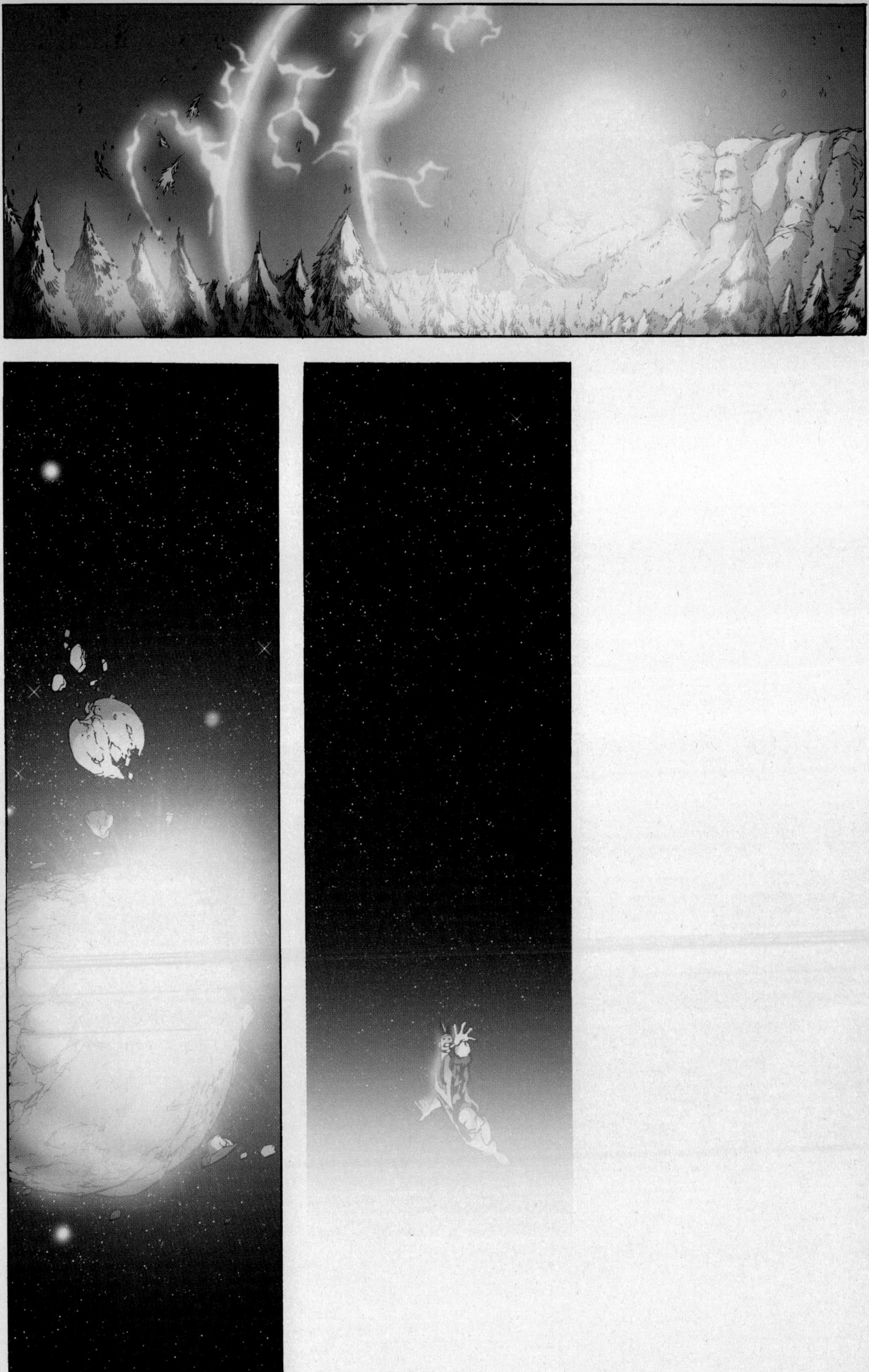

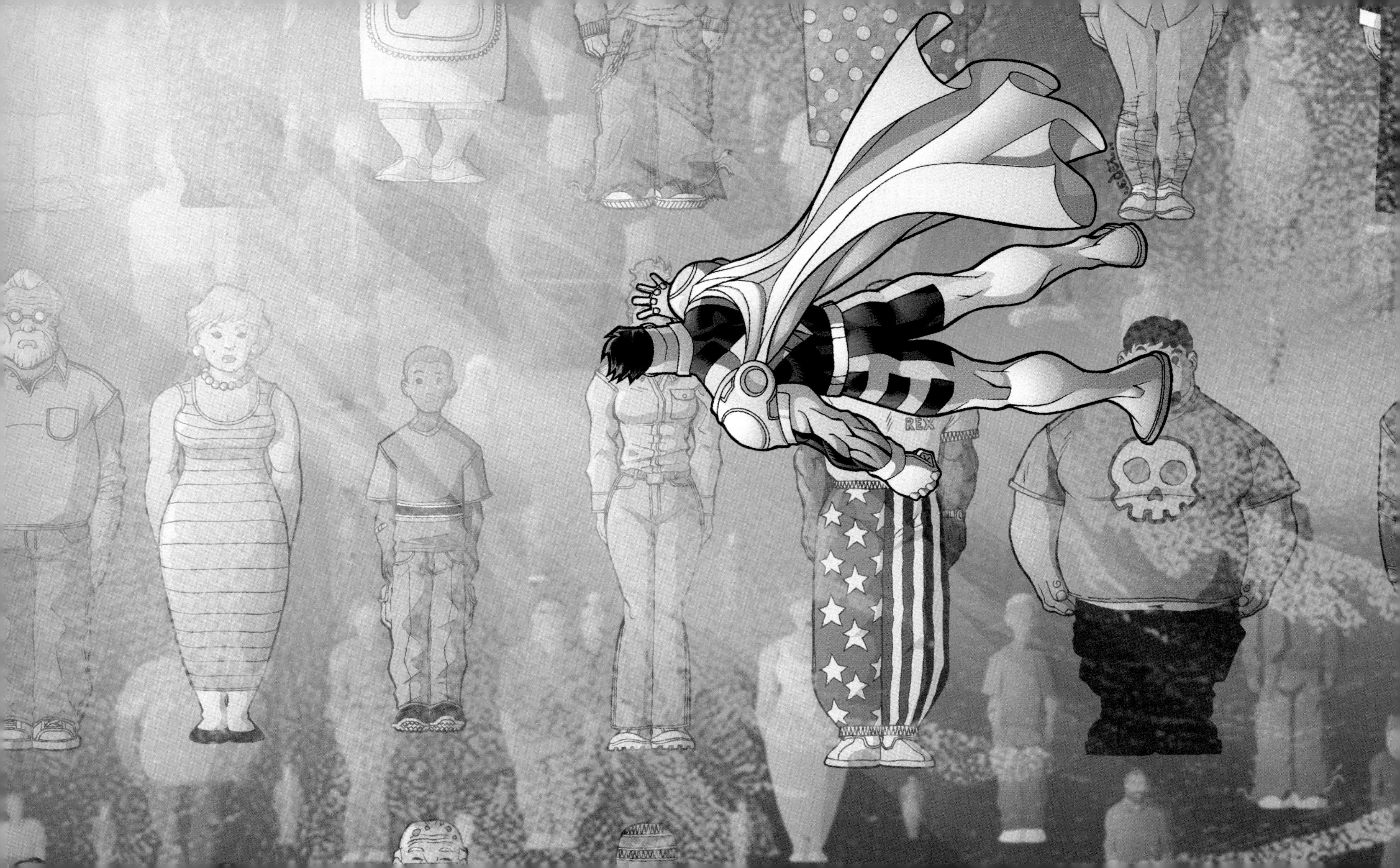
REX

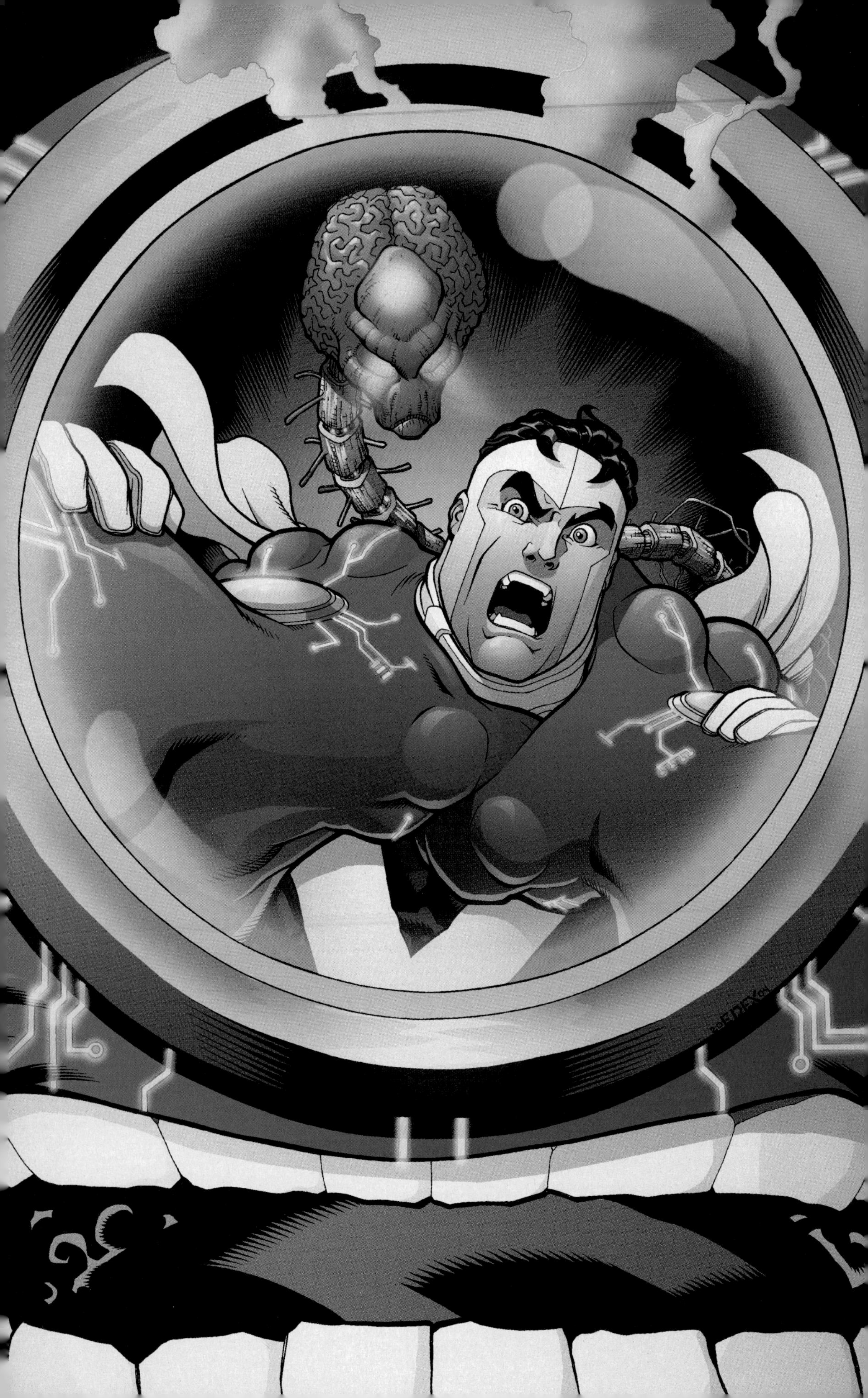

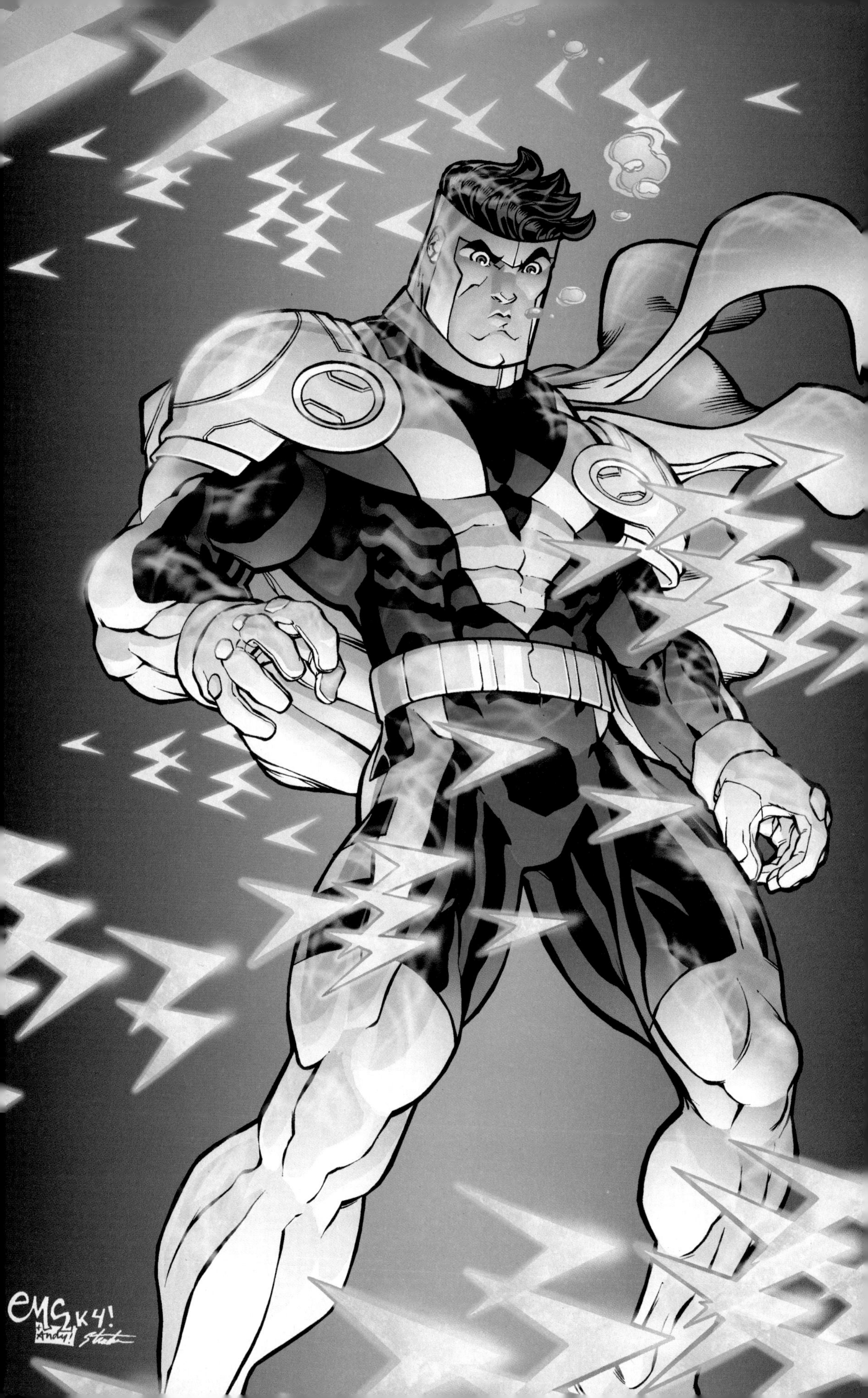

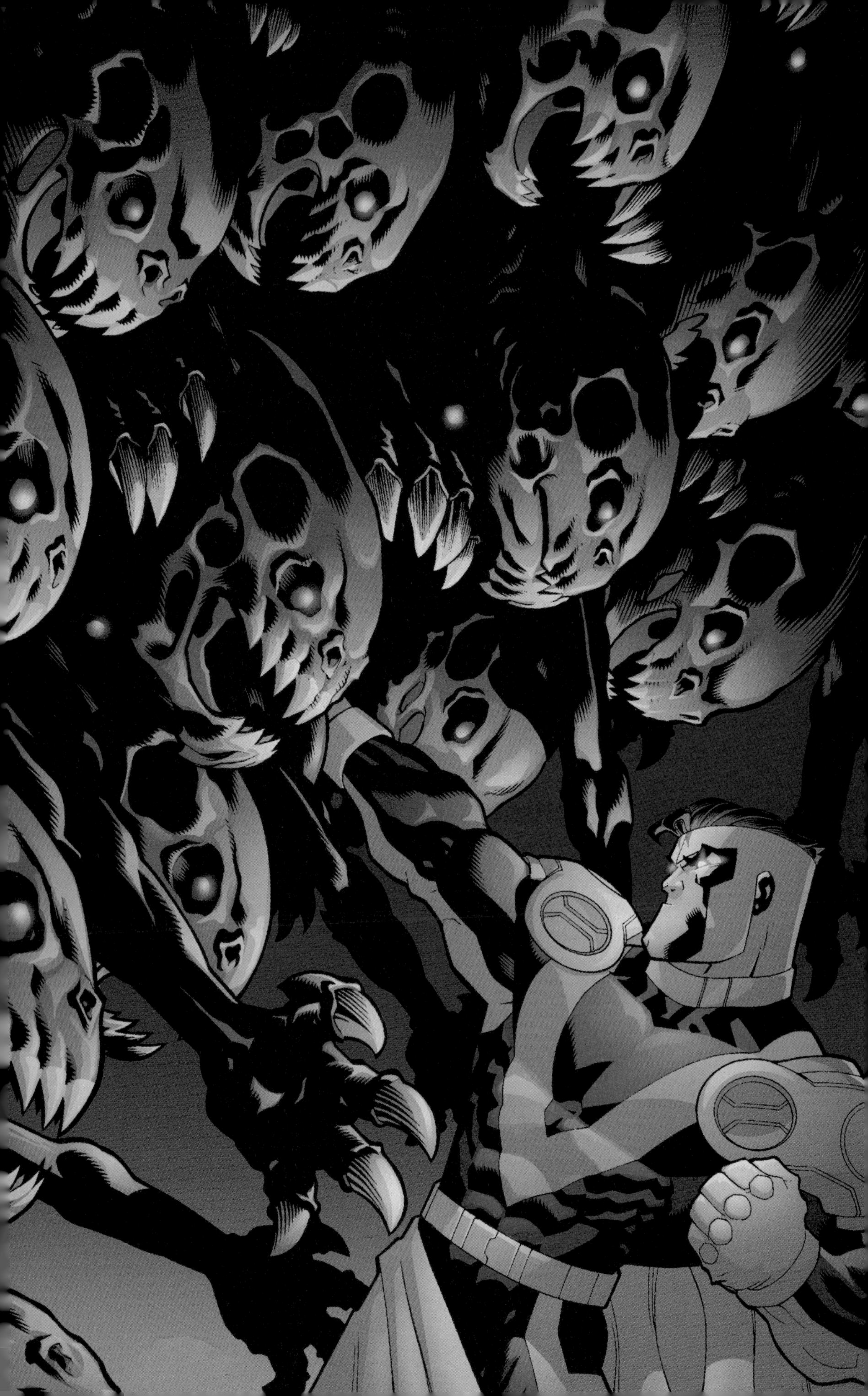

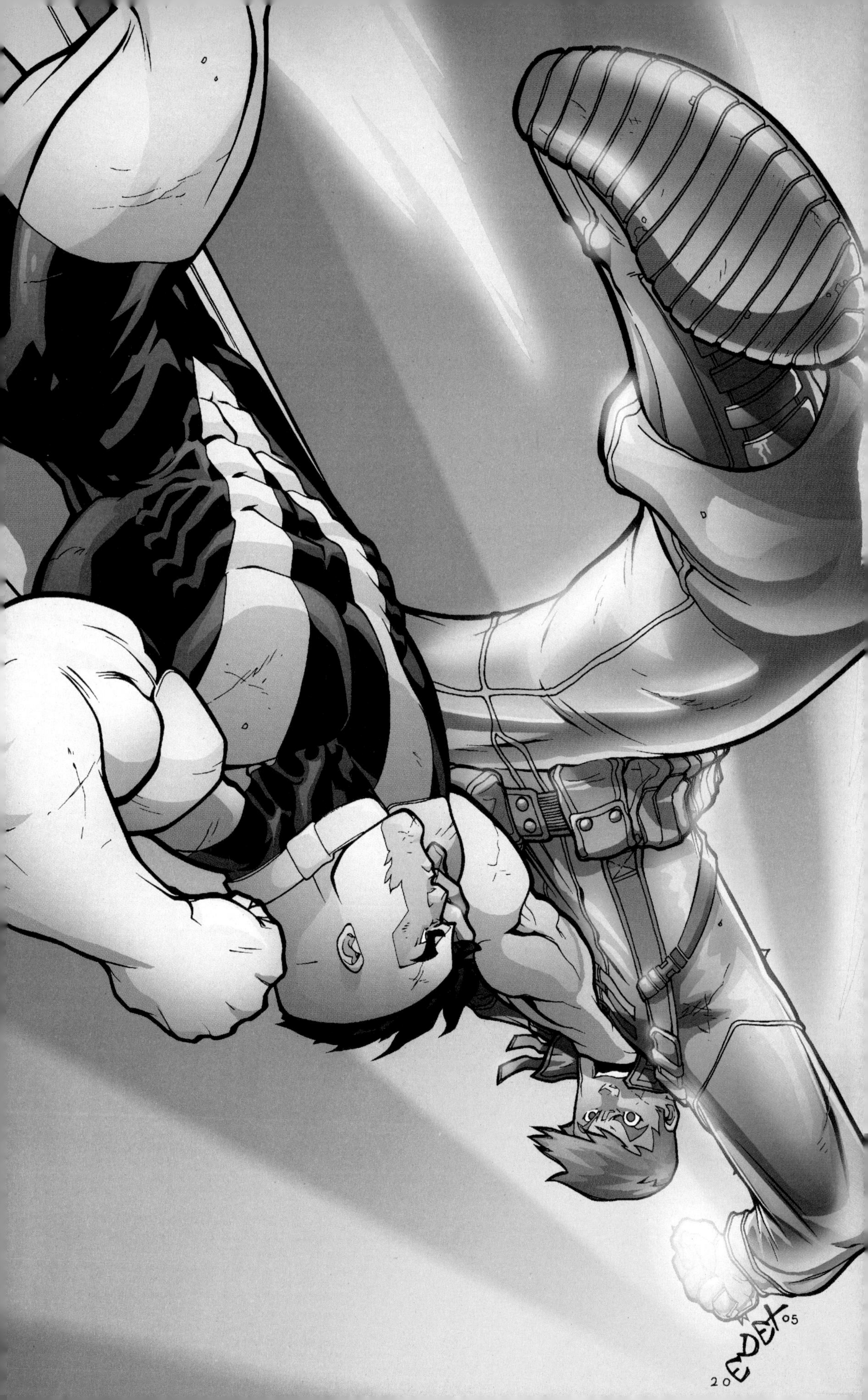

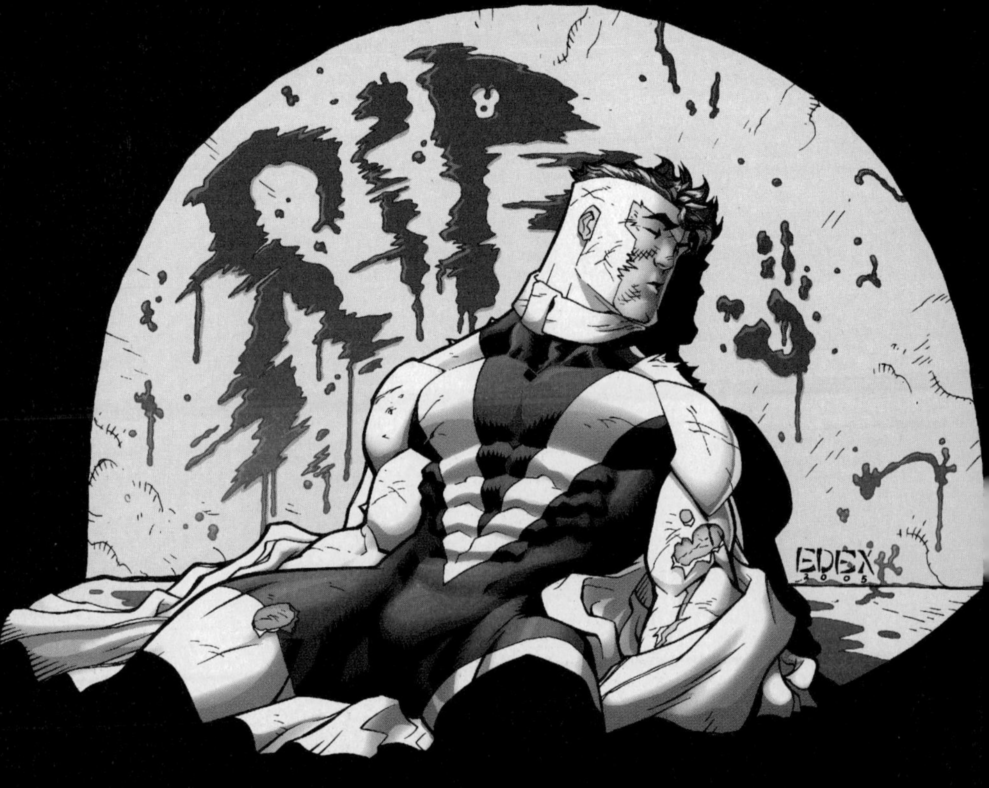
RIP

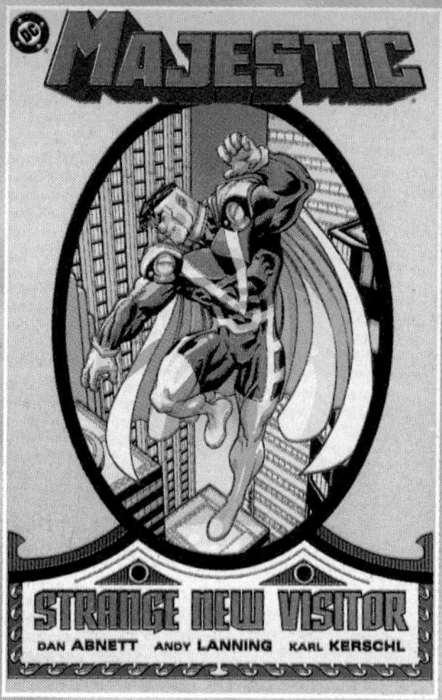
MAJESTIC
STRANGE NEW VISITOR
DAN ABNETT ANDY LANNING KARL KERSCHL

MAJESTIC:
STRANGE NEW VISITOR

ABNETT/LANNING/KERSCHL

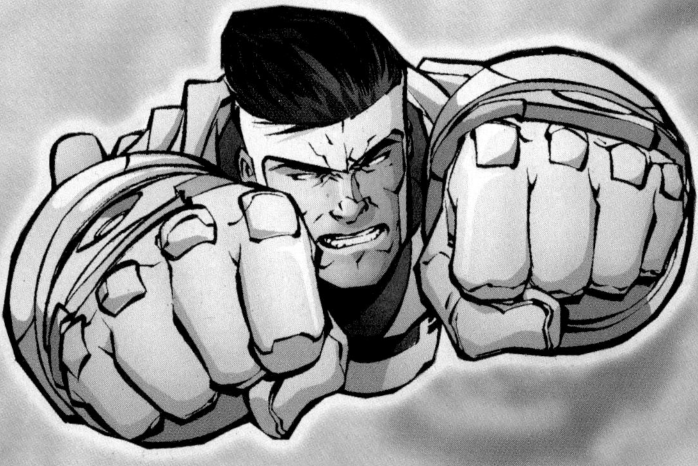

call 1-888-comic book for the nearest comics shop or go to your local book store.

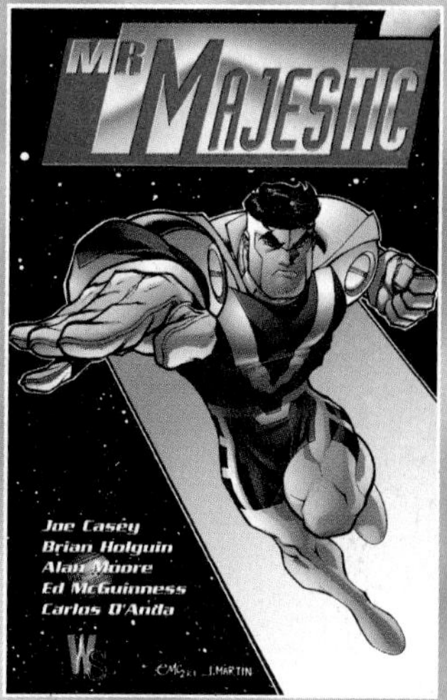
MR MAJESTIC
Joe Casey
Brian Holguin
Alan Moore
Ed McGuinness
Carlos D'Anda

MR. MAJESTIC

CASEY/HOLGUIN/MOORE
MCGUINNESS/D'ANDA

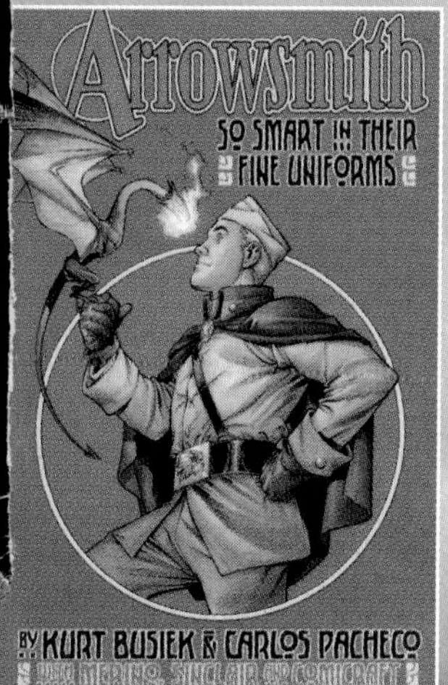
Arrowsmith
SO SMART IN THEIR FINE UNIFORMS
BY KURT BUSIEK & CARLOS PACHECO

ARROWSMITH:
SO SMART IN THEIR FINE UNIFORMS

BUSIEK/PACHECO/MERINO

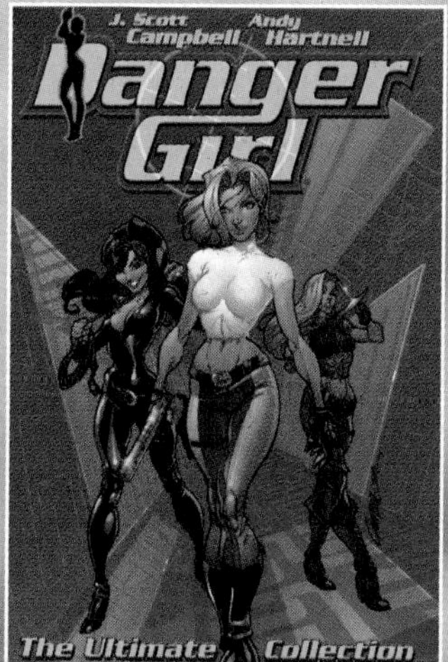
J. Scott Campbell
Andy Hartnell
Danger Girl
The Ultimate Collection
Introduction by BRUCE CAMPBELL

DANGER GIRL:
THE ULTIMATE COLLECTION

CAMPBELL/HARTNELL/GARNER

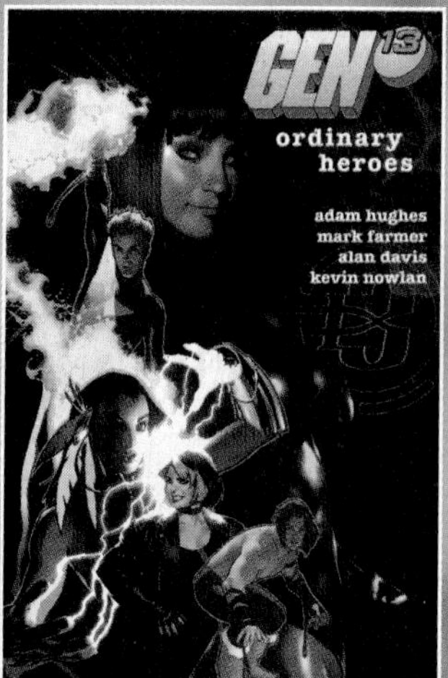
GEN 13
ordinary heroes
adam hughes
mark farmer
alan davis
kevin nowlan

GEN13:
ORDINARY HEROES

HUGHES/FARMER/DAVIS

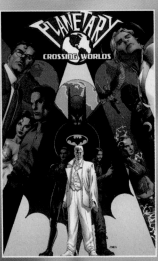